RESCUING THE FUTURE

Bequeathed Misperceptions in International Relations

RESCUING THE FUTURE
Bequeathed Misperceptions in International Relations

JAGAT S. MEHTA

MANOHAR
2008

First published 2008

ISBN 81-7304-752-9

Published by
Ajay Kumar Jain for
Manohar Publishers & Distributors
4753/23 Ansari Road, Daryaganj
New Delhi 110 002

Printed at
Lordson Publishers Pvt Ltd
Delhi 110 007

To my grandchildren Ananya, Ali,
Araddhya, Aṃir, Megnaa, Mallika and Ahilya.
They have made me proud. I am sure they will cherish
intellectual integrity and not
lose their commitment to social concerns.

We must not in the course of Publick Life except *immediate* Approbation and *immediate* grateful Acknowledgement of our Services. But let us persevere thro' Abuse and even Injury. The internal Satisfaction of a good Conscience is always present and Time will do us Justice in the Minds of the People, even of those at present the most prejudic'd against us.

BENJAMIN FRANKLIN 1772

Contents

Illustrations

Foreword

The twentieth century has seen half a dozen empires vanish. With all the empires gone, it would perhaps not be impolitic to state that there have been worse forms of governance. Given the human disposition to murderous tribal antagonisms, the intermittent intervals of regional truce brought about by some indigenous or external imperium have not been the worst experiences of mankind. Indeed, we have this from Gibbon on the subject of the Roman Empire:

> If a man were called to fix the period in the history of the world during which the condition of the human race was most happy and prosperous, he would, without hesitation, name that which elapsed from the death of Domitian to the accession of Commodus.

It is to be noted that only ninety-five years elapsed between Domitian's demise in AD 81 and the ascent of Commodus in AD 176.

The Indian subcontinent has seen its share of empires. Perhaps the greatest in extent was the Buddhist realm of Asoka which swept from Afghanistan in the north to the borders of present-day Kerala and Tamil Nadu in the south. At its apogee in the late seventeenth century, the Mughal Empire—nearly two millennia later—governed almost precisely the same territory, in geopolitical terms, both dominions ruled from the north. Asoka (273-232 BC) resided in Pataliputra, upriver on the Ganges from what would later be Kolkata. The Mughals ruled from there, but not for very long, thought themselves as conquerors from Central Asia. Babur, the founder of the dynasty had decreed that he be taken back to Kabul to be buried. However, throughout these periods, the large and important civilizations of southern India maintained their independence.

The British *Raj* was another matter. It began as a merchant adventure, which set up trading posts and gradually went on to acquire assorted territorial privileges which finally mutated into sovereignties of sorts. It did not become a proper affair of the British government until the mid-nineteenth century, an arrangement that persisted till the mid-twentieth century. Let us set aside the matter of just how 'happy and prosperous' the new subjects of the Crown were during this interval: let it suffice that there have been worse rulers. The main point is that British India, even at its close, was at best a work-in-progress. A map of the period looks like a half-finished jigsaw puzzle of daunting complexity. James Cameron writes, 'In the days of the Raj, the main railway line from Delhi to Bombay, almost a thousand miles, ran through only 150 miles of British India.' The capital was initially in Calcutta (now Kolkata). It was years before the British moved up north to Delhi, which the Mughals had reached riding south. New Delhi was a big twentieth-century city-planning project, completed at about the time the New Deal got going in the United States. Indeed, the principal architect there, Sir Edward Lutyens, also designed the British Embassy on Massachusetts Avenue in Washington.

At Independence, the new Indian government took up residence in the palaces and precincts of Delhi, just as its predecessors had done over the centuries. For all the familiar surroundings, however, there was something profoundly different about the new regime in independent India—a new era now commenced. For the first time ever, the Government of India was a government of entire India from Cape Comorin at the very south in the Indian Ocean to the foothills of the Himalayas.

It was a supreme achievement; perhaps 'only an Indian can conceive it.' Thus, Rabindranath Tagore, writing from Calcutta in the time still of the Raj, noted:

> . . . I draw your attention to the difficulties India has had to encounter and her struggle to overcome them. Her problem was the problem of the world in miniature. India is too vast in its area and too diverse in its races. It is many countries packed in one geographical receptacle. It is just the opposite of what Europe truly is, namely one country made into many. Thus, Europe in its culture and growth has had the advantage of the strength of the many as well as the strength of the one. India, on

the contrary, being naturally many, yet adventitiously one, has all along suffered from the looseness of its diversity and the feebleness of its unity. A true unity is like a round globe, it rolls on, carrying its burden easily; but diversity is a many-cornered thing which has to be dragged and pushed with all force. Be it said to the credit of India that this diversity was not her own creation; she has had to accept it as a fact from the beginning of her history.

This diversity was twofold. The first was of caste, a social hierarchy singular to the Hindu civilization, making even the most elemental modes of social cooperation unimaginably complex. (To a foreigner, that is. The modes are easily understood by those born under them.) Second, there was (and still is) the matter of Hindu-Muslim relations. Caste distinctions would seem to have originated, in part, by pre-historic tribal movements and conquest, but Islam arrived in medieval, as against ancient, times, and the resentments of conquest still persist. It is another matter that Muslims have long since ceased to be a ruling class, and, in fact, have become in many regions almost an oppressed section. When the British brought elections to India, there were property qualifications for the franchise, but then so had there been in Britain. What was different here was that seats were reserved for Muslims in local councils, a progressive idea of the 1909 Liberal government.

With Independence, the Indians had to deal with both these diversities, and multitudinous others, but these problems were only dimly perceived by outsiders. But they did manage to set aside the diversities. There were more than 350 'princely states' at the time of Independence and to cite Cameron, these states ruled about one-third of the population. In fact, many had their own armies, law courts, police, some their own customs, postage and currency. The departing British had urged that all the assorted rulers join—by treaty in many instances, formal agreement in all instances—the successor states of India and Pakistan, and this was done.

Hyderabad, the size of France, ruled by the fourth richest man on earth, or so it was said, held out for some time. As did Jammu and Kashmir, a state with a Hindu ruler and a largely Islamic population, a fault line which was present then and continues half a century later. The French held Pondicherry on the Bay of

Bengal, and the Portuguese Goa on the Arabian Sea. But the empire would absorb each of the southern enclaves. It was over in a historical instant. A new multinational entity, with eighteen official languages, not including English which was given 'associate status', and some fifty major regional languages was born. But this entity was also a democratic empire, secular and socialist, a state constitutional regime with a firm, unchallenged civilian control of the military, along with a vigilant and effective judiciary—something wholly new under the sun, an image not inappropriate to the Indian subcontinent.

Jagat S. Mehta was present at the creation of this new wonder of the world, and he has remained actively engaged with the Indian affairs down to this day. He has seen great successes, great failures, but most importantly the end of the Cold War between the Soviet Union and the Western democracies. The beginning of the Cold War coincided exactly with the attainment of Indian Independence and profoundly affected events on the subcontinent in the four decades that followed. The strains, the contradictions, the distortions and the costs of that world order are to be seen in India as perhaps nowhere outside the now-collapsed Soviet sphere itself. This is the subject of *Rescuing the Future: Coming to Terms with Bequeathed Misperceptions*, Mehta's collection of compelling and engrossing essays and manifesto.

The Mehtas are from Rajasthan, specifically the magical city of Udaipur in western Rajasthan's princely state of Mewar. Murray's *Handbook* records that the Maharana of Udaipur is the highest in rank and dignity of the Hindu princes, the 'head of the "Solar" Rajputs, the sun in splendour being emblazoned on his standard'. The ruling family was founded about AD 744. Cameron records it as 'the longest-established dynasty in the world', a ruling line of fourteen hundred unbroken years. Even if these dates don't exactly coincide, the point is sufficiently made. Needless to say, Udaipur was never under British rule, nor did the successive Islamic invaders ever hold sway there. Prince Khurram, who later, as Shah Jahan would build the Taj Mahal, took refuge in Udaipur in a period of revolt against his father, the Emperor Jahangir, but then such courtesies—and at times courage—mark the long history of this magical state. Whilst at

Udaipur, Khurram lived in a white marble palace that his host, Karan Singh, presented to Lake Pichola that sparkles, for miles seemingly, below the citadel. The palace on the other big island is now a hotel.

Mehta was born into a tradition of principled public service which flourished in India at the time of the Independence movement, and which carried over into the early years of the new state. His father, Mohan Singh Mehta, 'was an administrator, diplomat, educator, but is loved and remembered foremost for his pursuit of the ideals of the Servants of India Society, a movement devoted to social reconstruction in rural areas. His son was raised in this tradition and had the fortune—a Hindu might say the destiny, and a Hindu might be right—to be a member of the very first cadre of the Indian Foreign Service officers. (Jagat's supremely gifted wife, Rama Mehta, was one of the very first women members of that Service.) Jagat Mehta had prepared himself for the Indian Civil Service, first at the University of Allahabad, then at St. John's College, Cambridge. This must not be made to sound an everyday sort of thing. The Indian Civil Service was a sort of miracle, a perfectly modern, indeed prototypically modern organization, with admission based on examination and advancement dependent on achievement, and performed with efficiency, even parsimony, that no modern government could conceive. Surely not contemporary India!

The ICS, as it was called, administered the whole of British India (by the time of Independence most of its members were, in fact, Indians) but was constituted of less than a thousand members. It is difficult to imagine how the ICS then managed, but for a period the Indians still remembered the Service's achievement.

Mehta records that he could have joined the Service in July of 1947, but chose to wait for Independence, then not that far off. His father was a member of the Constituent Assembly and got him into the gallery on 14 August to hear Jawaharlal Nehru's legendary address proclaiming freedom at midnight. Mehta had already been interviewed by the new Prime Minister, one of a group of about thirteen to fifteen officers who would take India into the world's affairs. As was only proper, Nehru himself was issued diplomatic passport No.1, while Mehta's was No. 8. The reader might wish to bear this ranking in mind when reading that Mehta was 'the flunky around in . . . discussions with the United Nations Commission for India and Pakistan', that at the 1948 Commonwealth Prime Ministers' conference in London, his duties involved seeing off visitors 'and occasionally drafting unimportant summaries and telegrams'. And so on. (Nehru had determined that India should remain a member of the Commonwealth whilst forsaking allegiance to the British throne, a nice compromise in almost everyone's interest.) It is all there in one sentence:

> In the roulette of circumstances of my Foreign Service career, I make believe that through the entire seventeen years that he was Prime Minister of India, few officials had so many opportunities to see him so closely from the sidelines.

All a matter of chance; not necessarily so; sidelines and such. Clearly, these will not be the papers of, say, a typical American Secretary of State. (Mehta was Foreign Secretary for nearly four years.) Only Dean Acheson's *Present at the Creation* will compare in range and subtlety; not least as both were there at the beginning and lived to see the worst not happen. Just as clearly, as the reader will learn, few persons have been at the centre of so many of the defining events of that subsequent history. May I offer the judgement that none has?

Hence, the force of Mehta's judgement: 'The Cold War years may well prove to be the greatest intellectual failure in all of human history.' He lived it all, and has a right to tell what he saw. For the Soviet Union, the central intellectual failure was the fantasy that an outgrown Slavic tyranny on the edge of the Asian steppes could be the vanguard of a worldwide ascendancy of something called the proletariat. To be fair, the Russians did not think this up, others did that for them. But for a while they believed in their fantasy, with predictably unfortunate consequences. The more so, given a parallel and equally hopeless concept of how to operate a modern economy.

For the United States, the Cold War brought about a vast distortion in the size and scope of the national government, something against the American grain with the accompanying discontents that now characterize our national politics. Mehta was in Beijing at the time of the Vietnam War and found it incredible that the United States could not grasp that the Soviet Union and the People's Republic of China, far from being united in the comradely support of North Vietnamese cadres, were, in fact, bitterly antagonistic towards each other, concerned only that events in Vietnam not turn out to the advantage of *their* Communist adversary! Just so, the coming of detente in the 1970s was seen from Peking as a device which would enable Moscow to direct its energies towards the East! As Mehta will say, the CIA and the KGB have little enough to show for their trillion dollar extravagance. Both adversaries quite failed to see the essential instability of the Czarist/Soviet empire, vast reaches of which were in Central Asia. This failure was more costly to the Russians than to the Americans, but do not suppose it has nothing to do with the fact that ours is now the world's largest debtor nation.

And what of India in all this? It is difficult for an American not to feel that the new republic was caught up early on in the Cold War and ended up on the wrong side at considerable cost. Relations with the United States got off to a bad start and stayed that way. Dennis Kux has enquired into this matter with fine impartiality.* The United States was from the first an insistent supporter of Indian Independence. Why, then, did subsequent relations turn out so badly? At length the answer came and it was one word: Pakistan. Even as the Indian subcontinent was at last to be united under one sovereignty, it split along the Hindu-Muslim fault line. In an instant India acquired what seemed an implacable enemy astride the very Indus River whence came the designation India. Further, this was an enemy capable of rousing savage 'communal strife', and an enemy, finally, contesting control of Kashmir whence came the Nehrus. With the Cold War, the United States commenced a sequence of regional alliances which would encircle the Soviet Union. Pakistan was willing, even eager, to join the alliance. The United States thereupon entered a military alliance with India's seeming mortal enemy. President Eisenhower

* *India and the United States, 1941-1991: The Estranged Democracies*, Washington: National Defence University Press, 1993.

could tour the Taj Mahal at every full moon, but nothing could overcome that central political and military fact.

But that was not the whole of it. Ambassador Kux perceives the maddeningly elusive social and socialist bias, all British in origin, that produced an animus—is that, too strong a term? yes, probably—that would have caused difficulties in any event:

> Personally, Nehru had ambivalent feelings about America, a country he had never visited. The Indian leader had a considerable bias that seemed to combine the anti-American social prejudices of the British elite and the anti-American policy views of the left-wing of the British Labour Party. In foreign policy dealings, he found the United States too cocksure about the rights and wrongs of the Cold War, too insensitive to the aspirations of colonial peoples, and too patronizing in dealing with India. Despite disappointments over Kashmir and differences on anti-colonial issues, Nehru remained, nonetheless, hopeful about relations with Washington, believing the United States would be interested in friendly relations with India because 'it is well recognized today all over the world that the future of Asia will be powerfully determined by the future of India'.

Keep in mind that the reference here would be to the British Labour Party of the 1930s, and the left wing thereof, and most emphatically not to the Labour Party of Ernest Bevin, who conceived of the North Atlantic Treaty Organization, the first of the regional alliances. In 1948, the United States and India entered into a Treaty of Friendship, Commerce and Navigation, as befitted a newly independent State. In a note on the subject, Nehru wrote:

> America is the most powerful and richest country in the world and can certainly help India a great deal. There is no reason why we should not get that help and remove causes of friction between us. But it is true that America represents a reactionary policy in world affairs, I think a policy which will not succeed. . . . The safest policy, therefore, appears to be friendly to America, to give them fair terms, to invite their help on such terms, and at the same time not to tie ourselves up too much with their world or their economic policy.

There it is: 'a reactionary policy in world affairs. . . . A policy which will not succeed. . . .' The United States was, in fact, the revolutionary power on earth at this point, creating an international norm of a successful democracy—successful and prosperous democracy. This was everything India could wish to be, but Nehru could not have it. Instead, he helped to found the Non-Aligned Movement in 1961. This was an entirely reasonable measure on the part of new nations necessarily preoccupied with nation building. If only it were kept to that. Alas, it was not. Meeting by meeting, final declaration by final declaration, the Non-Aligned became objectively allies of the Soviet Union. India, on its part, was increasingly perceived in the West as *de facto* pro-Soviet. It spoiled a good many relationships. In his farewell address, George Washington had laid down, 'It is our true policy to steer clear of permanent alliance with any portion of the foreign world. . . .' Good advice for any new nation, but India allowed itself to drift otherwise. The time came when New Delhi swarmed with officials who were on the right side of history, and did not hesitate to let the Americans know that they were on the wrong side. Indira Gandhi sent one such official as the Indian ambassador in Washington so as, you might say, to spread the word. But then, a curious dichotomy arose. Slowly at first, but then in ever greater numbers Indians began migrating to the United States. By the 1980s Indians were a conspicuously successful and vital community in every major city in America. The ultimate sign of inclusion: an India Day parade in New York City. As with most immigrant groups in the United States, the newcomers kept up close relations with family at home, even acquiring a kind of caste status as Non-Resident Indians, or 'NRIs' as they were generally known. The success of the immigrants was and is a perfectly normal source of pride at home. The first- and second-generation Indians being so heavily drawn from the professions, notably medicine, research, science and higher technologies now have the highest social and economic status of any ethnic group in the United States. President Ford's ambassador to India, the distinguished former senator and attorney general William Saxbe commented on the complexity of it all:

> When I call on cabinet ministers, the President, or governors, they all love to talk about their sons, sons-in-law and daughters in the United States and how well they are doing and how well they like things. The next day I read in the papers that the very same people are denouncing the United States.

This latter class did not exclude Prime Minister Indira Gandhi, who was perfectly gracious and open to Americans, but was, for some reason preoccupied with the thought of United States involvement with Indian internal affairs. This could reach to the heights of the absurd. At one point during the time I was the United States ambassador (1973-5), a young Foreign Service officer was posted to the Consulate in Calcutta. It so happened that some years earlier he had been a Peace Corps volunteer in West Bengal, and upon his return made his way 'up country' to visit some of the villages and villagers he had known. Unfortunately, there was a spate of 'communal' strife at that time and a Communist newspaper in Calcutta hit upon the notion of accusing the young American of stirring it up. This notion made its way to New Delhi and the Government there literally decided to expel the American. It fell to me to call on the Indian Foreign Secretary to say that if he went home, I would go home with him and could not predict just when another American ambassador would return to take my place. We were not, I insisted, involved in any way in any such conduct. And we were not.

Alas, we had been, as the Prime Minister knew all too well. In the late 1950s, when she was President of the Congress Party, the United States had provided campaign funds in a situation where it seemed that Communists might come to power in a state election. It was a time of powerful indigenous Communist challenges in much of the world. Here was a new democracy; we were supporting it. But then we stopped. Stopped altogether. But how could Congress Party leaders know this? All they knew was that we were no longer giving campaign money to them. Who else, then? As Dennis Kux related in January 1976, Mrs Gandhi charged that the powers that had destabilized Chile, which is to say the United States, 'nurtured similar designs against India'. This was painfully wrong. First I, then Saxbe had been sent to India because we had opposed the Nixon administration's 'tilt' towards Pakistan when Bangladesh broke away in 1971. Saxbe was outspoken in the Senate; my actions were less public but no less emphatic.

In the summer of 1970, I was Counsellor (a cabinet position) to President Nixon. He asked me to go to the United Nations as our ambassador. I accepted at first, but then declined in November, saying it was time to return to Harvard where I held a teaching position. The White House turned to George Bush, a young Texan Congressman who had lost a Senate contest to Lloyd Bentsen. I played the most marginal part in convincing Bush that the post was worth his while. More generous than he need have been, but characteristically so, once installed the new ambassador to the UN asked if I would serve as the public member of the United States delegation to the 26th General Assembly that would convene in September 1971. I accepted with considerable enthusiasm. Unfortunately, the General Assembly had no more begun than the slaughter in East Bengal commenced as well. India absorbed—note well—some ten million refugees, and fed them, housed them, looked to their health and welfare as much as West Bengal could provide. The Nixon administration had inherited a now well-established notion of the Pakistanis as a warrior race and a Cold War ally. More importantly, the Pakistan government was serving as an intermediary in Nixon's opening to China. We 'tilted' towards Islamabad, without any consequence save moral outrage. I expressed this within our delegation, adding that it was one thing to be morally insensate; another to be stupid. If it came to war, the Indians would whip the Pakistanis yet another time. President Nixon learned of my views and called from Washington to explain that there was something else going on of great importance which could not be discussed on the telephone but which, if I knew, I would understand. I responded that nothing would make me understand our seeming complacence at the massacre, and we left it there. The following August, I was at home in upstate New York and watched the Republican nomination on television. My wife asked me what would happen now. I replied in the most casual terms that President Nixon would be re-elected and he would ask me to be ambassador to India. Which he did the following Thanksgiving Day. He wanted to get things right with that great democracy which always seemed so cross with us. President Ford felt exactly the same. Neither perhaps absorbed the central fact of our supplying arms to Pakistan; they did not see that as having anything to do with India! Still, there was no sustained animus. None whatever.

Nor did Indira Gandhi. In 1975 she had assumed emergency powers under the Constitution, and effectively shut down Indian democracy. This was hugely upsetting to the American opinion—the world's largest democracy—and equally to President Ford. The State Department, as state departments must do, thought in terms of power relations. The Soviets had gained a wholly unlooked for advantage. An end to Indian democracy might inaugurate an entirely new era of Indo-Soviet friendship. Kux writes:

> Through this period, Indo-Soviet relations remained cordial and close. The Russians applauded the imposition of the Emergency, labelling Mrs. Gandhi's opponents as right-wing reactionaries. Trade and cultural exchanges increased. The military supply relationship was stronger than ever. A vocal pro-Soviet lobby among intellectuals, journalists, politicians, and civil servants beat the drums to support Moscow and Marxism and to criticize the United States.

Then came the circumstances in which Mehta showed his abilities. He has remarked in private, but will not, I hope, mind my repeating that the likes of Molotov and Gromyko had had 'long innings' but their works are on the dustheap of history for they grossly misperceived their country's interests and capacity, and settled far too readily for protracted conflict. Mehta by contrast had a central vision and a defiant faith in diplomacy. The task of Indian diplomacy was to establish relationships with her neighbours such that peace could come to the subcontinent. In his years in office, he negotiated seven treaties—a lightning sequence by any standard and unprecedented for the parties concerned. The essential geopolitical fact and tragedy of the partition of the subcontinent was that the new national borders cut across the two great river systems, the Indus and the Ganges, that define the region. Water is everything, and now a measure of sharing, the rewards of sharing, and even the habits of sharing began to take hold. Within India itself the bonds of the vast multilingual state created at Independence frayed. The Nehru dynasty was nearly wiped out by assassination, but democracy did not collapse. The Cold War receded, and relations with the United States finally attained a normalcy that had for so long seemed distant, if not indeed unattainable. If it cannot be shown that one man did all this and no one person could have done, history will surely decree that what came about was what Jagat S. Mehta hoped for, and that he was there when it did. Blessed is the peacemaker.

Washington
July 2000

DANIEL PATRICK MOYNIHAN

Acknowledgements

The publication of this compilation has been delayed by more than ten years. It still requires grateful acknowledgement to those who encouraged me to bring it out. At a lunch with the Senator D.P. Moynihan, a former ambassador to India, in New York in 1990—the year after the Berlin Wall had been dismantled—in the course of the conversation, I remarked that 'the paranoiac analysis of the Cold War from 1947 onwards was the greatest intellectual failure in history. It had led to astronomical opportunity costs, needless distortion of international politics and overshadowed the constructive potential of decolonization.' Pat Moynihan almost jumped in his chair; he did not agree with me, but he said he had not heard this before and asked if I had ever stated it in print; he added, if I was prepared to repeat it, he would write a forword to the publication. Some years earlier, at a conference on South Asian Security organized by Prof. Stephen Cohen, then of the University of Illinois, after I had read my paper—included in this compilation—he had suggested putting together my occasional writings but I had not taken the idea seriously as I felt that such a publication would border on egotistical public relations. I must have mentioned to Stephen Cohen the conversation with the Senator and his suggestion. The combined persuasion of Senator Moynihan and Prof. Cohen overcame my bureaucratic hesitation. After returning to Austin the following year—where I was teaching for one semester every year—I sent the bunch of articles to Stephen Cohen and he set about painfully wading through them and making a preliminary selection and classification. I returned to India at the end of the Fall semester but Stephen pursued the suggestion directly with the Senator. Next year, when I returned to Austin, Stephen invited me to come and help edit the proposed selection. We spent two long days in the basement of his house in Urbana reviewing the manuscripts. Swarna Rajgopal and Chetan Kumar, who were Cohen's graduate students, in a labour of love, cheerfully helped and Swarna retyped the edited portions. In 1995, Prof. T.N. Madan a distinguished sociologist and an old friend of my late wife, brought Ramesh Jain of Manohar Publishers and Distributors to me to explore the possibility of publishing the proposed compilation. Ramesh offered me a contract in 1995 and Stephen Cohen, on his next visit to Delhi, also recommended publication, but the Senator's promised foreword was still awaited. In view of his widely publicized senatorial responsibilities, there was hesitation to remind him too frequently. Eventually the foreword did arrive. Although it was a fascinating overview on India, we thought it had only limited reference to the contents of the proposed book. Stephen Cohen sent another set of the draft compilation to the senator and requested him to consider revising his Foreword. The Senator agreed in principle to do so but this meant further delay. A somewhat refined version came but only in the year 2000.

I myself had virtually forgotten about the contract. Manohar Publishers must also have put it away on their shelves with other similar pending manuscripts. In the wake of 9/11, my book on Afghanistan moved up in priority at Manohar. Even so, Bhola Nath Varma, then editor with Manohar (who had become friendly with me), told me that many pieces in the compilation had what he called 'nuggets' of analytical originality and should not go unpublished. But a compilation on seven case studies had a more coherent unity and was brought out first as *Negotiating for India* in 2006.

As explained in the footnotes, most essays in this volume were done on 'requests' or to externally determined timing. The articles recalling Nehru were timed for his Centenary in 1989. 'The Two Cold Wars' and the general piece on fresh water diplomacy were written voluntarily when I was an Associate of the Woodrow Wilson Centre in 1981-82. 'Third World Militarization' is a reproduction of a keynote paper, which I circulated in advance of a conference at LBJ School in 1984. 'The Indus Water Treaty' is a reprint from a UN publication. The essay entitled 'The

Politics of Riparian Cooperation' was a contribution to the volume *Harnessing the Eastern Himalayan Rivers: Regional Cooperation in South Asia* edited by B.G. Verghese and Ramaswamy Aiyer published under the auspices of the Centre for Policy Research in 1993. (I have been an honorary associate of the CPR since I retired.) The 'Nepal' essay was suggested by the *Hindustan Times* after India reimposed a near blockade on transit trde in 1989. 'We Know the Past: Must We Live in it?' was for the conference on security at the University of Illinois in Urbana in 1984. The 'Kashmir' paper was in response to a request for a collection by Prof. Raju Thomas in 1992. The paper on retrospect and prospects in China was at the suggestion of the President of the Centre for Policy Research in New Delhi in 1992. The paper on Non-alignment was proposed by the India International Centre, New Delhi, for a book to coincide with the summit in 1983, but it was politely rejected by the IIC, presumably because of its title ('Will Non-Alignment Survive its Vindication'?) or its contents, but Nikhil Chakravarty published it in the *Mainstream* and subsequently Romesh Thaper carried it in the *Seminar*. The first part of 'Non-Proliferation' was written in 1986 for the *Seminar*, the second in 2004, and only the third has been freshly written after the passage of the Bush-Singh Agreement on Civil Nuclear Cooperation by the US Congress in June 2006. The essay on 'Cooperative Security' was written at the request of Prof. Joshua Cohen at the MIT, for a conference sponsored by the *Boston Review* in 1985. 'The Challenge for Democratic Statesmanship' was a paper prepared for a conference held in Dhaka to which I was invited in 1996. The long review of J.N. Dixit's book *War and Peace* was written as a private comment to an old colleague in 2002 but Mani Dixit himself suggested I publish it as a monograph. I was not keen on including the last paper on 'Volunteerism' but Stephen Cohen felt strongly it should be.

Inevitably there is an overlap in these papers, but I hope there is a running thread of consistency underlining the fact that the twentieth century has been a litany of tragic but avoidable misjudgements not just by India but by all major countries. They were traceable to the paranoiac anxieties generated by the Cold

War and the consequential hypnosis that diluted the expected potential of decolonization. As a direct result, decision makers have got into the habit of 'scapegoatism', which impedes rationalization for future rectification. India, with its civilizational heritage, is now uniquely well placed for the twenty-first century of people's power and modernization but, in my view, we must regain the confidence of all our neighbours, return to principled consistency and rely more on sophisticated diplomacy which focuses on priority for social justice at home and abroad.

This compilation truly is a jumble of old and new articles written between 1983 and 2006. I am aware that some are dated and many have repetitions, but they all underline the special quality demanded of professionalism in foreign policy, that of volunteering dissent at the advisory stage. We must aim to look well ahead, beyond populism, and anticipate the implications of galloping technology, show courage in reasoned prediction and be more self-conscious of the slow trot of comprehension. Only diplomacy can strengthen the scaffolding of international peace and help in conflict resolution.

Moynihan passed away in 2003. In the obituaries and in his biography *The Gentleman from New York* he was described as the greatest intellectual in the Senate. He had served four terms and on retirement in 2002, handed over the Senatorial baton of New York State to Hillary Clinton. I feel honour bound to include his Foreword. It is written in his own inimitable style but does reflect his strong empathy for India.

The book would never have got into print but for the interest and encouragement of Prof. Stephen Cohen, Prof. Madan, Ramesh Jain and his son Ajay, Bhola Nath Varma, more recently Siddharth Chowdhury at Manohar and, of course, originally Senator Moynihan. I must also acknowledge my gratitude to S.S. Bolia for his forbearance in typing and retyping the essays.

Even though personal reflections intrude into the articles, this book is not a 'memoir'. However, my experience as an observer was truly enriched by the privileged insights from various perches with the Foreign Service of India. I am now old and live mostly in Udaipur, far from the corridors of power. Whether my analyses will stand the test of time only the future will tell, but being able to set them forth itself does gratify me. Nobody tutored me even while in service, when I was doing policy planning, much less after I retired. It is, however, my private proof of the resilience of India's democracy and gives me some satisfaction that even after two decades and more, I can bear to publish it wholly unaltered for public scrutiny.

JAGAT S. MEHTA
7 July 2006

Introduction

COMING TO TERMS WITH A WASTED PAST

The world took many years to adjust to the lifting of the dark clouds of the Cold War; some are still nostalgic about a world where there were certainties about the enemy, confidence in ideologies, and the assurance that godfathers for aid and support will always be there. There were anxieties as well that peace had descended too suddenly. There is, of course, a search to find new paradigms and new conceptual frameworks to give meaning to the disorder—both actual and intellectual—which has broken out following the collapse of the dominant *leitmotif* of the post-War decades. The triumph of liberal democracy and the market forces over socialism and statism according to one judgement spells the end of history. From another perspective, the new tensions and conflicts overtook the faith in communism against democracies by a new international fault line between civilizations: Islam and Confucianism are seen as posing new threats to the West and its Greco-Roman Christian heritage. The question that is generally avoided is whether this long-drawn confrontation was unavoidable: or was it but the mindsets gridlocked in mutually reinforcing paranoia? Socialism in one country, Stalin's Russia, survived but the advent of the communist bloc, with Soviet Union and China and other states, stretching across the land mass of Europe and Asia in an ideological solidarity and a military alliance, did not hold together even for ten years. The security buffer of Eastern Europe against predatory imperialism/capitalism in fact carried the seeds of destruction in the resilience of nationalism and the inherent international diversity.

Some of the ablest in the present generation of decision makers and analysts who straddled the bloc politics and the post-Cold

War years, when they claim total victory of the 'West' over communism may well have a vested interest in rationalizing past misjudgements. Perhaps we are too close to these cataclysmic changes to get an objective picture of why we were so deceived. The world will have to wait for historians who come to maturity wholly unconditioned by the Cold War paradigm, to know the unvarnished truth. It is possible that, uncomfortably too soon, with the relevant Soviet (Russian) archives being opened for research, the depth and persistence of the rigid mindsets of those who were caught in the vicious grip of fear on both sides of the divide will be exposed. The Cold War years may well prove to be the greatest intellectual failure in the entire human history.

In moulding and rescuing the future, the deep reluctance to ask searching introspective questions about the past inhibits policy rectification. Notwithstanding the confidence in world revolution and the inevitability of communism spreading openly or surreptitiously across frontiers (and civilizations) was there really a danger to Western Europe in 1947 after the Soviet Union had retreated from Azerbaijan in Iran under UN and great-power pressure? Was there dependable evidence that the insurgency in Greece and Turkey was masterminded by the Kremlin, which created alarm and evoked the image of a new Carthage threatening old Rome, and which led to the proclamation of the Truman doctrine and global containment? Notwithstanding Eisenhower's prophetic caution in his farewell message as President of the threat from the military industrial complex, the momentum of militarization has continued, like a self-propelled monster, beyond the requirement of sufficient defence or even assured retaliation.

In retrospect, the four decades of the Cold War appear like an unprecedented squandering of the world's human and technological resources in a competition for self-destruction by the two great power blocs. The loss of China and the war in Korea effectively extended military containment to Asia and gave birth to McCarthyism and the extension of alliances to the Asian mainland. In the process it undermined professionalism in diplomacy and scholarship on Asia. Since then the West has 'lost' Iraq, Indo-China and Iran. The Soviet Union lost Eastern Europe, and itself disintegrated. Africa in a sense was lost by both powers and China found that the continent was not after all 'ripe for revolution' as it had prophesied in 1964. In the Third World, where ideologies and alliances competed, only the Far East and South-East Asia found the alchemy of economic progress but it was principally because of their own national exertions. Africa and South Asia could find a recipe for shoring up reconstruction in their own mix of plurality. In India democracy was not unshakably institutionalized but success depended critically on the culture of native statesmanship.

GREAT POWERS DO NOT HAVE A MONOPOLY ON MISPERCEPTIONS

Before discussing further I should unreservedly state that the great powers and the United States in particular did not have a monopoly on misjudgements in the story of these post-War decades. We, in the Third World, in the exhilaration of decolonization and affirming independence of judgement and non-alignment from the military blocs, actually got hooked to the misperceptions of the adversarial blocs. In distancing ourselves from the aligned philosophies, we quietly presumed that bloc rivalry, which gave us contrived importance, would last for ever. We did not anticipate the vindication and universalization of non-alignment; we almost banked on its failure. The major powers are now switching to peaceful economic priorities with a more measured calibration of defence and ideological agnosticism in their external political and economic relations. These were the essence of non-aligned principles, but in the meanwhile, non-alignment grew into a 'movement' and consequently became a pale imitation of the politics of the blocs. We dissipated the kinetic energy of nationalism which should have transformed our fervour against imperialism into a disciplined zest for accelerated development of our own people. The developed world frightened as well as flattered us to fall in line but we must acknowledge that we were also needlessly docile victims in becoming dependent and half-hearted towards our own social, economic and political emancipation. This dependency has gone so far that many areas in sub-Saharan Africa and Asia were dismissed as basket cases or beyond meaningful redemption. The end of the Cold War demanded a ruthless introspection on the origins of our misperceptions if we were to chart new courses.

THE UNEXPECTED INDIA-CHINA CRISIS

As a professional officer of the foreign service my realization of the penalties of misperceptions go back to 1959. By sheer bureaucratic happenstance, as a mere Deputy Secretary (the equivalent of a senior First Secretary) I found myself the chief operating officer dealing with China, Tibet, Nepal, Bhutan and the Far East when unexpectedly India's relations with China plummeted. I had not played any role in policy-making in the past, but for two years (1959-61) I had to handle all the manifestations of the crisis with only the head of the Foreign Office as my superior and, therefore, frequently I had to report and seek directions from Prime Minister Nehru. The Khampa revolt in Tibet had been going on for some time but it attracted international attention only when the Dalai Lama sneaked out from the Norbulinka palace in disguise. I must have been one of the first in Delhi to know of his escape and also of his arrival a fortnight later on our frontier. Two and a half weeks later I welcomed him on behalf of the Government of India when he arrived in Mussoorie. The Dalai Lama's escape led to an exodus of 100,000 Tibetans. Accusations were levelled by China that bourgeois reactionaries harboured by India had succeeded in fomenting the revolt deep inside Tibet. (This was unmerited flattery for capabilities of Indian intelligence.) The Chinese allegations triggered an angry public reaction in India: after ten years of crusading for the recognition of the People's Republic in defiance of Western disapproval. Such accusations amounted to ungrateful repudiation of India's consistent goodwill. In the months that followed there were some minor border incidents but the political crisis—like a Greek tragedy—moved inexorably to the India-China war three years later.

A review and prognosis of India-China relations produced in 1992 is included in this compilation. What is pertinent is that neither India nor China anticipated the sudden deterioration of relations; over the previous five years we had confidently proclaimed a fraternal, permanent friendship and held it up as a model for relations of peaceful coexistence between a communist and a non-aligned democratic state. However, Sino-Indian relations reached a political gridlock following the insensitive charges levelled by the Chinese, particularly after Nehru was personally criticized. It was therefore no surprise that no settlement was reached at the meeting of the two prime ministers in April 1960. Nehru was under constraint of being responsible to an aroused parliamentary democracy, and at the time, could not have obtained a mandate to concede territory previously openly notified in an official map as India. Contrary to many books written on the subject—all of them after our officials report of 1961—I remain convinced that the crisis was a case of mutual misperception. If either government had had a better understanding of the other nation's personality and sensitivity, there could have been a settlement in 1957, before the Tibet crisis and there would not have been an India-China war.

The India-China crisis marked the beginning of distortions in planned development in India. It also led to an unexpected China-Pakistan rapprochement, even while Pakistan remained a partner in the United States-dominated alliances (SEATO and CENTO). This non-ideological friendship, cemented by a common hostility towards India, encouraged Pakistan to launch Operation Gibraltar in August-September 1965, in an attempt to wrest Kashmir from India. There may well have been erroneous expectations in Pakistan regarding the kind of collateral aid China would provide in pursuit of Pakistan's purpose, particularly in the case of a military stalemate. I received the two ultimata on 16 and 19 September 1965, demanding the return of sheep and yaks as well as the demolition of bunkers in the Sikkim sector within three days.* The ultimata caused alarm in New Delhi that India may have to face a second front—a repetition of 1962—while the Indian army was engaged with Pakistan. I took the risk of forecasting before the deadline expired that China would not intervene to serve what was exclusively Pakistan's national

* See Chapter 4, *Negotiating for India*, Jagat S. Mehta, Manohar, 2006.

purpose. China did not intervene but for fifteen years it was engaged in the political attrition of India. China sided with Pakistan, even through the Bangladesh crisis, when the whole world (except the US administration) was critical of the military regime in Islamabad. Since 1976, India and China have been exploring the potential of friendly relations and functional cooperation with each other. The dispute over the alignment of the Sino-Indian boundary remains unresolved as it has been since India's independence and the establishment of the People's Republic. The India-China conflict has taken a heavy toll of militarization and hostility, which in all honesty both countries should introspectively regret as a needless failure of two-sided judgement.

VIETNAM AS SEEN BY AN OBSERVER IN BEIJING

Of far greater importance to the world was the protracted war in Vietnam. Though it falls outside the purview of South Asia related problems, I had occasion to follow Vietnam as a diplomatic observer in the 1964-6 period as head of the Indian embassy in Peking. Hundreds of books have been written on Vietnam, but I am not aware of any study of the nuances, differences and complexities of the conflict on the communist side, which to my mind were unmistakably plain in Peking. Had these deep differences been followed by decision makers and analysts, even from published information or through easy inferences, the tragedy of Vietnam may also have been averted, at least before the American combat troops were inducted into Vietnam in 1965. Till 1967-8, the official American view was that American intervention was against the united communist threat to South-East Asia, which otherwise would have fallen like dominoes. The history of Soviet detachment from the communist revolution in China in 1927 and in 1948-9 was so well known that claims of unity of purpose should not have been taken at face value. After Stalin's death and Khrushchev's denunciation of the cult of personality in 1956, the depth of ideological differences showed all the signs of sharp political differences. It should have been apparent, at least since 1960 when the Soviet Union summarily withdrew 10,000 Soviet technicians who took the blueprints of 250 odd major development projects with them, that Sino-Soviet relations had reached a nadir beyond any prospect of a return of mutual confidence. While neither side found it politically expedient to repudiate the Treaty of 1950, which was valid for thirty years, doctrinal differences were aired at the meeting of the International Communist Party in Bucharest in 1960. In the light of this background, it was evident to objective assessment that far from any united ideology or coordinated purpose, the Soviet Union and China were actually competing against each other even as the Democratic Republic of Vietnam (DRVN) faced the United States and its surrogate regime in the south. The failure to recognize these divergent goals was a vivid and tragic example of preconceived mind-sets, conditioned by the Cold War overlooking contemporaneously available evidence.

What bears repetition is how the question of nuclear weapons was central to Sino-Soviet differences and policies. Mao Zedong had felicitated the USSR after Sputnik's first space flight in 1957 and had declared, 'The East Wind prevails over the West Wind.' This was the high point of coordinated strategies against the West. In the confidence of the achievements of the socialist bloc, China believed in 1958 that the KMT forces could be threatened to evacuate the offshore islands, but Khrushchev cautioned China not to run the risk of provoking the United States which, even though imperialist was not a 'paper tiger', but had nuclear teeth. Apprehensive of China's independent belligerency, the Soviet Union had reneged on the agreement for the supply of nuclear weapons technology which was a part of the Sino-Soviet agreement concluded when Mao was in Moscow in 1957 for the 40th anniversary of the October Revolution. It may also be recalled that China had described the installation of missiles in Cuba as 'adventurism' and their removal under threat as 'capitulationism'. Incidentally, there was no appreciation in Bejing that during the missile crisis, the USSR had reverted to a pro-China tilt in the Sino-Indian border question, as the peak period of the two crises (October 1962) coincided with their outbreak. Within barely a few months of the Soviet climbdown, negotiations between the United States, the Soviet Union and the United Kingdom culminated in the Partial Test Ban Treaty (PTB) in July 1963. According to the Chinese view this agreement, arrived at behind their backs, between powers that were ostensibly sworn adversaries, as a conspiracy—a 'love feast' for a duopoly and calculatingly against China's own destiny.

The treaty brought Sino-Soviet polemics into the open. For the next year and a half, starting with 'Long live Leninism' at regular intervals, culminating in 'Khrushchevism without Khrushchev', doctrinal pamphlets were issued accusing the Communist Party of the Soviet Union (CPSU) of revisionism and of reneging on the shared ideology. One of the pamphlets criticized Soviet-India relations and argued that while for the Communist Party of China (CPC) the relations were tactical, the CPSU had begun to believe in the permanent existence of parallel social systems. What become transparent from these 'theological' arguments was that by 1964 China-Soviet hostility had become visceral, and while Vietnam was the testing ground, it was secondary to their rivalry.

The Democratic Republic of Vietnam (DRVN), which at the time was greatly dependent for food, arms and logistical support on the People's Republic of China, claimed that it was a 'lip and teeth' friendship, defied the Soviet Union and also refused to sign the PTB. This greatly outraged Khrushchev who feared that the ongoing conflict in Vietnam could easily lead to an impetuous use of a nuclear bomb by the United States. Such a contingency would pose an impossible dilemma for the USSR—to retaliate in defence of the socialist country and in the process invite destruction on the whole world, or remain detached and thus betray any claims to being the prime power and protector of the communist bloc. Concerned and angry Khrushchev significantly diluted economic assistance and stopped military supplies to the DRVN. This decision predictably intensified China's propaganda of denunciation of the Soviet Union and increased China's splitting activities within the world communist parties. The Japanese Communist Party switched to a pro-Peking stance. Therefore, when Khrushchev was overthrown in October 1964, his successors (Brezhnev and Kosygin) decided to supply arms to the DRVN to recover damaged Soviet credibility in the world communist constituency. It was with such a mission that Kosygin set out for Hanoi in February 1965. En route he stopped at Bejing to inform the Chinese and to outwardly show a united purpose. Having learnt about the visit of the Soviets, I decided to go to the airport. It was the coldest reception at the summit level that I have ever seen, but the tell-tale significance of this cool reception, obvious to all diplomats and careful observers, was never analysed in the West. To my mind, it confirmed that Mao had actually told Kosygin that Soviet help was not required in Vietnam and, in effect, Kosygin could return to Moscow.

Kosygin went to Hanoi despite China's negative counsel. The arms supplies started soon thereafter. However, weapons which could lead to air battles like fighter bombers and provoke the USA to escalate its efforts were not supplied. Initially, the equipment was dispatched by the quicker and safer land route through China. It was, however, suspected that some of the supplies were being held while in transit through China. Thereafter, even at the risk of delay, blockade and confiscation, the arms were shipped by sea to be unloaded at Haiphong. While remaining dependent for food and some supplies on China, in due course Vietnam's major supply source became the Soviet Union and this eventually led to the reassertion of Vietnam's nationalist purpose for a negotiated reunification and helped to save the country from further and needless devastation.

The antagonistic purposes of the USSR and China are not difficult to pinpoint in any objective analysis. The Soviet Union never obstructed, indeed quietly welcomed, the various initiatives for negotiations (such as U. Thant on behalf of the UN, the British Prime Minister Wilson's efforts after Kosygin's visit to London, deGaulle's suggestion and a Polish initiative). China, on the other hand, did not encourage the possibility of a negotiated end to the war, even though it was devastating Vietnam.

As Barbara Tuchman put it, the US betrayed itself in Vietnam. The American policy of Vietnam had an adverse impact on the rest of the world. India had to cope with a period of short leash in the despatch of food grains when it faced an acute shortage. As a result, gratitude for US support following the India-China war hardened into an anti-America stance. Once again, the United States and India, in response to divergent national priorities, became estranged because they were democracies while Pakistan under military rule, equally critical of US policies in Vietnam, did not receive flak even after it forged a close friendship with China which was antagonistic to the US.

MISPERCEPTIONS: THEIR ORIGINS AND LESSONS

As is argued in a separately published study,[1] there was a quadrilateral of misperceptions on Afghanistan—by the Soviet Union, the US, Pakistan and India. The result was a legacy of anarchy which continues, five million people were displaced; India and Pakistan got heavily militarized; the superpowers after 1987; all but forgot the plight of the subcontinent until after 9/11. Not having learnt the lessons from Vietnam and Afghanistan, Indian intervention in Sri Lanka led to similar military frustration and an adverse political fall out and the assassination of young Indian prime minister with promise of a great political future. There are scores of other cases around the world of mistaken threat perceptions and the wastage of human, material and technological wealth.

Having no pretensions to being an intellectual, I do not claim to present a comprehensive analytical picture. In this compilation of essays, I have drawn on my experiences or observations, sometimes in the scrum of decision-making and at other times from the sidelines as an officer of the Indian Foreign Service. I have benefited from readings and contacts which gave me a better understanding of the theory and examples of misperception in decision-making. I have referred more than once to Barbara Tuchman's *The March of Folly*,[2] of how 'governments act contrary to their own self-interest and against reason'. In analysing misperceptions I have also referred to Professor Jervis[3] whom I met at Harvard and whose writings on the psychological factors in 'perceptions of perceptions' impressed me. I would like to put on record that I found Vertzberger's[4] book on the Sino-Indian crisis extremely insightful. Recently I came across his latest book, *The World in Their Mind*,[5] wherein he examines the problem of information processing and decision-making.

Many misperceptions in our time, illustrate decision-making

processes, had no exact parallels in history. Among them, I would list the exaggerated importance attached to ideology in international relations, the unforeseen political consequences of the Information Revolution and the increased sophistication of military hardware which created illusions of victory but have proved unusable or potentially counter-productuive. The credence placed in universalist ideology may be compared to the doctrine of a universal faith in Catholicism, but even in this parallel one should remember it led to Protestantism and many churches. What should be noted by a secular, democratic observer is that every time a communist party in power faced the fork between Marxist-Leninist orthodoxy and national interest, ideology was jettisoned in practice but with a suitable or tortuous theoretical justification. The shared faith did not prevent tensions, diplomatic hostility and even conflicts between countries professing communism (the China-Soviet clash in 1969 and the China-Vietnam war in 1979). Fundamentalism and unity around shared Islam is being projected as a new internationalist force, but it failed to prevent the war in Yemen, or between Iran and Iraq, or the invasion of Kuwait. In Afghanistan, the irony was that the Soviet Union intervened because the advent of a local militant communist in 1978 had alienated the religious tribals in a country which for sixty years under a monarchy or an oligarchy had been consistently friendly to the USSR. The near unanimous belief that the Soviet intervention was designed to cut-off the supplies to the West and the US call for a Rapid Deployment Force and a new strategic consensus was the manifestation of a deep-seated paranoia. The irony about the role of ideology is that after the Soviet intervention, some extreme communist decrees promulgated by Hafizullah Amin, who was killed by the Russians in 1979, were actually dismantled to win popular acceptance of the Soviet intervention.

The other factor where historical analogy proved incorrect was the belief that with modern means of propaganda, an authoritarian government in an Orwellian fashion could effect mind control and make the people docile. In fact, modern media has proved to be a double-edged sword: it has given enormous power to the state, but has also promoted protest, aroused economic expectations and undermined arbitrary rule. Nuclear weapons have proved to be no more than a psychological asset. These weapons of mass destruction have not been used after Nagasaki. However, strategists have advertised reliance on massive retaliation and use even in a conventional war. Decades of politics based on the imperative for the continuing sophistication of nuclear and other such weapons of mass destruction is responsible for the present problem of checking proliferation. The great power example has led to redundant militarization in the Third World. It is clear that military power by itself cannot guarantee security to any country. Incidentally, non-nuclear powers are as influential, if not more, than nuclear power countries. Nuclear weapons have, however, become symbols of national prestige. On the other hand, they have diluted economic dynamism and are responsible for Russia's debacle today. Even confidence in sophisticated conventional weapons has proved ineffective against people's movements. Helicopter gunships failed against the Vietcong and the Afghan Mujahideen. Pakistan may well regret its role as the conduit and recipient of American support against the Russians in Afghanistan. Millions of Kalashnikov rifles and other military hardware, including stinger missiles, have been dumped in the country, paralysing the law and order machinery. The international bazaar is becoming bigger and more diverse, and arms trade is now a menace to well-established governments as it is only fuelling narco-terrorism. The present militarization of the Third World and only piecemeal progress in human development are attributable to misperceptions under the shadow of the Cold War. Indeed, rogue nationalism and chauvinism can be traced to impetuous partisanship of the great powers for non-representative governments such as in Angola. It would not have been too implausible to anticipate these ugly ramifications if the decision makers and non-official analysts of the Cold War, including amongst the non-aligned nations, had not developed mental blocks.

CATHARSIS MUST BEGIN WITH CONFESSION

If the future is to be rescued from the debris of explosive poverty, religion-motivated violence, ethnic and civil strife, the agony of failed states and widespread despair and desperation, it is important to recognize that there is always a better choice. Even the play of great power politics, bribes and inducements (foreign aid, free food, arms and war-making capabilities) never wholly smothered the margin for sagacity by independent governments with a genuine concern for the welfare of their own people. Whether poor or powerful, the point is that catharsis must begin with confession. Statesmanship should overcome the natural inclination to rationalize that under diverse compulsions, populist or otherwise, there was no alternative but to persist with the approaches adopted, which have only subsequently proved disastrous. In my paper presented at the 'South Asia at the Crossroads' conference held in Dhaka I had pleaded that political leaders even under the constraints of democracies should discover that political courage does not lead to political suicide.

PARTITION AND THE MARGINALIZATION OF INDIA

With the licence of retirement and over twenty years' detachment from any classified information I feel more strongly than ever before that India was well placed to avoid many of the pitfalls that tempted us into misperceptions. Having joined the Ministry of External Affairs in the very week of Independence I can recall the euphoric expectation of India entering the community of nations. No other country had struggled for decades to achieve freedom. At the time, Dean Acheson believed that the independence of India could directly affect world peace and prosperity for generations to come. Rising above acrimony under the inspiration of Gandhi and the leadership of Nehru, India openly proclaimed friendship for Britain and adopted the British Parliamentary system and Nehru persuaded the country to stay in the Commonwealth. When Vijay Lakshmi Pandit presented her credentials in Dublin (1956), the President of Ireland said to her, 'We greatly admire your brother, the Prime Minister and much in India, but we cannot understand how you could stop hating the British'! Even Churchill, after a lifetime of uncompromising resistance against Indians being granted self-government, in 1955 consecrated Nehru as the 'Light of Asia'.

At the Asian Relations Conference in March 1947, on the eve

of the transfer of power, projecting India's role in the future, Nehru declared Asia was the emerging continent of the future. Situated as it was near the sea lanes of the Indian Ocean and touching the continental land mass, and lying between the Arab world and the south-east archipelago, India would be the fulcrum of the continent. Today, by general consent Asia does appear to be the continent of the twenty-first century, which would dominate world trade and politics. At the Jakarta meeting of ASPAC and ASEAN, which was attended by many Asian statesmen and also President Clinton, South Asia was pointedly excluded when an Asian Forum was launched.

The political marginalization of India, even when it is perceived as one of the emerging markets and economic dynamos, can be traced partly to the whirligig of events and manipulations outside India's control, and partly to native misperceptions. The single most important one was the partition of a naturally united subcontinent. The partition of India was a legacy of old imperial policies, a war-weary Birtain as inherited by the Attlee government and Mountbatten's exaggerated alarm at the outbreak of communal tensions in 1947: even old stalwarts in favour of a united secular India like Nehru, Patel and the Congress leaders finally accepted that partition was the lesser evil. This was a fatal misjudgement even from the point of view of the Muslims of the subcontinent. The division could have been prevented if Nehru, having read the reports of the Truman Doctrine propounded on 12 March, eleven days before his speech to the Asian Relations Conference, had thought that his whole vision for India and Asia would be jeopardized by the subcontinent being continuously plagued by tensions and conflicts; it could become prey to great power politics, which he was trying to avoid in his approach of non-alignment. Quite apart from this, were it not for the coincidences surrounding the hundred odd days in the Spring of 1947, when simultaneously decisions vital to the future of the post-War politics were being taken in Washington and Delhi, Washington would not have been indifferent to the partition of India if it had been guessed that the whole of China would be communist and not remain divided and weak. In December 1946, when India pledged to become a democratic republic there was no Russian interest in India. When Stalin's advice was informally sought by Ernest Bevin, the British Foreign Secretary at the time, the Marshal was completely nonchalant and just wished the British 'Good luck'. The division of India brought about a perverse and wholly malevolent connection between the two military blocs on the one hand and India-Pakistan on the other. If India had not been partitioned it would have had influence both in the Arab world and in South-East Asia. The Soviet Union has had little role to play in the Gulf. The linkage of the Cold War bequeathed decades of myopia and psychological tensions, debilitating the subcontinent. The Kashmir problem is a legacy of a hasty partition and is an impediment to the optimal development of the Indus and Gangetic basins.

Nehru is readily blamed for many of our failures. His greatest mistake was that he did not realize that he was not immortal. This was compounded by the fact that his colleagues and civil servant collaborators did not see that he could not be replicated and so abdicated their duty of advice and dissent. There were many flaws in his intellectual genealogy. To understand his failures it is important to bear in mind that he was conditioned like pre-war British Fabians in believing that socialism was the wave of the future. The Soviet Union did not prove a worthy model in the delivery of social justice. Nehru was equally mistaken in taking the cold warriors too seriously and believing that any conflict anywhere would escalate into a world war between the blocs. He was wishful in thinking that nationalism after imperialism would always be constructive and cooperative. Even on the eve of the India-China war, he failed to anticipate that a socialist country could launch a massive attack against a non-aligned country like India. While acknowledging these flaws, I firmly believe that had he lived for a few more years, he would have been an incomparable mentor to the world. He would have anticipated and welcomed détente between the blocs, and would not have allowed a nuclear race to further complicate South Asian politics. Indeed, judging from the alarm he expressed at the non-aligned conference in 1961 about nuclear radiation from tests by the USSR and the USA and his enthusiasm for the Partial Test

Ban Treaty (1963), he would have been at the forefront of the movement to check nuclear proliferation. Even while, simultaneously but not necessarily conditionally, pressing for total nuclear disarmament by the weapon powers, even after the India-China war Nehru would not have permitted India to become militarized, and to abandon the moral and peaceful ingredient in the calculus of national strength. As one who had urged Nepal to join the UN and even maintained the independent status of Sikkim and Bhutan, Nehru would not have allowed India to be viewed as a regional hegemon. He had envisaged that instead of military alliances disciplining constituent members in their foreign, economic and cultural relations, the nation-state system should reflect plurality and equality.

Today the world comes close to the original vision of Nehru. Ideologies have been domesticated and external relations are healthily determined by economic, trade and technological complementarities. After decades of emphasis on security, with no visible enemy, there is a strong withdrawal symptom in the West which occasionally even negates the abiding reality of globalist interdependence. India did not provide international leadership against the regressive misperceptions because it, too, had deviated from Nehruvian enlightened internationalism. India commanded respect when it stood for decolonization, anti-racism, peaceful resolution of conflicts, and international social justice through economic cooperation. Serious global problems like ecological interdependence or degradation of human rights and genocide demand sustained commitment by and through the UN. India should resist every temptation of exceptionalism under the cover of domestic sovereignty. It should be seen as a country which seeks to transparently square precept with example and restraint through accommodation.

THE REVIVED ROLE OF DIPLOMACY

From this discussion it follows that India, indeed the whole world, should repose faith in the role of diplomacy. In the Cold War decades, with the multiplicity of international fora and the new reaches of the media, diplomacy had become a craft of public relations and propaganda. Not infrequently brave rhetoric abroad was simply for political impact on the domestic constituency. Professionalism stopped at declarations, resolutions, joint communiqués and banquet speeches. Diplomats only infrequently were called upon to negotiate, find compromise solutions and reach agreements between sovereign partners on vital issues.

I was involved in seven hard bilateral negotiations, mostly on issues gridlocked in impasse for many years.[6] This included negotiating with Idi Amin and his government to obtain compensation for Indian nationals whose assets had been confiscated following their expulsion from Uganda. My experience does not allow endorsing the generally held view that diplomacy in the age of jet craft and telephones has no useful role to serve national economic development. Given some latitude by the government. I learnt that it was possible to persuade Pakistan to agree to India building a hydroelectric project at Salal on the Chenab (a river in Kashmir which was allocated to Pakistan under the Indus Treaty) which provides 690 megawatts of power to the Indian grid.

The greatest challenge facing diplomacy is in relation to contiguous neighbours, particularly when they are of unequal size or strength. One of India's neighbours is of equal weight and great importance (China), but it has five substantially smaller neighbours. In the twentieth century, small countries with a large international audience have a propensity to revel in suspicion and defiance. The big stick has almost invariably proved counterproductive: sanctions generally fail and deceit or gunboat-like intervention inflicts disproportionate and lasting political hostility. This is more so where there are shared resources like transfrontier rivers straddling ethnicity and uncontrollable migrations. These factors exacerbate public opinion on both sides. Flexibility for negotiated compromises calls for transparent sincerity which needs to be lubricated with measured unilateralism. The withdrawal of the Farakka item, which Bangladesh had placed on the General Assembly Agenda of 1976 was, a unique event in the history of the UN as only the sponsoring country could do so. In bringing this about, what was crucial was the help from Pakistan with whom relations had been normalized in the previous months. It was possible because on behalf of Indira Gandhi's government a credible assurance could be offered that bilateral talks would follow immediately and new compromises would be explored with sincerity.

The détente between the USSR and the USA became a reality because Gorbachev and Shevardnadze gave unilateral concessions to win over hitherto hostile national opinions. These included the dismantling of intermediate range nuclear weapons in Europe, the withdrawal of Soviet forces from Afghanistan, the termination of nuclear testing, and concessions to China including accepting the Thalweg in the Ussuri. Only after a conducive climate has been created can diplomatic negotiations turn around and reach meaningful resolutions. In the post-Cold War world professional diplomacy could become not only more complex, but also more rewarding.

Diplomacy—bilateral and regional—is the critical challenge in South Asia. If South Asia does not advance together in trust and cooperation India will be dragged down and prevented from realizing its great potential. Whether it is power, poverty, ecology, or legal and illegal migration, South Asian nations should have a parallel stake in the stability and progress of all members of the SAARC. Only when political tensions were muted that ASEAN became a significant part of the globalizing economy. Whether it is realizing the potential from the Ganges/Brahmaputra basin or intra-regional trade, or resolving the Kashmir imbroglio, the first imperative is to create an all-embracing environment of trust. Making Kashmir or any other issue as a precondition for friendly relations is putting the cart before the horse. It would have condemned the South Asian region to continuing and vicious economic enfeeblement, social degradation and ecological destruction.

DIPLOMACY, DEMOCRACY AND VOLUNTEERISM HAVE A CONVERGENT ROLE

The lessons of the Cold War and the fate of the Soviet Union highlight that external security should never be compartmentalized and prioritized at the cost of the domestic agenda.

Global security depends on regional stability, understanding which facilitates national economic progress. The approach should not be of imposition from above, but political participation and economic development beginning at the grass roots. My primary interest in the last twenty years has been volunteerism in the rural sector and education for responsible citizens. I have been associated with an NGO working in comprehensive rural development in five hundred tribal villages near my home town Udaipur and with an educational society running eleven institutions. Volunteerism is part of the Indian culture and is central to the Gandhian philosophy of social and political regeneration. It is generally a commitment to a small area or a particular field for social, economic, human dignity, gender equality, for the civil rights of those suffering from inherent disabilities and the blight of poverty. In the wake of the acknowledged failure of socialism and disenchantment with the bureaucratic delivery system, after decades of suspicion, even official declarations have emphasized that NGOs play an important role in encouraging people's involvement in alleviating poverty and building a civil society. It would take years of patient effort for the peace dividend from diplomacy to reach the poor; people must be empowered to have the self-confidence to conserve and restore their common and natural resources. One of the great misperceptions has been to impose security and to export democracy. Citizens' awareness and self-confidence and grass-roots participation are the true guardians and guarantors of democracy.

India's greatest achievement has been that the will to freedom under Nehru's leadership was grounded in a democratic constitution. The masses have become aware of the power of their vote to choose and reject their leaders. They demand sagacity and integrity from their elected representatives. They are ready to accept discipline and are even willing to sacrifice to rescue the seemingly dark future if they see evidence of commitment and ethics from their chosen leaders.

To underline South Asia's ecological interdependence and space for volunteerism, I had once suggested that a South Asian Environmental Protective Authority should be set up under which around 10,000 youths in mixed groups of Indians and Nepalis (and later contingents of Bangladeshis and Bhutanese), living in austere camps spend a year planting trees, checking soil erosion in both the Indian and the Nepalese Himalayas. I had proposed that an endowment (as against yearly subvention) should be made by India (with or without supplementary assistance from foreign sources or other subcontinental neighbours). It should be controlled by an independent board representing governments but with an equal number of non-officials and voluntary organizations. To immunize the authority against political changes, it should be headed by a non-official from one of the member countries. Academic credit and even employment preference could be offered to those young men and women who participate in such regional volunteerism to save the regional ecology. One of the political parties in India included this idea in its manifesto but it has not been seriously considered. I remain an unrepentant dove as well as a defiant optimist. Misperceptions are neither divinely decreed nor built into human frailty. To despair of the 'Human condition' is unacceptable, as that way lies madness for men and nations.

NOTES

1. J.S. Mehta, *The March of Folly in Afghanistan*, New Delhi: Manohar, 2000.
2. Barbara Tuchman, *The March of Folly: From Troy to Vietnam*, New York: Knopf, 1984.
3. Robert Jervis, *Perception and Misperception in International Politics*, Princeton: Princeton University Press, 1976.
4. Yaacov Vertzberger, *Misperception in Foreign Policy Making: the Sino-Indian Conflict, 1959-1962*, Boulder: Westview, 1984.
5. His latest book is also extremely useful in understanding the problems of processing information in a decision-making system. See Vertzberger, *The World in their Minds: Information Processing, Cognition, and Perception in Foreign Policy Decisionmaking*, Palo Alto: Stanford University Press, 1990.
6. J.S. Mehta, *Negotiating for India: Resolving Problems through Diplomacy*, New Delhi: Manohar, 2006.

PART ONE
With Nehru

1

The Nehru We Loved to Serve
(A Personal Memoir)

Indians who grew up under the shadow of Jawaharlal Nehru are still sentimental about him. Those of us who came in contact with him are not ashamed of the willing suspension of our critical faculties. We have a sense of historic privilege to have seen and heard him. As Wordsworth felt about the French Revolution, it was an exhilaration for us to be alive and young to see India at a new dawn of history and have Nehru as the helmsman. In the nostalgia of his centenary year, the feeling grows that we will never see the likes of Nehru in authority. Gandhi we worshipped but Nehru we loved. Nehru embodied fearless courage in political strife and nobility of purpose in the quest for India's freedom. He gave us pride and confidence in independence, but it is only now that we see he had a prophetic vision for the world.

Attempting an intellectual balance sheet of his place in history is naturally hard, but the present and future turns in international politics will progressively vindicate the validity of his ideals. We in India must not belittle his faith, and never stop asking the question, 'What course would Nehru have followed were he alive today?' We are in danger of praising him ritually and forgetting the essence of the convictions behind the ends and the means he urged on his fellow countrymen. This personal recollection only recalls Nehru the man, which comes from the experience of serving Nehru the Prime Minister.

In the roulette of the circumstances of my Foreign Service career, I make believe that through the entire seventeen years

* Paper presented at a seminar in Toronto in 1989, and published in Milton Israel (ed.), *Nehru and the Twentieth Century*, University of Toronto, Centre for South Asian Studies, South Asian Studies Papers, Number 4, Toronto, 1991.

that Nehru was prime minister of India, few officials had so many opportunities to see him so closely from the sidelines. I have half a dozen albums of photographs with him taken on different occasions. I also have two eight mm films of Nehru—both in some ways unique.

One film is of a ten-day trip during a general election tour in 1957 when, as an official not in his personal secretariat, I had the unusual privilege to see, at close quarters, Nehru interacting with the Indian masses. The trip included staying in Anand Bhawan, the ancestral Nehru home in Allahabad, and following him as he stumped through his own constituency (Phulpur), then to Nagpur in the Central Province, Telangana, which was part of the domain of the Nizam of Hyderabad, and Karnataka, which used to be the princely state of Mysore. He did not have a helicopter for his use, as has become available to his successors, but even so he made three air-stops every day and some twenty million Indians must have seen and heard him in those ten days. The most interesting part of the journey was by road and rail through the length of Kerala, where the crowds went wild with enthusiasm, though those were the only elections that Nehru lost in his time.

We travelled mostly by an Ilyushin-14, which was the first Soviet aircraft in India and had been presented for Nehru's personal use by the Soviet government. On the last day but one of the ten-day tour, while in flight from Mangalore off the west coast, to Jabalpur back in the centre of the country, the port engine caught fire and Nehru (and what mattered less, the rest of us) came very near to a violent death. Fortunately, the fire extinguishing system worked before the flames could reach the fuel tanks. Nehru never lost his cool—in fact, if I remember correctly, he was reading the full text of Krishna Menon's nine-hour long speech on Kashmir delivered in the Security Council.

The Air Force pilot made a skilful landing on one engine on an unused, unmanned and isolated airstrip. The strip had been built during the Second World War by the US Air Force for emergency landings for military aircraft on their way to deliver supplies over the Burma (now Myanmar) hump for the Kuomintang forces in China fighting the Japanese. For once one was grateful for bureaucratic delays, as the state government orders to plough up the airfield had not been implemented. There were cattle grazing on the overgrown airstrip, but they moved away with two buzzing runs. This was fortunate, because on one engine it would have been difficult to regain height. Nehru had to be helped down as there was no aircraft gangway at hand. All that Nehru symbolises for me is encapsulated in the remark of the lone herdsman as Nehru was being helped down. He exclaimed, '*Are ye to Panditji hain! Hame to kisi ne bataiya bhi nahi, ki wo yahan aa rahe hai*,' which translates as: '*Are*' [an exclamation], 'This is Panditji, and no one even told us he was coming here.' The herdsman immediately rushed to touch Nehru's feet, but Nehru forbade him to do so. Instead the Prime Minister put his arms around the unknown Indian. The herdsman's response was representative of the deep respect that Nehru the beloved leader enjoyed even in remotest corners of India. We walked to a lone schoolhouse where a few hundred villagers quickly gathered from nowhere and Nehru squatted and talked to them for a couple of hours. We were rescued by an Air Force transport Dakota of Second World War vintage, with no seats. A chair was tied to the floor of the aircraft with ropes for Nehru's use, and, though much delayed, he insisted on addressing the scheduled public meeting at Jabalpur.

Several seconds of my film strip, taken out of the window as the fuselage near the engine was crumbling, were considered useful by the Court of Enquiry ordered by the Chief of Air Staff. A deeply embarrassed Air Marshal Mukerjee awaited us when we landed the next morning in New Delhi where the entire cabinet was also present to greet Nehru—the morning newspapers had described the incident a miraculous escape from a national tragedy. Nehru, cheerful as a lark, was almost irritated at the fuss. Incidentally, the Soviet Union promptly, and somewhat secretly, took the Ilyushin back and within weeks replaced it with another, even better equipped craft for the Prime Minister's use.

The second film is of three-week journey on hill ponies and yaks to Bhutan and back, but more about the Bhutan trip later. Panditji thought my film on the Bhutan trip was better than the official one, and so I have given a copy to the Nehru Library.

I first saw Nehru as part of a cheering crowd. I was an undergraduate at the University of Allahabad during the War years, and he had come home in an interlude between imprisonments. Thanks to a Kashmiri friend, who was distantly related to the Nehru family, I was fortunate to be invited to one of the functions held after Indiraji got married to Feroze Gandhi in the spring of 1942. My first face-to-face encounter with Nehru happened when, as Vice-President of the Governor-General's Council and Minister of External Affairs (1946-7), he interviewed each one of us in a group of 13-15 officers. We had been selected for the Indian Civil Service but had expressed a preference for the old Indian Political Service, and were thus considered as the first entrants to the new Indian Foreign Service. I remember how the awe, anxiety and nervousness quickly turned to relaxed adulation. He asked me why I had chosen to go to St. John's College at Cambridge. As a sort of undergraduate humour, I claimed superiority over the next-door Trinity and reminded him of the territorial encroachment of his college on St. John's which required in repayment that the Trinity clock chime twice—once for Trinity and the second time for St. John's. In a sort of an equally undergraduate reaction, he affirmed the superiority of his own college. What nonplussed me was his question why I wanted to join the Foreign Service. After some hesitation, I muttered something about wanting to travel and enjoy myself. It was my first experience of his famous quicksilver half-anger. Nehru reacted, 'What! Is that what your interest is in this career?' I replied, 'Sir, if I had made more pretentious claims you would not have believed me anyway.' He smiled in his characteristically affectionate way and said that I had better be prepared for hard work, etc., and graciously signified his approval.

I could have joined the Service in July 1947. However, I decided to defer it till immediately after the transfer of power which was to take place in a few weeks' time. As my father was a member of the Constituent Assembly, he got me a gallery pass and I heard Nehru's historic midnight address, proclaiming that while the 'world sleeps, India awakens to keep its tryst with destiny'. Without a day's training, I was yoked to work as Private Secretary to Sir Girja Shankar Bajpai who had been appointed as Secretary-General of the Ministry. Nehru had criticized Bajpai when as Agent-General of India in Washington (which was, of course, part of the British embassy), he had carried on a propaganda against India's independence during the War years. The rehabilitation of Bajpai and his appointment to a specially created super-secretary post, in effect a sort of Vice-Foreign Minister, was itself a tribute to Nehru's magnanimity in overcoming his earlier prejudice.

When Nehru took charge of the External Affairs portfolio in September 1946, he found that most of the officers of his department, headed by Sir Hugh Weightman, the immediate successor of Sir Olaf Caroe, were British.[1] Even as a constituent part of the Empire and under the East India Company, there was a sort of sub-Foreign Office under the Governor-General in India. This department, with its separate service, had more say than Whitehall in the running after British interests in the circumference around India. British representations in the Trucial States of the Gulf, Tibet, Sinkiang, Afghanistan, Nepal, partially in Persia and to some extent on both coasts of the Indian Ocean were managed from Calcutta, Delhi and Simla. To underline the importance of his position, the official head of the British Indian External Affairs Department was designated Foreign Secretary, a title equivalent to that Secretary of State for Foreign Affairs in the United Kingdom. Knowing the prestige which went with the post, Nehru decided to occupy a small room rather than displace the British Foreign Secretary from the vast room with a private verandah with Corinthian columns, facing the Viceregal Lodge. Nehru knew that Sir Girja had the same sort of sensitivity about the style in Government and so he allowed him to occupy in June 1947 what was considered the most prestigious office in the Imperial Secretariat. Nehru moved into the present office occupied by successive prime ministers only in 1952 when Bajpai left Delhi to become Governor of Bombay.

Even though his foreign policy approaches were to be radically different from those of the old British Imperial ones, during the Interim Government period, Nehru did not summarily ask for replacement of the British officers. Humphrey Trevelyan, one of the senior officers, quickly won Nehru's confidence and was asked to prepare the plans for the constitution of a Foreign Service for India. Nehru even asked him to stay on after the transfer of power but Trevelyan did not think it was appropriate for a non-Indian to be in the Foreign Office and switched to the British service dropping by two ranks in equivalence. But he made a great second career, ending up as head of the British embassies in China, Egypt, Iraq and the USSR. After retirement, he became Governor of Aden and finally Keeper of the British Museum. He was elevated to a peerage and made Knight of the Garter, something that is unusual for any British civil servant.

Nehru, of course, was never infected by the virus of position and protocol of office. Rather than summon an officer, he would frequently walk down the corridor or around the first floor of the quadrangle and see him in his own office. He invariably dropped in to see Bajpai when he came or left the building for Parliament or for outside engagements. He never objected to the nameplate outside Bajpai's room with the imposing string of British titles KCSI, KBE, CIE, ICS. (Only after our Republican Constitution came into force and the use of titles was officially forbidden was the nameplate changed.) Both Nehru and Bajpai worked longer hours than any other officer—and invariably all through Saturdays and at least till lunch on Sundays and other special holidays. Theirs was a powerful duet with great mutual respect and intellectual rapport even if they did not have a total concurrence of views. Bajpai, who was known to be ruthlessly critical of most people, found in Nehru someone who was more than his intellectual equal. Both were superb draftsmen dictating down to colons, semi-colons and exclamation marks. Their literary styles were very different, but they enjoyed comparing each other's draft replies to important telegrams. Occassionally, I would be in the room with Bajpai when Pandit*ji* walked in. On more than one occasion I heard Pandit*ji* graciously say, 'Your draft to B.N. Rau (the Permanent Representative to the UN) better expresses what I wanted to say. Let your draft go' (which of course was sent as from the Prime Minister). This characteristic of Nehru's self-confident generosity enthused the officials who worked for him.

Those first months of Independence are terrible to contemplate even now. I saw the stream of telegrams and at times had to act as a courier to the Operations room established by Lord Mountbatten in the Governor-General's residence, where the cross-border migrations and the communal incidents were plotted and for daily decisions taken by the Emergency Committee of the Cabinet. Cycling back late at night after curfew hours was eerie. The mental agony of those holocaust days was writ large on Nehru's face, but so much has been written about it that I can scarcely add anything new.

From the perspective of the ante-room and the peephole, I recall the flurry of meetings and the air of ominous urgency as reports came in of the tribal incursions from Pakistan into the Valley of Kashmir in October 1947. It led to the accession of the state of Jammu and Kashmir to the Indian Union and the despatch of a battalion of the Indian Army which landed just in time to save Srinagar from being overrun. Nehru had insisted that Sheikh Abdullah, the popular leader of Kashmir, be released and inducted to form the government before the accession could be accepted. Once the state became a part of India, there was no compulsion to couple it with any conditions about its finality. While for Nehru there was a special sentiment about his ancestral homeland and its symbolism for his secular ideals, the idealist in him showed his abhorrence for the need to use force in the first months after Independence and the seeming compromise with the cherished principle of self-determination.

I was also witness to the series of meetings around Christmas 1947, discussing the question of whether or not Pakistan's involvement in Kashmir should be referred to the United Nations Security Council. I remember being asked to fetch a copy of the UN Charter when the question came up whether the reference to be made should be under Chapter VI (Pacific Settlement of Disputes) or Chapter VII (Threat to Peace and an Act of Aggression). Bajpai handled the diplomatic side of the Kashmir dispute in the ministry during the initial discussions in January 1948. I accompanied Bajpai in the delegation for the second round of the Security Council meetings in March-April 1948. I was also the flunky around in the subsequent discussions with the UN Commission for India and Pakistan which led to further exchanges in Paris during the General Assembly and culminated in the ceasefire on 1 January 1949.

Much has been written in India questioning the wisdom of making the reference on Kashmir to the UN Security Council. There are good reasons to believe that Mountbatten was an important factor. Mountbatten obviously wanted to avoid the prospect of a war between the two Dominions while he was still Governor-General. His plan to advance the date of the transfer of power from June 1948 to August 1947 to not one but two successor states was accepted because of the implicit assumption that communal tensions could only thus be diffused. Mountbatten was able to overcome Churchill's opposition to the Indian Independence Bill because he brought the assurance that Nehru was agreeable to India having Dominion status after the transfer of power. Faced with infiltration in Kashmir, Nehru was hesitant to launch a war because it was abhorrent to him that in the first year of freedom there should be a departure from a commitment to peaceful resolution of international problems. The Hamlet in Nehru became evident when he had to decide between cherished principles and urgent military action. He thus also hoped that the UN reference would deflect the possibility of war with Pakistan. Alas it came and continued anyway.

In October 1948, I was part of a small delegation accompanying Nehru on his first visit abroad as prime minister to attend the Commonwealth Prime Ministers' Conference in London. For the first time, the heads of the Governments of India, Pakistan, and Ceylon (now Sri Lanka) sat as equals with those of the old white Dominions like Canada, Australia, South Africa and New Zealand. It was the first time that Indian diplomatic passports were used: Nehru's passport carried the number 1, Mrs Vijayalakshmi Pandit's passport was no. 2, Sir Girja's no. 3, and I think M.O. Matthai's was fourth in the series, and my own first diplomatic passport was no. 8. Nehru almost always travelled commercial even on long flights abroad. Normally Air India flew straight west from Bombay (now Mumbai), and the only concession in order to save time was that the routine service was diverted to pick up the Prime Minister and his party from Delhi. The other courtesy was to keep the adjoining seat vacant and improvise a bed for him for what was then an eight-hour flight to Cairo.

Nehru had run great risks of being killed in the post-Partition frenzy by rushing into the middle of murderously inflamed communal riots. Sardar Patel, as Deputy Prime Minister and Home Minister, had succeeded in overcoming Nehru's resistance to a personal security officer being attached to him in India. Nehru had reluctantly accepted the decision but he could not understand the point of an Indian bodyguard abroad. He thought Scotland Yard could do the job better. The Indian Deputy Superintendent assigned to him as security officer was left behind in Cairo to have a holiday until he rejoined the party on the way back! Incidentally, Nehru and the particular Scotland Yard inspector—I forget the name—developed an equation of mutual respect and, thereafter, the same inspector was always attached to him on his visits to London.

In London, Nehru and the small party were booked to stay in Claridges, with Nehru occupying the corner suite on the second floor. My own duties involved being a mix of an archivist for the conference papers, a resident clerk, ADC, and a protocol officer for receiving and seeing off the stream of high-powered visitors and occasionally drafting unimportant summaries and telegrams. I remember Panditji asking me to invite Ernie Bevin, the then British Foreign Secretary, to breakfast and instructing me to ask his private secretary what he would like for breakfast. The reply came back: 'The Foreign Secretary would like chicken curry!' Always a good host and particular about food and fruits and culinary excellence, the Prime Minister asked me to make sure that the Claridges chef knew how to make a proper chicken curry and not to send up an Anglicized imitation of it: 'Otherwise arrange to get it from elsewhere'. I cautioned the catering manager, and Bevin had a hearty breakfast. Anyway, I was not going to risk getting it from a restaurant and appropriating the blame if it did not come up to Nehru's exacting taste.

Nehru certainly was the most handsome amongst the prime ministers. In his custom-made three-piece pre-War suits, he was also one of the best dressed around the table. Hats were still in vogue and Nehru acquired a homburg from Scotts the best hatters in the West End and wore it with natural aplomb. Over the weekends, however, he always used an old, weatherbeaten felt hat, which was not so smart but was an obvious favourite, and a Burberry mackintosh (both seemed pre-War acquisitions). After 1953 Nehru stopped using Western clothes on his trips abroad, but over the weekends he would revert to tweed jacket and grey flannels. (One could see he had not discarded the old hat and the old 'mac'.) At the Commonwealth Conference I picked up a scrap of paper from 10 Downing Street slipblock in which Sir Stafford Cripps, then Chancellor of the Exchequer and of course an old friend, had asked Nehru if he would come to his country house for the weekend. Nehru wrote back that he was going to Broadlands, the Mountbatten home in Hampshire. On every subsequent visit to England, Nehru would go to Broadlands over the weekends. Even when he was invited to Chequers, the country home of British prime ministers; he would spend part of the weekend with the Mountbattens.

I was also part of the delegation for the Prime Minister's visit to London for the shorter but historically more important conference in April 1949 which considered and decided that even after India became a republic under the new Indian constitution, it would remain a member of the Commonwealth. Historians have described at length how the decision was shepherded in the face of opposition in India and in some parts of the White Commonwealth. Finding the right basis and semantic formula was not easy. Nehru's own persuasion and drafting improvements were the critical factors but credit must also go to Cripps, Krishna Menon and the telling support of Prime Minister Malan of South Africa. Canada played a very important role both in overcoming the opposition from Australia and New Zealand (because they felt there was no place in the Commonwealth family if there was no allegiance to the Crown) and in evolving the final formula of words. There were many drafting sessions between Lester Pearson who as Foreign Minister was accompanying St. Laurent, the Canadian Prime Minister, and Bajpai (who alone amongst all officials then present was at the London meetings in 1927, which led to the Statute of Westminster). Pearson and Bajpai had known each other from the War years in Washington; both had a facility with words. Somewhere I have on scraps of Claridges letterheads drafts and corrections in the attempt to find the ultimate formula: 'The King as head of the Commonwealth and the symbol of our association.' The credit for the way the Commonwealth has grown over the years goes certainly to Nehru. The Commonwealth now has a membership of over fifty countries, big and small, rich and poor, from different continents, belonging to diverse races and religions. Had Nehru's political courage in persuading India to stay in the Commonwealth been voiced a year and a half earlier, it is possible that Myanmar might have remained in the Commonwealth and not shut itself up in suicidal isolation.

The sequel to the Indian decision to stay in the Commonwealth was the historic reconciliation between Churchill and Nehru. After the decision was announced, Churchill's Secretary rang to say that the great man wanted to call on Nehru. I remember receiving the call when we were due to leave London the next morning. Characteristically, Nehru said he himself would call on Churchill on the way to the airport. Nehru described the meeting on the flight after we took off from Heathrow. Churchill, he said, was emotional, almost sentimental, and said something to the effect, 'Sir, I have done you great wrong. You are like the prodigal who has returned to the fold of the family.' The great Churchillian tribute ('Mr. Prime Minister you have conquered two great human infirmities: you have conquered Fear and you have conquered Hate') was to come later. But that meeting in 1949 was the beginning of a remarkable friendship between the two great forgiving statesmen. Nehru would telephone Churchill even if he was only passing through London. I cannot help speculating that Nehru might have wanted Churchill to visit independent India. Churchill, of course, was too old to do so, but one can safely conjecture that Nehru would have ensured the warmest welcome for his old political adversary, symbolizing a historic reconciliation and the grand finale in the downs and ups of Britain's relations with India. I was not in London when Churchill and Nehru together went to their old school and sang Harrow songs. Their new-found mutual regard speaks volumes for the greatness of the two fearless fighters.

My next memory is of Nehru's personal interest when I got married. Rama, my wife, was one of the first women members of the Foreign Service. Panditji was strongly supportive of women working in the civil services. When Rama and I decided to get married, we were confronted with the provision in the new Indian Foreign Service rules which (copying the prescriptions in the rules of the British Service at the time) laid down that if a woman entrant decided to get married she should seek permission with an accompanying letter of resignation. My wife wanted to stay on in the Service and we knew the Prime Minister was sympathetically inclined. However, the higher echelons in the department, notably my own chief, Sir Girja Shanker Bajpai, were socially conservative and stated quite categorically that a married woman's place was at home, and in a diplomatic career her duty was to play the hostess. However, thanks largely to Nehru, Rama was allowed to continue while we were both serving in the Ministry. But the rule was enforced and she had to resign when, after four years at headquarters, I was transferred abroad.

In subsequent years, every time the Prime Minister saw Rama he would say she should be working. When I was posted in London, Panditji seeing her 'doing nothing', sent a minute to the Foreign Secretary that she be appointed in the High Commission on an ad hoc basis. For all his domination of foreign policy, Nehru would seldom overrule matters of administration when the bureaucracy was firm. The regulations and traditional arguments were respectfully presented to the Prime Minister and Rama remained a hostess, scribbling articles for Indian papers. Occasionally, Nehru would see these articles in print and would often give words of encouragement, especially for the writings on social problems. Rama and my children received many marks of his thoughtful and indulgent affections. Often, especially when as director of the division during the China crisis I was obviously overworked, he would ask Mrs Indira Gandhi to invite the whole family including our four children (ranging between four and ten) for breakfast. What my daughter remembers is how Nehru would butter the toast and pass on slices of fruit to her.

By a quirk of circumstances, the Prime Minister intervened in my first posting abroad in a comparatively lowly capacity as First Secretary. In the spring of 1951, the Foreign Service Board had nominated me as Head of Chancery and number two in our embassy in Bonn. Just before I was to hand over, following the death of the first Minister to Switzerland, there was an ugly incident of internal feud in our legation in Bern. It is unnecessary to recall the details here but *Blitz*, the weekly from Bombay, blazoned a report of factionalism almost leading to physical violence, and that too under the gaze of Swiss dignitaries and prior to the funeral of the late Minister. The Foreign Affairs Committee of the Cabinet quickly took up the embarrassing report. The Committee, apart from Nehru, included Rajagopalachari, who after having been Governor-General had joined the Government as the Home Minister, Maulana Azad, the Minister for Education, and some other senior members of the government. Without being given a reason, I was asked by the head of the administration in the ministry to present myself before the Cabinet Committee where I was given a once over. The next day, at the National Day party at the Dutch embassy for Queen Juliana's birthday—in the early days he attended such parties—Nehru called me aside and said that my posting had been changed. I was to go as soon as possible to Bern instead of Bonn and relieve all four or five officers of the mission and 'clean up' the place. We were then expecting our daughter in a few weeks' time but none of us dared to put forward our personal wishes before public duty. Our daughter was born while I was on a ship approaching Aden. I did not eventually regret the change to a politically less interesting post, as from Bern our mission also covered Austria, the Vatican, and international organizations in Geneva. I specially enjoyed unravelling the workings of the Vatican and wrote the first report on the Vatican's foreign policy.

In 1953, as First Secretary and number two in our mission in Bern, I found myself responsible for organizing the meeting of the heads of Indian missions in Burgenstock near Lucerne. The meeting was fixed to follow the Commonwealth Prime Ministers' Conference which was timed to coincide with the coronation of

Queen Elizabeth. The ambassador, Asaf Ali, had died suddenly just six weeks before the proposed conference. When Nehru and Mrs Gandhi went to London, Rajiv, the future prime minister, and Sanjay were left behind and I took them to spend time at Paul Geheeb's famous school which had quit Hitler's Germany and established itself in the Bernese Oberland. (Almost no one other than the Nehru family in India would have known about the Oldenwald Schule.) The whole family and some fifteen heads of our diplomatic missions gathered in the spectacularly located hotel that we had entirely to ourselves because the season had not yet begun. Nehru revelled in the setting overlooking Lake Lucerne on one side and the snow-capped mountains at the back with only cows at pasture in between. The Burgenstock meeting was memorable for many reasons. While we were discussing the international situation, Nasser displaced Neguib in Egypt and the workers rioted in East Berlin. Nehru's international prestige was then near its zenith. We arranged for Dr Grueber, the Austrian Foreign Minister, to call on Nehru at Burgenstock. This meeting was followed by Nehru instructing our ambassador to the USSR to appeal to the post-Stalin Soviet government to settle the Austrian question and end the four-power occupation of the country. It is now generally recognized that Nehru's efforts contributed to the conclusion of the Austrian State Treaty in 1955.

There was a visit by Charlie Chaplin after the conference concluded. I fetched Chaplin from Lucerne and brought him across the lake by boat rather than by the long, tortuous road route. Chaplin spent the night in the hotel. I remember Nehru telling Rajiv and Sanjay about Charlie Chaplin before the latter arrived. There was instant rapport between the Prime Minister and the actor because, in essence, both were committed social idealists with natural empathy for the downtrodden. They talked at length in the large sitting room with a view of the mountains at the back. It was then that Chaplin complained, 'I like everything about you, Mr. Prime Minister, except that you don't drink.' Nehru replied, 'Is that all you have against me?' and promptly ordered a sherry. Next day, on the way to Geneva, we had lunch at the beautiful Chaplin villa near Vevey, where Oona Chaplin and Claire Bloom were also present.

Burgenstock was the first time that I saw Nehru in the mountains. He was obviously relaxed as he went up in a funicular across a little lake and then on a chair lift. The boyish sixty-four-year-old Prime Minister played with snowballs with his grandsons on the high slopes of Engelbert. He remained youthful in so many ways all his life.

In 1955, when I was posted in London, Nehru came to attend another Commonwealth Prime Ministerial Conference. He accepted an invitation to visit Cambridge. His nephews (Harish and Ajit) were both in residence. He spoke in the Union but I remember well that, like any old Cambridge man, he insisted on walking through the Backs, even in freezing temperatures.

My posting in London was enjoyable, especially after I became head of the External Department at the High Commission where, unlike in Bern, there were no administrative responsibilities. I had been in the post for barely two years when Lady Mountbatten told me at a reception that I was to leave London almost immediately. I rushed next morning to Mrs Pandit, the High Commissioner, gingerly trying to find out why I had not been told of my premature move and whether it signified some sort of disapproval. She protested that no such transfer was known to her, nor would it be agreed to. Apparently Lady Mountbatten had got to know about my transfer directly from the Prime Minister even before we had received any official communication from Delhi. The ministry was then making preparations for the possibility of a revival of the Kashmir debate in the UN Security Council. It had, therefore, been decided at a high level to set up a special cell on Kashmir. Having been associated with the early phase of the Kashmir discussions, I was selected, with the Prime Minister's approval to head that cell. As it happened, another officer who was looking after the public relations side of the work during the Security Council discussions suddenly became available. So I didn't do the Kashmir assignment. However, my immediate transfer was not rescinded. I had to pack up and report back home within ten days of the orders but, thanks to the tip from Lady Mountbatten, we had a few more days to prepare.

After a few months in the Personnel Division, I was attached to Krishna Menon for the Suez crisis and served as Secretary of the delegation for the first London Conference in August 1956. I remember in the briefing session how surprised and horrified Nehru was that liberal democracies should conspire to re-establish control over the Suez after the process of decolonization was inexorably underway.

At the end of 1956, I was moved as Deputy Secretary to the Eastern Division, which dealt with our northern neighbours (Nepal, Bhutan, Sikkim, Tibet) and East Asia (China, Japan, Korea, Mongolia), and also administered the North East Frontier Agency (NEFA—since named Arunachal Pradesh). Having been only in Europe till then, I was scarcely qualified in terms of background much less expertise for the Eastern Division. Apparently I was chosen because of previous experience in administration, and we were to create a new pattern of administration for the tribal belt. But the move also initiated my involvement with China which in one way or the other continued for twenty-three years and covered all four seasons of our relations with that country.

Incidentally, it is worth digressing on why Nehru insisted on retaining the administration of NEFA and Nagaland under the External Affairs Ministry for all the years he was prime minister. (The responsibility was transferred to the Home Ministry only after his death.) It provides a clue to Nehru's special concern and sensitivity for the tribal people of India. He appointed Verrier Elwin, the famous anthropologist, as adviser and after seeking counsel with him, gave detailed directives for our guidance. The thrust of his instructions was that the distinct and diverse tribal structures and customs should be respected. He insisted that development should be gradual, and the tribes should be protected from encroachment and exploitation by plainsmen and Marwari merchants and moneylenders. He resisted the imposition of the standard district administrative pattern, which, he thought, would destroy the way of life of the tribals. His approach was a ready contrast to China's approach to Tibet, just across the Himalayas.

In January 1959, three middle-level officers (one from the Air Force, one from the Army, and myself) and Shobha Kanwar, belonging to the princely state of Jodhpur, decided to go to Gulmarg for a rather rough skiing holiday. All of us had skied before, and Shobha had been at a finishing school in Switzerland. The Prime Minister heard about this planned adventure because Shobha, with her multilingual fluency, was working off and on with Mrs Pandit in the Prime Minister's house. He suggested that we should take along Rajiv, then fourteen, who was home from Doon School. Rajiv had never skied before and since we were not exactly qualified instructors, we were somewhat nervous about being responsible for the Prime Minister's grandson. But we obviously couldn't say 'no'. Gulmarg, at a height of 9000 feet, was beautiful and invigorating in the winter sun but deathly cold (minimum –20°-25°C) at night. Staying in a hut with no more than a wooden stove and no servants was a far cry from a Swiss chalet in winter or the prime minister's residence in Delhi. There were then no skiing facilities in Gulmarg and we did not tell the golfers in Delhi that we had planned to ski on the famous course—we knew we would be the only ones around. When we felt really energetic, we had the option to put skins on our skis and trudge up to Khilan Marg, taking three hours in order to get a fifteen-minute run down the slopes. Rajiv Gandhi turned out to be tougher than the rest of us and, of course, more of a daredevil, hurtling down, without even learning how to stem turn and stop. The sort of encouragement and subsequent benediction Nehru expressed on our return was characteristic of his own inclination for out-of-the-way adventure.

My most intense and direct contact with Nehru was after the Sino-Indian crisis erupted in the spring of 1959. This is not the place to discuss the substantive problem in detail. When our relations with China plummeted, aside from the Foreign Secretary and in the absence of a Joint Secretary, even as a Deputy Secretary (the equivalent of senior First Secretary), I found myself as the Principal Operational Officer dealing with China and Tibet. All at once, we had to deal with the arrival of the Dalai Lama and his cabinet, and the migration into India of one hundred thousand Tibetans through widely separated mountain passes. The most difficult part was responding to the sudden and often angry Parliamentary interest, which was aroused after some incidents on the border and the public confirmation that the highway from Sinkiang in the north to western Tibet cut across Aksai

Chin in Kashmir. There were daily detail-seeking short notice questions, and sometimes several adjournment motions in a week. I was in the official box almost every day in one or the other House of Parliament. Nehru personally handled all questions in both Houses, often on the same day. Sometimes there was only a minute or two to brief him and that too when he was going from one House to the other. I could not accompany him by the shorter route which is across the Central Hall as officials are debarred from it. He got furious because when he wanted some clarification I was running round the long outer gallery. When I explained the reason he ordered that, as an exception, I should be given a pass to use the Central Hall so that I could walk with him when he went from the Lok Sabha to the Rajya Sabha or vice versa. At least until then no other officer had been authorized this intrusion into the sanctum of the parliamentarians. Preparing briefs for the visit of Zhou-Enlai in 1960 while the budget session was on was a particularly demanding period. Since I could not risk taking highly secret files home, I actually slept in the office for a month. Somehow Nehru got to know that I was working through the night, and he would periodically throw in a word or gesture of encouragement. Sometimes I had to go and see him after dinner with urgent drafts or to seek directions. I was touched when the senior personal assistant at the house told me that the Prime Minister had ordered that I should be allowed to see him even after dinner and late at night.

I would like to mention one of the many incidents illustrating Nehru's graciousness which made us all his willing slaves and deeply grateful for the privilege of working for him. In the third and concluding round of the official talks on the Sino-Indian boundary held in Rangoon, we had to make our final statements, scrutinize each other's reports, and make sure that we did not supplement or detract from what we had stated in the substantive sessions in Beijing and Delhi. In the Rangoon session, the full text of both reports had to be reviewed and then copy-typed for signing by the leaders of the two official teams. The Burmese government, we learnt indirectly, wanted us out of Rangoon because a large Chinese delegation was expected to come and celebrate the signing of the Sino-Burmese Boundary Treaty. The two reports together were over six hundred printed pages and perhaps twice as long in type. Our team had only four stenographers. Within a week or so the four typing for about nineteen hours every day, had the report completed in a form that was suitable for signing—which meant not even a single correction on any page. (Needless to say this was almost twenty-five years before the Ministry acquired its first computer.) I do not know if any other stenographers in the world could have matched the zest and competence of our much-derided *babus*. As leader of the team, I felt immensely grateful to have the report completed in time. I wanted some reward for the monumental exertions of our stenographers. I could have, of course, got them a few hundred rupees as a special honorarium for their labour. I reported to the Prime Minister that, aside from the ability of the senior colleagues from the Historical Division, these functional members of the team had truly excelled themselves. I requested him to meet the delegation, but especially the stenographer typists. He readily agreed and I remember he came to the office specially on Christmas Day 1960 to be photographed with the group. For the rest of their lives, the lowly officials boasted of the privilege of possessing a photograph with the Prime Minister in his office in the Secretariat. They never asked for any monetary reward.

Like all who worked for Nehru, I too had to occasionally face his proverbial temper. On one occasion I had the temerity to tell him that an off-the-cuff statement he had made in Parliament was not consistent with our interests. Perhaps I mangled my words and was less than coherent in his presence. He did not grasp what I was trying to say and interrupted me and snapped, 'I thought you were an intelligent boy. You are a damned fool.' I had seen enough of him over the years not to be totally flummoxed and quietly said, 'I am glad, Sir, you have not forgotten your Harrow idioms'. He kept quiet and silently walked out of the room and as he reached the grand staircase of the Ministry, he put his arms around me. It was Nehru's way to react spontaneously and then give it some thought. Having later grasped what I was spluttering about, he corrected his earlier statement in Parliament.

Nehru had, of course, something of the Anglo-Saxon sense of humour. Before leaving for Rangoon (now Yangon), I had hurriedly prepared the summation of our case. It formed the basis of the long concluding chapter of the Indian report and was as close to a political statement as we could get in our exercise to provide supporting evidence for the Indian stand. It was, therefore, important to get his prior approval. Sitting in his upstairs drawing room after dinner, near the original Tang horse presented by Zhou-en Lai, he patiently and, as we discovered, carefully read through the forty-odd pages of a hurriedly typed draft. Suddenly he raised his eyes and peering over his glasses and said, 'You say, "For our parts, the Indian case stands vindicated" —what about "your" parts?' The typist had added the 's'. My colleague Gopal and I didn't know where to look. After the report was submitted to Parliament, he was more than generous about the efforts of the Indian team in upholding our stand which of course was consistent with the broad outlines contained in Nehru's letters to and conversations with Zhou-en Lai.

Perhaps the most memorable experience for me was while accompanying the Prime Minister on a trip to Bhutan in September 1958. We knew from our Consul General in Lhasa that a formal invitation for Nehru to visit Tibet had been sent by the Dalai Lama to Beijing for onward transmission, but months went by and it was not received in Delhi. Meanwhile, three weeks in September 1958 had been blocked in Nehru's calendar of engagements. Finally, the Chinese told us that because of possible difficulties in ensuring the Indian Prime Minister's security, the visit to Lhasa would not be convenient. I had something to do with the suggestion that a visit to Bhutan in lieu of Tibet be made.[2] The visit, even to Paro, the capital of the western province of Bhutan, also required a minimum of three weeks—a week each way in the journey and a week's stay in between. At the time, the quickest and easiest way to Bhutan was through Yatung in Tibet. Earlier, in 1958, there had been some anxiety about Nehru's health and so attempts were made to discourage him from what was bound to be an arduous trip, involving crossing over several passes over ten thousand feet. There would be no hospital within a week's march. Nehru, of course, was not to be deterred. The Chinese could not deny a short transit through the Chumbi Valley salient across from Sikkim.

The visit had obvious political importance, but Nehru's exhilaration was in the long traverse under the shadows of the Himalayas that he loved. The accompanying party was small. Apart from Nehru and Mrs Gandhi, there was Apa Pant, our Political Officer in Sikkim, G.C. Dutt, the Senior Officer-in-Charge of Prime Minister's security, Major Malhotra, a doctor from the Army Medical Corps, Rustomji, the Chief Executive of the Sikkim Government who was a friend of Jigmi Dorji, the Prime Minister of Bhutan, and myself from the ministry. During the six-day trek from Gangtok, the arrangements for our stay were simple and sometimes primitive. At two places Nehru and Mrs Gandhi stayed in little wooden huts, and some of us in tents. The halts for lunch or mid-morning coffee were in places with spectacular views of the snows and valleys. At one such halt, Apa Pant decided to do a difficult Yoga Asan—the Surya Namaskar. Somebody matched it with a headstand and Nehru, not to be outdone, demonstrated his capacity with a handstand. In one valley we passed through, there was a whole mountainside covered with edelweiss. Nehru and Mrs Gandhi, with their old associations of Switzerland, were thrilled and Mrs Gandhi climbed up and picked a handful and gave some to each of us to carry home.

Nehru was pleased to have confounded the doctors and showed that he was demonstratively fit. He outpaced the rest of us who were all much younger. The senior party was provided with specially caparisoned horses for the comparatively easy pathways. Where the slopes were steep, we got on to the ungainly-looking, slow but very sure-footed yaks. For considerable stretches in steep descents we had to walk using sticks or each other to keep a steady balance. We were followed by a train of two hundred-odd mules led by their tough muleteers, bringing the baggage, rations, crockery and even some folding furniture.

A couple of mules carried a Heath Robinson wireless unit, but we had left instructions not to repeat incoming telegrams except in an emergency. For three weeks the Prime Minister of India was more or less cut off from domestic and international politics, and he never seemed to fret for the affairs of the state.

On the other hand, for us in the party the most exhilarating part was after we reached our day's destination. In the long evenings, from teatime to dinner, Nehru would talk on serious and not-so-serious matters in a relaxed manner. Every day was a quiet seminar on politics and international relations, giving us insights into his thinking and his vision—a rare and perhaps unmatched opportunity for the rest of us, similar to what some who had shared a prison with him must have experienced.

When Nehru went to Bhutan, the country was probably still the way it must have been for one thousand or more years. No one had seen a wheel except the prayer wheels. (There was not even a bicycle in the place.) The entire valley did not have a single shop. One old man sat on the approach to the bridge selling safety matches, torches and knick-knacks. The valley was one expanse of rice fields each with a wooden hut on stilts. In the background were the old and new *dzongs* (forts), and high above were the monasteries. In the entire valley, especially next to the *chortens* (stupas), fluttered Tibetan-style prayer flags. Nehru was deeply moved by the country and the grandeur of the surroundings. Mrs Gandhi told me that she had seldom seen him so relaxed and carefree. One of my treasured photographs is of Nehru in Bhutanese dress, with long, embroidered soft boots and the tucked up skirt, which he inscribed *Jagat ko* (to Jagat) in Hindi. Once, in the Bhutanese dress he got into the spirit of revelry and tried his hand at archery, the Bhutanese national sport. The late King with the Queen, now Queen Mother, made a striking couple and completely won over Nehru and Mrs Gandhi. The present king was then about three years old and his sisters were only a little older. Nehru addressed a public meeting with the king acting as his interpreter. Thereafter he and Mrs Gandhi were hosts at a giant tea party to which all the inhabitants of Paro and the adjoining valleys were invited. Nehru and Mrs Gandhi walked down the line serving *Chang*—sweet butter-laced spiced tea—and biscuits (which we had brought with us). Since everyone carried a decorated metal mug, there was no need for a caterer to arrange for the crockery for a party of a thousand or more. By such informality, Nehru completely won the trust of the Bhutanese and even now, after thirty years, that visit provides the anchor to India's good relations with the country.

I would like to recall one incident from this trip which came close to being a sacrilegious disaster. Having refused him a visa for Lhasa, the Chinese really did not like Nehru making the trip to Bhutan. A strong Chinese military escort, ostensibly for security but in reality for surveillance, accompanied us through the Chumbi Valley in Tibet on the way to Bhutan. After his visit to India in 1956, the Dalai Lama had decreed that Nehru was also a Rimpoche, an incarnate high lama. Defying the Chinese attempt to isolate Nehru, Tibetans came in hundreds to see him and pay silent obeisance in Tibetan style as the Nehru cavalcade on horseback passed through. The Tibetan *Kashag* had deputed a representative to meet Nehru and had especially invited him to stop at the Kargyu Monastery a few miles on the descent from the Nathu La Pass. After the cold biting rain, a halt and a hot drink in a warm room was most welcome to all of us. On the Dalai Lama's instructions, the most holy room reserved, only for His Holiness himself, was to be opened for Nehru Rimpoche and the party. The escorting Chinese colonel, with some flourish and deliberate purpose, pulled out a Tienanmen packet and lit a cigarette. Nehru also wanted to smoke after the cold ride. The Chinese watched Nehru to see if he would follow the colonel in offending the sanctity of the monastery and betray his Rimpoche status. Suddenly Nehru, as if prompted by some inner instinct, stopped and put away his cigarette case leaving only the colonel guilty of outraging Tibetan sentiments. In the eyes of the assembled monks, it confirmed their faith that there was something of the Buddha about Nehru.

The other incident posed a different problem and showed a different kind of sensitivity of the Nehru family. While we were halfway through our week-long stay in Paro, a message from Delhi was brought to me by the communication operator, that Feroze Gandhi (Mrs Gandhi's husband) had suffered a heart attack, his first. I knew there was no way by which anyone could get back to Delhi in less than six days. (Yaks are sure-footed animals but they do not gallop.) There was no airstrip and no metalled roads in or out of Bhutan, and India then had no helicopter which could climb ten thousand feet to cross even the low range along the south of Bhutan. I was in a cold sweat as I did not know what I would do if the Prime Minister and/or Mrs Gandhi decided to return to India in a hurry. I took the message to Nehru. I assumed he would go over to Indiraji's room and break the news. Instead he just told me to take it to Indu. I hesitated and suggested that perhaps he would himself like to tell her. He said that she knew me and I could do so. I duly climbed the stairs to the top floor of that Paro guest house and showed the message to Mrs Gandhi. She read it with no show of emotion and said nothing. I nervously asked whether I should explore possibilities of a quicker return. She knew this would not be easy, but more importantly, she knew the special importance of the visit. She simply said that the planned programme should not be changed. It was a small insight into the Nehru code of values. Neither father nor daughter would even contemplate personal wishes intruding into the course of public duty. Fortunately, the next day a message came that Feroze Gandhi was improving and was no longer in danger.

In this expression of nostalgia for Nehru, I can recall many other little incidents where I happened to find myself close on the sidelines. I cannot, however, conclude without recalling my last meetings with Nehru. After five years of dealing with China, East Asia and our northern limitrophe, I was transferred abroad in 1961. I was in Bonn at the time of the Forward Policy and the India-China conflict of 1962. However, in 1963 it was decided, apparently at the Prime Minister's express instructions, that I be transferred to take over as head of our mission in Peking. I spent nearly six weeks in November-December 1963 briefing myself, visiting our frontier posts all along the border from Leh to Tawang before taking up the post. Instead of the customary single call by outgoing heads of missions on the Prime Minister, he called me on four or five occasions and each time said I should come again. He also invited me to meals at his house. Once he called me to his house at the last minute simply because he happened to be free and wanted to talk. The specific questions I put to him for directions were few but at these meetings, he just thought aloud expressing his worry about the future, not just about our relations with China but for Asia and world politics as well. On two occasions during the morning or afternoon, his eyes closed in the middle of the meeting, and he seemed to doze off. I sat there silently and did not know whether to withdraw or not. After a while he came to and resumed his talk. We now know that his kidneys were already infected. One could see that it was not the Nehru of the vigour and sustained intellectual buoyancy that we had seen over the years. One dared not even allow the thought to cross the mind that some day our beloved Panditji would be no more. In a few months' time, while I was in Beijing, he passed away. After the deterioration in India-China relations Zhou Enlai is supposed to have said, that Nehru was arrogant, but when he came to sign the condolence book at the embassy, he said to me as he was leaving, 'He was a great man and my good friend.'

On my last call on Panditji around Christmas in 1963, I requested him for a souvenir, a talisman. He took me to his bedroom and more or less asked me to choose something. I asked him for one of the swagger sticks he always carried. He pulled one from the cupboard and I muttered that I hoped he had used it. So he gave me a second, the one he was currently using and two white handkerchiefs with his initials, J.N. Those Nehru swagger sticks will be my most precious bequests to my children.

I am, of course, only one among thousands who will never tire of clutching at the memory of having lived under Nehru. We who had the privilege to work for him think he was great because he never made us feel small. He could be authoritarian but we knew he was a democrat. He never evoked fear and never expected sycophancy. Perhaps in our adulation we were hypnotized into thinking that *Panditji knows best.* We are thus not blameless for some of the mistakes. But what we remember is that when he was angry, we loved him all the more.

NOTES

1. Weightman was an ICS officer, and served as Foreign Secretary (Secretary of the External Affairs Department, Government of India), 1946-7.
2. See 'Catalyzing Graduated Modernization through Diplomacy: Nehru's Trek to Bhutan—1958' in Jagat S. Mehta, *Negotiating for India: Resolving Problems through Diplomacy*, New Delhi: Manohar, 2006.

2

'Panditji Knows Best': The Abdication of Advice and Dissent by the Bureaucracy

Outside India, the world took surprisingly little note of the Nehru centenary. It was a far cry from Churchill consecrating him as the 'Light of Asia' near the end of the first decade of India's independence. More so now than in the many centenary seminars organized in 1989, we can better appraise how Nehru will appear at the bar of history as the architect of independent India.

The Berlin Wall came tumbling down on 9 November 1989—in the very week of one hundred years of Nehru's birth. The end to the contending ideological and military blocs came close to Nehru's non-aligned perspectives and his insistence that, in the twentieth century, the aroused political consciousness of the people will reject alien authoritarian domination, and that their aspiration to liberation and democratic participation cannot be denied. Nehru, like Gorbachev who would do so forty years later, had urged that real defence must find a balance between 'sufficient' military capability, and social justice for the majority, if defence is not to impede the march to economic dynamism. Nehru's commitment to a world of non-ideological and non-imposed diversity flowed from a fundamental faith in constructive nationalism. In refusing reparations from Germany and Japan, Nehru showed instinctive deference for their national personalities even if he did not anticipate that they would rise to become economic superpowers. But the revolution of 1989 also saw the dramatic repudiation of socialism which Nehru had believed would be the wave of the future. As a democrat he had long seen the flaws in communism but he would have been taken aback by

* Unpublished paper delivered at the University of Texas in 1990.

the development people who had enjoyed egalitarian social benefits clamouring for the capitalist market system. The Cold War did not; lead to a hot war as he had feared; nor were the conflicts in the Third World countries necessarily proxy wars of the superpowers. Though Nehru had correctly prophesied that the arms distributed under bloc competition would be abused, he did not expect that some newly independent poor countries would use their sovereignty to overmilitarize and risk economic suicide. He would have been distressed at the rogue nationalism which embarked on aggressive adventures against other Third World countries.

In India, soon after the culmination of the Nehru centenary, the ninth general elections were held. Charges of corruption were levelled against Nehru's grandson which, though unproven, contributed to the defeat of the Congress Party at the Centre and across the Hindi belt at the hands of a loose coalition of opposition parties. At the same time, in the south, it brought back the Congress Party to power, repudiating some regional parties. Taken together, the elections were proof that the tender plant of democracy that Nehru had nurtured had taken root in Indian soil; and universal suffrage had come of age. But the protest vote was also indicative of the atrophy of values which Nehru, and before him the Mahatma, had sought to imbue in the political life of the country. The second non-Congress coalition at the Centre fell in less than three years. Everything on which Nehru had laid primary emphasis seemed to be crumbling—secularism, anti-militarism, non-violent and non-communal politics, national unity embodying the plurality of India, and priority for economic development and social justice through planned development. The burning flame in Nehru's life was to exhort pride and national self-confidence. Within a quarter century of Nehru's death, there was a pervasive cynicism towards political leadership in general and even despondency about the future of the country.

History is bound to ask whether the tribulations that India faces today, including the multiple threats to its integrity, the erosion of cherished values, and the uneven progress in modernization, are entirely due to the degeneration that set in after Nehru's departure from the political scene. Or were Nehru's blueprints themselves faulty, and the institutional foundations that he had laid not sufficiently deep and secure?

It is being acknowledged that the socio-economic design embodying Nehru's ideals and aspirations for the future of India had flaws which were not foreseen in his time. When the Westminster model was constitutionally adopted, Nehru and his colleagues, revelling in the unifying role of the Congress Party, discouraged the growth of other parties and provide safeguards to make democracy de-personalized. Nehru himself acquiesced to the undermining of the first elected non-Congress government in Kerala. He did not foresee that in a federal structure, with a continental scale of diversity, it was not only possible but inevitable that, in the future, the party in power at the Centre would be different from the complexion of the elected governments in the states. Nehru wanted a strong Centre to enable planned development of the country. According to Durga Das[1] even Krishna Menon had urged that the central government should have only limited powers, somewhat on the lines proposed in 1946 by the British Cabinet Mission. He had suggested that the country be divided into fifty to sixty smaller regions or counties. Nehru gave in to the linguistic-based division of Bombay, Madras and Hyderabad, but going back on his assurance, he did not accept other recommendations of the States' Reorganization Commission. A Pandora's box of tribal, religious and sub-nationalist demands has now been unleashed, not only in the peripheries but even in the heartland of India.

The Hindu Code Bill, which is truly one of the greatest piece of social legislation, anywhere, was largely thanks to his personal commitment, but Nehru did not adopt a uniform civil code for all religious communities, though such a code exists even in some Muslim countries. A step in that direction might have controlled the virus of fundamentalism and communalism. There were other progressive social and economic reforms, notably in the field of primary education, which were contemplated but not sufficiently funded in his time. Future historians will thus be tempted to castigate Nehru for the many problems that now beset India, but the blame must be shared fairly by other elements in the post-Independence political structure. An objective assessment of Nehru as prime minister must steer between idolatry and blind prejudice.

It cannot be denied that until the China crisis in 1959, Nehru enjoyed the unquestioning confidence of the Indian people. His personal charisma, his political standing from his years in prison, and his being the anointed heir of Gandhi were the factors that gave him an almost unmatched mandate in the history of democracies. Like the Pied Piper, he could have led the nation in more or less any direction he willed. He had definite notions about where he wanted to go but his temperament did not let him seek counsel on policy goals. Most people around him were intellectually and morally too dwarfed to refine with correctives his openly declared purposes and concepts. Frank Moraes,[2] the distinguished journalist/editor, contrasted this to the open-minded approach of Lal Bahadur Shastri, who was prime minister when the book by Durga Das, *India from Curzon to Nehru and After*, was written. But it is more important to underline that everyone around Nehru knew he was no Stalin who demanded submissive sycophancy from his colleagues and subordinates. Nehru was too compassionate a person to banish anyone to a political Gulag for reasoned advice. Sometimes, the Hamlet in him hesitated to action or, for want of support, yielded to erroneous advice even against his better instincts. After the deaths of Gandhiji and Sardar Vallabhbhai Patel, and after Rajagopalachari relinquished the Home portfolio (1953), he had no political equals around him. Rajendra Prasad, Maulana Azad, Radhakrishnan and Govind Vallabh Pant, etc., differed on some issues, but even they seldom gave clear alternatives on foreign, economic, and social policies. His many political colleagues must, therefore, share part of the blame, that the democrat Nehru was allowed to be overwhelmed by the Nehru who had himself long ago acknowledged having the propensity of a dictator. Nehru's great limitation was that, unlike Gandhi, he never thought of India without Nehru.

This essay dwells primarily on Nehru's administration of the Ministry of External Affairs. It refers to foreign policy issues only illustratively but highlights the characteristics of Nehru as the departmental head which illuminate his general style as prime minister.

INHERITING A BRITISH SUB-FOREIGN OFFICE

When the Interim Government was formed in September 1946, Nehru became the Vice-President of the Governor-General's Council and retained the Foreign Affairs portfolio as his direct charge. A Political-cum-External Affairs Department had been established by the East India Company as early as 1784—the year after Pitt's India Act. After the British Government took over from the Company in 1857, and began functioning directly under the Governor-General/Viceroy, the Department developed into a Sub-Foreign Office. Though theoretically subordinate to Whitehall, the Department had considerable latitude in policies, especially before the era of instant communications. The perspectives were Indo-centric rather than determined by the global British interests and were often at variance with those received from Calcutta/Delhi and Simla.

Though its name was changed from time to time, the broad responsibilities of the 'Foreign and Political Department' remained threefold: (a) regulating paramountcy relations of the crown with princely states; (b) superintending diplomatic and consular relations in the limitrophe around the Indian Empire; and (c) administering the north-west frontier and the Pathan tribes along the Afghan border. Since the 1920s, following concern over the disabilities suffered by Indians sent to different parts of the Empire, an Indians Overseas Section had been created in the Government of India and Agents had been appointed in Ceylon (Sri Lanka), South Africa, Malaya, etc. This section, renamed the Commonwealth Relations Department, was transferred to the charge of Nehru and so for some years Nehru's portfolio was called the Department/Ministry of External Affairs and Commonwealth Relations.

A Foreign Service cadre separate from the ICS to service the Foreign and Political Department, most of the time simply called F&P, was started as early as 1820. The Agents to the Governor-General, the Residents and Political Agents in the princely states and, at one time, the British representatives in Basra and Baghdad, Meshed, Aden, Canton, Penang, Singapore, and Mauritius were of this Service. Many who were engaged in the Great Game in Central Asia belonged to the F&P Department. Until the transfer of power, British relations with Nepal and Afghanistan were superintended from Delhi. The Department, consisting of approximately a hundred and thirty officers who were 'picked from the pick' enjoyed even more prestige than the ICS. Two-thirds of the officers were selected from the Sandhurst-trained officers of the Indian Army and the others from the ICS, but all were chosen personally by the Viceroy. After the 1935 Government of India Act, when the External Affairs and Political Department were finally split, the Service was named the Indian Political Service (IPS), but continued to serve both departments. Durand and MacMahon, names associated with the famous (or infamous) boundaries, were Foreign Secretaries who belonged to the IPS cadre. Sir Olaf Caroe was the last to hold a full tenure as Foreign Secretary before Independence. By 1939, a little less than half of the officers in the ICS cadre in the provinces were Indians, but there were less than twenty Indians in the IPS cadre, K.P.S. Menon being the senior-most Indian in the IPS.

Nehru thus took over one of the most exclusive bastions of British Imperial policies. Only two Indian IPS officers were in the Department when he took over and they too were no higher in rank than that of deputy secretary. It would have been understandable if Nehru had asked for a summary transfer of the senior British officers and chosen his own Foreign Secretary, as is now becoming the practice with governmental or even ministerial changes. But he accepted the departmental structure as he found it, never slighting the British officers or questioning the patriotism of the Indians who till then had served the British rule in India. The British officers also quickly developed admiration for Nehru's ability and personality. Appointing Sir Girja Shankar Bajpai to the specially created post of Secretary-General was early proof that Nehru respected the ethics of political neutrality in dealing with the civil service.

BUREAUCRACY LEFT TO MOULD THE NEW FOREIGN SERVICE

Nehru took an active interest in the constitution of a foreign service to execute the policy of independent India. He asked Humphrey Trevelyan (later Lord Trevelyan) of the IPS, who was then Joint Secretary in the External Affairs Department, to compile the original Foreign Service Regulations. All Indian members of the old Political Service were automatically transferred to the new service (as the ICS officers were embodied in the IAS cadres of the states); thirteen officers with the War Service who were selected for appointment to the ICS and had given the option for the Political Service (of which I was one) were the first to be appointed to the new Foreign Service. In February 1947 a committee was constituted to consider volunteers from the ICS and other services of the central government who wished to be seconded to the Foreign Service. It was presided over by Sir Akbar Hydari (a senior civilian who was the Governor-designate for Assam) with K.P.S. Menon (soon to take over as the first Indian Ambassador to KMT China) and Hugh Weightman (the then Foreign Secretary) as members. After the decision on Partition had been taken, most Muslim officers of the IPS, including three of the War Service officers, opted for Pakistan and became the nucleus of the Pakistan Foreign Service. Hydari and Menon left to take up their respective appointments, and Weightman retired to the UK. A successor committee presided over by Bajpai, the newly appointed Secretary General, with the Cabinet Secretary (H.M. Patel), the Commerce Secretary (Sir N.R. Pillai/Sukhtankar), and Joint Secretary, Establishment of External Affairs (S. Ratnam) as members reviewed the previous selections. Out of the initial list of sixty approved officers and twelve on a reserve list for permanent secondment, the number that could be spared had to be pruned to just over twenty. All but one of these officers were from the ICS and provided the controlling hierarchy of the new Foreign Service for the next twenty-nine years. Eight officers (who had crossed the age limit to appear for the normal competitive examination) were Federal/Union Public Service Commission recruits.

In 1948, on the recommendation of the higher echelons of the Ministry of External Affairs, Nehru was persuaded to bypass the Public Service Commission and launch an ad hoc recruitment without the preliminaries of the usual advertising process. Out of a little over one hundred interviewees about eighty over-age candidates were selected. As far as I know, only one name—(P.N. Haksar) who subsequently proved to be an exceptionally dynamic and influential civil servant—was recommended by Nehru himself to this committee. Two more (M.R.A. Baig and Mohamad Yunus), with strong old political connections, were inducted into the Service. A few officers were taken from the Indian National Army of Netaji Subhas Bose (because Nehru had conceded that they should not be restored to their regiments in the Indian Army). To help the integration of the princely states, on the recommendation of the Deputy Prime Minister and V.P. Menon, seven ex-Maharajas or their sons were summarily appointed to the Foreign Service. From 1948 onwards, the intake into the Foreign Service has been through competitive examinations only, supplemented by promotions from the subordinate IFS(B) which was initially constituted by selective detachment from the Central Secretariat Service.

There were problems in inter-leaving officers selected from these different sources. For the parallel problem in the IAS, a careful formula was adopted by the Home Ministry in consultation with the Public Service Commission. There was considerable dissatisfaction with the ad hoc way in which the External Affairs Ministry determined the *inter se* seniority of officers, who could not obviously be treated as cadets with year of allotment determined by the date of appointment. Nehru had given broad indications of a new Service, but he lacked the aptitude and inclination to go into the bureaucratic chores of selection procedures and seniority determination. There was some truth in the criticism sometimes made (for example, by Walter Crocker)[3] that India could have had a more uniformly excellent service. In the present context, it need only be noted that Nehru did not determine or interfere in the bureaucracy-controlled processes.

Nehru took keener interest in the issue of where diplomatic missions should be opened and who should head them. The appointments to Moscow, Washington and Chungking were made during the rule of the the Interim Government itself. The choice of Mrs Vijayalakshmi Pandit for the USSR, Asaf Ali (a senior Congressman and member of the Interim Government) for the US and Krishna Menon for the UK was deliberately 'political', but there was no prejudice against the bureaucrats. Only four non-officials participated in the 1951 Paris Conference of the Heads of Missions. At the Burgenstock Conference (1953), except for the High Commissioner to the UK (B.G. Kher), all ambassadors in twelve European countries were members of the ICS. In fact, during Nehru's tenure, there were never more than ten or twelve non-career heads of missions.

The Foreign Service and the Foreign Office revelled in working in Nehru's ministry. They quickly developed the confidence that under Nehru's tutelage civil servants enjoyed full security of tenure. Some officers no doubt had easier access to Nehru than others, but often it was because of those officers' conscientious zeal. What is important to recall here is that Nehru never allowed the notion to gain ground that officers must have a sort of ideological 'commitment' to the pseudo-socialist policies of the government—a notion which was to be promoted some years after Nehru died.

With the bureaucracy enjoying full administrative autonomy and a decline in the numbers of ICS officers, some healthy old aditions and efficiency of the Civil Service in British India were diluted. Earlier, while covenanted members had an assured tenure and time scale increase in salaries, higher promotions were based on an officer's record and performance. Not all ICS officers became commissioners or joint secretaries and very few rose to the position of secretaries in the central government. After 1947 an unconscious sense of solidarity developed among the residuary members of the old services, and promotions to higher grades became more or less automatic. In general, after sixteen years of service all officers became joint secretaries or ambassadors to posts of medium/high importance. While Nehru, in theory, was impatient with the rigidities of the seniority principle, career advancement in his own ministry came to be on the escalator principle, where with age and years of service, an officer could claim the top grade. Thus, the fundamental administrative principle of reward for merit and performance was diluted with obviously adverse consequences on efficiency and uneven quality of reporting and policy implementation. This atrophy of administrative principles was not because of Nehru's interference and directions. On the contrary, it was the degradation of self-management by the bureaucracy which Nehru, partly because of lack of administrative acumen and partly on account of his magnanimity of spirit, failed to detect or correct.

THE DISADVANTAGES OF NEHRU REMAINING HIS OWN FOREIGN MINISTER

There were obvious advantages to having the Prime Minister as the departmental minister. Senior officers and the ambassadors abroad could obtain first-hand directions from the head of the government. At the same time there were many adverse consequences, simply because Nehru was the departmental minister. The most obvious was that with the sheer burden of his responsibilities—as head of both the government and the Congress Party and the ultimate decision-maker in all things—Nehru could not spare the time for departmental supervisory functions in the formative years of an important ministry. Since there were no real precedents for diplomatic establishments, there was resistance in the finance ministry to the provision of the necessary infrastructure and adequate allowances for effective functioning abroad. Many missions reported that the Pakistan embassies had more generous latitude where entertainment was concerned than the Indian missions. One suspected that on administrative and financial questions, Nehru was self-conscious about being a spokesperson seeking allocations for his own ministry at the cabinet level.

The Foreign Office did not physically equip itself for efficient performance. In the Nehru years, there were no telex connections with the missions abroad, and except for secret telephones reserved for senior officers, there was no intercom within the ministry. There was not a single electric typewriter and the first Xerox machine came to the Foreign Secretary's office in 1977, and that too was acquired from the surplus equipment for a non-aligned conference! The first computers came after Rajiv Gandhi launched the modernization drive. Because the capital budget was meagre, the ministry acquired only a few properties abroad when they were inexpensive. On the other hand, China, the USSR and other countries with much smaller involvement in international politics were more far-sighted with regard to the acquistion of real estate.

More importantly, the proposal to build a Foreign Office which would bring all External Affairs offices under one roof, conveniently located near the South Block, was never seriously followed up. New buildings for Agriculture, Industry & Commerce and Railway ministries, and Air Headquarters were authorized during the Nehru years. (The offices of External Affairs Ministry are still spread out over four or five locations. Until recently, the administrative offices were in temporary structures built during the Second World War. Senior officers, indeed even junior ones, seldom go to the ministry's excellent library because it is housed in a building two miles away from the main ministry.) Within the Indian diplomatic missions there was a strongly felt need to strengthen the political side and reduce the size of purchase missions in London and Washington which had many delegates from other ministries, but this was never rationalized in Nehru's time.

While higher policy questions on the political side received Nehru's careful attention, commercial and foreign economic problems were not included in planning the foreign policy. In Nehru's time there was no economic division in the Foreign Ministry. The Economic Ministries filled the lacuna and came to enlarge their operational latitude. To some extent, unconsciously, there was a certain policy method in this incongruity. The Foreign Ministry under Nehru's direction took up bold independent political postures, disregarding the economic consequences, and the Economic Departments were left to quietly plead for aid, promote trade, and even make direct approaches for aid to the State Department or Foreign Ministries. As an unintended consequence, the Finance and Commerce Ministries never received the 'political' support that they merited. The policy towards foreigners and on immigration was riddled with the old conservatism of the Home Ministry. Had Nehru not been his own Foreign Minister, the organizational and policy rationale would have been more realistically integrated and correspondingly become more effective.

The more serious consequence was that the opportunity for positive responsibility and organizational innovations in policy-making was lost because the one-man think-tank was the direct decision-maker. The best moment to initiate the process of institutionalizing foreign policy planning and undertake systematic long-term studies was when Nehru's authority and charisma were at their zenith. It was well known that the State Department had established a Policy Planning Council under George Kennan in the spring of 1947. I was asked to set up the Policy Planning Division in the Ministry in 1966, two years after Nehru's death. I do not want to make exaggerated claims for the policy planning organizational innovations begun after the Second World War. Policy planners frequently end up writing speeches, or making surveys of problems which straddle geographical and functional bureaus. Policy planning establishments can be useful when policy-makers have the self-confidence to ask unloaded questions and can spare the time to debate long-term projections, and have the courage to modify an inherited approach. George Marshall, having won the highest laurels as the five-star Army Chief of Staff, had that kind of natural self-confidence and gave George Kennan the latitude from which emerged the Marshall Plan in 1947, which was probably the most enlightened initiative of the post-War decades. The US had also begun the practice of governments consigning studies to non-official experts and interacting with scholars, journalists, and specialists, but such non-official consultations never got started in Nehru's time at the professional level.

Nehru saw himself as mentor to the nation. He thought aloud on all problems including those on foreign policy, often at public meetings. Sometimes, we distilled policy directions on major issues from press reports of his extempore speeches. Unavoidably diplomatic indiscretions crept in when policy approaches were spontaneously articulated in public or Parliament. The point, however, is that Nehru would certainly not have objected to coherently prepared policy statements which he could amend or merely use to marshal in his own inimitable style of presentation. But he was not the kind of person who would ask for a draft. My experience tells me, however, that he would not have cast aside a carefully prepared assessment or suggested statement. If the tradition of obligatory submission of a draft of statement had been established in the Foreign Ministry in Nehru's time, the subsequent corrosion of the rights and responsibilities of the professional Service could have been better resisted. The bureaucracy did not use the opportunity of direct access to the head of government to recommend institutional processes, envisaging a situation when the Prime Minister may not be the Foreign Minister. In contrast, Homi Bhabha, the first Chairman, of the Atomic Energy Commission, insisted that the Commission be in the Prime Minister's portfolio. He used his personal equation to get Nehru's benign support to bypass red tape, obtain generous allocation of resources, and enlarge the space for dynamic and imaginative scientific policies. This independence of the Atomic Energy Commission survives from Parliamentary scrutiny even to this day.

There is no doubt that Nehru was easily accessible and regularly consulted his senior officers individually and collectively. But the brief 'morning prayer meetings' of secretaries were necessarily hurried and unsystematic. They were largely confined to instant decisions on important incoming telegrams. If the practice of in-depth studies demanding responsible professional judgement had started in Nehru's time, the process could have prevented adhocism and centralization in decision-making, so common in subsequent decades. The irony is that this hesitancy in providing professional inputs started as genuine respect for Nehru's ability and knowledge but de-generated into professional non-accountability. The relationship of Nehru with the permanent civil service was the very opposite of the 'Yes Prime Minister' and 'Yes, Minister' syndrome. It was not a case of the the policy inclinations of the minister being torpedoed by the civil service, but the bureaucracy instinctively and uncritically saying 'Panditji knows best'. Nehru's position as prime minister was somewhat akin to the authority exercised by Winston

Churchill during the War years. Both were exceptional leaders who were deified by their official subordinates as well as by their political opponents. But while Churchill superseded or sacked his generals if they did not perform effectively, Nehru generally accepted whoever was presented to him from the bureaucratic shuffle of the cards even to the point of being tolerant of mediocre officers for surprisingly long periods.

It should be clarified, beyond any implied misunderstanding, that even if there had been a separate Foreign Minister and professional inputs, the fundamentals of Nehru's foreign policy—non-alignment, decolonization, anti-racialism, non-militarism, and nuclear restraint—would have remained unchanged. Some interesting political consequences, however, can be traced from the administrative accident of Nehru having direct departmental responsibilities.

Sikkim and Bhutan had Maharajas, the former with a fifteen gun salute like middle level princely states. Before Independence, relations with these principalities were left to the External Affairs rather than the Political Department primarily because the Political Officer in Sikkim had supervisory responsibilities over the British Consulate in Lhasa and the problems relating to Tibet. But for this factor, the responsibility for handling relations with Sikkim and possibly Bhutan might have gone to the Ministry of States (the successor to the Political Department) which after the transfer of power became part of Sardar Patel's portfolio. It is not inconceivable that, consistent with the overall policy towards the princely states (and Patel's strong apprehensions at the Chinese presence in Tibet), Sikkim and even Bhutan might have been induced to accede to India. Nehru, however continued to treat Sikkim as a protectorate. With Bhutan, the 1949 Treaty only reproduced the ambivalent clause in the 1909 Treaty which laid down that Bhutan would be guided by India in its external relations. This approach, however, was consistent with Nehru's policy that new India must demonstratively respect the national and distinct political personalities of Asia.

With Nepal, Nehru authorized a near 'equal' treaty in 1950 and that too with the oligarchic Rana regime. Following China's military attack on Tibet and recalling that the Ching Dynasty considered Nepal (as also many other separate national entities around China's rim) as a tributary, the Rana regime itself debated whether it was not in the country's interest to surrender to Indian protection. In my own view, notwithstanding what happened subsequently to Sino-Indian relations and especially recalling that after forty years China has failed to win the honest acquiescence of the Tibetans, Nehru's instincts were prophetically wise. The subsequent integration of Sikkim has added political problems without improving the security options for India that were guaranteed under India-Sikkim Treaty of 1950.

But one must acknowledge that there was also a heavy debit side which flowed from solitary decision-making. The fundamental mistake of Nehru and Patel was to accept Partition as the lesser evil. This cast a shadow on the totality of Nehru's hopes for independent India and his vision for Asia. The offer of plebiscite and the reference of the Kashmir question to the UN was authorized by Nehru because so soon after Independence, he did not want to outrage the principles of self-determination and peaceful arbitration of international disputes—principles which, with Nehru's active support, were embodied in the constitution as a directive principle. The most vicious consequences came later when the India-Pakistan problem became enmeshed in the Cold War. Even after the US–USSR détente, the subcontinental tension continues to bedevil the future of both countries. Nehru did try to seek limited rapprochement with Prime Ministers Liaquat Ali Khan and Mohammed Ali Bogra, but in general, the bureaucracy was more hawkish towards Pakistan than was Nehru.

There are many examples when professional advice might have averted damage to Nehru and India. If, for example, the senior Indian envoys and secretaries had advised that in the Hungary situation in 1956 there was no likelihood of intervention by the West (and so there was no danger of a world war) or had volunteered that not criticizing the USSR—when Tito had done so—would discredit non-alignment, Nehru might well have not fallen out of step with international outrage at the Soviet repression of a nationalist process. In 1961 Nehru himself was reluctant to authorize the use of force to dislodge the Portuguese from Goa. If there had been strong counsel that such an action would produce serious adverse international reactions, and that the alleged involvement of Pakistan or NATO was merely convenient disinformation, Nehru might not have been pushed into approving the military operations that the Defence Minister Krishna Menon favoured. Giving accurate assessment on what would do disproportionate harm to India's standing and Nehru's image was a professional obligation, not a policy-making issue.

The greatest setback in foreign policy during Nehru's tenure was, of course, the crisis with China. The report of Sumal Sinha, the Consul General in Lhasa at the time of the Chinese occupation of Tibet (1950), on the serious implications that the Chinese action held for India was a courageous assessment, but was very summarily dismissed because it went against Nehru's hopes from new China. The letters sent by Bajpai, then Governor of Bombay, prior to the negotiations on the Tibet region (1953-4) disagreed with Panikkar's advice, and urged that the Sino-Indian boundary issue be raised in the discussions. No other non-wishful assessment of the prospects of relations with China was offered by the officials until the crisis actually came to a head. Nehru did raise the boundary question and the MacMahon line issue when the Chinese prime minister was in India in 1957 at the height of Sino-Indian friendship. Had this initiative been followed up at the official level, the Sino-Indian territorial dispute might have been brought into the open and possibly settled before 1959 while Nehru had the political latitude to do so. At least, the crisis would not have come as a shock leading to the criticism that Nehru was naïve and that the Chinese had deliberately lulled him into a fake sense of security and then betrayed India's pledge of friendship. After the Dalai Lama's arrival in India (March 1959), China's ill-conceived accusations, and the strong Indian reaction in Parliament and the media, it was not possible even for Nehru to settle the border dispute. Academics or officials who in hindsight argue that the problem could have been settled in 1960 (when Zhou Enlai and Chen Yi came to India) discount the vigour of aroused democracy and ignore the then prevailing political atmosphere in India. It was also a professional failure of the bureaucracy which acquiesced without reasoned dissent to the Forward Policy. The judgement by Nehru and Krishna Menon that China may make minor advances but would not attack on a two-thousand-mile front was the accepted conventional wisdom.

Nehru was not like some heads of governments who wanted all policy issues to be summarized on one double-spaced page! On any dissenting verbal suggestion, Nehru could react impetuously, sometimes in seeming anger, but he reflected far more carefully when he had a reasoned paper before him. Generally, officers who had the experience of working with Nehru knew that any paper, regardless of its length, would be read and returned within a day or two and invariably with a thoughtful minute. With his facility in dictation, Nehru redrafted parliamentary replies and even prepared letters for his private secretary to sign. In any given year of his prime ministership, he probably dictated more words than all of his senior advisers put together. He was always impatient to do the job himself rather than improve the organization and demand higher quality from his supporting staff.

THE LACUNA FILLED BY KRISHNA MENON

The lacuna of professional advise on critical foreign policy issues was filled by Krishna Menon. As is well known, Menon had an old and rather special relationship with Nehru. Even as High Commissioner in London he volunteered advice on issues which went beyond his diplomatic charge. Later, without holding an appropriate official position, he became Nehru's energetic foreign policy counsellor. Menon's approach on international politics was close to but not identical with Nehru's own perspectives. Both were old Fabian socialists and had a kind of British Fabian dislike for the materialist values permeating the American democracy. But Nehru had stronger reservations on communism and some Soviet policies and publicly articulated his deep distress with China, which Menon never did. Nehru found in Menon an intellectual support against the 'rightist' and suspected pro-American tilts. However, Menon's abrasive personality and provocative diplomatic style were very different from Nehru's and this certainly compounded the prejudice in the West against

India and Nehru personally. There were critics inside India who felt that Menon should not have been allowed the latitude he appropriated, particularly in the UN General Assemblies. Mrs Pandit did not conceal her irritation with Menon who poached her responsibilities even when she was leader of the delegation and later when she became High Commissioner to the UK.

Barring a small band of Menon loyalists, the Foreign Service hierarchy was generally uncomfortable at Menon's intrusions in their realm but they acquiesced silently or at best made muted complaints when the embarrassment was serious. Everyone knew Nehru was indulgent towards Menon. This was vividly confirmed when Nehru stood by him even when General Thimmaya, the Chief of Army Staff, tendered his resignation because Menon habitually bypassed the military command structure. Only following the defeat by Chinese forces, when the political uproar threatened Nehru's own position, was Menon dropped from the cabinet.

But Nehru had a sufficiently sensitive political antenna and Menon was excluded from the Cabinet Committee discussions on relations with China. A meeting was, no doubt, fixed between Zhou Enlai and Foreign Minister Chen Yi in April 1960 with Menon but the Home Minister, G.B. Pant, had a more central role in the internal reviews on India-China relations. However, in July 1962, at the Geneva Conference on Laos, Menon got an opportunity for his personalized diplomacy with Chen Yi. What is more relevant to this thesis is that the senior officers of the Foreign Ministry were never excluded by Nehru from decision-making throughout the period and, therefore, there was no reason for the senior bureaucracy to have abdicated its professional duty of providing advice and dissent.

On some issues there might have been corridor criticism amongst officials that Menon should not be allowed to needlessly irritate the democratic West, whose economic support was necessary for development. The professionals, however, also failed to perceive the inner contradictions of global bipolarity, the irrelevance of ideology, the stirrings of nationalism within the blocs, and the more resilient economic and technological dynamism of the West.

THE NEHRU LEGACY AND THE CONTEMPORARY CRISIS IN INDIA

Nehru would himself be surprised at the suggestion that the atrophy of the policy-making processes started with his years in office. He was, after all, responsible for inviting Professor Paul Appleby, an American public affairs specialist, to prepare a report on how to revamp the machinery of the Government to fit in with the challenge of a dynamic developmental state. The fact, however, is that Nehru as the helmsman was unaware that he was more or less left alone on the bridge to chart the course for India. Even his few critics (the socialists, the communists, the Jan Sangh) did not claim to be his serious political opponents on foreign policy. In their uncritical admiration for Nehru's single-minded zeal, they lost the opportunity of creating institutions and traditions which could have warned him of the shoals and withstand the degeneration of men and politics, when he himself would be no more.

Under our constitutional system, the judiciary, the armed forces and the civil services were envisaged as the non-political guardians of continuity. Following the British model, it was expected that the civil service would be free to give professional advice and then to implement faithfully the decisions of the government which enjoyed the parliamentary mandate. In Nehru's India, even though he did not invite objective policy advice, there were no constitutional, political, or administrative impediments for the bureaucracy to tender internal advice and offer divergent viewpoints at the policy determination stage.

The erosion in the morale, efficiency, respect and public-spirited ethics of the civil service is both the cause and the consequence of the larger malaise that has enveloped the political system. It is speculated that only a small fraction of the officers in the senior services remain conscientious, honest and positively earnest. These 'few' frequently carry a disproportionate share of the initiative and responsibility in the central and state governments. Many under pressure or lure of ambition, or just with the instinct for self-preservation, become politically identified with a particular leader or political party. Many more shirk difficult responsibilities and shrink from righteousness in public duty. Tenure security and automatic promotion to the highest level dampen optimal performance. When the regulatory role of the government was on the increase, especially in the developmental fields and the industrial and public sectors, there was greater potential and temptations for monetary benefit and corruption. According to former Prime Minister Rajiv Gandhi, only fifteen *naya paise* out of one rupee reached the intended beneficiaries from projects for the rural areas. But this degeneration in the bloated bureaucracy, with its frequently half-hearted and sometimes needlessly politicized approach, its proneness to illicit gains, inclination to drift and career coasting, originated or got compounded in great measure because the civil service itself did not collectively try to preserve its traditional ethics and independence.

The paradoxical legacy of the Nehru era in those early 'golden years' is that policy-making and, in important respects, implementation have slowly moved away from the Foreign Ministry to the Prime Minister's Office. It is true that after Nehru's death, a separate senior Cabinet Minister has held the Foreign Affairs portfolio, but even so there has been a marginalization of the Foreign Ministry and frequently even of the Foreign Minister. Psychological inhibitions have crept in with the frequent changes of Secretaries. In all of Nehru's seventeen years most senior Secretaries had at least four years' tenure in their posts. Bajpai was Secretary-General for five years, N.R. Pillai for eight years; K.P.S. Menon was Foreign Secretary for four years, S. Dutt for six years, and M.J. Desai as Secretary and later Secretary-General for a total of eight years. As against this, in the decade 1980-90, there were seven Foreign Secretaries. What started as a voluntary reluctance to intrude with advice in decision-making because of a hypnotic admiration for Nehru has developed into a situation where advice is frequently not sought from the Foreign Office and, whether from fear or instinct of self-preservation, professional recommendations are not volunteered. The deterioration has, of course, varied with individual ministers and senior officials, but the contrast in the psychological climate from the Nehru years can scarcely be denied.

While the lack of policy direction can be traced to opportunity not seized because of Nehru's special interest in foreign affairs, the excessive and secretive centralization of decision-making with the prime minister and his/her office is a post-Nehru phenomenon. In Nehru's time, the Principal Private Secretary, later designated Secretary (for a while held at the Joint Secretary level), was the only professional officer in the Prime Minister's Secretariat. The Prime Minister's Office (PMO) expanded somewhat with two additional joint secretaries during Lal Bahadur Shastri's time. In contrast, now the PMO has about fifteen IFS/IAS officers and specialist advisers, including several Secretaries, an Additional Secretary, and many Joint Secretaries. The PMO is headed by the Principal Secretary, with the status equal to the Cabinet Secretary and so, unlike in Britain, he is superior to the civil service heads of other ministries. The PMO now scrutinizes the considered decisions of the departmental ministers. The access to the Prime Minister by Ministers or departmental Secretaries has been restricted. The PMO has, in fact, developed the character of the Presidential White House and has correspondingly emaciated the role and responsibility of the entire structure of ministerial and departmental government which go with the parliamentary system.

NEHRU IF WERE ALIVE IN THE 1990s

Nehru would have flowered in the post-Cold War world. In 1961, at the Non-Aligned Conference in Belgrade, Nehru was already groping towards a new emphasis on policies for the Third World in the post-colonial era. When Sukarno, the Indonesian leader, was calling for the unity of the emerging Progressive Forces to continue confrontation against Western imperialism, Nehru perceived that the new focus must have a constructive emphasis. He urged the end of nuclear testing and the diversion of resources through disarmament on economic development. Nehru enthusiastically welcomed the Partial Test Ban Treaty (1963) and saw in it a giant step towards lifting the shadow of the nuclear war.

The real tragedy for India and the world is that we squandered the years when Nehru was in command. Nehru knew he had miles to go before he slept but, one suspects, he thought he had the health and stamina to keep going for a long time. Those around him also let him believe that he was immortal. We, the professional bureaucrats, cannot affirm that we rendered unto Nehru or our subsequent 'Caesars' the obligation that comes from the security of our tenure. Nehru was not warned to diplomatically prevent the US-Pakistan alliance in 1954, or to open the concealed time bomb of relations with China, and at least explore Ayub's offer of joint defence in 1959 and thus prevent the subsequent Sino-Pakistan rapprochement. Nehru was wrong to think that the regional conflicts would escalate into a world war, but he had some foreboding of the eventual Sino-Soviet rift. He neglected sustained attention on our immediate neighbours and to South-East Asia and the Far East. On the other hand, he would have allayed South Asia's fears of India's hegemonistic propensities. He would also have been horrified at the rampant militarization of the Third World. However vaguely, he was aware that the technology of destruction and the balance of terror could change the nature of world politics. He was totally and unconditionally against nuclear weapons for India and had he lived five months longer, to hear of the Chinese explosion in Lop Nor, his conviction would not have altered. Nehru might well have gone to great lengths by giving timely unilateral assurance to prevent Pakistan from going nuclear.

I saw Nehru several times in November and December 1963, to get his directions before proceeding to Peking to take charge of our embassy there. He was shaken by the betrayal of his hopes by China and the damage to his vision for Asia. But he was still worrying about the world and the future as he had done since the 1920s. Had he lived a few years longer and been supported with reasoned counsel, he might have reoriented some of his own judgements. According to Frank Moraes, before he died Nehru may well have given the green signal to Sheikh Abdullah to explore modalities to resolve the Kashmir problem and rationalize India-Pakistan relations.

Had Nehru remained Prime Minister for as long as Churchill or Adenauer held office, he would have been in the vanguard of détente and would not—as much of the Third World does today—have looked upon the end of the Cold War with helplessness and dismay. The 'lonely long distance runner' (as Milton Israel so aptly described Nehru) deserved not just adulation from the cheering multitudes, or the hypnotic admiration of his political colleagues and bureaucratic subordinates but also, in return for his dedication and concern for India and the future of the world, forthright advice and the moral courage of dissent.

NOTES

1. Durga Das, *India From Curzon to Nehru and After,* New York: John Day, 1970.
2. Frank Moraes, *Nehru: Sunlight and Shadows*, Bombay: Asia Publishing House, 1964.
3. Walter R. Crocker, *Nehru: A Contemporary's Estimate*, Oxford: Oxford University Press, 1966.

PART TWO
The Cold War and Its Shadow

3

Two Cold Wars: Myopia and Misperceptions in the Great Powers and the Subcontinent

We are not fighting to hold the British Empire. In the light of what you are doing in India, how do you expect to talk of principles and look at our soldiers in the eye. Forsake your side of this war and join our side. Our side is plenty big, bigger than the Raj or Empire, bigger than both of us combined.

Life Magazine, *Open letter to the People of England*,
10 November 1942

While we recognize the reality of the fear of the Muslim League, we do not accept that the setting up of a separate Muslim state is a solution to the communal problem. . . . In conclusion I will repeat and emphasize what to me is a fundamental issue. The future of India and how that future is inaugurated are matters of vital importance not only to India herself but to the whole world.

Lord Pethick Lawrence, Secretary of State for India in
His Majesty's Government, 16 May 1946

I feel most strongly that it will be in the interest of India, as well as the whole world, for its leaders to grasp the opportunity for a stable and peaceful India. . . . The United States has long taken a sympathetic interest in the progressive realisation of India's political destiny. . . . We have expressed in tangible form our confidence in the ability of the Indian leaders to make vital decisions that lie immediately ahead with full awareness that their actions at this moment in history may directly affect world peace and prosperity for generations to come.

Dean Acheson, on 3 December 1946 in a press
statement on the eve of the London talks

* Paper written at the Woodrow Wilson Centre in Washington DC in 1981.

> A highly possible Soviet breakthrough [in the Near East] might open three continents to Soviet penetration. Not since Rome and Carthage had there been such a polarisation of power on earth.
>
> Dean Acheson on 27 February 1947, to Congress, to secure support for the Truman Doctrine

> A divided India augurs ill not only for the Indian people but for all Asia and the whole world.
>
> Aung San, future President of Burma, 4 June 1947 (the day after British announcement on the Partition of India)

This analytical study is part of an endeavour to explore the potential role of India in a divisive but interdependent world. The paper seeks to trace the origin of the partition of India and the parallel developments of the 'big' Cold War, concentrating on the post-War period (1945-8). While internal developments are relevant to understanding these developments, the focus is primarily on international relations and the unforeseen distortions in the foreign policies of countries involved in or affected by their interaction.

The independence of India was of historic significance. It was the first non-white British dependency to wrest freedom and the only one where there was a sustained movement for self-government dating back to the nineteenth century. India had imbibed ideas from Western political thought and British and American examples, and brought to its independence status definite convictions on fundamental human rights, social reform, planned economic progress, as well as the determination to graft on to an old society and civilization the institutions of parliamentary democracy, an independent judiciary and a federal structure. The political struggle was unique in its emphasis on disciplined non-violent protest and a moral appeal, and this led to a dramatic reconciliation between an old imperial power and a former colony.

Indian independence set in motion the era of decolonization. Indeed, India actively supported the process and became its spokesperson in the UN, even before its own freedom. There were hopes amongst governments and liberal thinkers that India's advent in the international community would give a mature leadership to international democracy where nations, new and old, would, as equal partners, create a new force against international conflict and provide an impetus for enlightened cooperation amongst independent nations. As a country with old traditions of ethnic and religious assimilation, as well as tribal and social diversity, the Indian civilization had been a kind of cultural melting pot. It had no tradition of isolation and superiority as in China and no nostalgia for an empire as in Vietnam (towards Cambodia and Laos), and Europe (towards its colonies). Its self-confidence had been reinforced by Mahatma Gandhi's political leadership, which aroused a mass awakening and combined it with a movement for social reform. India was seen as likely to prove a bulwark of peace and stability in the world.

India remains important—its achievements have in many ways exceeded Indian or international expectations. It has domesticated democracy. It has modernized without coercion; it has institutionalized fundamental rights and an independent judiciary; and it has provided sanction for radical social change in a traditional society. Apart from Sri Lanka, it is the only country of a non-European ethnic complexion where there have been changes of government within the framework of constitutional legitimacy. Perhaps the greatest achievement is that the people have become aware of their rights as guardians of democracy. India has also become the biggest laboratory for the development process—the only country where all the sequential stages of economic growth exist and struggle simultaneously. But India faces enormous problems, made worse by an ever-growing population. As in other parts of the developing world, independence has whetted economic expectations—political rights and social reform have spurred dissatisfaction and there is protest at the sluggish fulfilment of their expectations. India advertises, as only democracies do, its failures.

For all its achievements, today India has lost a great deal of its positive international importance, at least in the West. Much of this downgrading of India in its international position can be traced back to the bifurcation of its geographical unity which damaged the historical synthesis of its old civilization. Had Partition taken place in earlier centuries, India and Pakistan, with or without a reunion, might in thirty years have rediscovered the logic of their interdependence and developed a relationship of trust and cooperation between them. If the beginning of such a denouement is no more than a distant goal of public policies, it is very largely because the artificial division of India got fused into the other great divide—the post-War bipolarity of power politics.

The Partition took place in bitterness, left a legacy of suspicion, and started a kind of cold war between India and Pakistan, which has continued ever since. It led to not only periodic conflicts but also persistent militarization, and has resulted in sluggish progress and the economic emasculation of both countries.

The contenders in this little cold war sought to exploit competitively, but in different ways, the big Cold War. The end result today is that there is neither a natural relationship of harmony within the subcontinent nor are the superpowers comfortable or confident with their relations with the countries of the subcontinent. The subcontinent remains one of the most tense if not explosive regions in Asia and the world. The reason is neither entirely due to the inability of India and Pakistan to resolve their problems (as argued by the major powers) nor due to the quarrel of the great powers alone (as explained in the subcontinent) but due to the interaction of both cold wars.

COLD WAR BEGINS IN EUROPE BUT IS GLOBALIZED

The most fateful decisions in both cold wars were taken precisely in the same three and a half months (February-June 1947). This coincidence seemed to have blurred any recognition of the future interaction between the two developments. It is only now realized that the connection between the great power policies and the problems in the subcontinent started with the almost inexplicable compartmentalization and intellectual non-linkage of the two issues.

The steps and stages in the deterioration of relations between the wartime allies are familiar ground. In the aftermath of Yalta, where Roosevelt, Stalin and Churchill met for the last time, the problems in Eastern Europe, the future of Germany and developments in Iran and Turkey vitiated the relations. These culminated in the appeal of the British government to the State Department on 21 February 1947 to take over the burden of assisting the Greek and Turkish governments to fight the communist insurgency in the these countries. In response, after intense internal consultations, on 12 March, President Truman in his speech proclaimed the doctrine named after him to assist free institutions and governments anywhere against minority violence—in effect, a commitment to contain communism and bolster non-communist countries everywhere. Although Churchill's Fulton speech of February 1946 and the Truman commitment managed to contain the globalization of communism, hardly any attention was paid in early 1947 to the contemporaneous developments in Asia. It was not foreseen, or rather available evidence was ignored, that there were problems outside Europe too. The Cold War started with a Western response to the perceived threat from the USSR to countries outside the Soviet orbit. Even though the dimension of the pledge was enlarged, attention was in fact switched off from the developments, then on the anvil, regarding the future of the subcontinent.

NATIONALISM AND SEPARATISM IN INDIA

In India, the growth of nationalism, and of political communalism, and of the sense of Muslim separateness, is a long story which need only be recapitulated briefly. The first important official decision that sowed the seeds of separation was in the reforms enacted by the British Parliament in 1909. The reforms conceded separate electorates to the Muslims against the better judgement of the liberal political philosopher, Lord Morley, who was then Secretary of State for India. He reluctantly agreed to provide for a separate franchise for the minority community because a conservative Viceroy (Lord Minto) had unilaterally committed himself to weighted separate Muslim representation. Even then it was half hoped that this departure from the British political tradition would be only temporary.[1] A Whitehall

Government committee recognized such provisions as contrary to democratic practice but they could not be undone in the next legislative Act (Montague-Chelmsford Reforms of 1919) towards a progressive self-government in India. In the subsequent decades, while the Indian National Congress under Mahatma Gandhi's leadership launched various movements to marshal people's support for freedom, the Muslim League under Jinnah's guidance concentrated on creating consciousness of the separate identity of the Muslims in India.

The 1935 Act provided for provincial autonomy and a federal central government in order to bring the Indian princes into the political superstructure, as a step towards progressive self-government. The principles of safeguards and weightage for minorities became even more entrenched in the administrative system and political processes of the country. The provisions for provincial autonomy were implemented and cabinet governments based on elections in 1937 were formed, bringing in representatives of political parties for the first time.

The Viceroy (Lord Linlithgow) seems to have prevaricated unnecessarily in implementing the provisions for a federal structure, and the War further provided an excuse for deferring progress towards self-government. One hypothetical question that has been asked in this regard is that if the federal provisions of the Act (even though only partially democratic and based on restricted franchise) had also been implemented before the War, would not the nucleus of a coalition central government of a Union of India been created for the future.

INTERNATIONALIZATION OF INDIAN INDEPENDENCE AND THE BRITISH ATTITUDE

The independence of India became a question of 'international' concern only after the Pearl Harbor incident and when Japan quickly overran South-East Asia, and India became critically important to the prosecution of the War by the allies. In 1942 the Churchill government, partly under pressure from the Labour members and partly to satisfy American public opinion, sent Sir Stafford Cripps to try to associate political India to join a wartime

Interim Government in India. The Cripps negotiations were a bold effort but Cripps had a constricted brief from the War Cabinet. The negotiations failed on the question of the composition and powers of the Interim Government and whether India was to be treated fully like other Dominions. There was also a continuing ambivalence on the pledge for independence even at the end of the War. In a confidential analysis made in the State Department at the time, the judgement was that His Majesty's Government (HMG) and the then Viceroy (Lord Linlithgow) were really interested in sabotaging the success of the negotiations.

The Quit India Movement of 1942 followed the failure of the Cripps Mission. The Congress leaders and Gandhi were imprisoned and remained there for the rest of the War in Europe even though people like Nehru wanted to collaborate in the defeat of Fascism. During these years, Jinnah enlarged the demand for safeguards for the Muslims into one for a separate Pakistan and received sympathy and encouragement from the British Indian administration.

It was only when the Labour government came to office in 1945 that serious initiative got underway for the transfer of power in India. The Labour party was committed to independence for India. The War had destroyed the illusions of permanence of the British Empire at least in Asia. Up to 1947, many in the British government (and also in the Congress) had thought that the League's demand for Pakistan was a bargaining ploy for a greater weightage and a weaker central government rather than an absolute precondition to the transfer of power in India. The cabinet delegation nearly hammered out an acceptable compromise (16 May 1946) on the basis of a federal structure limited to Foreign Affairs, Defence and Communications with maximum autonomy for the provinces including the right to form subunions. Differences persisted on the representation in the Interim Government and the prerogative of the proposed Constituent Assembly in drawing up the post-Independence constitution. Even when given parity for the Muslim League with the Congress—a heavily disproportionate weightage—Jinnah sought to deny the Congress the right to nominate a Muslim leader as one of its own representatives. This was critically important for the Congress, as a symbol of its faith in secularism in politics. Following the failure of the Cabinet Mission and efforts of the Viceroy, consultations to resolve the differing interpretations were held in London in December 1946. However, the impasse between the Congress and the League could not be resolved.

On 20 February 1947 Clement Attlee the British prime minister, announced the decision that power would be transferred anyhow to 'responsible Indian hands' not later than June 1948 and that Lord Mountbatten would be appointed as the last Viceroy to replace Lord Wavell. The possibility of partition was hinted in the announcement but even then there were hopes, amongst both the Labour government and the Conservative opposition, that the Cabinet Mission's plan envisaging a single sovereign state of India might remain the basis for the transfer of power.

Mountbatten had exceptional personal credentials and came to India in March 1947 armed with plenipotentiary powers to modify the Cabinet Plan. He went back to London after two months of consultations and secured approval for his plan which became the basis of the Indian Independence Bill. On 3 June (two days before the Marshall Plan speech at Harvard), the House of Commons was told that power would be transferred earlier than planned, but not to one but two Dominions—India and Pakistan. The next day, at a press conference in Delhi, Mountbatten announced that the date would be 15 August, the anniversary of the victory over Japan with which his wartime command was associated. When he came to India, Mountbatten had been told to make his assessment and any new recommendations after six months. He advanced the final date of devolution by ten months in view of Jinnah's obdurate demand and his fears at the prevailing communal tensions. Even so, this advancement, after decades of prevarication, was unnecessary or at least avoidable. There was admittedly exasperation in Congress circles, especially as Mahatma Gandhi and others had done much to ease communal tensions.

The above is a brief chronological summary of the developments leading to the decision to create two Dominions instead of preserving the unity of India. The manner in which it withdrew undermined what was Britain's proudest boast about its Empire—to have given an administrative unity to India.

The primary focus in this paper is on the international attitudes towards Partition and the inability to anticipate the future implications of that division for the foreign policies of the countries involved as well as for world politics. Whatever may have been the policies and reasoning up to the end of the War, the British government, from 1945 onwards, did want to avert Partition but succumbed to the division without any thought on its international implications. Why did HMG agree to Partition and that too in such a precipitous manner?

THE US ATTITUDE TO INDIAN INDEPENDENCE

The US attitude towards India before 1947 was almost the opposite of British policy. It is a story of sustained and enlightened interest in independence and unity. The importance of Anglo-American accord during and after the War led to tactical reluctance to speak against independence, but not support for perpetuating British rule. In the Philippines, the US conceded independence as soon as the War ended. Up to February 1947 there was no mistaking that the US wanted to see the division of India averted.

Direct commerce between the British, American and Indian colonies developed from the sixteenth century onwards. Missionary interest in India was evinced soon after American independence but was discouraged by the East India Company. In the nineteenth century intellectual interest developed in the Indian philosophical heritage. With America's deeply held anti-colonial ethos, sympathy also grew for Indian political aspirations. The only exception was when President Theodore Roosevelt in 1909 complimented the British administration in India as the 'most notable achievement of the white race during the past two centuries'. But this attitude was isolated and untypical. From President Woodrow Wilson's time, an undercurrent of feeling against British and other European imperialism started growing even if it found no official expression.

Within the US administration, interest in India's independence manifested itself unmistakably during the presidency of Franklin Roosevelt. It was not just for the better prosecution of the War, but as a 'peace aim' and the future world order. Roosevelt thought decolonization must be a basic purpose for the US and the fulfilment of nationalism in India and Indo-China was considered symbolic of the broader purpose of the War and eventual peace for the world. The strength of the conviction was apparent in the initiative President Roosevelt took in sending a long telegram to Churchill on the eve of the Cripps Mission (1942). He recalled how the American Union of thirteen sovereign states also came into existence during the War of Independence and this eventually facilitated a strong federal structure for the US. Ignoring British reservations, Roosevelt sent his friend Colonel Louis Johnson as his personal representative and encouraged him to be actively involved in supporting Cripps to hammer out a solution by which a politically representative Interim Government could immediately hold the reins. Churchill, according to Harry Hopkins and Averell Harriman, reacted 'more wrathfully' to Roosevelt's interest in Indian independence than on any other issue during their entire wartime association. Learning of Churchill's reaction, Roosevelt himself became hesitant in directly broaching the subject with the British Prime Minister.

But Congressional and public opinion in the US was not so easily subdued. It looked upon British policy towards India as a critical test of whether the War was a fight for democracy or to save and enlarge the British Empire. The presidential candidate Wendell Willkie, did not visit India during his wartime 'One World' tour but spoke in passionate terms arguing for the end of empires and of India being immediately conceded self-government. *Life* magazine published an open plea to the British people to make it 'Our kind of war'—for freedom and equality for all peoples. FDR's personal conviction and public pressure led him to send another special representative (Ambassador William Phillips) to Delhi. Phillips maintained an active interest in the political situation in wartime India. While in Delhi, Phillips sought to intercede with the Viceroy Linlithgow when, in 1943,

Mahatma Gandhi embarked on a twenty-one-day fast. The US was deeply concerned at the moral and political consequences of Gandhiji's possible death.

After the death of President Roosevelt in April 1945, however, direct interest of the White House in India declined. The focus was on Europe and assessing Soviet intentions and countering its moves. Ambassador Phillips, however, who had become deeply persuaded of the urgency of Indian independence, was supported by the American officials. The Near East Bureau continued to vigorously press for an early transfer of power to one Indian Union. Soon after FDR's death, Phillips wrote a memorandum to the Secretary of State urging that the Indian leaders should be released and political negotiations should recommence. During the visit of the Cabinet Mission to India and afterwards, there was active involvement of the American mission in Delhi. As late as December 1946, Dean Acheson, as Acting Secretary of State, sent direct telegrams to Nehru and Jinnah urging for a federal solution, with the same kind of modalities urged by FDR. In a press statement supporting this approach, he said the decision of India 'was of momentous importance as it may directly affect world peace and prosperity for generations to come'.

At a time when there was no Cold War rationale to bring India on 'our side', this interest in India was remarkable for its persistence and its far-sightedness. It was apparent as late as 26 February 1947 in the conversation between the first Indian ambassador, Asaf Ali, when he made his initial call on the Secretary of State, George C. Marshall. And yet, after February 1947 and the Attlee announcement (and just when the process had reached a critical point), there seems to have been a blanket indifference in Washington to the future of the subcontinent and its subsequent importance. The reporting from the US mission in Delhi continued but, unlike during the previous stages of constitutional negotiations (in 1942, 1945 and 1946), there were no personal contacts, no enquiries, and no instructions from Washington. The present American indifference to India can plausibly be traced back to that interlude of indifference in 1947.

When the Labour government approved the Mountbatten plan even though it shared the global perspectives of Washington, it never gave any thoughts to the future international implications of a divided subcontinent. The India Office and the India Committee of the British Cabinet never seemed to have consulted the Foreign Office. Bevin (the then Foreign Secretary), in a letter to Attlee in his own personal capacity, questioned the wisdom of a precipitous and disorderly disengagement and even suggested US mediation, but never seemed to have got a written reply. The fact that both India and Pakistan were to remain Dominions and continue to be associated with the Commonwealth was looked upon with such satisfaction that the more important geopolitical consequences were wholly overlooked.

ABSENCE OF INDIAN ANTICIPATION OF THE INTERNATIONAL IMPLICATIONS OF PARTITION

During the war years, the Indian political leadership had come to recognize and even depend on the enlightened interest of the US Administration and public opinion in the achievement of independence of the country. The fact that President Roosevelt, disregarding Churchill's interpretation, believed that the Atlantic Charter was a pledge of the principles of freedom, not just for European countries but also for India and other colonies had been widely welcomed in India. Col. Johnson, Ambassador Phillips and the US Chargé d'Affaires (George Merrell) had established strong personal relations with Nehru and other Congress leaders. Public opinion in the US was looked upon as a telling pressure on the British Government. Both Gandhi and Nehru wrote personal letters to President Roosevelt after the failure of the Cripps Mission. There were penetrating exchanges of views between US officials and Nehru, Jinnah and others through 1946, but the Indian leadership made no contact with the US mission after Mountbatten's arrival in India.

The Indian leadership must have read reports of Truman's speech of 12 March, but they never saw its pregnant importance for India. Even Nehru, who had maintained a deep interest in international developments during the interwar years, did not foresee the likely consequences of the looming global Cold War, and its relevance as a factor in deciding whether or not to acquiesce to the division of India. The non-official Asian Relations Conference started the day after Mountbatten's arrival in India (22 March 1947). Despite his responsibilities as head of the Interim Government and as principal leader of the Congress Party, Nehru took an active part in it; indeed he presided over the Conference. He delivered one of his most impressive speeches to delegates from all over independent and colonial Asia. His theme was the emergence of Asia; he foresaw an Asian Federation and unity around the Indian Ocean. But he did not foresee that the chances of such hopes of unity were being undermined by the Cold War heralded by the Truman Doctrine. He did not see that his dreams for India would be enfeebled by accepting partition, which had not yet been decided. He did not raise with Mountbatten (a former supreme commander with a feel for Asian resurgence) or with the US chargé d'affairs the possible international consequences of the division of India in the light of Truman's speech. Had he done so there might have been a pause before the fateful decision. Only Maulana Azad, President of the Indian National Congress and Education Minister in Nehru's cabinet, seemed to have had some premonition of the international consequence of partition.

The intellectual compartmentalization in Washington, London and in Delhi—a sort of mental fatigue in the face of sudden alarm (in Washington) or weary exasperation with a seemingly intractable problem (in London and Delhi) seemed to have smothered the depth and breadth of vision and laid the seeds for future frustration and disasters for India, Pakistan, the UK and the US. Personality traits and entrenched convictions seem to have played a part in restricting vision and wiser policies—Churchill's faith in the permanence of the Empire; Roosevelt's propensity for pragmatism and political expediency in the face of stern opposition; Truman's lack of broad interest in foreign policy problems; Jinnah's single-mindedness; Mountbatten's self-confidence and the commando operations style in the face of political problems; and the impatience of Nehru and Sardar Patel, the deputy leader in the Interim Government, to get even truncated independence. The sheer overload of immediate problems and pressures of democratic or constituency politics, the sudden loss of will and administrative self-confidence to face communal tensions seemed to have blanketed foresight and led to impetuous urgency in dividing the subcontinent. In the final reckoning, however, it seems to me, that the coincidence of the two fateful decisions can explain the surprising myopia of all the decision-makers.

PARTITION AND ITS UNFORESEEN AFTERMATH

The partition machinery, working under the personal direction of Mountbatten, has been one of the most remarkable achievements in administrative history anywhere. The separation of Burma from India had taken five years. But the entire machinery of both the Central Government of India and the two provinces (Punjab and Bengal) was divided within just seventy-three days. It was, however, inevitable that some major problems could not be forced into resolution. Most, but not all, princely states were persuaded by Mountbatten's skilful efforts to join one or the other successor states. Only a standstill agreement was made regarding the integrated irrigation system of Punjab.

The major error of judgement was to imagine that the shock therapy of overcoming political wrangles by loading the burdens of responsibility and the lure of power would dissipate or minimize communal tensions. The violence in the civil strife and the tidal migration which followed (two hundred to five hundred thousand killed; fifteen to twenty million uprooted) were not foreseen. The critical question at the heart of the rationale for dividing the country—whether Pakistan was to be a homeland for all Indian Muslims or only a state where Islam would be the official faith within its frontier—was ignored in the impatience to divide and quit. Indeed, the issue could not be resolved. While West Pakistan was almost purged of minorities, thirty million Muslims in India remained back and felt abandoned and, indeed, became suspect in their own homeland, and especially because there were no balancing hostages left in the dominant wing of Pakistan.

For foreign policy implications, the most important unresolved problem left over from the precipitous partition was that the state of Jammu and Kashmir did not immediately accede to either country. The tribal intrusions into the state were organized and encouraged by Pakistan to compel its incorporation. This led to the hurried accession of the state to India and the subsequent successful defence of its valley against an unconstitutional takeover. In the spirit of his idealism, Nehru authorized an appeal to the UN Security Council that the tribal intrusions organized by Pakistan were a violation of international law and the UN Charter. The Western powers under advice of British expertise sought to treat the Kashmir question as if it was still a kind of internal problem—whether Kashmir with a Muslim majority should or should not remain a part of India. The legality of the accession could not be questioned under the Indian Independence Act; it was no longer a pre-Partition decision but one of international law. There was deep disappointment in India at the ideas of mediation and self-determination under outside supervision in a part of a country which was facing aggression. It was the first shock to India's relations with the West, but even so there was no serious slide in the general climate of relations with the UK or the US. The real deterioration of the Indo-US relationship happened only after the Cold War when globalist perceptions intruded into the subcontinent.

It may be mentioned that the Soviet Union in the Stalin period was almost distrustful of Indian independence and contemptuous of the Indian leadership. During the first stage of the Kashmir debate, the USSR did not take an active part even in the behind-the-scenes mediatory efforts, much less see in it an opening to be exploited for its own diplomatic advantage. In fact, up to 1949-50, the USSR made warmer gestures to Pakistan than to India. The Indian embassy under Mrs Pandit was treated correctly but with cold disdain by the Soviet hierarchy. On the other hand the Pakistan premier, Liaquat Ali Khan, was extended an invitation to visit Moscow in 1949. He deferred it and in the next year he was assassinated. In fact, the Soviet Union developed its standing in India only after Pakistan was accepted as a military ally of the US on the basis of the latter's anti-communist pretensions (1954).

In brief, in 1947, when the Cold War began and partition was decided, the Soviet Union remained indifferent to nationalist

India. The present Soviet standing in the subcontinent followed the interaction of the two cold wars, and not because of the USSR's own aggressive ideological or strategic initiatives or the intra-subcontinental problems.

WHAT IF THE COLD WAR AND PARTITION HAD NOT COINCIDED?

Even assuming that the big Cold War was inevitable—the debate has gone on for two decades on this point—what might have happened if the fateful decisions that started the two cold wars had not coincided? What might have happened if the containment policy had been adopted a year earlier (on the basis of Kennan's long telegram in February 1946) or a year later after the takeover (in Czechoslovakia in the spring of 1948) or after the Berlin blockade? What if the constitutional discussions to explore a federal structure in India (underway since at least 1945) had continued as originally envisaged till June 1948?

One can concede that in the frenzy of prevailing communal tensions, internal strife in India would have continued through 1947, but its magnitude would have been infinitesimal as compared to what actually followed partition. During this period the Indian Army would have remained under the unified command of Field Marshal Auchinleck, the then Commander-in-Chief (who was distressed, indeed alarmed at the prospect of the army's division). The army could have tackled the problems as it had done when required in the past to assist the police forces. As it was, the army was caught halfway through a hurried and necessarily confused division of regiments, staff and stores. Ian Stephens in his book *Pakistan* argues that there might have been a fullscale civil war.[3] But with the army detached from politics—even if it could not be actually trusted to prevent or suppress communal strife—the problem would have been manageable. There was only one accidental, short-lived altercation between a Muslim and a Sikh army unit. The 'civil war'—even if it came to that—would have been less bloody than the Biafra conflict. The pockets of tension did not add up to a separate base like Yenan as in the Chinese civil war.

Everyone in India and Pakistan will recall the sense of revulsion and shame in both countries when Gandhi became martyr to Hindu-Muslim unity on 30 January 1948. It is not inconceivable that the political leadership, including that in Pakistan, might have retreated from the brink of partition if India had not already been divided. Jinnah was quite seriously ill then; he succumbed to a terminal illness in September 1948. (The illness was known only to his personal doctor in Bombay till June 1947 but was more widely suspected by the beginning of 1948.) Even Jinnah was known to have been deeply affected by Gandhi's assassination.

Important international developments took place in the second half of 1947 and the first half of 1948 which could have shaken the complacency about the division of India. On cooler reflection the British government might have recalled that all British imperial strategists from Clive to Curzon had recognized India's geopolitical importance. The US government would have surveyed the global picture implicit in their policy of containment. In September 1947, the theoretician Zhadnov of the USSR answered the Truman Doctrine and Marshall Plan with the founding of the Cominform. He asserted that the world was indeed facing a struggle between the 'imperialist and capitalist forces' on the one hand and the 'socialistic democratic anti-imperialist camp' on the other, and there could be no coexistence in this confrontation. By the end of 1947 and early 1948 it became clearer (as it was not in early 1947) that the Kuo-min-tang (KMT) could not defeat the People's Liberation Army (PLA) in China; in fact, perceptive observers began to foresee the eventuality of communist victory over the whole of China. Mao-tse-tung claimed in a speech that the civil war in China had reached a turning point during this period. Mao was later to make plain that he saw no middle or third way between the two camps and China must tilt towards and ally itself with the USSR. The prospects of a US-CPC rapprochement had been abandoned and the likelihood of China turning to the USSR was more evidently on the cards. Would democratic India have been partitioned if China, instead of being feeble and divided, was likely to emerge united and strong under communism?

By the spring of 1948 Washington was more alive to the crumbling post-war dispensation in Asia; the Attlee Government was always unhappy at the prospect of division; Mountbatten, awakened to geopolitical importance, might after all, as Wavell had urged, have continued discussion rather than adopt a policy of 'divide and quit'; the international perspective would have steeled the political and intellectual grit of diverse decision-makers, including Nehru, the unchallengeable leader in India after Gandhi; there would have been, despite all internal exasperation, a stronger rationale to preserve the natural unity of India. Thus, the chronological separation, in time, of the decisions on Partition and the Cold War might have 'tilted' the scales against the division of India.

THE UNFORESEEN CONSEQUENCES OF PARTITION

No one can accurately calculate the opportunity costs of Partition. An undivided India, if it were to divert fifty per cent of the resources expended by Pakistan and India on their conflicts and defence against each other towards development and productive investment, might have obtained an additional growth rate of say three per cent. If a steady compounded growth rate of seven per cent over three decades (within institutionalized democracy) had been obtained—no more than that of the less dynamic countries of South-East Asia, like Malaysia—India may by now have reached a stage of self-sustaining growth. Pakistan would of course not have suffered the agony and humiliation of the breakaway of Bangladesh, and Bangladesh in its independence would not be facing the problem of development with a dense population and very limited natural resources.

Undivided India would, of course, have been non-aligned but it could have kept the Cold War competition more effectively at bay even under the pressures of the Dullesian phase of containment. It may be recalled that Pakistan also started by being non-aligned. Its early foreign policy pronouncements had pledged 'friendship for all'. Despite American pressure, it supported the seating of China in the UN and kept aloof from contributing to the UN force in Korea. Eventually, after twenty-four years as an American ally, Pakistan actually joined the non-aligned group in

1978 and has apparently been resisting the idea of endorsing the strategic consensus or making available its territory for military bases to the US.

With differing emphasis, because of different connections built during these decades, the present policies of both India and Pakistan have some similarities. Although not officially described in these terms, the policy is of simultaneous, non-ideological beneficial bilateral relations with the US, the USSR and China. India rejects the idea of being in Soviet tutelage as Pakistan now repudiates any suggestion of being a US ally for anti-Soviet strategy. In the absence of the subcontinental cold war, India's non-alignment would not have been as seriously misunderstood or tactically deflated. Trade, aid, and economic relations with the Soviet Union would have broken new ground as they did in the 1950s, but the US would have become, as indeed it is today, the foremost trading partner of India because of natural, economic and technological complementarities.

Both India and Pakistan have suffered disappointments and frustrations in the process of voluntarily or involuntarily seeking national advantage from the big Cold War. Pakistan had expected that the US would come to actually support it militarily during the 1965 conflict. As it happened, the US took an even-handed approach and stopped aid to both Pakistan and India. India found the USSR reverting to a tilt towards China during the crucial week of the Sino-Indian conflict because the Soviets did not want to alienate China at a time when they were confronting the USA on whether to continue the installation or withdraw the missiles in Cuba (October 1962). The people in Pakistan were to burn the US embassy, possibly with the acquiescence of their government (1979); the people in India, without the encouragement of the government and despite official policies, were to demonstrate against Soviet invasion of Afghanistan (1980). In relations with other countries, Kashmir and Indo-Pak relations would not have consumed the greater part of the diplomatic energy of India only to find that the world remained neutral on what for a while had become the touchstone of India's international friendships. Africa and the Arab world do look to India for support in their regional problems, but they shirk from any categorical reciprocal support on subcontinental problems.

An India not enfeebled by the subcontinental cold war would have been a stronger bulwark of stability in the wider context of Asia and a more powerful voice for international détente. It could also have had a more effective role in the North-South economic configuration.

SUPERPOWERS—ALTERNATION OF BENIGN ATTITUDES AND IMPOSED COMPETITION

An analysis of superpower relations during the entire period of their interaction with the subcontinent is also instructive and different from conventional wisdom in the West and in the subcontinent. When there were moments of actual conflict within the subcontinent or periods of hopeful improvements in Indo-Pak relations, both superpowers showed a parallel interest not to exacerbate the relationship but to encourage the easing of tensions. In the period 1945 to 1947, neither power foresaw any future advantage in the division of the subcontinent. The ideological prescription of proletarian internationalism was not to divide in order to infiltrate; it banked on the economic determination of Marxist philosophy and not on the diplomacy of state relations. In 1960, after the Sino-Soviet rift, and in 1962-3 after the Sino-Indian conflict (when the US and the UK urged resolution of India-Pakistan problems through the Averill Harriman-Duncan Sandys efforts), the USSR did not try to frustrate the efforts of the West. In 1965-6, after the Indo-Pakistan conflict, the US actually seemed to have prompted the Soviet Union to play the honest broker. Washington welcomed Kosygin's role which resulted in the Tashkent Agreement. (Curzon and all the British imperial statesmen must have turned in their graves when a successor government in the UK encouraged Russian political mediation in the subcontinent!) Similarly, both the US and the USSR made the same kind of approaches urging India and Pakistan to subscribe to the Non-Proliferation Treaty (NPT) and publicly and privately sought to discourage nuclear explosions by both countries as undermining regional stability.

The intrusion of the superpowers into the subcontinent actually came during periods of high intensity in their own global competition and not with a deliberate desire to exploit Indo-Pak tensions. The countries of the subcontinent admittedly sought to take advantage of this competition and thus provided the opening for the involvement of the superpowers. Pakistan was accepted as a military ally and armed in the pursuit of the American policy of military containment of the USSR and China, and the menace of communism. It is now acknowledged that accepting at face value Pakistan's credentials for a real anti-communist crusade or vigilance began the process of the cooling in Indo-US relations. It eventually led to the India-Pakistan conflict of 1965. It was in response to this policy that, as Barnds puts it, the 'Soviet Union chose India.'[3] India and the Soviet Union found a convergence of interests and chose each other, and a military supply relationship was forged between them. Later, Pakistan befriended China disregarding its obligations as a member of SEATO.

In 1971 the US Administration did not see the Bangladesh crisis as a nationalist upsurge—a kind of sub-decolonization from a geographical anomaly created by Partition. By deliberate decision, the US 'tilted' towards Pakistan. This, however, was primarily because the US was in the process of seeking to fashion a Washington-Peking (now Beijing) axis for its own strategic advantage. Islamabad had been a useful go-between for Kissinger —and so the White House was inclined to keep it as an intermediary for the perceived strategic goal. The dispatch of a carrier unit to the Bay of Bengal to frighten India was also to assure China, warn the USSR and obtain 'a new global geopolitical equilibrium'. As an exercise in coercive diplomacy, it proved an embarrassing failure. It did not save the old Pakistan but has left indelible suspicions in India. The rationale of that disastrous policy was born of globalist objectives, not on the merits of the regional problem.

The present India-Pakistan arms race and the deterioration of bilateral relations came because of the Soviet invasion of Afghanistan. In this case, the Soviet Union ignored or underestimated the adverse consequences of its intervention in Afghanistan including public reaction in India. There was a compounding error in the US judgement in concluding that the Soviet action was a move on the strategic chessboard directed against the West. The Soviet move, no doubt ill-conceived, was to tidy a local situation which had gone awry. It outraged Afghan nationalism and invited strong reactions in the entire Third World. It also prompted the US to press for a strategic consensus, the constitution of the Rapid Deployment Force and for Pakistan to get arms against India. In turn the Soviet Union used these arms supplies, as an ex-post-facto justification to 'save' democratic Afghanistan from the West and perpetuate its uncomfortable presence in the country. The real damage has been to the prospect of stability in South Asia, and this was not accurately anticipated. From globalist perspectives, Afghanistan was an intellectual challenge for interpretation but because of its diminishing security significance, it was on the way to becoming an international sideshow. But for the region of South and South-West Asia itself, its persistence increased the propensity of chain reactions and internal ferment. It carried the danger of mounting consequences and a serious longterm fallout.

In sum, the interaction between the two cold wars was because the subcontinent hoped to exploit the big Cold War. Both superpowers probably wanted stability in the subcontinent but in the process of their global competition, the paradoxical result was that of destabilizing the subcontinent without really securing their own interests.

The situation had become unsatisfactory from any point of view. The benign intentions of the great powers were suspect; they may not have wanted a conflict but in the course of their global competition and arms aid policies, they increased the likelihood of provoking one. For all their leverage, they were powerless to prevent it. They must recognize that neither power is likely to have the whole of the subcontinent as a military surrogate or political dependency even if they had the will or capacity to carry the full economic burden, the military liabilities and the political hazards that such an ambition would entail. On the other side, the mutual fears of India and Pakistan increased. Pakistan feared an Indo-Soviet pincer and India suspected US malevolence wanting to encourage Pakistan to belligerency in Kashmir. Both India and Pakistan speculated that the other country was preparing a preemptive strike against its own nuclear installations. Both superpowers shirked from the policy dilemma that this could pose for each of them. Neither the USA nor the USSR could now be effective with their counsels of restraint. In the prevailing state of East-West relations, they could act together.

The lessons of these decades is that, in the short run at least, the tail wags the dog and arms supplies do not enable control in the use of arms. In fact, there was probably neither candour nor confidence to define the scope and limitations of any of the bilateral relationships. Thus, in a potentially explosive situation in a strategically important area, the whole web of relationships has got riddled with ambivalence, ambiguities, and apprehensions for the future.

These complexities can all be traced back to the myopia that led to Partition and the misperceptions that yielded to the temptation of inviting or imposing the Cold War into the region. One of the foremost American scholars, W. Norman Brown, states: 'The partition was the greatest disaster which the subcontinent has ever suffered.' Sir Penderel Moon[4] (a former civil servant in India and who edited the multi-volume *Transfer of Power* archives) commented ruefully about its origin: 'The Congress passionately desired to preserve the unity of India; they consistently acted to make its partition certain.'

The lessons of these last decades at the time of writing are (1981) beginning to register in the subcontinent itself. It is more widely appreciated that Partition has belied the hopes of its most vigorous advocates because it made the countries more vulnerable to extraneous politics. This is recognized by sober leadership at every end of the political spectrum in both countries. The leadership of the erstwhile Hindu party (the Jan Sangh), which for three decades remained unreconciled to Partition, now urges good relations with Pakistan. A growing body of non-official opinion in Pakistan feels that ultimately national security and progress of their country hinges more on good relations with India than on American arms or exclusively Islamic connections. For the first time, relations with neighbours is the dominant issue for public and private foreign policy analysts. However, the question still remains whether the two Cold Wars can be disentangled and whether and how good neighbourly relations can be established. The reunification of India, Pakistan and Bangladesh by any means, direct or indirect, must be ruled out as neither feasible nor desirable. The violence in Ireland would pale before any attempt to unscramble the divisions in the subcontinent. The challenge to statesmanship now is to find an alternative goal than to look back in nostalgia or just be resigned to a diplomacy of complaint. The superpower approach of using the subcontinent whenever convenient but pretending that the subcontinental problems can be put on the back-burner under the assumption that they would somehow defuse and disappear or at least never erupt is nothing but wishful thinking.

The feasible broad approach to stability in South Asia is to recognize the region as the microcosm of world politics—an area of diverse and sensitive national sovereignties of unequal strength, who remain tied to each other in physical, ecological, hydrological and economic interdependence. The lessons of the big Cold War, as often perceived by the subcontinent, are valid for the subcontinent itself. The conceptual notion of world politics as a polarized struggle between 'a new Rome and a new Carthage' and a new threat to Christian civilization from a militant, monolithic, expansionist, revolutionary secular dogma was proved false fairly early in Yugoslavia and more significantly by the Sino-Soviet rift. Ideology and theology are important factors—but in domestic rather than international relations. Nuclear weapons and a strategy of deterrence are admittedly a new feature in international politics. Whether the nuclear balance is considered stable or not, the international system has reverted to something akin to the old pattern of nations confronting or cooperating with each other, regardless of ideology or social systems. Each country perceives and pursues its interests with its own mix of security anxieties and economic compulsions. The new international democracy—a much bigger conglomerate after decolonization—is more disparate in economic and military strength than any in the past, and yet even the poor and economically dependent nations are strong in defiance of coercion and imposition.

Nehru's vision before and at the time of Independence was more prophetic than the one advanced by communist ideologies or by those who feared an unending challenge from communalism. Nehru had argued then that ideologies will have to be domesticated; national self-determination will assert itself against bloc discipline; nations big and small will have to learn to coexist and cooperate with each other. He had also constantly emphasized the overriding importance of geographical compulsions and that socio-economic growth and political participation were more critical for national strength than military might.

The vision was vindicated but India's own stature as an advocate and spokesman for enlightened internationalism has got enfeebled and deflected by the cold war nearer home and the complications and distortions from the intrusion of the great powers. Non-alignment at times became tactical; self-determination became associated with the problems with Pakistan; respect for other nationalisms became qualified; security through primacy of development succumbed to excessive militarization. But for all that the validity of the vision remains and is not repudiated.

Today, situation prevails where nationalism and regionalism are asserting themselves everywhere in defiance of the global strategic perceptions. The superpowers are slowly getting estranged from most regions and from every country where there is a national consensus, including from their respective allies. The superpower quest for superiority and balance is having the paradoxical result of becoming a competition in losing political influence. Regionalism based on economic pulls and complementarities has, however, made strong beginnings and looks like the wave of the future.

The answer in the subcontinent itself is economic regionalism which adjusts to political diversity. The lesson of these decades is that the superpowers cannot impede such efforts if the initiative is taken and it becomes common ground and an agreed purpose of the countries of the region.

The real problem is to find the alchemy of trust in the web of bilateral relations, which have got so vitiated because of a search for security. It demands nothing more and nothing less than that the principles of mutual respect, so often urged in other international problems including those between the superpowers, but not scrupulously nurtured. It requires the mutual recognition of the political reality of 'other nationalisms' including the element of false fears and entrenched misperceptions. Non-alignment is now a common commitment in South Asia although its essential spirit of detachment from big-power politics remains vitiated. Regionalism predicates that no set of bilateral relations would be directed against another country of the region. Pakistan must give up the notion of wanting to balance its military capability through continuing leverage from the big Cold War. The challenge and burden depends critically on India because it is a neighbour to all the concerned countries. But the hardest thing in diplomacy is negotiation between unequal sovereign neighbours.

The problem of the region is not different from the logic of survival and progress through the recognition of economic and ecological interdependence. In the North-South strategy to which all countries of the subcontinent are committed, the arguments rest on diverting resources from excessive militarization to economic development, survival and progress in an interdependent world. The logic of strategic disarmament between superpowers and diversion to productive investment to avoid self-destructive militarism applies to the subcontinent also. The axiom of the French author Seay has a universal validity—'A wise nation fosters with all its might, the progress of its neighbours.' The US is neighbour to the whole world just as India is to South Asia. Both have potentially enormous markets if they are open and can be fostered to growth. In brief, South Asia must by common determination agree to allow regionalism to thrive. Partition cannot be undone but security globalism must be kept at bay.

The contenders of the big Cold War must also learn their lesson. The partition of India took place because the vision of the USA and the UK and India were neither broad in their contemporary judgement nor farsighted enough in their forward perspective. Fostering, exploiting or perpetuating regional tensions should be seen as a frustrating exercise; it has not made dependable allies or self-confident friends for either superpower. Pakistan invited disaster under the pretension of being a bastion of US strategy. India can progress only haltingly if it thinks a two front war with Pakistan and China, is inevitable. The subcontinent and South-West Asia is a region where agreed restraint in competition and arms supplies could make an easy beginning. (Arms vendors, motivated primarily towards commerce, would have to be persuaded or obliged to turn some of their exported swords into exported turbines or tractors.) The superpowers must see—as they have done in the past or only in moments of reflection and not at the height of their own paranoia—that the lesser evil points to disengagement from anything that fuels tensions in the South Asian region.

Finally, it is worth mentioning the continuing resilience of the Indian democratic system. India brought to Independence a faith in pluralism and secularism, and has developed intrinsic strength from the political participation of the people. It was able to graft a federal democratic structure to an old tradition of tolerance and assimilation. The safety valve of adult franchise has absorbed and moderated religious tensions and acute violence from social change and rising expectations in the face of economic insufficiency. In its federal structure, it is riding the strains of regional and sub-regional pulls. It remains a bold and almost unique example in the developing world of a large subcontinental country modernizing in agriculture and simultaneously in industry without revolution. The backlash of tribalism and fundamentalism is unavoidable in new states embarked on modernization and national integration, but in India it has been contained and at least partially resolved. Partition came in the way of the democratic system of government being allowed to take early root in other parts of old India, notably in Pakistan. But where country after country is crumbling to authoritarianism, militarism and violence, the prospect of the extension of civilian rule and constitutionally determined succession, and the return to socio-economic priorities in the subcontinent depends on the easing of regional tensions and not being continually buffeted by extraneous cross pulls and entanglements.

Neither wisdom nor myopia have been the exclusive monopoly of either the great powers or the lesser ones. But it is equally clear that while the great powers can destabilize countries and regions, only national governments working together can find the basis for constructive resolution of their own regional problems. From any point of view the first step in this direction in the subcontinent points to the separation of the two Cold Wars. This would lead to healthier relations all round and give a chance to stability in the interconnected region of South-East and South-West Asia which has acknowledged importance for global policies. What started with naïve 'non-linkage' and was vitiated by perverse 'linkage' can only be defused by the deliberate 'de-linkage' of the two Cold Wars.

NOTES

1. Stanley Wolpert, *Morley and India, 1906-1910*, Berkeley: University of California Press, 1967.
2. Ian Stephens, *Pakistan*, London: Ernest Benn, 1967.
3. William J. Barnds, *India, Pakistan, and the Great Powers*, New York: Council on Foreign Relations and Praeger, 1972.
4. Penderel Moon, *Divide and Quit*, Berkeley: University of California Press, 1961.

4

Third World Militarization: A Challenge to Third World Diplomacy

Not since Hiroshima and the Second World War have statesmen, scholars, scientists and thoughtful people everywhere been so concerned with the fate of the earth, international security and human survival. All share a sense of alarm; alarm at nuclear destruction by miscalculation, alarm at the 'Poverty Curtain'[1] which is more profound and real than the Iron Curtain that was perceived as polarizing the world into a new Rome and a new Carthage, alarm at the world's ecological future and the threatened exhaustion of its critical resources. There is broad agreement that providing for the future—for each country and for the interdependent community of nations—will require a more rational balance between productive outlays and national defence in the use of the world's physical and human resources.

The oil price hikes of the early 1970s made nations vividly aware of global interdependence. For the first time, modern industrial states were held at bay and seemed at the mercy of a few poor nations which controlled the resources essential for developed economies. The Third World came to relish the new bargaining strength of some in its fraternity and hoped that this strength would lead to a restructured international economic relationship and an enlightened view towards the developing world. The energy crisis, however, proved perverse. The industrialized world, after the initial jolt, has all but overcome its difficulties and has regained economic supremacy. But most

*This is basically a production of a keynote paper circulated for a conference on the subject held at the LBJ School, University of Texas, Austin, in 1984. As holder of the Tom Slick Professorship, the author was responsible for the choice of subject and the participants. There were twenty outside invitees from all the continents.

of the oil importers of the developing world, and now many of the exporters, remain disabled and are in dire economic straits. The oil shocks, instead of fostering interdependence, have created a Hobbesian world bent as never before on beggaring its neighbours far and near.

The consequential international malaise has been exhaustively analysed. Urgent blue-ribbon recommendations have been made for renewed economic dynamism in an interdependent world. The reports, Common Crisis (the 1983 review of the Brandt Commission Report) and Common Security (the Palme Commission Report on Disarmament and Security) complement each other in their focus on international economic and security problems. No international conclave has mustered greater weight of experience and authority than was assembled in these commissions. The membership of the Palme Commission even included representatives from communist countries. After years of debate in all possible forums, the outlines for a New International Economic Order were hammered out and have been adopted by the UN. In the *Global 2000* report, the US itself has projected a dreary future if urgent international efforts are not immediately launched. The substance of these reports was endorsed by the South-South Summit in New Delhi in 1982 and the Non-aligned Summit in New Delhi in 1983. As chairperson of the non-aligned fraternity of nations, Mrs Gandhi reiterated in 1983 before the UN General Assembly the need for North-South cooperation in changing international institutions and turning today's disadvantaged of the South into tomorrow's consumers for the North. There is a consensus that the problems are global and that solutions are urgently needed. Unfortunately, beyond damage control and crisis management, there is little cooperative effort forthcoming along the lines of these recommendations—not, at least, to arrest the downward slide of the developing world.

A meaningful dialogue has been notably absent. The 1981 Cancun Summit was a response to the Brandt Commission, but it produced only palliative sympathy for and half-hearted commitment to the problems of the South. The United Nations Conference for Trade and Development (UNCTAD) conference in Belgrade in 1983 also did not bring forth any promise of substantive global negotiations. The 1983 Williamsburg Summit was preoccupied with intra-OECD problems and expressed only reluctant concern for the structural, financial and trade problems of the developing world. The 1983 session of the UN General Assembly reiterated its past position, but pledged no breakthrough.

The fact is that the post-war hopes, designs and fears have degenerated into political bedlam and intellectual confusion. The communist monolith has not advanced inexorably, implanting its standard model around the world; it has been resisted by nationalism abroad, but it is really disintegrating from within. The policy of containing communism and 'making the world safe for freedom and democracy' has resulted in a diversity of dictatorships and authoritarianisms. But the superstructure of the Cold War and the intellectual hold of old ideological antagonisms and military fears continue to propel mutual paranoia. Nuclear peace, at least, has been preserved, albeit under the awesome fear of mutual destruction. The rationale of old policies is now challenged by an articulated demand for build-up freezes, dialogue and arms control between the superpowers. The change is the result of the exasperated weariness of the great powers and their creeping but patent indifference to the socio-economic problems of the Third World. Coinciding with this comparative unconcern and the demand for enlightened restructured international economic relations is the Third World's rush to militarize. While the North remains obsessed with security when it ought to be concerned about human survival, the South, which should be occupied with social progress for economic survival of its populations, is squandering its resources on the quest for internal and external security, even at the obvious cost of human development.

This matching myopia—of uncontrolled build-up and indifference to global interdependence in the industrialized world and self-inflicted accentuation of problems in the Third World—is a grim reality. Some observers doubt whether parts of the Third World can be saved from starvation, stagnation and chaos. Some of the afflicted within the Third World even wonder whether decolonization was a mistake and a failure, a question cynically echoed in the developed world.

The challenge is to both the Third World intellect and Third World politics. It should be plain by now that the old mix of angry complaints and helpless pleas is as ineffective and outdated as the old Cold War rhetoric against coexistence and diversity. The Third World nations must learn a lesson or two from the industrialized world's attention to self-regarding priorities. The Third World nations' demand for enlightened reorientation in international relations is not credible when their own domestic priorities remain equally distorted, if not more self-damaging. They must recognize that the great powers cannot resolve Third World domestic or regional problems. The contribution of the great powers to resolving Third World problems can, at best, be collateral and subsidiary to self-regarding efforts in the developing world itself. In this context, Third World militarization should be seen as the most critical threat to its future and, therefore, as a challenge to its diplomacy. A simultaneous challenge exists for the great powers—whether, with their experience of failures and frustrations, they can better safeguard their own goals and interests through benign encouragement to Third World diplomacy.

Before dwelling on the consequences of Third World militarization, one must look at the backdrop of how it came to be.

THE BACKDROP OF GREAT POWER RELATIONS

In the last two decades, the great powers have rhetorically acknowledged the imperative of coexistence and détente but then reverted to the old attitude of menacing competition. The international climate has clearly deteriorated in the last few years. The Cold War rhetoric has been revived. The arms race of the superpowers is accelerating; expensive weapons systems are being deployed and ultra-sophisticated space weapons are on the drawing boards. Some new and ominous paradigms have arisen: pre-emptive nuclear first strikes are now considered possible, and, in a minority view at least, nuclear war deemed winnable. Some in the West even analyse that the arms race was a means of economic attrition of communism in Soviet Russia. In the continuing vigilance and political competition between the two superpowers, every problem—Afghanistan, Central America, the Caribbean, Lebanon—is, in a sort of conditioned reflex, interpreted in Washington and Moscow as another move on the East-West checkerboard. All conflicts, regardless of local factors or socio-economic realities, were blanketed in the superpower strategic syndromes. When superpowers rationalize the existence of their own burgeoning military, they forget that such interpretation budgets and exaggerated fears had once led to the disastrous involvement of the US in Vietnam and to the foreign policy setback and the agonizing military experience that baffled the Soviet Union in Afghanistan.[2] With their assured capacity of mutual destruction, they know only too well that for them, in a Clausewitzian sense, war can no longer be politics by other means. Yet, even though Washington and Moscow are compelled to depend upon diplomacy as their only chance, the habitual conviction that politics must rely on unending preparation and the contingent sanction of force persists.

The Third World has taken the rhetoric and intellectual misjudgements of the superpowers seriously, and this has affected the evolution and the actuality of its own politics. The developing countries have also tended to overlook the occasions when the superpowers have pulled back from confrontations and have even recognized a community of interests with their adversary. For example, the US and the USSR converged and even acted in parallel in disciplining France, Britain, and Israel in the Suez crisis of 1956. The Austrian Treaty was signed, and in 1955 the four-power occupation of Austria was ended after the USSR modified its previous stand. Similarly, more than a decade later, both Germanys were recognized. The superpowers have negotiated and concluded, at times behind the back of their allies, some arms limitation and disarmament agreements. The Partial Test Ban Treaty (1963), restrictions on the development of biological weapons (1972), restrictions on the deployment of nuclear weapons in space (1967) and on the seabed (1971), and the first of the Strategic Arms Limitation Talks (SALT I) are examples of such agreements. Significantly, the US and the USSR jointly and separately canvassed the endorsement of the Non-proliferation Treaty (NPT). The provisions of the SALT II Treaty, even though not ratified by the US, are said to have been observed by both powers. Complacent satisfaction, of course, cannot be drawn from these limited agreements: on the contrary, the general trend has been to develop new sophisticated weapons systems even while conducting negotiations. It still looks like what Alva Myrdal called it—*The Game of Disarmament*.[3]

In four decades of mutual apprehension, the superpowers, in addition to being militarily prudent, have also been more and more economically self-regarding. Most of the sanctions imposed in the wake of Afghanistan and Poland have been unilaterally eased. Eastern European debts were rescheduled and, similarly, the Western European participation in the Siberian pipeline was finally approved by the US. The US itself has contracted to give the USSR the first option on US grain surpluses for five years. To be sure, restrictions continue on the import of Russian nickel and export of technology, but when large-scale economic interests are at stake, confrontation has yielded to the logic of interdependence. The Korean airliner Flight 007 incident (1983), for example, initially generated demands for punitive retaliation, but the actual reaction was more limited in scope. Even the duration of the boycott of some air links with Moscow by the US was reduced.

Moreover, in Western democracies, a strong popular movement has grown which demands an arrest of the arms race. The movement varies in strength from country to country and oscillates in the intensity of protest, but it has become such a significant factor in domestic and intra bloc politics that even the most conservative governments cannot ignore it. Not only was the earlier practice of shelving SALT talks modified, but the US Administration has been obliged to try to assuage internal and allied opinion by adopting more conciliatory postures. This change does not necessarily signify that arms control agreements are around the corner or that present prospects are auspicious, but there is at least heightened awareness in the industrialized North that arms reduction must be taken seriously for political and economic reasons.

Even those who earlier questioned the wisdom or possibility of international détente are aware of the dilemma caused by increased military expenditures competing with social and economic demands at home. Outside the peace movement, there is a widening spectrum of opinion that recognizes that the arms race is not only dangerous but also self-debilitating. There is growing realization, even among the old proponents of nuclear defence, that an unending search for military superiority is neither necessary nor attainable. At least in Western democracies, defence and security is less and less consigned to the confidential discretion of national security establishments.

THE COLD WAR AND DECOLONIZATION

Generally speaking, in the Third World there has been little blending of economic sensibility with scrutiny of defence policies and programmes. This can be traced back to the unprecedented transformation of the international system after the Second World War. Two parallel and conflicting developments shaped the post-war scene. On the one hand, international society became globally pluralistic when the countries outside the European heritage gained independence. On the other hand, two superpowers, each with global reach, emerged. Each sought, in a mutually reacting determination, to dominate the international system in accordance with its own strategic and ideological perceptions. Indeed, these powers came to expect a kind of imperial subordination from other independent nations.

When the Second World War ended, the era of European empires was already doomed. Bipolar competition between the superpowers undoubtedly accelerated the process of decolonization. The coincidence of global competition yielded both attendant benefits as well as perverse consequences. At the height of the ideological and strategic struggle in the world arena, the two blocs sought to persuade or induce the newly independent countries to join their respective military orbits, or to at least refrain from turning to the other. Even when localized tensions had origins in historical regional animosities or purely national ambitions, the contending blocs tended to line up behind their respective proxies; and this only exacerbated the problem. The client states were rewarded with government-level military and economic aid by the respective superpowers. This aid and political cultivation gave the decolonized nations an exhilarating sense of participation in international politics, but it also undermined their sense of independence and enfeebled their determination to become self-reliant. Policies came to be predicated on the Cold War competition by not only those countries that consigned their security and foreign policies to the great powers through pacts or military arrangements but even by nations asserting non-alignment. But for the Cold War, the UN might have been more effective in preserving peace and resolving non-great power conflicts under global rules. The UN could have contributed more significantly in promoting regional and world economic cooperation and development.

One is tempted to speculate that had the Cold War not intervened, the newly independent countries would have been left, to a much greater extent, to evolve gradually according to their respective national personalities and circumstances, to fashion their own destinies, as did the US after its own independence. The industrialized world might have confined its interests to raw materials or minerals and not intruded into the domestic policies and external politics of the new countries; thus disappointments and frustrations on both sides might have been minimized.

In a digression, the consequences of the overlap of the Cold War and decolonization can be illustrated by the problems of South Asia. India was ripe to become at least a self-governing Dominion in the 1930s. If representatives of the Indian National Congress and the Muslim League had begun to work together in the central government and the provinces before and during the Second World War, a federal Union of India might have emerged in the same way as did the United States of America from the thirteen colonies that cooperated during the American War of Independence. The partition of India and the consequential Indo-Pakistani tensions have dominated the external politics of the two countries. The penalties of delayed decolonization were more seriously exacerbated because these tensions became enmeshed in the politics of containment and the Cold War. After over thirty years of independence (and three Indo-Pakistani conflicts), both countries were beginning to recognize that the Cold War had vitiated their problems and solutions could only come from their bilateral diplomacy. The process again suffered a reversal because of the Soviet intervention in Afghanistan and the reimposition of the Cold War analysis on the whole area. The subcontinent is today riddled with revived suspicions and fears that have in turn precipitated a new arms race in the area, diluting and jeopardizing the prospects of a more stable polity in the region.

Almost worldwide, the outcome of the interactions of the Cold War competition in the Third World has generally proven frustrating for the great powers and disastrous for the developing countries. Looking back, for all the assistance that the US provided to Iran, Vietnam, Cambodia (now Kampuchea), Ethiopia and Pakistan, and by the Soviet Union to China, Egypt, Iraq, Indonesia and Somalia, these countries did not prove to be security assets much less reliable allies. Indeed, the record shows that ultimately the reverse leverage of the recipients has become more significant than the influence of their donors and suppliers through aid and arms.

As the Iran-Iraq war vividly illustrates, future Third World conflicts may start more in defiance of the superpowers than at their bidding and convenience. Even with dependence on foreign arms, such conflicts will not be easily managed or defused. In the present climate, the great powers are unlikely to be able to agree on self-denying restraints, much less coordinate their policies in an erupting rash of conflicts.

The easy flow of military hardware was calculated to buttress the strategies of the donor nations, but this tactic has all too frequently fanned regional ambition and thus precipitated conflicts in the Third World. It has also had another unforeseen consequence. Just when countries began trying to establish democratic structures and modernize traditional societies, the military, a comparatively better-educated and better-disciplined element, was tempted by political ambition. The military was modernized faster than the social institutions and generally before inherited economic stagnation could be transformed through developmental momentum. According to respected compilations, some 90 out of the total of 114 Third World countries are either directly controlled by the military or provide backing to one-party governments.[4]

Some military regimes have tilted towards radicalism, but more frequently they have been conservative and have intervened to preserve their oligarchic privileged positions. Some takeovers were justified by impatience with the sluggish progress and corruption of the civil governments. Most such regimes started with declarations of temporary involvement in politics and affirmed pledges to return to the barracks after putting the house in order. Some sociologists look upon military authority in the Third World as a tolerable or even a desirable vehicle for modernization. They argue that, even while making disproportionate demands on the scarce resources for arms, the military promotes education and skills and contributes to social welfare and economic progress. Sample studies have used diverse variables and show a wide variety of relationships between defence expenditures and economic growth rates. But countries which have indeed shown spectacular economic development even while expending very heavy outlays on their military, like South Korea, are exceptions. Rapid militarization has generally increased the polarization between the rulers and the mass of the people and so intensified the social tensions in the developing countries. The quest for legitimacy in a post-coup scenario has generally proved elusive. Moreover, the return to participatory civil democracy has been rare and, where obtained, as in the recent case of Nigeria, has again been overwhelmed by the military. One can but hope that Argentina will prove a long-lasting exception. At all events, military or authoritarian regimes of the right and the left are necessarily inclined to exaggerated chauvinism and adventures abroad (for example, in the Falklands). Their increased dependence on outside arms suppliers only erodes the substance of independence. In fact, in the wake of disproportionate militarization, even civil governments come to rely more and more on the weapons and loyalty of the security forces, not so much against external dangers as against internal disaffection. On the whole, and especially in a longer time frame, military priorities have had, and are likely to have, a negative correlation with development, particularly in the face of reduced outside assistance. The obvious opportunity costs in neglected priorities are evident almost everywhere in military or one-party states.

Few parts of the Third World face as grim a prospect as sub-Saharan Africa. Most of these nations are under either military regimes or one-party governments which bank for survival on the security forces. The prognosis for Africa is negative or of minimal growth and unprecedented starvation. This can be traced partly to population growth, urbanization, and serious droughts, but the failure of agricultural modernization must also be attributed to distorted priorities, unnecessary militarization, the neglect of internal infrastructure and, in some case (like Tanzania), external military adventures. The result is a general paralysis or at the least a slowing down of developmental momentum and increased dependency.

All said, the hopes and fears of the Cold War that initiated or facilitated the militarization of the developing countries proved too simplistic and have been generally discredited. The world remains a plurality of nation-states. The international interdependence of the arms-supply relationship and worldwide militarization goes hand in hand with instability, tension and defiant political independence. The great powers have thus far failed, except in select areas, to obtain reciprocally cherished and stable relationships in the Third World. They are left exasperated and perplexed in determining effective policies. The Third World countries on their part are unable to adjust to policies which oscillate between active concern for and callous indifference to their developmental problems. It is in this context, with ever more pressing socio-economic problems, that the Third World must undertake an examination of the dimensions and consequences of its own militarization.

THE SCOPE AND CONSEQUENCES OF MILITARIZATION

Although there have been crises and near-direct confrontations between the superpowers (for example, on Berlin, Korea and Cuba issues), they were prevented from erupting into active conflicts. Actual international conflicts since the Second World

War—and there have been nearly 150—have all involved Third World countries. In the last two decades, while the increase in military expenditures of the developed states rose by 48 per cent, defence spending in the Third World as a whole increased by about 400 per cent. More recently, according to the Palme Commission, in the period 1975 to 1979, the Third World expended $416 billion on military budgets and arms acquisitions, $169 billion of which were by non-oil-exporting countries. The Third World's share of global military outlays increased from 19 per cent in 1975 to as much as 25 per cent in 1980. Ninety-five per cent of arms transfers originated in the industrialized countries, including the Eastern bloc, but only one quarter were intra-bloc sales and transfers; nearly 75 per cent were to the developing continents of Asia, Africa and Latin America. Even after the energy crisis and in the face of oil price hikes, military outlays increased three times faster in the developing countries than in the industrialized nations. Terrorism and insurgency have increased with the spread and easy accessibility of modern weapons. Meanwhile, outlays on social programmes—education, health, nutrition and safe water—have proportionately remained stagnant or even declined. Military aid from great powers has continued, but its value in fixed dollars has gone down and the number of recipients has become fewer. In any case, the total outlays on arms imports by the Third World exceeded the military-cum-economic aid received.

Significantly, most of the recent arms acquisitions by aid transfers to the Third World have been through commercial transactions. Estimates for the current worldwide arms trade are of the order of $20-25 billion per year. Arms exports were deliberately stepped up to recycle petrodollars. Such sales have become a purposeful component of the foreign-trade strategies of the US, the Soviet Union, France, the UK and Germany; some other developed countries have a smaller share. Arms exports are considered a necessary method for reducing unit costs in production, rescuing failing domestic defence industries and protecting jobs at home. In the pursuit of this arms-export drive, agreements have been readily concluded with Third World countries to manufacture arms under licence or under co-production contracts. Although political and security rationales for arms sales and transfers persist, competitive commercial reasons are more and more on the ascendant. Another trend is evident. Out of a desire for self-reliant defence and for the same commercial compulsions that affect the developed countries, some Third World countries (for example, Brazil, Israel and India) have themselves become exporters of military hardware. They are small contributors to the total arms trade, but in a few years they too may face the political dilemmas associated with hawking in the international arms bazaar.

In view of the commercial motivations, it is not surprising that arms sales and transfers to the Third World now include high-priced, overly sophisticated weapon systems which, until the 1960s, both the US and the Soviet Union were reluctant to market or transfer. Ironically, even if the price tag is not prohibitive, the complexity of the systems actually increases the dependence of the recipient on the supplier nations because of the need for outside technical advisers, spare parts and ammunition; thus, the goal of self-reliant national defence is jeopardized.

The overall economic problems of the developing countries were discussed exhaustively in the last two UN 'Development Decades'. Despite the obvious connection, the opportunity costs of defence outlays by the developing world were only lightly or obliquely addressed in these deliberations. The Group of 77, the non-aligned declarations, and the other documentations for the North-South dialogue have generally ignored military-related expenses in arguments for the New International Economic Order. Similarly, the Brandt Commission barely referred to military burdens in the developing world. Although the Palme Commission did acknowledge the excessive diversion of Third World resources for defence purposes and pleaded for rational regional initiatives, its main focus was to urge arms-control measures on the power blocs. Both these commissions primarily addressed their recommendations to the industrialized nations. One cannot help but suspect that these commissions simply did not want to offend Third World sensibilities. In effect, the Third World's dilemmas of defence and development were more or less left for developing countries themselves to examine.

UN studies on disarmament, including those on its economic and social consequences, have also dwelt mostly on the arms race of the great powers and on making funds saved through arms reduction by the great powers available for international economic development. In fact, only the Stockholm International Peace Research Institute (SIPRI) and World Priorities (which publishes Ruth Sivard's *World Military and Social Expenditures*) have endeavoured to systematically collate military and social expenditures of the developing countries along with the industrialized nations.[5]

In the current international climate, notwithstanding concessionary postures for reasons of democratic politics, one cannot be confident that the trend towards great power militarization can be easily arrested or reversed. Even if negotiations are resumed and agreements reached on limiting the deployment of theatre nuclear weapons or on the Strategic Arms Reduction Talks (START) and the Mutual and Balanced Force Reduction (MBFR) talks, the resultant 'saving' will not automatically be diverted into transfers of resources and technology or imaginative trade concessions for development in the Third World. Outside the Scandinavian countries and the Netherlands, aid of all kinds now has shrinking electoral support among the donor nations. This tendency is especially true regarding untied development assistance. In the face of powerful recommendations alluded to above, it must be recognized that the trend of the developed nations toward domesticating foreign economic relationships is not likely to be reversed in the foreseeable future. The lobbies and intermediaries that promote the buying and selling of arms will not easily be curbed. The Western humanitarian sentiment that is readily activated in disaster situations is far removed from the logic of international cooperation aimed at re-stimulating developmental momentum. Other than crisis management, like not allowing Third World debts to precipitate the collapse of the world banking system, the prospects for enlightened restructuring of the North-South economic relationship are clearly not promising.

It must also be noted that both the US and the USSR are becoming less willing to assume long-term responsibility for the developmental needs of even 'friendly' countries which are ostensibly important to them (the exceptions being where urgent strategic interests are perceived to be immediately threatened). Whether the Kissinger Bipartisan Commission's recommendation of an $8 billion programme for economic assistance to Central American countries will win bipartisan national support remains to be seen. But even this belated counsel—based on alarm at communist infiltration in the area—cannot controvert the long neglect by and the general reluctance of the US to prevent similar internal crises in regions of actual or potential importance around the world. Similarly, even though Vietnam, after its defeat of the US and in its newly perceived role of containing China, is thought to be a great asset to the Soviet Union, the USSR has not spared the economic resources for reconstructing the country. Cuba, Ethiopia, Angola and Yemen, like Vietnam, get full military support, but the economic help they receive, though sufficient for survival, is inadequate for development.

The US is the most critical nation with respect to world economic growth. Still the strongest military-cum-economic power, the US is uniquely anomalous. It is besieged with expectations of assistance from all the developing world, and, at the same time, it has become—in an invidious kind of flattery—the foil to all nationalisms. But it would require great statesmanship for any US president to cajole the domestic electorate into sparing significant resources for economic development in the Third World. Present policies, in fact, point in the opposite direction. The Third World countries must, therefore, be reconciled to the reality that the leverage to persuade the great powers to undertake purely developmental programmes has greatly declined.

The Third World, has not fully registered the implications of the withdrawal syndrome prevailing more or less all over the industrialized world. One explanation for this failure to comprehend the trend is the mixed Third World mindset of the simultaneous condemnation of and dependence on the Cold War competition. The superpower presence has come to be looked upon as the ultimate *deus ex machina* for all problems and all solutions. Sheer political realism, however, warrants that the developing nations break out of this intellectual hypnosis and become as self-regarding as the industrialized world. If flows of aid are not likely to revive and economic priorities are not to be more dangerously diluted, national efforts will have to be geared to diplomacy aimed at reducing defence burdens. There must be a brutal recognition in the Third World nations that there is no alternative to taking the initiative themselves to arrest their own militarization.

A TWO-TRACK POLICY

The answer lies in the Third World adopting its own enlightened goals. On the one hand, pressure must be maintained towards great-power disarmament and the restructuring of international economic relations, and on the other hand, immediate and simultaneous diplomatic efforts must be initiated by the Third World nations to reverse their own punishing militarization through graduated arms-control agreements. While endorsement by the superpowers might be sought, the initiatives should proceed regardless of great-power approval. After all, it is the non-aligned who consistently argue that national and international security depends more on national and world economic progress. In the present economic and political climate, to focus only on great-power disarmament is suicidal diversionary scapegoatism. It has to be acknowledged that intra-Third World arms races (like those between the superpowers) have generally provided less and less security at more and more cost. It would be pertinent to recall two notable exceptions. Mexico and Costa Rica have resisted the Latin American proclivity for militarism and have remained secure, stable and democratic despite the tensions and dangerous bush fires around them. The per capita income of Costa Rica is more than twice that of its Central American neighbours. Japan has proven the effectiveness of the non-aligned approach to independence and security through its initially imposed and more recently voluntary decision to limit its national defence forces. Perhaps recognizing that the balance of terror is more stable than what its protector nation—the US—contends, Japan has emerged as a commanding economic world power and a stable democracy.

In their inner counsels, the Japanese probably believe that either the whole world will be destroyed or all countries might enjoy a free ride under that awesome umbrella.

Some political scientists have argued that Third World arms control is feasible only through supplier restraints with the collateral support of the recipients where possible. No doubt the principal suppliers are few and given their accumulated experience they should recognize the futility of fuelling the competitive tensions in different regions. The Conventional Arms Transfer (CAT) negotiations undertaken by the Carter Administration were based on this approach. Indeed, in the four sessions of talks between the US and the USSR, progress was made in defining the scope of restraining, both quantitatively and qualitatively, the supply of arms to certain tension-ridden regions of the Third World. Even 'market-sharing' agreements were discussed. In the present vitiated atmosphere, it is salutary to recall that much progress was made. The CAT round of talks was summarily terminated during the Mexico meeting by a unilateral change in American policy. This promising, if unfruitful, beginning discounts the notion that such agreements between adversary powers can never be revived. In any future exercise, talks might be enlarged to include other suppliers and, in later stages, the principal regional recipients. In the present polycentric world, any suspicion of a two-power condominium approach will be no more successful than the unilateral or competitive arms aid policies of the past decades.

The argument that the Third World countries are helpless victims of arms trade and competitive-supplier politics is, at best, only a half-truth. While arms flows may have started with military containment policies, the Third World has never fully shared, if at all, the threat perceptions of the supplier nations. Their motivations were primarily parochial, and the most recent acquisitions have been voluntary, not induced. It is unrealistic for the Third World to depend upon self-denying restraint from the suppliers, especially when there are both obvious economic incentives to sell abroad and growing moral indifference to the consequences for the recipients. Should they be promulgated, supplier restraints would be welcomed, but arms control in the

Third World hinges on sagacious resistance from the demand side. Any serious attempt at arms-control measures in the developing countries—conventional or nuclear—can succeed only if it is initiated by the Third World countries themselves. Similarly, determined Third World resistance to arms dumping can only flow from purposeful volition between constituent nations.

The catalyst for such a realization is a fuller recognition of the price and penalties of the present policies. No nation in the past has faced the kinds of problems that confront most Third World countries in the wake of their recently won independence. Internal weaknesses (that is, lack of resources, population pressure, inadequate political and administrative structures and traditions) are, no doubt, inherited disabilities in most countries. The communications revolution has internationalized political consciousness and the levels of economic aspirations. Demands for education, health, housing and economic opportunities cannot now be smothered or quarantined, however backward a country may be. The development process had already whetted Third World expectations when the energy crisis and the changed international atmosphere reduced many nations to the present level of economic stagnation, compounding the already grave problems. Increased arms acquisitions have generated a major share of the crushing and unserviceable debts of the Third World. All these factors—errors of perception and compounding errors of politics—make the Third World an explosive tinderbox of instability and revolution. The First and Second Worlds might ignore or be complacent about the ominous threat to their interests, but the challenges to the governments and peoples of the Third World in terms of their political and economic interests can be ignored only at the peril of their own nation.

There can be no facile confidence that obtaining graduated arms-control agreements between the Third World countries will be easy. In a world of armed nations, every country must have its own national security perceptions and appropriate capabilities. Every nation claims that its historical, political, economic, territorial and even religious, tribal, and cultural features make its own security problems unique. The running dichotomy between intention and capability presents the most difficult decision for any government. Each country's armed forces staff is professionally inclined to prepare for worst-case scenarios, disregarding other demands on public expenditures. Even if a statesman heading a strong civil government can overrule the demands of the military, the ghosts of appeasement and past reversals are recalled, nationalism fanned and threats to national independence invoked. All too frequently, there is a failure to recognize that objective circumstances may have changed. National and international military-industrial complexes and a host of intermediaries with vested interests in profits and commissions from international arms sales and purchases are only too ready to influence decisions for their own not quite enlightened motives.

There is also no denying that the legitimate needs of security have increased. Many countries face fissiparous regional, provincial, tribal and minority demands which challenge national unity and consolidation. Such problems will, no doubt, persist in the process of change and modernization. Since economic demands can seldom be satisfied in the short run, modernized security forces will remain essential to keeping political protests from becoming violent and disruptive.

In most Third World countries, however, the quest for arms is often unrelated to the realistic security needs; hypothetical external threats and the responsibility to preserve law and order are only convenient arguments for extravagant militarization. The desire for prestige and the determination to stay in power have been, more often than not, the true incentives for many governments to build up armed forces and acquire unnecessarily sophisticated and expensive military hardware. While military governments, as mentioned earlier, are inclined to give unreasonable priority to the need for security forces, the rate of increase of military expenditures is not invariably slower in a democractically governed country or one that has returned to civilian direction. Excessive militarization, in fact, is a contagious infection against which few countries have been farsighted enough to develop vigilant resistance.

Another pertinent fact is that the military muscle of an authoritarian or military regime does not ensure political longevity. Where there has been long neglect of developmental and social priorities and suppression of demands for political participation and human rights, governments have found themselves powerless against people's protest and desperation. The fall of the Shah of Iran in 1979 demonstrated that the might of an elitist military (even with the powerful backing and endorsement of a superpower) cannot prevent an internal revolution. A similar scenario seems to be developing now in the Philippines after the fall of Marcos.[6] The size of the army has quadrupled, but can it, even with modern weapons, suppress the political ferment catalysed by the murder of Benigno Aquino, the notable Phillipines leader? The present agony of Iraq in the conflict with Iran also shows how adventures against a neighbour can recoil and come to be regretted. These are extreme cases, but the phenomenon of rapid arms acquisitions under false or exaggerated rationales, with the inevitable danger of increased internal disaffection, is pervasive all over the Third World.

The political fortitude of Third World leaders to strike a balance between reasonable and exaggerated security needs must be imbued with the recognition of the penalties of social underdevelopment in their countries. Responsible governments, be they civil or military, must weigh their competing socio-economic and political responsibilities along with security considerations. The Third World governments must demand more objective assessments of external threats from their civil and political advisors, and direct efforts toward diplomacy, thus seeking a balance between economic development and legitimate defence against the likely (not hypothetically exaggerated) threats. The cynical view that history does not reveal many instances of disarmament cannot be allowed to prevail in the face of unprecedented expectations and present international realities.

Finally, it bears mention that the justification of public expenditure is subject to people who are the victims of erroneous priorities. In democracies, informed organs of public opinion bear this responsibility, but, where there are no constitutional outlets and safety valves, the demand has found and will find expression in diverse forms of desperation and violence.

The Cold War, with its security-conscious, politically motivated aid flows, has obscured the fundamental premises of independence. Even the non-aligned have flattered the great powers with deliberate imitation. Of overriding relevance is the premise that, whatever the odds, the burden, not only for security but also for internal stability and social development, is a national responsibility. This duty, involving critical choices, can no longer be shirked or shifted; it is, in fact, nothing less than the essence of the demand for decolonization and the pledges affirmed in gaining independence.

ARRESTING MILITARIZATION THROUGH REGIONAL DIPLOMACY

Easing the defence burdens in the Third World and reorienting the national priorities cannot obviously come through unilateral disarmament. My own limited experience has convinced me that Third World diplomacy need not despair at such efforts if the temptations of Cold War gamesmanship are seriously resisted.

Developing countries can draw some confidence from their record of political sagacity in facing post-war international problems. Many were prophetically incisive in rejecting *ab initio* the great power analysis of a new Rome and Carthage. The world has remained a community of nations acting independently, regardless of their military weaknesses or economic dependence. After gaining independence, it was the non-aligned leaders (in this, by a long lead, Nehru was the first) who pleaded for ideological agnosticism in international relations and called for coexistence between differing social systems. Development was affirmed as critical to stability and security in their definition. The Cold War notions of a permanent global bipolarity, of ideological universalism, and of unrelenting confrontation across the international arena, which were challenged by the non-aligned, stand exposed and falsified. Even the Kissinger Commission (1983) seems to accept that, in Central America, military measures by themselves are not sufficient for long-term security. Notwithstanding the revived Cold War rhetoric and moral denunciation of other socio-economic systems, this recognition has now become the conventional wisdom among most cognoscenti in the world.

Another valid argument must be anticipated. The differences among the developing countries—in politics, economic capabilities and security perceptions—are so immense that any generalization about their interests in arms control is meaningless. The grouping of all the Third World countries is a simplification for convenience of analysis only. So indeed is the notion of the 'free world' or of the communist bloc. The Third World countries, however, are on the same side of the Poverty Curtain; they have hammered out collective positions in the Group of 77 and share a declared faith in non-alignment with the demand for a restructured world economic order. While resources and threats do vary from country to country, all of them (except for a handful like Saudi Arabia, Kuwait, the United Arab Emirates (UAE) and perhaps South Korea) face constraints in resources and development. Moreover, almost all have distorted priorities and are pinched financially, or are being overwhelmed by excessive military burdens.[7]

The question remains—what is the strategy that could initiate the change in priorities and reversal of the present trends toward militarization? The first major precondition is the need for public debate and official recognition of the social costs of the present distribution of available resources on mounting defence outlays. The Third World governments, after deliberate effort to educate and lead the people, must start by examining—as does the peace movement in the West—whether the unrelenting quest for military security is not self-defeating for national goals. Sparks of reason cannot be the prerogatives of the idealists in the industrialized world. Indeed, this awakening must be looked upon as a new freedom movement: it is a protest against the wrong kind of internationalism—of global military culture and the tentacles of international military-industrial complexes. The contention that this brand of internationalism is unavoidable must be challenged with the counter-argument that to succumb to military modernization at the expense of the basic needs of people is a threat to the freedom gained and meaningful independence.

Second, Third World conflicts and areas of tension must be segregated into pairs or groups of nations by identifying the local and regional factors that motivate militarization. Each such pair, subregion or region is unquestionably linked with not only international politics, but also the politics of the connected subregion. (Lebanon, for example, cannot be separated from the Arab-Israeli problem, nor the Indo-Pakistani problem from Afghanistan.) Even so, it is possible to define and separate the different areas of tension into fairly clear regional negotiating regimes.

Third, regions must seek to decouple from the global strategies of the great powers. With the legacy of the Cold War, detachment from great power politics will not be easy. In the present climate, one can anticipate that any such initiative may be looked upon with great suspicion by the superpowers. Any objective appraisal of the diverse experiences of these past decades will reinforce this goal of disengagement from Cold War politics.

In reality, such a movement may not meet with as much resistance by the great powers as is sometimes asserted. Contrary to conventional wisdom, while the superpowers have competed against each other, they have not necessarily opposed the quest for regional stability, as long as the strategic interest of one or the other is not perceived as being jeopardized. The old suspicions against non-alignment have all but evaporated. More often than is remembered, in the past the superpowers adopted parallel approaches to contain or end conflicts and facilitate regional stability. (Consider, for example, the Indo-Pakistani conflict of 1965. Even in Vietnam, the USSR did not oppose negotiations, but encouraged them.) Detachment from their strategic preoccupation should not, as is often done, be dismissed as far-fetched. Disentangling from the great power confrontation does not, of course, preclude the options of beneficial economic relations with one or both blocs.

Fourth, as is recognized in great-power arms-control negotiations, regional diplomacy must start with confidence-building measures. This will require an initial small, unilateral step, or a deliberate act of restraint to be a catalyst in giving diplomacy a chance. It should be recalled that the Partial Test Ban Treaty came about when President Kennedy of the US unilaterally suspended further air and underwater tests. Similarly the Anti-Ballistic Missile (ABM) Treaty followed an agreement to limit the planned deployment of such systems. In each region, the critical role will have to be played by the stronger regional power. The notion that some 'Regional Hegemons' (Richard Ullman's phrase[8]) can play the role of regional policemen—and therefore must be disproportionately armed—stands exploded with the fate of the Shah's Iran. The hegemons encounter the same nationalistic opposition against coercion as have the superpowers. The influence of a regional power depends more on its own political stability and its own economic, industrial, and technological capacity and infrastructure than on its capacity to militarily threaten and conquer. A five per cent reduction in defence budgets or the resistance to the temptation to introduce a new generation of modern weapons could have prevented an escalating arms race in many regions. Examples abound. The acquisition of Jaguar aircraft in the Indian subcontinent in 1978—long resisted by the previous government—and supersonic aircraft in Peru stimulated competitive acquisition by other countries in the respective regions. The prescription for regional détente in the form of arms control and conflict resolution is, in fact, no different from that urged on the great powers by the Third World.

It would be naïve to suggest that all Third World problems and consequential militarization in Asia, Africa and South and Central America are similar in origin or amenable to a model solution which can be universally applied in an identical time frame. Specific problems within each continent exhibit different power dynamics and complexities. A discussion of these problems, together and separately, would bring out both the differences and the similarities in a plausible approach to their resolution.

The Indian subcontinent is one such distinct area of tension. The problem originated in the partition of India, which sought to then form two distinct cultural entities. As stated earlier, the situation there became vastly complicated because of the globalism of the contending power blocs. Indo-Pakistani tensions were, however, moderated after the conflict of 1965 by the Tashkent agreement. Hostilities erupted again in the wake of the nationalist protest in East Pakistan (a case of sub-decolonization). The essential conflict of the Bangladesh crisis was local, and the partisan tilt of the US had no effect on the end result except to estrange and disappoint both India and Pakistan. Since 1971, and especially after 1976, the subcontinent has been groping towards regional diplomacy. But the old scenario was resurrected in the wake of the Soviet invasion of Afghanistan. Interpreted as an imminent threat to Western interests, the invasion led to the revival of military aid to Pakistan.

South-East Asia, the mainland peninsular countries Malaysia and Thailand and the island nations of Indonesia, the Philippines and Singapore form another interrelated group of nations. Contrary to expectations, at the end of the Vietnam war and the American withdrawal, the dominoes did not fall. The Democratic Republic of Vietnam and ASEAN began groping towards more stable and mutually beneficial regional economic relations. However, the extension of the Sino-Soviet rivalry and the Vietnamese invasion of Kampuchea ruptured the process. Vietnam as a regional hegemon has encountered typical problems—nationalist resistance, overstretched military commitment, and consequential economic stagnation.

On the eastern seaboard of Africa, the Horn states of Ethiopia, Somalia and Sudan and the East African community countries of Kenya, Tanzania, and Uganda are and will remain economically interdependent. Ethiopia and Somalia effected a switch in allegiances, but the essentially regional problem remains unresolved. The two subregions have, in the meantime, over-militarized while their economic problems have become more acute.

In Western Sahara, including Mauritania, Morocco, Algeria and Tunisia, the ongoing conflict is also basically regional. Chad was disrupted by a civil war with religious and tribal overtones fuelled by Libya, not by the superpowers. The major issue in the African continent that has united all of black Africa is, of course, the confrontation against South Africa over apartheid and Namibia. Regarding South Africa, the Organization of African Unity (OAU) has readily found common ground, but on the other problems, the organization has been powerless to mediate in these regional conflicts.

In South America, several distinct areas of tension can be isolated. Peru, Chile, Argentina and Bolivia form one comprehensive region, where interacting security perceptions have been responsible for their debilitating militarization. Superpower competition has had a minimal role and where it has been involved, it has been mostly at the initiative of the Third World countries.

The Middle East is probably the most complex Third World region. The area contains a mesh of so many old feuds and newly lighted fuses that it has become an explosive powder keg. The Arab-Israeli problem can be traced back to the Balfour Declaration of 1917, but after the Suez conflict in 1956, the regional problem became more vicious, especially when the parallel approach of the two superpowers turned to strategic competition. The intra-Arab rivalries, the problems of dispossessed Palestinians, and the potpourri of minorities and confessional fanaticism in Lebanon have not proved amenable to management by any outside power. A particularly complicating factor is the linkage with domestic politics in the US, but the US has suffered unforeseen setbacks to its policies. The American predicaments in Lebanon since 1982 only reinforce old lessons. The introduction of the US Marines was intended to be for neutral peacekeeping, but it resulted in the identification of the US as partisan, the deaths of innocent Marines and massive hostility towards the American presence. American political strategic interests and credibility have been eroded in the entire region and gains have been almost gratuitously achieved by Syria, the USSR and anti-US political factions.

On the other hand, the breakthrough in Egyptian-Israeli relations and the US mediation in the Camp David agreement (1978) highlight the potential for regional diplomacy. Ultimate stability in this vital region cannot come by attempting to make the area a part of the exclusive strategic domain of one of the two superpowers. It will require either military detachment or the kind of joint approach exemplified by Suez (1956), Glassboro (1967) and the Gromyko-Vance Communiqué (1977).

Aside from the Middle East, the most serious problems are those that lie in the front – or backyards of the superpowers. The interests and stakes of the Soviet Union in Afghanistan and of the US in Central America illustrate the inadequacy of interpreting these situations as essentially East-West strategic problems. As mentioned earlier, the problems that have been essentially local and socio-economic in origin, through misjudgements and peremptory interventions, led to the igniting of nationalism and undermined the inherent advantage or long-term interest of the neighbouring superpower. Each superpower's attribution of the root cause of the problem to the overt or covert involvement of the other superpower only transposes cause and consequence.

It bears repetition that the solution to any or all of these problems will not be the result of the attempts by the great powers to permanently occupy or even militarily intervene in these regions. Such involvements have proven politically counter-productive and less than cost-effective; they provide no long-term blueprint for the future. The distilled lessons of the past suggest that it would be less hazardous if the countries themselves took (and were allowed to take) responsibility for regional stability. Regional diplomacy, by holding the ring against interventions and counter-interventions, could create a more propitious climate for internal political evolution.

The regional approach emanating from regional initiatives has, in fact, achieved unexpected success in South-East Asia. Indonesia was at one time feared by all its neighbours; these suspicions have at least been muted. ASEAN has also demonstrated the potential of economic growth through regional cooperation. Together, the members of ASEAN have made a commitment to neutrality and non-alignment and have harmonized their approaches to world problems. Once ASEAN made a go of cooperation, it was accepted not just by the US and the European Economic Community (EEC), but also by China and the Soviet Union which were initially hostile to this regional grouping. The problem now facing the region is to persuade Vietnam, Myanmar and the Indo-Chinese peninsula to become part of South-East Asia and to see the interests of the countries of the region as detached from the rivalries and strategies of the USSR and China.

Regionalism is beginning to appeal to many parts of the tension-ridden world in South Asia, Central America, the Caribbean, around the Niger basin, in East Africa—but it has barely gotten off the ground. If stability is to be ultimately achieved, the chances of success will rest on the initiative and involvement of the countries affected. Only they can reverse the priorities from militarization to fundamental social and human needs. The challenge boils down to the sagacity and skill of Third World diplomacy and statesmanship, inspired by enlightened concern for national futures.

PREVAILING ATTITUDES TOWARDS THIRD WORLD MILITARIZATION

I have not hesitated to acknowledge that the Third World countries have justified their militarization with rationalizations of uncontrollable pressures and inducements. Even intellectuals within or from the developing countries have asserted that disarmament is not important for the Third World. Proponents of this perspective argue that if the developing countries were left militarily weak and ill-equipped, they would not be able to exercise any moral and political leverage on the great powers. Demilitarization in advance of world disarmament, they conclude, need not be given serious priority, whatever the damages to the economic development of their countries.

Prevailing analyses in the developed world with respect to Third World militarization reflect many different attitudes. Public declarations of the Eastern Bloc indicate little interest in the problem or its link to the economic prospects for the developing world. In fact, the East has always asserted its detachment from Third World economic problems: these issues are dismissed as wholly the legacy of imperialism, and the West alone must pay 'reparations' for its past exploitation. The Eastern Bloc diplomacy is confined to discretionary bilateral relations and more and more use of arms supplies for political advantage and to balance its bilateral trade. The Eastern European countries have remained silent and aloof from any commitment or contribution towards a multilateral programme for the reorientation of the New Economic Order.

Contrary to general impressions, however, the Soviet Union has not been averse to non-aligned regional stability. In South Asia, without alienating their own interests, the Soviets have quietly advocated easing of the prevailing tensions. In the past, Moscow has also exercised restraint in not arming countries in areas of tension with offensive weapons (as in Egypt in the 1950s and 1960s). Similarly, although Soviet anti-aircraft guns were provided in Vietnam, Soviet fighter aircraft were not sent despite incessant bombing by the US, lest it further escalate the conflict and jeopardize the chances of negotiations. In short, to assume that the Soviet Union is implacably committed to increasing tensions and is necessarily opposed to regional solutions does not correspond to the record. Future Soviet reactions, one can safely assume, will be conditioned by its own perceived security needs, not ideological interests.

Among analysts in the West, the 'radicals' view the Third World problems, including militarization, as resulting entirely from the economics of profit and the deliberate imposition of dependency relationships all over the developing world. This approach more or less dismisses any voluntary motivation in arms acquisition in the Third World. Others despair of the success of participatory, democratic political systems in the developing countries. For such analysts, militarization and military regimes are seen as the only available instruments for national consolidation and progress in these countries and, therefore, as a lesser evil than chaotic governmental incompetence.

Many liberals in the West also avoid focusing on the social costs of militarization of the Third World. This group feels that it is improper to urge on others a kind of behaviour that their own countries have failed to practise. The nonchalant failure of the US to honour the commitment to seriously embark on disarmament under Article 6 of the NPT is an embarrassment for these well-intentioned crusaders of arms limitation. This group concentrates on pressuring their own democratic governments to engage in a more earnest approach to arms control with the Soviet Union. In turn, they hope this will generate more enlightened perspectives on North-South issues.

Another significant perspective should be noted. There are those who are indifferent to conventional militarization anywhere and focus only on the dangers of nuclear proliferation in the Third World. This view even justifies making conventional arms available to reduce the security incentives for a Third World country going nuclear. Compared to the hazards of regional nuclear conflicts or the uncontrolled spread of nuclear-weapon technology, the economic and political costs of fuelling the arms race in developing regions are ignored or discounted.

Most of these analytical strains either betray indifference to the Third World economic problems or share the belief that their solutions are wholly contingent upon and subordinate to the progress, or lack of it, of great-power relations and the superpower arms race; this paper argues against this contention. These arguments, sometimes explicitly but more often implicitly, amount to an arrogance of power (that world problems can only be solved by the superpowers), or an arrogance of conscience (that all the Third World problems are basically the fault of the Third World countries themselves). Both discount the sovereign capacity of the independent Third World countries either to inflict suicidal damage upon themselves or, alternately, to better manage and improve their own destinies against the present odds. Whether or not the great powers effect a turnaround in their own present short-sighted policies, experience and reality must reject this slur on the sovereign discretion of the poor but independent nations.

It must be repeated that the militarized industrial countries, armed to overkill with nuclear weapons, have all but forfeited their right to counsel restraint in national arms acquisitions by the poorer nations. Their diplomacy, even when supported by plausible political and economic arguments, has not been effective in even arresting the threat of nuclear proliferation; in fact, their example and counsel have provoked defiance instead of agreement.

In the light of this, a further obvious observation must be reiterated. Third World diplomacy will be doomed if it is pursued in a way which deliberately disregards or harms the interests of one superpower and facilitates the promotion of another. Shrewd and skilful regional diplomacy does not have to offend the vital strategic interests of either superpower. The superpowers, in trying to maintain vigilance and credibility and at the same time not be dragged into local politics and conflicts they did not create, may find it less counterproductive to acquiesce in regional military non-alignment and give regional diplomacy a chance. As stated before, the ASEAN region, in its military non-alignment, did succeed in developing equally healthy economic relations with the USSR, China, and the West. An eventual end to the Iran-Iraq War through bilateral or regional diplomacy (possibly after some change in leadership), coupled with regional neutrality, may be the best guarantee for the oil flows and Western interests in the Gulf. The 'Swedenization' of South-West Asia—voluntary declaration of neutrality—may be the only possible way to bring about the 'Finlandization'—accepting a treaty obligation—for Afghanistan and contribute to stability in South Asia. Such a task may also be the means to relieve Pakistan of the dangerous burden it carries with the presence of three million Afghan refugees. Detachment from the Cold War in the developing world, if combined with regional stability, may, in fact, facilitate a more stable strategic balance between the superpowers. The Third World is off the superpowers' horizons; with the present range of missiles, the Third World can be off the horizons of concern of the superpowers. The poor, weak Third World, by its exertions, may ease the superpowers from their anxieties and facilitate global détente.

CONCLUSION

To sum up, the contention urged herein is that there is both scope and urgent need for successful diplomatic initiatives within different regions and the specific tension areas. Despite certain differences, there are common features in the widely separate problems in Asia, Africa and Latin America. All these countries belong to the South and face grave economic obstacles; in every area there are reservations about remaining militarily dependent on a superpower and running the risk of becoming victims of intervention or competitive strategic moves. Even where there are some contingent anxieties about external security, there is a decided preference for denying superpower presence on their own soil. On the other hand, all these nations expect economic support from the US and the West, supplemented by Eastern Europe. But the aid flows are turning into trickles. When non-commercial external resources are available, there is a preference for multinational sources like the International Monetary Fund (IMF) or the World Bank or regional banks, which constitute a kind of donor regionalism. These inclinations reinforce opportunities for intraregional diplomacy to tackle hardy old tensions and establish comparatively more stable relations with the superpowers and the developed nations.

The basic rationale for urging earnest diplomatic efforts to arrest Third World militarization through regional diplomacy is that, in a dismal international situation, this approach may be the only feasible means of achieving national progress and national self-preservation in the Third World countries. Acknowledging that 'the fault, dear Brutus, is not in our stars' may be a contribution, not only to their own future but also to that of the superpowers and to international peace and stability.

NOTES

1. Mahbub ul Haq, *The Poverty Curtain: Choices for the Third World*, New Delhi: Oxford University Press, 1976.
2. March 1984.
3. Alva Myrdal, *The Game of Disarmament; How the United States and Russia Run the Arms Race*, New York: Pantheon, 1982.
4. Ruth Legard Sivard, *World Military and Social Expenditure*, Washington DC: World Priorities, 1991, 14th edition.
5. Since the 1990s, the UN brings out the *Human Development Report*, which highlights the point more effectively.
6. March 1984.
7. Since this was written, the problems of sub-Saharan Africa and South Asia have greatly deteriorated. The economic capabilities of the Far Eastern Tigers and ASEAN alone have improved.
8. Richard Ullman, *Rural Development*.

5

India and the United States
United or Divided by their Democracies?

The art and craft of diplomacy depends on understanding and anticipating the misperceptions of partner sovereign nations. This can avert problems, minimize consequences through damage limitation and, within the realm of the feasible, show the way to improve relations. A detailed view of the story of Indo-US relations vividly illustrates the penalties of the failure to do so. Future stability in their relations will come not from explanations and complaints but by patiently clearing the accumulated layers of past perceptions of the national concerns of each other. The paradox of Indo-US relations is that both sides expected too much, little realizing that the affinities and similarities were in fact divisive. The euphoric expectations precipitated irritations, which with better judgement, need not have turned relations into suspicions and even crises bordering on antagonism.

India and the US have been in fundamentally two different orbits with respect to their policies. The public postures and rhetoric of a natural friendship between the two great democracies obscured the fact that since the Second World War and Indian Independence, the two countries have had different perspectives and divergent goals. When the Second World War ended, the US was taken up, all too suddenly, from its historical isolationist detachment to the game of international politics and feared the globalist reach of the USSR, which proclaimed that socialism resulted in an overriding solidarity and globalization of communism. The US was engaged militarily, politically and economically in containing the perceived threat of the communist monolith. Anyone who claimed to share this dread was

* An article published in *Seminar* 1986.

indulgently befriended and any country that honestly saw the world in different terms was suspect. India had an international perspective of its own—to keep its independence, and this meant not being squeezed or smothered by the ideological-cum-military confrontation between the two worldwide power blocs led by the US and the Soviet Union. India was ideologically agnostic in its international relations. It did not want to lose its own discretion in global politics or be prevented from cooperating with countries which may have been competitive adversaries themselves. These approaches, which came to be defined as non-alignment, were consistent with the historical approach of leaders like Nehru and understandable from the point of view of India's own interests and aspirations. In the wake of the agonizing partition, these international principles got coloured, often distorted, and in any case conditioned by the imperatives of the regional problem with Pakistan. Indo-US relations thus found themselves in a running conflict between the globalist perspectives of the US and the regional priorities of India.

To illustrate this divergence let us look back on the misperceptions that have bedevilled US-India relations. Initially, the Soviet Union suspected the USA's partiality for democratic India (especially following the Indian decision to stay in the Commonwealth and Nehru's visit to the US in 1949). The US was not exactly sympathetic to India in the Kashmir discussion in the Security Council, but it largely followed British guidance in determining its approach. The USSR under Stalin, however, was neutral and indifferent on Kashmir. Stalin refused to receive Mrs Vijaylakshmi Pandit, the prime minister's own sister, who opened the Indian embassy in Moscow, in April 1947, even before the formal transfer of power. It looked like a calculated cold-shouldering of India. The sea change in the Soviet attitude towards India began after Stalin's death but more particularly after mutual security arrangements were reached between democratic America and the military-dominated dispensation in Pakistan in 1954. The US accepted Pakistan as an ally not because it was moving towards a democratic form of government—in fact in 1955 the military summarily dislodged the outward form of a civilian president—but because it advanced its pretensions to combat

Communist USSR and China. Anyone with even the most superficial understanding of Pakistan could have seen that its chief foreign policy and security concern was the perceived threat of India and Pakistan's inner anxiety about its own independence and survival. India, however, banked on the professed American faith in the democratic system and did not recognize the distortion of Washington's approaches to other nations after the growth of the Macarthyist paranoia of anti-communism, and the commitment of the US government and especially under the direction of Secretary of State John Foster Dulles' policy of military containment of Soviet power. India was not vigilant or at least not effective in preventing the development of this non-ideological military relationship between the US and Pakistan. This was to cast a long shadow on India's security and its internal and external aspirations. It was only the American military aid to Pakistan which subsequently led to the balancing relationship between India and the USSR. Thereafter, disregarding ideological considerations, the USSR has consistently supported India on crucial votes on Kashmir in the UN and the debates at the time of the Bangladesh breakaway from Pakistan. The USSR thus established a position of firm trust in the national opinion in India which would have seemed impossible in the Stalin years. The fact that India always had a non-communist central government never impeded the growth of the Indo-Soviet relations.

During the 1960s, the American globalist paradigm was falsified. The communist bloc splintered; when the Indo-China crisis erupted it was independent of US/USSR competition. Pakistan befriended the People's Republic just when China was militantly hostile to the American involvement in Vietnam. Much as India had feared, American arms were used against India in 1965. In the meanwhile, India and the USSR had found it to their mutual interest to reinforce their relations. In order to demonstrate that non-alignment was not naïve but could have credibility in resolving problems, India assiduously sought to win the trust of the socialist powers and break new ground in promoting economic relations with the socialist countries. It also tried to avoid antagonizing the USSR, as on the question of

Hungary (1956). But India remained non-communist at home; indeed, it demonstrated that despite poverty and illiteracy it could work a democratic system. When Nehru and Shastri died, the succession was determined by prescribed constitutional procedures. On the other hand, while Pakistan under Marshal Ayub toyed with the idea of a basic democracy, it continued to maintain a military regime. Under Bhutto's direction, Pakistan, even joined in the then policy goals of China (which were actively endorsed only by Sukarno) to forge a tricontinental solidarity of the 'villages' of Asia, Africa, and Latin America to confront the US, the USSR and the entire group of industrialized nations—'the cities of the world'. India was slow to see through the disintegration of the Soviet-led monolithic bloc and the seriousness of the Sino-Soviet ideological rivalry. It was thus taken aback when, even at the height of the US confrontation with communist Vietnam (which for entirely differing reasons was supported by the USSR and China), the Soviet Union decided to supply heavy arms to Pakistan for a brief period. The Soviet Union was trying to neutralize the influence of communist China, and not so much that of anti-communist US. To the surprise of both India and Pakistan, in the regional crises between India and China (1959-62) and India and Pakistan (1965), the attitudes of both super- powers were similar, if not identical. President Johnson of the US is reported to have claimed that he was an unseen presence in the mediation by Premier Kosygin of the USSR at Tashkent. The US and the USSR were more openly united on the Non-Proliferation Treaty (NPT) of 1968 and made parallel pleas urging all nations including Pakistan and India to sign the Treaty. All this was a far cry from the Cold War syndrome when US globalism in 1954 first developed into what was perceived as a US-Pakistan line up in the South Asian region.

Meanwhile, the Cold War had changed its character, and for a while, following the Cuban missile crisis, the great powers were even groping towards a dètente. Even so, the American-Soviet mutual paranoia continued and manifested itself in the build-up of nuclear overkill with new systems like Polaris submarines and multiple independently targetable missile launchers (MIRVs). In their political competition the superpowers seized every target of opportunity which presented itself to either power (Cuba, Egypt, Somalia, Ethiopia, etc.). But at least in South Asia the shared fear of China muted their own competition.

From time to time, the old intensity of the Cold War was revived. One such occasion was during the Bangladesh crisis (1971) and another after the Soviet intervention in Afghanistan; on both occasions, Indo-US relations touched a new low. The Bangladesh crisis was internal which went back to the false concept that religion can bind a country when geography, economics and culture were repugnant to a unified national identity. It posed a serious problem for India with the inflow of ten million refugees. The situation was a regional crisis; it did not warrant globalist interpretations. The despatch of the American aircraft carrier *Enterprise*—a kind of old-fashioned exercise in gunboat diplomacy—proved an abysmal failure, but it left behind an indelible fear in India that American hostility towards democratic India would not even hesitate at direct military intervention. The real reason for the pro-Pakistan tilt was that Washington was tailoring its attitude to the regional crisis to further its global objective of forging a strategic relationship with China against the USSR. India, too, gave way to a nervous fear of US globalism. Instead of a confidence that the Bangladesh problem was not of its making and that nationalism could not be frustrated, India concluded a treaty with the Soviet Union and compromised, in the eyes of the US and even its own friends like Yugoslavia, the spirit of non-alignment. The American strategic goals in China have not been realized. China has remained studiously independent and the US has been by far the most important aid giver to Bangladesh. But the 1971 crisis showed that both the US and India, in their instinctive reactions, were conditioned by the failed hypothesis of the old Cold War that there were only two players and only one game on the world chessboard.

In the following years, the problems in Indo-US relations were moderated largely because the intervention of the global powers in regional affairs was muted. There was a move away by Washington from its partiality towards Pakistan. The prejudice against India, however, was revived with the Indian underground nuclear explosion in Pokharan (1974). It raised the spectre of proliferation of nuclear weapon capability around the world and threatened to destroy the nuclear regime established by the NPT. This led to the US Non-Proliferation Act of 1978 and a unilateral modification of the 1962 US-India agreement for the supply of fuel for the Tarapur reactor. India did not recognize that the US motivations were global. The US Administration and Congress have also sought to deter Pakistan in its quest for weapons capability, but the memories of the US alliance with Pakistan and the tilt against India have led to deep suspicions that the American attitude was a manifestation of a discriminatory prejudice against India.

The present phase in the hesitant attitudes of both India and the US to their relations followed the Soviet intervention in Afghanistan in 1980. What happened was almost a re-enactment of the 1953-4 syndrome, only this time the critical initial mistake was made by the Soviet Union by invading a non-aligned country. What compounded it were the misconceptions and erroneous reactions not only in the United States, but also in India and Pakistan. It was not in the pursuit of the alleged seventeenth-century Russian aim—attributed to Peter the Great—to reach out towards warm water ports; nor, recognizing the obvious hazards involved, to seize or control the vital flows of oil for the West and Japan. It was also not for simple territorial expansion or a preventive action against Islamic fundamentalism spreading to Soviet Central Asia. The irony was that the ill-fated Soviet action took place because of defensive security anxieties resulting from the ideological fanaticism of a pro-Soviet Marxist Hafizullah Amin who controlled the government that had come to power in 1978, unaided by the Kremlin. It was the height of mis perception—as was then alleged by the Carter Administration—that the Soviet invasion was a threat to world peace and the territorial integrity of Pakistan. The constitution of the Rapid Deployment Force, and the attempt at forging a strategic consensus, was unnecessary and its consequences were incorrectly assessed.

The change from this erroneous interpretation was the revival of US military aid to Pakistan. It was the old Cold War mindset that any move by the Soviet Union on the international checkerboard must have a strategic purpose directly hostile to the West.

The Government of India, too, made an incorrect appraisal in accepting that the Soviet action was provoked by American intentions and interference within Afghanistan. Instead of decrying the invasion and the violation of non-alignment and remembering the traditional anti-foreigner nationalism of the Afghan people, India initially all but condoned the Soviet action.

In Pakistan, as in much of the Islamic and non-aligned world, there was genuine alarm at Soviet actions and intentions. But Pakistan showed diplomatic perspicacity in seizing the opportunity created by the prevailing mood in the US to repair the low credibility and standing of its military regime, and its poor human rights record the revulsion created by the execution of Bhutto in the face of worldwide appeals and the burning of the US embassy. The surreptitious build-up of a nuclear weapons programme was glibly set aside. The Carter Administration, which earlier had a very negative attitude to Pakistan, diluted its old repugnance, and saw the country merely as a front-line state against Soviet expansionism. But it was a whole year later—when the Reagan Administration came to power with a domestic mandate (unpopular with even American allies) to establish military superiority over the USSR and militarily contain the Soviet threat—that massive arms aid to Pakistan was pledged. The point to underline is that the perceptions in the US attitudes that followed the Soviet intervention were erroneous but could have been anticipated. India could have been more agile and perceptive of developments which threatened to strengthen Pakistan's military capability against India.

Indian diplomacy lost a rare opportunity to rationalize South Asian relations and insulate the region for non-alignment and minimize the induction of sophisticated arms in her neighbourhood. Instead of extenuating Soviet action, there should have been quick overtures to assuage Pakistan that India was not in conspiracy with the USSR. In January 1980, Mrs Gandhi as prime minister could have issued the kind of statements she subsequently made—asking for Soviet withdrawal. The gestures of friendship as offered by the foreign minister, Narasimha Rao, when he visited Pakistan in June 1981 could have been made earlier—when Pakistan was truly even if falsely alarmed about its security. Another opportunity to improve the climate of India-Pakistan relations was missed by not agreeing quickly to the no-war declaration offered by Pakistan. Instead, after some delay, India made a counter-suggestion for a more comprehensive Treaty of Friendship. The diplomatic battle over rival suggestions has still not been resolved after four years.

The result, as we know, of the pledge of $3.2 billion military and economic aid package to Pakistan in 1981, including supersonic aircraft like the F-16 with offensive capability, revived and intensified the arms race in the subcontinent. In the wake of Washington's support to Pakistan, India launched a massive arms acquisition programme of its own. India tried to diversify its programme, and turned to France to contract for the Mirage 2000, advanced submarines from Germany, and Sea-Harriers from the UK for air-sea operations. India is also shopping for other sophisticated military hardware. The US alone, no doubt because of the Pentagon's reluctance, prevaricated or refused to respond to democratic India's requests. On the other hand, the Soviet Union once again showed its willingness to meet India's demands for weapons, offering easier terms for payment and agreeing to further build up India's capability to improve its internal ordinance industries. The result was a confirmation that socialist Soviet Union was a more reliable friend of non-socialist India. Pakistan may remain affiliated and even active in the non-aligned fraternity on international issues like Africa, North-South and the Middle East, but with these new arms flows, the situation has resurrected the 1950s syndrome of US-Pakistan military relationships confronting the Indo-USSR arms supply relationship. Once again globalism has complicated and obscured the region's problems, which are intrinsically independent of the US-USSR Cold War.

Before we can get out of the present trough in the Indo-US relations, it would be worth identifying, in a crude simplification, the present web of misperceptions in the quadrilateral relationship of the US, India, Pakistan and the Soviet Union. The US thinks that India disregarding its own security interests and non-alignment, India invariably subserves Soviet global strategic interest, and behaves like a client state. Pakistan still fears that India, in a diabolical conspiracy with the USSR, is only waiting for an opportunity to further dismember what remains of Pakistan and establish a hegemonistic domination which would all but destroy the independence of the Islamic state. India is unconvinced that the US really believes Pakistan can meet a purposeful attack by the USSR. India therefore thinks that the US is only bent on encouraging Pakistan's belligerence against India. Indeed apprehensive of India's strength and potential, the US may well be using the Afghanistan issue—so it was at times argued—to curb the potential progress of India and its future role in the Indian Ocean area and in world politics. The Soviet Union, taking at face value the anti-Soviet rationale of the US aid to Pakistan and increased support for the Mujahideen, suspects that the claimed sympathy for the Afghan struggle against the USSR is really being used as a step to subvert, if not detach, Central Asia politically and militarily in the soft underbelly of the USSR.

Each country denies the malevolent designs attributed to it but clutches self-righteously to its own fears. The Soviet Union and Pakistan, however, have the advantage of being closed societies with a controlled press. Their private fears may not necessarily be as great as their public alarms. The former has, no doubt, sometimes warned and occasionally even threatened Pakistan, but outside the direct compulsions of the military operations in Afghanistan, Soviet-Pakistan relations have not been as hostile as their declarations would suggest and which many US analysts prefer to take at face value. The USSR has, in fact, never looked like precipitating a direct conflict with Pakistan or even taken steps to slow down the ongoing economic cooperation between the two countries. Baluchistan has not been subverted as was anticipated by a notable expert. A Soviet-built steel plant was opened with considerable publicity and offers of further friendly cooperation were extended to Pakistan. Pakistan similarly almost deliberately underplays the fact that all political parties in India now accept the independence and frontiers of Pakistan.

The paradox is that the open press of the two democracies of India and the US, which debates the future potential of their nations' bilateral relations, has justified the false rationalizations and reinforced old misperceptions. At least the open press has not acted as a corrective to misjudgements. In the US, the suspicions have persisted that India did not act from its regional imperative but was a voluntary Soviet satellite, under orders of the Kremlin for the latter's global objective. The evidence against this fear is fairly weighty. India, for example, has consistently refused to echo the Brezhnev doctrine for Asia. The India-China talks go on not because of but despite Indo-Soviet relations. On the other hand, India suspects American encouragement for Pakistan's nuclear programme. There appears to have been leniency in taking action against Pakistan's surreptitious purchases in which India suspects, probably erroneously, that the CIA and the Pentagon may have prompted some indulgence. But the official attitude of the US on Pakistan's response of polite innocence does not carry much credibility. Both India and the United States, for different reasons, have played down and almost ignored the rampant anti-Americanism in Pakistan. The result has been that populist opinion in India and the US has constricted the scope for bilateral diplomacy in India-Pakistan and India-US relations.

The clue to this record of misjudgement can be traced to the Cold War and the hypnosis of the alleged role of ideology in international relations. By now it should be clear that ideology and internal social and political systems—be they communism, democracy, free enterprise or state control, military rule or other forms of authoritarianism—do not play an overriding role in determining foreign policy. The appeal of a chosen ideological or political system is that it has of course provided good material for public speeches but 'national interests' often determined by national paranoia are not ideological but determined by domestic political structures. It is as well to recognize that US governments, be they Democratic or Republican, will continue to base their foreign policy vis-à-vis the Soviet Union on the global perception of US interests. India will continue to view the superpowers, indeed at crunch moments all countries, through the prism of its regional priorities. This divergence of perspectives cannot be bridged, but if they were objectively understood, the oscillations between hope and disenchantment could be narrowed. India is not unique in not being convinced of the Reagan Administration's single-minded approach of military superiority as a viable way to world peace. However, ultimately, only the domestic electorate can bring about a change in US policies. When even the allies of the US have not succeeded in moderating US strategic policies of neo-containment (and Strategic Defence Initiative (SDI) plans), India is not likely to be able to change the extrapolation of this policy as it affects the subcontinent. With this background, to nurture euphoric expectations of a dramatic turnaround and convergence between India and the US may be a public relations temptation but really only a continuing manifestation of political naiveté. Mrs Gandhi's visit to the US in 1982 was a major media event but it is worth remembering that the belief that it had cleared the way for providing a friction-free basis for future relations proved to be a fallacy.

What, then, is feasible, out of the forthcoming meeting (1985) of the Prime Minister of India and the President of the US? If we can untie the tangle of mental knots, some preliminary steps could be taken to improve the prospects for less hostility and some substantive agreements between the US and India. It must start with the acceptance of the divergence in the national priorities of the two countries. India has to recognize that India-Pakistan mistrust is an India-Pakistan problem. The long-term goal of our foreign policy should have been and must be to decouple the subcontinent from the big Cold War. Success hinges on removing the pervasive fear of Indian hegemonism amongst our neighbours—and not diplomacy in Washington or Peking. Once it is possible to demonstrate a turnaround in the political climate of the subcontinent, India would be in a better position to demand that the subcontinent's problems should not be complicated by the United States. We cannot expect the Reagan Administration to do a Tarapur to Pakistan, as the Carter Government did to India—unilaterally repudiating or modifying the subsisting military aid commitments to Pakistan. To assuage both Pakistan and the US, and to promote South Asian harmony, we could take a non-aligned initiative on Afghanistan. It is a convenient but false perception that Indo-Pakistan relations can improve only after a US-USSR détente or a change in their global knee-jerk reactions and strategies and competition. With a sense of the interdependent destiny of South Asia, India and its sovereign neighbours could dilute or even defy the malevolent involvement of the outside powers in its affairs.

This will require an intellectual reorientation and skilful patient diplomacy over a period of time. India, under Rajiv Gandhi in 1985, and with non-alignment as his touchstone, is in a position to make a beginning. In the wake of the film on Gandhiji and other films and television series, and the Festival of India, for the moment the old indifference towards India has been significantly corrected. We do not have to flatter ourselves any more by suspecting perverse hostility towards democratic India. Rajiv Gandhi, with an unprecedented mandate and an image of a modern mind and with no inherited blind spots, can speak with authority reflecting a persuasive vision of domestic and foreign policy goals of India.

The fact of democracy may be almost irrelevant as a rationale in foreign policy. But the reality of demonstrating that by rooting the democratic system India has achieved greater stability and progress than almost anywhere else in the wider arc of Asia, Africa, the Middle East and Central and South America makes it uniquely important to global politics.

India, like the Third World, no doubt faces great economic odds. The logic of the New Economic Order is irrefutable but the promise of its realization is an exploded hope. International interdependence notwithstanding, we are back in a world of nation states following short-term goals of national economic and political interests. But India is a success story compared to most decolonized countries. It is one of the few countries that has the infrastructure to survive the deteriorating international economic circumstances. It is one of the great potential markets, and even a shrewd economic power like Japan has now got over decades of half-hearted interest in India and recognized the scope of meaningful cooperation with it. If the US can rid itself of its old inhibitions and India, without agreeing with the US, can be realistic in its understanding of the US, bilaterally beneficial agreements can be reached on the flow of technology and productive investment. But again, such agreements on technology, trade and even arms supplies will not give the relations such strength and health to make them immune to relapses of the kind that occurred in the past. Despite 1985 being the year of India, with the Festival revealing to millions India's great heritage and its continued vitality, it may not be a permanent insurance for political good relations between the two countries.

The one important purpose should be to shed the old habits of suspecting a CIA agent in every scholar and student who wants to study India. It will be a long time before India has a coherent (and not divisive) ethnic lobby in Washington. In fact, the ethnic Indians in the US may be a complicating factor as they will be prone to exploit America's democratic system to play the domestic politics of India in the streets of New York and with the lobbies in Washington. With the success of our Green Revolution, the US is no longer looking to India as a steady grain market. (The USSR has taken its place!) Even if investment flows increase, India will have a negligible corporation lobby compared to countries like South Korea or Singapore. Unlike Brazil, Mexico and Argentina, India did not borrow commercially, so American banks have no stakes in the country. The most important friends of India are in the media and a diverse body of academics. The pledge of more liberal facilities for intellectual exchange—and we could certainly outmatch China—would have minimal risks but considerable potential dividends in cementing the basis for a firmer Indo-US understanding.

On the other hand, we cannot, indeed we must not, accommodate with US-dominated globalism and seek to gratify American opinion by diluting Indo-Soviet relations. But then we should have greater confidence that non-aligned India can have simultaneous good relations with both superpowers. We merely have to stick to our own interests and principles and keep away from US-USSR postures and their separate bilateral problems.

In the final instance, the most important common element between India and the US—we might remind them—is the original faith and confidence in a world made safe for diverse nationalisms. The US and India must separately recognize their respective traditions against militarization and reverse the American propensity to export it. Let the United States recognize that the non-aligned India is after all pursuing the modern variant of the policies embodied in the Act of Neutrality of the union of thirteen states in 1792 which confidently rejected involvement and nervousness at other nations' ambitions, perversions and quarrels. India and the US should not, as they have in the past, allow their similarities to separate them. In brief, stabilizing Indo-US relations requires above all an intellectual effort to not live in an ugly past. We must rejoice in the real strength of democracies which predicates that honest differences and divergent priorities may still serve common international goals. It would suffice if both countries could acknowledge that peace is best safeguarded by functional international cooperation and political equality in the international democracy.

PART THREE
Fresh Water Diplomacy

6

The Challenge of International Riparian Politics

Water and air have traditionally been the two elements associated in the human mind with purity and abundance. We have only in these decades come alive to the spectre that they may yet be polluted and that both may become a constraint on life and progress. Sovereignty in the air is a comparatively recent concept—the product of the age of air flight and air combat. The seabed and space are also new frontiers for diplomacy, even though the limits of territorial waters have been extended, in many cases, beyond the capacity of countries to police them. The new opportunity is to exploit the economic potential of the oceans. Since this was a new frontier, it was possible to declare the oceans as the common heritage of mankind, and the regulation for their exploitation was thrown into the fora of multilateral rather than national diplomacy. International opinion and agreements reaffirmed that space should remain the preserve of all. The Seabed Convention and the Space Treaty of 1967 are both a challenge to how national interests and technological advantages can be balanced with the concept that they should not be wholly appropriated by terrestrial, military or economic strength.

Diplomacy for fresh-water resources, however, is a mix of old and new diplomacy; of old notions of territorial sovereignty and new concepts of international interdependence. Fresh water is almost uniquely symbolic of the complexity of old nationalistic self-conscious territorial sovereignty and new awareness that fresh-water resources cannot be controlled by terrestrial authority. Sooner or later, fresh-water use and purity will demand

* Article written at the Woodrow Wilson Center for Scholar at Washington DC in 1982 and published in *Seminar*, New Delhi, 1986.

cooperation between neighbours and eventually husbanding water will become an international ecological problem.

Water has been at the heart of human progress and history. Ancient civilizations were born around rivers (the Nile, the Euphrates, the Indo-Gangetic Basin and the Hwang Ho); many of them died out because water became scarce or the land was overwhelmed with floods. In old faiths, water was associated with every ritual—from baptism to death. Rivers were looked upon as the divine protectors of nature and are woven into fable and literature.

Rivers have divided lands, provided firm frontiers, provoked wars and become the barriers for keeping peace. If the countries in the temperate latitudes progressed faster (the developed North of today), it was because they were well endowed with rain and the precipitation was not torrential or seasonal. Streams were the motors for power and industry which in turn led to agricultural modernization with comparative ease and without heavy investment in irrigation. Water was neither scarce, as in the tropical deserts, nor destructive, as in the monsoon or in equatorial climates.

Today, water looms as a problem for the industrialized nations and even more for the developing world for building the basic infrastructure. Consumption has increased with population, but even more with the requirements of industry. In the US thirty-two billion gallons of water are required for industry—twenty billion more than for domestic consumption. Seventy gallons of fresh water are required to refine one gallon of gasoline; thirty thousand gallons of water is required in the manufacture of a single car! All other basic resources—land, minerals energy—require water for their productive use.

However, the deeply embedded psyche of individuals—that water is free and plentiful—has not come to grips with the new revelations about the impending crisis of water shortage. National governments have not seriously raised alarm signals for conservation and against pollution. There is insufficient recognition that there are no substitutes for water; there are no means to add a single drop to the water available on the planet within the hydrological cycle.

Scientific research has, of course, opened new vistas on the availability and better husbanding of water. Ice caps could be melted and icebergs may be towed to Saudi Arabia. Geology has confirmed that there is twice as much fresh water underground than on the surface. Rain could be induced and run-offs can be better prevented. Seasonal shortages of rainfall can be overcome. Desalination of ocean waters could become cheaper. But all this does not detract from the consensus that there is a severe water crisis ahead which will make it difficult to meet the demands of world population and progress.

For some countries, availability of fresh water will be a less serious problem than for others. The US and developed nations are not only economically and technologically better endowed but the surface and ground water there is more abundant. In the developing countries, because of their growing population and paucity of financial resources, the problem is more grave. Lack of economic resources comes in the way of providing even drinking water for vast segments of people.

But whether countries are developed or underdeveloped, 90 per cent of them will face future fresh water problems as not just a national problem but an international one. What can be available or harnessed depends on cooperation with neighbouring nations. What prophylactic steps may be called for—in conservation, storage, ecological correctives, flood control—will demand working with co-riparians regardless of political relations or social systems. Water is thus the ultimate symbol of the 'global village'. Nations barely recognize this new dimension to diplomacy. This study will concentrate on the international implications of optimal management of the available water resources.

The physical and chemical qualities of water make it critical to national (indeed subnational, regional and local) politics but has ultimate dependence on international cooperation. Surface water has to be under national territorial jurisdiction, and yet no sovereign power can totally control groundwater. The basic qualities—that water flows and that water, more than any other element, has the capillary qualities of seepage—underline once again the limits of sovereignty and become the best symbol of interdependence. Yellow rain is a problem enough; but at least it can be detected and traced to its source: a polluted international river like the Rhine or even largely enclosed seas like the Mediterranean or the Baltic have brought about a sense of shared concern and attempts at regulation by international agreement. But the problem of underground pollution, which after decades may surface in a different region of the same country or across the frontier in a neighbouring country, will totally defy traditional attributes of sovereignty. These are the negative factors. The more positive challenge will be of husbanding water resources such as international rivers or aquifers for increased domestic and industrial use. This will demand diplomacy and agreement between sovereign nations.

In the past, the chief international problems have been around rivers which flow from one country to another. Where rivers became frontiers, any shift of the water course becomes a source of conflict (for instance, the Sino-Russian incident in 1969). The chief peace-time problem was navigation rights on international rivers. Agreed navigation arrangements were reached even in ancient Babylon and on the Nile and under the Roman Empire. Freedom of navigation covering several domains was worked out in the seventeenth century for the Rhine, the Danube and other European rivers because rivers were the principal means of transport. Conventions and agreements for the common use of rivers like the St. Lawrence were reached between Canada and the US during the nineteenth century. The problem, however, acquired a different character after the non-navigational use of water was discovered and affected other co-riparians. The multiple use of water and the idea of basin-wide development—as in the case of the Tennessee Valley Authority (TVA) which was, of course, only a national project—opened up the possibility of national and international basin development around rivers which were not nationally self-contained.

Wherever there is a hydrological connection—be it on the surface or underground—the most natural unified entity is a basin unity. This is something more than a watershed determined demarcation.

Island countries like Japan, Great Britain and Australia have a special advantage because they have domain over their surface and underground waters. However, of the major continental nations in the world, only the USSR is fortunate in having all its rivers exclusively under national jurisdiction. The Ussuri, where there was a military conflict between the USSR and China in 1969, provides the frontier, and so, according to the Thalweg (midstream) principle, is a shared river. It is not a historical accident but a geographical compulsion that where there are large mountain ranges, the watershed has come by tradition to demarcate the frontiers between neighbours (as in Italy, Spain, France). The essence of the Sino-Indian dispute was that while India claimed that the historical frontier of India coincided with the Himalayan watershed, the Chinese claimed that in some sectors the traditional frontier of Tibet marched with the edge of the plains of the Ganges and the Brahmaputra. This gave the dispute an economic as well as a strategic dimension. The more vexing problem is in Ladakh because it is on a high altitude (16,000 feet) flat plain where there are no river flows. The Sino-Indian territorial question amounted to a conflict between the demarcation along the vague watershed of the Kuen Lun range or a subsidiary demarcation along a dry bed in the Lingji Tang plain.

International riparian law recognizes the evolving versatility of water resources. The principal concepts advanced have been: (a) territorial integrity over national water courses which imply absolute sovereignty over rivers, regardless of downstream need; (b) limited territorial sovereignty; and (c) a recognition of the community of waters, based on the principle of equitable sharing of international rivers.

In 1895, US Attorney-General Harmon advanced the opinion, in relation to the US-Mexican dispute over the Rio Grande, that the US had absolute right to use and divert any amount of waters while it flowed inside its own frontiers. This was an extravagant claim and led to serious political friction with Mexico. Ever since, the US Government has tried to live down this notion without disowning it altogether. In essence, this concept of absolute sovereignty was in conflict with the policy goals of good neighbourliness.

Since the end of the Second World War, after a series of meetings of the International Law Association, the Helsinki concept—which recognizes that there must be an equitable utilization of shared water resources—has emerged. It envisages that after weighing existing and contemplated use, national governments can only enjoy limited sovereignty. The social and economic needs of all co-riparians must be equitably appraised. While even now this concept is not universally accepted, a case law is being slowly built up around the Helsinki rules.

In almost all international riparian flows, there is conflict between national sovereignty and interdependence, between the rights of the lower and the upper riparian states. The impending shortage of water and the internationalization of pollution has led to a creeping recognition of the validity of the concept of equitable utilization.

In the twentieth century, the technical and economic compulsion to harness rivers for optimal use has engaged international and national civil servants, lawyers, engineers, ecologists, economists and social scientists. Blueprints for development around the Nile, the Jordan, the Indus, the Ganges and Brahmaputra, the Mekong, the Amazon and the Niger have been drawn up. Most of these affect up to five or more countries.

One could almost generalize and say that the long-term future of much of the Third World depends on the regulation and development of these river-basin systems. Yet almost all such regulation and development are bedeviled by political hesitations towards realizing the optimal benefits. Meanwhile, in most cases, there is serious physical and ecological deterioration underway and grave dangers are developing due to the delay and drift. These dangers will multiply the economic and opportunity costs as time goes on. A close examination of each case brings out special individual problems but also illustrates the universal need to transcend the existing political boundaries, as solutions are outside the national capacity of management. Specialist international organizations like the UN Water Resources Division, regional organizations like the Economic Commissions for Asia, Africa and Latin America), the World Bank and the UN Conference on Water (Mar del Plato, 1977) have done excellent studies on the principles and possible steps for the optimal management of these international water resources. Models for institutional and legal arrangements have been drawn up. The critical factor is the political one—the will to cooperate. This, in turn, hinges on the balancing of short-term politics with long-term potential and the recognition that international cooperation alone can bring about economic benefits to all and avert the disasters that are implicit in the deferring of any solution for narrow nationalistic reasons.

In this summary, the lessons that emerge from each of these major problems will not be detailed. However, it is worth noting that where there have been international agreements on the multiple use of common rivers (such as between Columbia and Colorado) or on reducing pollution (as on the Rhine), the gains are transparently obvious. In each case, the negotiations were tortuous and the results were based on a compromise of competing considerations. Sometimes there were conflicts arising out of internal regional, as opposed to federal politics. But in each case the benefits were optimized by the advent of international cooperation.

The resolution of these problems can only follow by very detailed economic and technical studies. In the developing world, where energy, food, flood control, siltation, and deforestation are much bigger problems, the imperatives for water diplomacy are greater but nationalism is even stronger and more short-sighted. The challenge for statesmanship and diplomacy is to build around a distant vision, overlooking considerations like established user rights or purely national economic alternatives.

For our purpose here, briefly described, the real overriding challenge is whether nationalism can be squared with the patent logic of interdependence. The problem is critical to South Asian polities but it is not unique to the Indian subcontinent. The example of short-sighted confrontationist attitudes is set by the globalism of the Cold War. Perhaps it is time for lesser nations and regions to ignore or defy the great-power game and look ahead at least in their own nooks and rediscover the God-given basin unity. We cannot fiddle while the wells go dry, the river beds rise, the flood plains spread, and the rich forests become totally denuded. Water must, one day, through diplomacy, bring home the lesson of survival through interdependence.

7

The Indus Water Treaty: The Resolution of an International River Basin Conflict

The Indus Water Treaty (1960) is one of the few examples of a successful negotiated settlement of a major international river basin conflict. The dispute between India and Pakistan on the river issue erupted unexpectedly in 1948, the negotiations started in 1952, and the treaty was finally concluded in 1960. The problem, as is well known, arose because the frontiers drawn for the division of the Indian subcontinent to create the independent states of India and Pakistan cut across a canal system which had been built over the previous hundred years in the Indus basin. The treaty assigned for consumptive use the three eastern rivers of the Indus to India and the three western rivers to Pakistan. The treaty gave the new countries the freedom of independent development of the waters flowing through their lands. Had the treaty not been concluded, it would have remained another major contentious issue in the political relations of the two countries, and the massive economic aid for subsequent development might have been wholly or partially withheld.

The World Bank volunteered to act as a benign go-between; it did not intend, at least initially, to bifurcate the existing canal system and the basin's unity. The original approach was predicated on the rationale of joint management of the inherited integrated assets and cooperative attitudes in the planning and optimizing of future development. As a result of the treaty, the trans-border canal linkages were replaced and the basin interdependence for surface flows was legally ended in perpetuity.

* Paper written for the UN magazine on National Resources, 1981. See also Chapters 5 and 6 in J.S. Mehta, *Negotiating for India*, New Delhi: Manohar, 2006.

To reach this agreement, the World Bank was able to bring to bear its own independent expertise and enormous financial resources. Further, the Bank was able to supplement this financial inducement with pledges of substantial support as grants and loans from other Western nations. The World Bank became, in effect, an independent arbitrator.

The agreement was a triumph, but a triumph of the lesser evil. Judged from the point of view of optimum gains which could flow from the total waters of the Indus basin by recognizing the ecological and economic unity of the river basin, one must recognize the great opportunity costs in repudiating the investment in the existing network of irrigation canals. However, in the prevailing circumstances in the subcontinent, the agreement is considered as one that was the most politically feasible.

BACKGROUND TO THE DISPUTE

The Himalayas and the glacier-enriched southward flowing rivers created the natural frontiers of what for millennia was known as India. The Ganges-Brahmaputra and Indus systems gave India its multi-religious civilization and its distinct economic and social life.

In 1947, prior to Partition, the subcontinent was about the only sizeable area on a mainland continent (as distinct from island nations) where, broadly speaking, the political authority and the economic market coincided with integrated river basins. When the independent Dominions of India and Pakistan came into existence, the historic and natural unity was thus artificially severed. The two halves of Pakistan itself were one thousand miles apart, the West belonging to the Indus and the East to the Gangetic-Brahmaputra basin. While it was recognized that the lines of division were not based on optimum economic viability, the full consequences of the frontiers cutting across the major river systems were not foreseen. Indeed, it is seldom recalled that in the years of constitutional negotiations which led to Partition, none of the main negotiating parties—the British Government, the Indian National Congress, and the Muslim League—ever seriously considered the far-reaching implications of trans-riverine boundaries. The Indian Independence Bill passed by the British

Parliament made no provisions relevant to the administration of the Indus irrigation system. The inter-Dominion Partition Committees which met in the weeks before Independence and separated the assets of undivided India—from the regiments of the Indian Army down to office desks and typewriters—failed to decide on the management of the canal system sharing the proposed boundary. Sir Cyril Radcliffe, the British jurist who was called out in July 1947 to make, within barely six weeks, the detailed delineation of the boundaries for both West and East Pakistan, seems to have been the first to realize the implications of a frontier which ran counter to the basin logic and the existing irrigation infrastructure. The basic political decision and the principle on which the country was to be divided (which also involved the division of the two provinces/states of Punjab and Bengal) had already been taken and announced and lay outside the terms of reference of the Radcliffe Commission. However, in his award, Sir Cyril ominously expressed the hope that by agreement between the two states, some joint control and management of the irrigation system might be found for what he termed 'a valuable common service'.

One cannot but suspect that if Partition had not been rushed, this omission of a short-term-cum-long-term agreement on the Indus system might also have been negotiated before August 1947 at the highest level. The professional irrigation engineers, the bureaucrats and the political decision-makers seem to have assumed that at least the existing canal system would not be disrupted. In fact, as soon as the monsoon flows receded and the time for sowing of the winter crops arrived, the chief engineers of West Punjab (by then a province of Pakistan) and East Punjab (in India) met in December 1947 and readily agreed to a Standstill Agreement to last until 31 March 1948, to continue discharges from the headworks in India for waters which traditionally flowed into what was now Pakistan.

THE HISTORICAL RECORD

The six rivers—the Sutlej, Ravi, Beas, Chenab, Jhelum and Indus—have an aggregate length of 2,800 miles. The Indus system carries 90 × 10^6 acre-feet of water, covering a drainage area of 4,50,000 square miles. Once out of the Himalayan and sub-Himalayan ranges, the Indus and its tributaries flow steadily on a southward slope, with no impeding ranges, until the Indus reaches the Arabian Sea near Karachi. In 1947, forty-six million people lived in the basin. The beginnings and the construction of the Indus canals go back to the apogee of British rule in India. By the middle of the nineteenth century, the Sikh empire had collapsed; Sind had been conquered, and the entire basin, with vast arable areas between the rivers of the Indus basin, came under British authority. British army engineers were quick to perceive the technical potential for irrigation, and the administrators saw not just the revenue-earning possibility but, following serious famines with ominous threats to the newly established rule, also the politico-economic rationale for developing the canal system between the Indus tributaries. The new canal settlements could provide a method of settling the Sikhs, who had been disbanded from the defeated armies of the Sikh kingdom.

From 1850 onward, the canal system was steadily developed into a vast and complex irrigation network. The economic benefits that followed were visible in the agricultural production and progress of the Punjab. Some time before independence, professional engineers and provincial administrators in the Punjab had become aware that the potential for perennial, non-perennial, and run-of-the-river inundation canals was well-nigh exhausted. The body of pre-Partition Punjab irrigation engineers (British, Hindus and Muslims) agreed that further extension would require storage dams to open up new areas for perennial irrigation in the eastern part of the basin. With that idea in mind, the Bhakhra storage project on the Sutlej for hydroelectric power and irrigating parts of East Punjab and north Rajasthan was being planned since the 1920s. It was also a pre-Partition legacy that these proposals brought forth complaints that such upstream utilization could pre-empt the development of agricultural potential in the Sind and in the lower regions of the Indus Basin. In fact, a judicial commission was appointed by the British government to consider the upstream/downstream priorities.

After surveying many national and international lower-upper riparian conflicts, Sir B.N. Rau (who was later to become the adviser to the Constituent Assembly drafting the Indian Constitution) as Chairman of the Commission, gave an important adjudicatory judgement in 1941.[1] The commission recognized the needs and claims of the Sind, and the proposed storage capacity of the Bhakra dam was therefore scaled down; however, the proposal to develop the power potential and a canal system in East Punjab was accepted in principle. The commission underlined the view that water utilization in rivers should be planned by treating the basin as an integrated whole.

At the time of independence, the Indus basin irrigation system was the biggest in the world. The layout of the system was such that the headworks were at the outer fringe of the Shivaliks and the sub-Himalayan ranges which remained in India, whereas the actual area irrigated was further west—in what was to fall inside Pakistan. Specifically, the biggest anomaly was that the headworks of the two big canal systems (the Upper Bari Doab Canal starting in Madhopur on the Ravi and the Dipalpur Canal starting in Ferozepur on the Sutlej) were left in India, whereas almost all of the area irrigated by these canals was on Pakistan's side of the border. Out of the total waters carried in the canals, 80 per cent, or 64.4 million of acre-feet, was committed to the irrigation of land which was to fall inside Pakistan, whereas only 8.5 million acre-feet (m.a.f.) was earmarked for land that was to fall inside India. On the other hand, while twenty-five million people who were directly engaged in agricultural production and benefited from the canal system lived in Pakistan, the Partition resulted in as many as twenty-one million people in India being cut-off from a great part of their traditional source of foodgrains. Herein lay the embryo of the Indus dispute.

There seems to have been an implicit expectation by the British government that once Pakistan was established, the communal frenzy would become muted, there would be a balance of minorities as hostages on both sides of the border and only a small number would uproot themselves from their traditional homes and move to the other country. There was, of course, a conceptual lacuna in the partition. No one asked, much less answered, the question of whether Pakistan was to be a homeland for all the Muslims of the subcontinent or whether the state, created from the provinces with Muslim majorities, had its primary rationale in permitting a part of the subcontinent to have Islam as its official religion, thereby assuaging the anxieties of all Muslims. Neither was it foreseen that about half a million people would die in communal killings or that seventeen to twenty million would migrate from one side of the new frontier to the other.

Even after this horrendous saga of killings, migration and human distress, the atmosphere might have eased except that in the wake of this grim situation the Kashmir problem came to the fore. It started with the infiltration by tribals from Pakistan into Kashmir and later escalated into an armed conflict between the two countries. The atmosphere remained tense and created a climate where reason and economic realism were obscured by suspicion and bitterness. In the wake of such bitterness Gandhi was assassinated by a Hindu on 30 January 1948 because he demanded protection of the Muslims.

All these events are relevant to the understanding of why suddenly the question of the Indus canal system erupted in the spring of 1948, when earlier it had not been foreseen by any government.

The charged emotional atmosphere at the time must be kept in mind in order to understand the reasons why the provincial government of East Punjab stopped the flow of discharges of water from the headworks in the canals on 1 April 1948, after the Standstill Agreement concluded in December 1947 had expired. There was a legal rationale—in a sense typical of upper riparians everywhere—of trying to establish a claim to waters which flow through one's territory before downstream utilization became a prescriptive right. The decision for the stoppage of flows was taken without the approval of the central government in Delhi. Nehru, the prime minister, was sensitive to the moral and international implications and was quick to disapprove of the provincial-level decision. Subsequently, an inter-Dominion meeting in May 1948 agreed to the resumption of flows from the canals on payment for administrative costs by Pakistan. While

India had established, in principle, proprietary rights on the eastern rivers, the brief stoppage aroused alarm in Pakistan. It was suddenly realized that India, as the upper riparian, had the capacity to turn West Punjab into a desert! In Pakistan as a whole, it germinated the idea of securing economic independence from all linkages with India. Pakistan, therefore, took the position of asserting a veto on the utilization of all waters on the Indus system. In effect, Pakistan's Punjab, reversing the earlier position, took over the lower riparian brief of the Sind and abandoned the idea of integrated economic development of the river's potential.

The irony, hypothetically speaking, is that had the canal system not been built in the previous century, Pakistan's economic viability as a state would have been very dubious. The agricultural production generated by the canal system was West Pakistan's greatest asset.

A VISION ERODES

After the transfer of power, the idea of further developing the Indus basin was first mooted by David Lilienthal, the former chairman of the Tennessee Valley Authority (TVA), and the US Atomic Energy Commission, in articles published in *Collier's* magazine. He visited India at the invitation of Nehru. Lilienthal wanted Pakistan's fears for its economic future to be assuaged. He argued that by using modern engineering skills and building storage dams and linked canals on the Indus and its tributaries, the benefits for both countries could be enormously augmented. He even hoped that by developing the full potential of the Indus system, the ongoing Kashmir problem could be muted, if not resolved. He argued: 'the rivers pay no attention to partitions; the Indus just keeps rolling along through Kashmir and India and Pakistan'.[2] The Indus system, he urged, should, like the TVA, be administered by a joint India-Pakistan authority or by a supranational international agency as in the Schumann Plan. Lilienthal urged that such an imaginative comprehensive plan should be financed by the World Bank with support from a consortium of friendly nations. Lilienthal's standing evoked widespread interest in the proposal and persuaded Eugene Black, the then president of the World Bank to explore its possibilities.

The Indus dispute negotiations started in Washington in 1952. The initial approach was based on the Lilienthal rationale of the exploitation of the basin's economic potential for the optimum benefit of both countries. The Bank representative asked each country to put forward its comprehensive proposals. The Indian plan, from the pre-Partition idea of basin unity, suggested storage and linkages from East to West on the Chenab. The plan identified sites for storage and power potential in the areas that were under India's control and suggested that Pakistan could have proportionate share in the costs and benefits. Pakistan's own comprehensive plan projected proposals that exceeded the total availability of waters in the whole Indus system. Pakistan wanted India to have no rights on the three western rivers (Indus, Jhelum and Chenab) and very limited rights (up to 30 per cent only) to draw waters from the eastern rivers. In effect, Pakistan sought to claim historic rights to the waters of the eastern rivers but was not prepared to countenance any share of the waters of the western rivers for consumptive use by India.

The negotiations revealed wide divergence between the disputants. The Bank eventually resolved the crisis by coming forward with its own proposals. The idea of treating the Indus as an integrated river basin which should be jointly administered by India and Pakistan was abandoned by the Bank in 1954. The fact that there were six rivers in the system offered the simple solution of the three rivers lying to the west (Indus, Jhelum, and Chenab) being reserved for consumptive use by Pakistan and the three rivers lying to the east (Ravi, Beas, and Sutlej) being reserved for consumptive use by India. Each country would thus be free to go ahead with the construction and further development of the rivers in its own territory. The World Bank pledged to underwrite financially the construction of canals and storage in Pakistan to the facilities and canals emanating from the headworks now in India. The pre-Partition withdrawals were to be continued from the headworks in India during the transition period until the replacement works were completed. As the negotiations proceeded, Pakistan demanded that, beyond the assurance of historic flows, it must have the bonus of improved capabilities as part of the resolution of the dispute including a vast storage dam at Mangla on the Jhelum. India insisted that its own financial contributions to construction in Pakistan must be limited to what could be recognized as the cost of replacement of the pre-Partition canals. This was fixed at £ 62,000. In the treaty India was also pledged US $56 million towards the construction of the Beas dam, but India's proposal to draw part of the flow from the Chenab was ruled out. After much discussion, it was also agreed that India could make non-consumptive use for power generation on the western rivers while they flowed through India. To meet Pakistan's enhanced demands, the Bank was able to obtain pledges of grants and loans to supplement its own support from Australia, Canada, New Zealand, West Germany, UK and the US. In drafting the treaty, the Bank skillfully bypassed the political issue of the status of Kashmir which was especially sensitive because the Mangla dam straddled the line between the part of Kashmir controlled by India and the part controlled by Pakistan.

Both Pakistan and India expressed dissatisfaction with the Indus Treaty. In India it was widely felt that, as finally concluded, Pakistan obtained from the treaty a better position for potential development. Seventy-nine per cent of the total volume of waters (the statistical average for the three western rivers) was earmarked for Pakistan, whereas the eastern rivers reserved for India had only the balance of 21 per cent from the Indus system. Following the treaty, in a supplementary agreement (1964), Pakistan was able to get an additional commitment for an ambitious storage project at Tarbela on the Indus. The fact that Pakistan had become a US ally in CENTO and SEATO gave it an intangible political advantage and diplomatic leverage. However, the overriding consideration that propelled the Bank and friendly countries was the fear of consequences of an Indo-Pakistan war precipitated by an Indus waters dispute.

The treaty was finally signed by President Ayub and Prime Minister Nehru in 1960. The treaty has eight annexures which cover financial and transitional arrangements; it makes specific provisions relating to agriculture and hydroelectric power and embodies priorities for appointing neutral experts for technical appraisals, and for arbitration to resolve any major dispute which may arise between the two countries. The annexures specify three dams, eight link canals, three barrages and 2,500 tubewells and other minor works to be built in Pakistan. Altogether Pakistan pledged $1.21 billion to pay for all the envisaged construction. The treaty also established a Permanent Indus Commission, which has met regularly ever since. It handles the exchange of data on flow discharges and generally monitors the implementation of the treaty.

The Indus Treaty is the single biggest international riparian settlement negotiated so far and matches the Aswan dam on the Nile in its financial outlays. It has increased agricultural production in the Indus basin by 33 per cent, and it is projected to further add to it in the next fifteen years. India has gone on to develop the irrigation system on the eastern rivers, notably the first stage of the Rajasthan canal. As a result of the treaty, India became free to use 12 m.a.f. from the eastern rivers, which in turn contributed to the Green Revolution and the present food surplus estimated at approximately 30 × 106 tons. Had there been no treaty, following on the human distress caused by the partition, there might have been even greater political and economic ferment in the two countries.

OPPORTUNITY COSTS AND THE DECISION-MAKING PROCESS

When the treaty was signed, both heads of government expressed satisfaction and hoped it would be a new beginning in their relations. If the political Partition is considered as having been unavoidable, if one concedes that the process of division had to be rushed and could not have been protracted to allow more comprehensive anticipation and agreements, and if the emotional trauma for millions on both sides has to be accepted as part of the empire of circumstances surrounding the dispute, the Indus Treaty must be hailed as a great success. However, it cannot be denied that the many compromises reached departed from the enlightened approaches and reduced the potential benefits as initially projected by Lilienthal and envisaged by the World Bank. Having said that, even recognizing that it was not the optimal economic solution, one must reiterate that there was great political gain in removing a major problem with the potential to threaten the amicable relations between the two neighbours. It should be added that even in the circumstances of Independence coinciding with Partition, a different solution might have been reached if economic considerations had not been subordinated by a climate of political hostility and apprehension. The investments in the existing canal systems might have been accepted as valuable assets for both countries which face gigantic threats of poverty and paucity of resources to meet them. It will be recalled that prior to April 1948, neither at the political nor at the technical levels was the need for substitution of infrastructure contemplated by either country. Had the unity of the system been maintained; the Bhakra and the Sutlej valley project, which were planned prior to Partition, could have gone ahead; the technical viability and the economic benefits of a canal from the Chenab to the Ravi had been clearly established and need not have been abandoned, Tarbela could have been built as a project to give irrigation acreage not only for Pakistan's Punjab but also for the lower basin areas of the Sind, and the nucleus of joint management of the existing network might have facilitated hydroelectric projects of benefit to both countries. There could also have been storages on the Skardu, Indus and Dhiangarh on the Chenab and smaller reservoirs on the Monavar and Ravi tributaries, and even the development of the Marhu and Palchar. The provisions of the treaty as they stand foreclosed optimal gains in agricultural production and power generation. It is clear from the above that the benefits of cooperation are such that some day the two countries will have to join together to share in using and safeguarding their common ecological heritage.

NEGOTIATIONS AND DECISIONS[3]

In both countries there must have been serious inter-departmental differences within the respective governments, but published information gives limited insights into them. In neither country was there any impediment from the judicial system (as happened in the implementation of the agreement on exchanges of territorial enclaves between India and East Pakistan/Bangladesh). In both countries the data available was copious and comprehensive. India engaged a non-national lawyer who was a specialist in international water resource problems. Pakistan had several American legal and technical consultants. By and large, the two countries had equal professional skills and experience for understanding a very complex problem.

The critical decisions were taken at the political level, but the protracted and complex negotiations were between senior professional officers or engineers. The chief Indian negotiator was always an irrigation engineer. Pakistan replaced the engineer who initially led their team with a senior administrative civil servant. Pakistan canvassed its position more effectively at the diplomatic level. The greater myopia, born of suspicions and exasperation, was in the parties to the dispute.

I would be bold enough to suggest that the World Bank, in coming forward with its mediating position, gave up the optimal solution too readily. It could have canvassed its own proposal based on the Lilienthal approach more strongly with the political leadership. Even so, one must concede that the success in hammering out the agreement was due to the skill and ability of the World Bank team and the financial leverage to underwrite the agreement. The Bank could commit $1 billion for the replacement canals, plus a substantial bonus of advantages to Pakistan. This third party role was critical in obtaining compromises where the parties to the dispute were sharply divided. In the Nile-Sudan agreements of 1929, Great Britain had a similar leverage: it had an imperial position and brought to bear its power and influence and so compelled the resolution of the differences between the upper and lower riparians. The World Bank did not have political power, but its ability to bring in friendly countries with financial commitments was a kind of quasi-imperial third-party inducement to the successful resolution of the dispute. At various stages, the World Bank politely threatened that it would withdraw from the negotiations if its independent proposals were not accepted. Pakistan, being the lower riparian, was not prepared to risk such a breakdown. India's own Second Five Year Plan depended on massive economic aid from the World Bank and from the other developed countries which were also members of the Bank. These exogenous factors enhanced the effective role of the World Bank in the negotiations.

However, international and economic circumstances have changed in the decades since the Indus Water Treaty was signed. The World Bank, for example, is obliged to tread more gingerly in approaching water management and riparian development plans between India and Nepal and India and Bangladesh. Except in select countries, aid availability, especially after adjusting for inflation, is much smaller from both multinational and bilateral sources. In other words, it is difficult today to foresee the World Bank or any outside power commanding the same position of inducement or leverage in mediating a major international riparian conflict as was the case in the Indus Water Treaty negotiations.

LESSONS OF THE INDUS AGREEMENT

The lessons that emerge from the Indus Water Treaty and the negotiations leading up to the treaty are applicable to the decision-making process in other riparian conflicts and can be summarized in the seven points set forth below.

First, as a generalization, all riparian conflicts must be conditioned by the recognition that fresh-water diplomacy is a symbol and the test for international relations. How do we balance national interests (including the competitive domestic demands that go with the availability of water) and the emotions that go with the notions of territorial sovereignty on the one hand and the uncontrollable imperatives of international interdependence on the other? We now know that the 'beggar thy neighbour' approach, which ignores the logic of the integral unity of river basins and common stakes in the optimal progress of upper and lower riparian partners, is self-destructive. The reason for this is clear. Ecology and groundwater potential do not respect political frontiers and do not necessarily give advantage to the upper riparians.

Second, the circumstances of the Indus dispute were loaded against a more rational approach. The dispute might not have taken shape if it had been anticipated and negotiated in advance, or the long-term economic optimization on the basis of the integral unity of the basin been kept at the forefront. The lesson is that a recognition by the political-cum-economic community of the interests between competing riparian partners is a precondition and the overriding motor for equitable agreements destined to control the present and future development of a river basin.

Third, the prevailing political climate and therefore the timing of negotiations will always be crucial in determining the solutions to international riparian conflicts.

Fourth, public opinion at home has to be led towards rational compromises and not be inflamed into chauvinistic self-righteousness. To illustrate this point, one might refer to the problem of another river basin in the northern part of the Indian subcontinent. Deforestation and near desertification in upstream Nepal is leading to extensive soil erosion in that country, causing ever-increasing flood damage, imperilling development and aggravating socio-economic problems downstream in India and Bangladesh. The solution is the development of the Ganges-Brahmaputra basin in a planned and managed manner. The benefits of the solution are clear because there is a perfect complementarity in the power potential in Nepal and flood control in India. The challenge is for the independent countries of the Ganges-Brahmaputra basin to resolve the problem.

Fifth, it follows that in sensitive issues involving rivers shared by nations, the decision-makers at the highest level of government must be brought into the negotiating process from time to time. The Indus river negotiations, which were conducted at the bureaucratic and professional levels, were therefore bound to be less flexible. While marshalling great technical and professional expertise, more frequent references to the political level would have probably increased the chances for optimally beneficial compromises.

Sixth, most of the Indus river negotiations were conducted in Washington, London and Rome—away from the Indian subcontinent. There are obvious advantages in negotiating on neutral ground. But, as nations become more self-conscious, it may be propitious to choose a small country capital for the negotiations. Alternatively, in preference, the negotiations might be rotated between the capitals of the riparian partners.

Seventh, while third-party mediation proved a powerful influence in the Indus river case, bilaterally negotiated solutions should not be ruled out, as they could bring better trade-offs in confidential give and take.

THE SALAL PROJECT: AN EXAMPLE OF CONFLICT RESOLUTION

Does bilateral fresh-water diplomacy have a chance? Or is an outside power or a multinational institution like the World Bank essential for the resolution of a riparian conflict? Let me give one small but revealing example which arose out of the Indus Treaty itself. This pertains to a run-of-the-river hydroelectric project at Salal on the Chenab river, which lies thirty miles upstream inside Kashmir. The Chenab is one of the western tributaries assigned to Pakistan. Under the treaty, consumptive utilization of hydroelectric development on the Chenab is permitted to India but only after the designs have been scrutinized and approved by Pakistan. The Salal project envisaged a 690 megawatt power dam on an especially attractive bend of the river. In the climate of political suspicions that prevailed at the time when the proposal was made by India the instinctive reaction in Pakistan was that the project was not primarily for economic benefit but for contingencies in military operations. For almost eight years, the design of the project was discussed between the Indus commissioners and the heads of the foreign offices, but Pakistan strenuously withheld its consent to the project. The proposal was on the point of being referred to arbitration when, in the summer/autumn of 1976, relations improved and bilateral negotiations were resumed. The rigidities of the professional engineers of both sides were overcome by a new negotiating team with a somewhat more enlightened economic and political brief. India made concessions on the height of the dam and accepted a corresponding reduction in the power potential of the project. Essentially what effected the turnaround were not, however, technical modifications in the design but successful efforts to assuage the unexpressed military suspicions of Pakistan.

This agreement could not have been reached if it had been urged by a third party. Indeed, friendly countries or the World Bank did not try to intervene or even expect that the Salal dispute could be overcome with or without outside mediation.

The negotiated agreement on Salal has worked satisfactorily. The hydroelectric project is now almost complete.[4] The military fears of Pakistan are never reiterated and the direct economic benefits in India are probably of the order of several million rupees a day. While the suspicions in Pakistan were assuaged, the negotiated compromise was never projected as a one-sided victory. This provides an important lesson for such sensitive negotiations. What one also learnt about the negotiating process was that although professional engineers should provide the technical inputs, they must not be allowed to dominate and determine the strategy or inhibit longer-term goals. The resolution of the Salal conflict came about because broader, more enlightened and bolder decisions were taken at the highest level of the governments involved.

CONCLUSION

In riparian conflicts, decision-making requires long-term projections of national interests and socio-economic cost-benefits. The economic penalties of non-agreement must be put side by side with optimal or even suboptimal benefits. The new elements and new technology are still not known to many older generation engineers. While chemical pollution reinforces the advantage of upper riparians, the impending scarcity of fresh water and the unknown implication of ground water pollution point to a recognition of joint interest in basin management and the need to overcome the myopic notions of national interest.

The Indus Treaty is a success but a suboptimal one. Twenty-five years from now, India and Pakistan, as independent countries, may find it worthwhile not necessarily to scrap the treaty but to go on to rediscover that additional benefits from this river system may be possible through new projects financed and managed jointly. It would require recognition, which must come one day, that good neighbourliness is good international politics and may well be the only way to assure the internal economic progress of the two countries. Indeed, optimal use of waters may be the ultimate key to political stability at home. All this may seem a long shot now, but decision-making must not remain an exercise in improvisations to deal with short-term issues.

My submission, therefore, is that the fundamental factor in resolving river-basin conflicts is enlightened political perspective and direction. Politics is bound to permeate the negotiating process. What is crucial is the projection of a far-sighted vision. Collateral efforts by professionals, publicists, analysts and academics can play a role in what must be repeatedly stressed: water affects the lives of people. Public opinion must be educated to give political decision makers the necessary latitude for conflict resolution to reach optimally beneficial and equitable compromises.

NOTES

1. For background see B.S. Minhas, et al., *Scheduling the Operations of the Bhakra System: Studies in Technical and Economic Evaluation*, Calcutta: Statistical Evaluation Society, 1982.
2. Henry Hart, *New India's Rivers*, Bombay: Orient Longman, 1956.
3. N.P. Gulati, *The Indus Treaty*, New Delhi: Allied Publishers, 1973.
4. It has since been completed and 650 mw flowed into the northern grid. This may be the biggest such power project constructed with the consent of a neighbour.

8

The Politics of Riparian Cooperation

The tragedy of our times is that just when there was unprecedented breakthrough in technology and unforeseen availability of resources, the politics of military security overtrumped and subordinated the politics of socio-economic development. Nationalism was fulfilled by decolonization, but the quest for development in the newly independent countries which hinged on functional regional economic cooperation did not generally go beyond verbal homage. The Third World countries became militarized as a by-product of the mutually reinforcing fears and competition of the great powers, but they were also inhibited in using the latitude of their sovereign discretion to optimize economic progress which required harnessing natural resources jointly with their neighbours. The irony is that the enormously enhanced military capability stands paralyzed not just in the balance of nuclear terror, but also against violent internal disaffection which can be traced to people's unfulfilled expectations. The Revolution of 1989 in Eastern Europe has been followed by the general acknowledgement of the folly of the Cold War. In its wake, defence is being downgraded and economic rationale is getting primary focus in national goals and in international relations, but the developing world is still trapped in the mindset discarded by the industrialized countries. In the emergent calculus of world politics, the non-aligned principles, in their original concepts of peace and development uninfluenced by global military strategies and unaffected by borrowed ideological models, look prophetically wise. However,

* First printed in B.G. Verghese and Ramaswamy Aiyar (eds), *Harnessing the Eastern Himalayan Rivers: Regional Cooperation in South Asia*, New Delhi: Konarka, 1993.

the policies and achievements of most non-aligned countries have been poor examples of the principles which they profess.

South Asia has had a unique civilizational unity. Most countries of the subcontinent subscribed to non-alignment from the very beginning, but under inducements or the impact of the Cold War were enmeshed in the game of great-power politics. Even Pakistan, which joined the Western alliances while fearful of communism, was never serious about fighting communism on the global stage. Even though the ideological struggle was really extraneous to the problems of the subcontinent, by reactive osmosis the developmental priorities of the region were obscured and socio-economic progress was enfeebled. After four decades, the results are tragically plain. According to the UN Human Development Report of 1990 and Ruth Sivard's *Military and Social Expenditure,*[1] even compared to sub-Saharan nations, South Asia has the lowest rating in social indicators and about the highest per capita increase in military expenditure amongst the non-oil exporting developing countries. The other contrast is that while South Asia has the world's most dense concentration of poverty, with over five hundred million under or around the poverty line, it has the greatest potential in agriculture and energy, and thus an unrealized possibility of raising living standards. Clutching to their sovereignty, the countries of this naturally integrated region have yielded to myopic perspectives and pursued a diplomacy which has failed to pursue their own enlightened goals.

DIPLOMACY AND SHARED NATURAL RESOURCES

The challenge of diplomacy has always been how to make not just power but intelligence and persuasion serve national interest beyond national sovereignties. The present problems of international relations highlight two old and enveloping dilemmas for decision-makers which have acquired an entirely novel and awesome significance. The first dilemma is that the political frontiers, as they evolved after millennia of turbulent human history, do not coincide with the logic of physical geography, optimal economic progress and ecology. The other dilemma flows from the fact that politics, as the craft of getting power and keeping it, leads to an instinctive predilection for what is feasible and domestically palatable in the short term, but the demand for social justice and fulfilment of people's expectations require cooperation on a widened basis and an ever-lengthening gestation period for economic progress. The dichotomies of space and time which confront the nation-state crystallise into a conflict between sovereignty and its limitations and between the pressures of populism and the imperatives of long-term solutions.

Nothing brings forth the essence of the challenge for decision-makers and diplomacy as cooperation around international rivers. Here, the cherished notions of independence and domestic jurisdiction come face-to-face with interdependence with neighbours which requires a deliberate effort to insulate temporary bilateral problems from the quest for long-term answers to poverty alleviation and economic development. The high ground of nationalistic independence becomes the enemy of rational solutions for national futures. For millennia, the control and use of river flows was looked upon as if the river was a terrestrial property to be appropriated by whomever had access to it, disregarding claims of those downstream. This attitude aroused furious conflicts between one farm and the next homestead; one province and the adjoining one; the selfish harnessing of advantage against the building of social assets and the 'commons'. The problems within a country are replicated and compounded when rivers traverse frontiers with domains coming under different sovereignties. Economists and planners fully recognize that the optimal use of flowing waters is possible only through a planned and equitable use of surface (and even groundwater) over an entire integrated drainage basin. Since international rivers are in this respect different from oceans and space where there is no traditional notion of national domain, it has been possible for member nations to show rare collective sagacity in the UN and affirm that the ocean seabed and space must remain the common heritage of mankind. (Since these declarations were made, even this enlightened pledge has been under threat of erosion and repudiation.)

The new reality is that economically usable fresh water may soon be in short supply for the exponentially growing demand for human consumption and the needs of industry and agriculture. Nature also demands that some part of the water must remain in the ground to facilitate natural purification, retain earth's regenerative chemistry, and preserve the planetary environment. The nub of the problem is that flowing rivers and groundwater, like air, defy human authority. Any attempt to disregard the legitimate claim of riparian neighbours to river flows becomes a peril to the general climate of good relations within the region.

INTERNATIONAL DRAINAGE BASINS AND THE EVOLUTION OF EQUITABLE SHARING

There is a long history of penalties from international riparian conflicts but there are also instructive examples of the benefit of cooperative agreements and compromises. The Harmon doctrine of absolute rights over flowing rivers within a country was advanced as an extension of the principle of territorial sovereignty during the negotiations between the US and Mexico in 1896 over the utilization of the waters of the Rio Grande (and by extension the Colorado). This assertion reflecting the stronger upper riparian power's chauvinism bedevilled relations between the two countries for decades. The doctrine had to be modified many times (in 1906, 1944 and 1972) with concessions to the weaker lower riparian state on the quantity to be made available and eventually even guarantees offered on the purity of water when it reached Mexico. The starkest contrast in the US approach was when the country had to negotiate—this time as a lower riparian—with Canada on the harnessing of the Columbia. In the treaty concluded in 1964, the US, after weighing the costs and benefits, agreed to pay not just for the storage dams and hydel power, generated in a location in Canada, but even for the downstream benefits within the US for the consequential mitigation of flood damage. Both sides are now pledged not to divert the waters without the consent of the other.

In Europe, the Danube basin, encompassing twelve countries, has a three-hundred-year-old history of international navigational arrangements. Even when the countries of the basin became members of opposing military blocs (with some neutral and one non-aligned country), agreements were reached on the comprehensive management of the river. The European Economic Commission (EEC) has made striking progress, admittedly after difficult negotiations, to control and reverse pollution on the Rhine which flows through four heavily industrialized countries. In South America, the Brasilia (1968) and Itapu (1973) Treaties have created the framework and institutions to develop the del Plata basin and its tributaries for hydel power and navigation, which involves Brazil, Paraguay, Uruguay, Bolivia and Argentina. In Africa, a bilateral agreement, improving on earlier arrangements was reached between Egypt and Sudan prior to the construction of the Aswan dam (1959).

The Mekong, Niger and Jordan are other examples where plans have been prepared on sharing and development of a common river, holding promise of enormous benefits to all or most riparian partners, but political problems have deferred a purposeful beginning. On the other hand, it has been argued that, aside from the bonus of economic gains, coordinated riparian development on the Jordan, Tigris and Euphrates could be a way to buttress permanent political solutions in the Middle East.

There are two hundred and fourteen rivers that are shared between two or more countries; indeed outside island nations there is no country that has all its rivers originating within and flowing to the oceans on its own coast line. In the earlier centuries, the problem was chiefly of navigation rights of the upper riparian states, but with growing populations, industrial and agricultural needs, the potential of multipurpose valley developments like that on the Tennessee, and the new realization of the threat of groundwater pollution, differences between riparian partners are legion and frequently cast a shadow on harmony and peace amongst neighbours.

International lawyers have long been engaged in trying to evolve principles which could provide guidelines on the rights and obligations on rivers which flow across frontiers. The International Law Association constituted under the UN auspices, after addressing itself to the problem in several sessions, adopted a set of rules for the utilization of waters of shared rivers at its 1966 meeting in Helsinki. The UN Conference on Water held in

Mar de Plata (Argentina) in 1977 and a subsequent Conference in Dakar (Senegal) prepared a draft convention embodying the principles and presented it to the UN General Assembly in 1984. The underlying approach of the Helsinki rules is that the drainage basin must be taken as an integrated whole with a view to optimize the benefits and balance competitive national needs. The crucial Article IV lays down that each basin state is entitled to a 'reasonable and equitable share in the beneficial uses of waters of an international drainage basin'. In defining 'reasonable and equitable use' many factors are listed such as physical geography of the area, population, climate, as well as the potential social and economic needs of all the basin states. The rules also cover problems of pollution, navigation, weightage to existing operational use and so forth.

THE PAST AND POTENTIAL OF RIPARIAN COOPERATION IN SOUTH ASIA

In dealing with internal river disputes, India had long ago adopted approaches which were broadly consistent with the Helsinki rules and the recommendations of the International Law Commission. There is no clearer enunciation of the principles governing the use of waters between upstream and downstream neighbours than the judgement of Sir B.N. Rau given in 1942 when the Sind province of British India protested against the planned construction of Bhakhra and the proposed diversion of waters of the Sutlej in the Punjab. The judgement stated that the 'the most satisfactory settlement of this kind is by agreement with the parties adopting the same technical solution as if they were a single united community, undivided by political or administrative frontier[s]'.[2] Even in the nineteenth century, the British inspector of irrigation works, in considering the proposal of the State of Patiala (described then as a Foreign State) to draw water for the eventual Sirhind Canal, conceded that a reasonable share of waters should be allowed by the British 'to give the greatest aggregate advantage with the smallest outlay'. After Independence, the principle of equitable share and allowing for downstream benefits is recognized in the Indian River Boards Act 1956.

After independence, South Asian countries, in determining their approaches to their common rivers, have overlooked the bonus of a national advantage in adopting cooperative attitudes. This is particularly tragic because, prior to 1947, the subcontinent was the largest area in the world where the controlling political authority coincided with the broad logic of a major watershed. (Nepal and Bhutan were outside the British Empire but under exclusive British tutelage.) This monsoon-defined unity—where its rivers gave old India its pluralist civilization—was shattered by the impetuous partition of India. It incidentally negated the British imperial boast of having given administrative and rational unity to ancient India. What is relevant to our purpose is that Partition artificially splintered the natural integrity of the drainage basins of the Indus and the Ganges. The satisfactory working of the Indus Treaty has at least eliminated a major irritant in India-Pakistan relations. It demonstrates that a settlement on natural resources can be insulated from the continuing political tensions.

This background of benefits which flowed from the Indus Treaty and other negotiations on shared rivers did not permeate the approach of India, Nepal, and Bangladesh on the Ganges-Brahmaputra basin.[3] There are, no doubt, manifold technical, seismic and ecological problems, but many, if not all, experts do not consider them insuperable. The constraint of resources has not been an impediment. The potential benefits in renewable sources of power, agricultural productivity, soil conservation, flood control, transportation and, above all, poverty alleviation and social progress are so astronomical that projects have always been considered patently viable. Indeed, engineers, economists, social scientists around the world were enthused at what looked like one of the greatest developmental El Dorados. The idea of the integrated development of the Himalayan waters was commended without ulterior motives by President Carter of the US, British Prime Minister Callaghan, President of World Bank MacNamara, etc. But this outside enthusiasm only aroused fears because of the Cold War-generated psychosis and sapped the political will to give the urgency and zest needed to pursue the projects. The waters and the electricity could not after all be taken away, but India, disregarding its own interests, suspected

Western malevolence and Chinese mischief. Nepal, equally self-disregarding, baulked at the consequential dependence on and benefits for India. Behind this hesitation, there was a myopic parochialism and unrealistic security anxieties. The following paragraphs, which briefly recapitulate the story of India-Nepal and India-Bangladesh riparian relations, have this common thread of beggaring the neighbour even when the penalty was mounting national impoverishment.

INDIA AND NEPAL: THE POLITICAL BACKDROP

With the British imperial policy of exclusive control and influence over the landlocked state, Nepal, under the Rana oligarchy, rejoiced in an introverted independence insulating itself from the world at large. When independent India concluded the Treaty of Friendship in 1950 with the Rana regime, it gave proof of its respect for Nepal's separate international personality and of its desire to continue the special relations that were predicated on the economic, ethnic and security interdependence between the two countries. After the overthrow of the Rana regime, India under Nehru's leadership assisted Nepal to establish modern communications with India and thus opened it to international horizons, especially with decolonizing Asia. India also encouraged Nepal to embark on all-round economic development and adopt democratic constitutional structures. There was an underlying assumption that with the virtually unsubstitutable dependence on India, the economic and political modernization of Nepal would only reinforce the permanent coincidence of national interests between the two countries. Following China's military occupation of Tibet, it was the expectation that nationalism in Nepal would consider it in its own interest to tailor its international attitude with an abiding sensitivity to the common security of India and Nepal. In this confidence, relations between the two countries in the 1950s were characterized by friendship and faith in each other. But modern nationalism, regardless of national weakness, is irked by subordination, its external dependence notwithstanding. There was some early irritation in the body politic of Nepal against the thoughtless manifestation of an overbearing Indian diplomacy. This should have been perceived as a warning of the emerging and unprecedented complexity of relations between the two unequal powers. The banner of non-alignment, which had been raised by India, was itself an assertion by the weak and poor newly independent countries against the strategic and ideological hectoring by the great powers. The story of India-Nepal political relations has been a sort of reverse mirror image of US-India relations—sensitive nationalism baulking at economic dependence and the logic of beneficial bilateralism being inhibited by postures of political reserve.

After becoming a member of the UN, Nepal became alive to the international climate where economically handicapped and militarily weak countries demanded respect for their independence and their own claims and rights. But because India was, in a manner of speaking, midwife to the modernization and political liberation of Nepal, there was an insensitive grasp of the maturing of Nepali nationalism.

It was in the early stages of trusting relations that the Kosi and Gandak projects were negotiated between India and Nepal. Nepal did not then have the technical resources to appraise the projects or undertake construction on its own. The primary concern of the Indian project engineers, from what was wholly an Indian investment, was to bring about a moderation of floods in India (especially from the Kosi). However, they were short-sighted in not anticipating India's potential power needs and, more to the point, in overlooking the consequential harm in the extent of submergence within Nepal. No one in Nehru's time would have been so non-chalant as to authorize such flawed projects if either Indian expertise or Nepalese representations had correctly spelt out the possible damage to Nepal, especially if an alternative proposal of building barrages further upstream had been put forward frankly at the political level. As it was, when the unforeseen flooding and damage took place in Nepal, it cast a dark shadow on all subsequent proposals, even though the potential benefits to Nepal were unquestionable.

A feeling became entrenched in Nepal that until its own technical capabilities were enhanced, it should avoid turning to India for support and advice. Indeed, the more nationalistic decision-makers felt that Nepal should go slow in further riparian cooperation with India. Thus, Nepal turned to the US International Development Agency (IDA) to renovate the Chatra Canal (which was originally part of the Indian Kosi project) and politely excluded India's participation.

The determination to demonstrate that Nepal was not a 'satellite' of India came to the surface when Sino-Indian relations deteriorated in 1959. Nepal then had a democratically elected government led by B.P. Koirala (who had an old association with the Indian National Congress and had actually participated in the Indian freedom movement), which first took a 'neutral' attitude towards Nepal's two neighbours. In the mid-1950s, China had not openly disputed, but nor had it ever unreservedly accepted,—as had been done to a greater extent by the USA and the USSR—that Nepal was an area of special Indian interests. Beginning with the visit of Zhou Enlai and the establishment of diplomatic relations in 1956, China started making overtures of friendship and aid to Nepal. To symbolically wean Nepal from its exclusive reliance on India (and incidentally get essential supplies for Tibet which traditionally came from India through Sikkim and the Chumbi valley), China offered to build a direct road link from Kathmandu to Kodari on the Tibetan border. Nepal's apprehension of China posing a security and ideological threat to Nepal was patiently assuaged by China's largely 'correct' political approach. The Sino-Nepal boundary agreement was quickly negotiated in 1960, which incidentally sought to show that it was India which was being intransigent in the Sino-Indian boundary dispute. This boundary was even declared as 'traditional'. It coincided with the watershed and so was in fact consistent with the Indian case, particularly in the Eastern sector, to that which had been delineated in Simla in 1914 (and is referred to as the MacMahon Line) and was also along the watershed.

A different kind of irritant arose when India criticized the abrogation of the democratic constitution and the dismissal of the Koirala government by King Mahendra in December 1960. Thereafter, for a while, the Nepali Congress members and sympathizers embarked on raids into Nepal from the adjoining Indian states which compounded the fear that when it came to Nepal, India was not scrupulous in adhering to the principle of non-interference.

Nepal did not dispute India's contention on the border with China. However, Nepal's staying aloof during the biggest crisis in India's foreign policy led to suspicions in India that the former was insensitive to India's security perceptions. King Mahendra's government, by a show of friendship to the powerful northern neighbour, tried to ensure that China, in contrast to India, would not aggressively encourage the communist factions to undermine the non-party Panchayati Raj which he had established after the democratic constitution had been abrogated.

The Shastri visit to Kathmandu in 1965 assuaged the fears of Indian interference that had been festering since 1960. For a while, during the Cultural Revolution, the Chinese embassy irritated the Nepali government by holding defiant demonstrations in Kathmandu. There was also a wilful intrusion along the border in the Mustang sector. China was, however, quick at political damage control such as in semantically compromising on the ownership of Mt. Everest (Sagarmatha) and by paying compensation after the border intrusions. The suspicion remained in India that Nepal was engaged in a naïve but dangerous flirtation with China. India felt that Nepal had overlooked the many privileged economic concessions extended by India. It became more irritated by the abuse of such concessions by official encouragement or connivance in the smuggling of banned products, such as the electronic products, synthetics and other items into India across the open India-Nepal border.

The gulf of mutual insensitivity is also illustrated in the reactions following the integration of Sikkim into India. India saw it as an entirely internal affair but in Nepal it aroused fears that, in a similar manner, first Bhutan and later Nepal could become victims of India's hegemonistic ambitions. Bhutan showed no public reaction, but in Nepal there was strong criticism which was suspected as having been inspired officially. Along with a strong diplomatic representation by India, restrictions were imposed on the supply of essential items like POL and coal for Nepal's domestic needs. But instead of bending under pressure, the Nepalese authorities became more sullen and determined to adopt further independent postures in international politics. It was in this half-nervous and half-defiant state of mind that King Mahendra proposed, at the Algiers Summit of the non-aligned

(1973), that Nepal should be accepted as a Zone of Peace. Though it was a seemingly innocuous and unexceptionable demand, especially when the developing world was endorsing the idea of continents and oceans being declared zones of peace or free of nuclear weapons and insulated from great power strategic competition, India perceived it as pointedly balancing it with China and departing, in letter and spirit, from the Treaty of 1950.

In the two decades following its entry into the network of international organizations, Nepal had come to understand that it, like all, landlocked countries, was entitled, in peacetime, to unrestricted transit for its newly developing seaborne imports and exports across India. Up to the 1960s, in the periodic commercial agreements between India and Nepal, trade, transit facilities and measures calculated to control illegal trade were in an omnibus agreement. Reflecting Nepal's determination to wriggle free of Indian control, Nepal asserted that under international practice, transit was an unrelated permanent right, and must be delinked from trade and smuggling. India felt that the open border was a special and unusual privilege which justified bracketing the provisions on trade and transit, especially when insufficient efforts were made to curb the export of imported goods which were prohibited in India. The impasse resulted in no new treaty being concluded for eight years.

India had denounced the Barcelona Convention on Navigability on International Rivers in 1956, at a time when the Farakka plan for flushing the Hooghly was being contemplated. Apprehensive of Pakistan (on behalf of the Eastern wing) trying to establish a pre-emptive claim on the Ganges flow, India turned down the Nepalese proposal to have the Ganges declared as an international river. India, therefore, looked with grave suspicion on Nepal's proposal that it would like to establish a waterway connection across a small neck of Indian territory with Bangladesh and thus have access to the Bay of Bengal, bypassing the traditional route through Calcutta (now Kolkata).

THE DOWNS AND UPS OF RIPARIAN COOPERATION

The combination of these bilateral irritants so vitiated the political attitudes on both sides that the progress on riparian cooperation got inhibited or reduced to periodic formal reiterations. The consequence has been decades of delay in the start of the Karnali project. The cost benefits to both India and Nepal for a high dam at Chisapani on the Karnali—4,500 megawatts of power at a meagre cost of approximately Rs. 300 crore—had been confirmed by a Japanese report way back in 1966. Further studies were entrusted by Nepal successively to an Australian group, some Norwegian consultants and more recently to a World Bank-selected Canadian firm. In all of them, India which had vital interests and enormous experience and expertise, was deliberately excluded. All the studies reiterated the technical feasibility and vast benefits to both countries; indeed, the last study, in the light of more recent technology, recommended upgrading the project to realize 10,500 megawatts from the Karnali system. The economic viability of the project hinged on the Indian purchase of substantial surplus of power. With the time consumed in undertaking a succession of feasibility studies, the estimates of costs continued to mount geometrically. Other major projects were also identified by India and presented to the Nepalese authorities. Amongst the notable ones were the Pancheshwar on the Sharda and Barakshetra on the Kosi, but all of them suffered the same political hesitation on the part of Nepal, albeit the objections were defined in technical obscurities.

In this mood of mutual suspicion, India overlooked the desperate and growing power shortage for the north Indian grid and Nepal ignored the increasing resource crunch that it faced in development. As a collateral consequence, Nepal's forest wealth, which was its traditional source of energy was rapidly depleted and the country visibly moved towards desertification. India was also nonchalant about the downstream damage by erosion and the floods that were aggravated by Nepal's deforestation. Indeed, the problem was compounded by the purchase of Nepalese hardwood for India's domestic needs of railway sleepers. If Karnali had been started in the 1960s and completed by the 1970s, it would have yielded something like $10 billion to Nepal's annual revenues. On the Indian side, even after making the utmost reservation for Nepal's domestic use, India might have saved perhaps $20 billion in costs of imported oil in the subsequent decade after the oil price hikes of 1970s. Future generations may well wonder why this compact of self-destruction was not overcome by sagacity and foresight.

Contrary to what has often been asserted, it was not impossible to cut through these psychological barriers of mistrust. When the Janata government came to office in 1977 and made a determined effort to improve relations with India's neighbours, it agreed to delink trade and transit by concluding separate treaties—the former for five years and the latter for seven years—along with a colateral agreement on the control of illegal trade (smuggling). All the old substantive provisions were incorporated and the freedom of transit through Indian ports and territory was conceded, and so the political climate was dramatically transformed. Nepal interpreted this separate transit treaty as the symbolic acceptance by India of the full independence of Nepal, even if it was landlocked by India. Following the treaties there was a more purposeful willingness to discuss Karnali and the Pancheshwar project. The Janata government, however, fell in July 1979. When the Congress government came back to office in January 1980, relations between the two countries suffered a setback, once again for reasons extraneous to India-Nepal relations. Nepal, like all India's other neighbours, voted against the Soviet intervention in Afghanistan (1980). India's acceptance, if not defence, of Soviet actions was interpreted as following the *droit de limitrophe*, viz., that a great power had the right to intervene in a neighbouring country if it did not like an internal dispensation or was apprehensive of a possible danger from a third country. It looked like a departure from the Nehruvian policy of respect for independent nationalisms. The perceptions that India, as a regional power, would exercise a similar option at some future time, intensified the determination among India's neighbours to find common ground and in 1983 this fructified in the Bangladesh proposal to constitute the South Asian Association for Regional Cooperation (SAARC). Always suspecting the Indian hand behind the opposition to its Panchayati Raj, Nepal persisted with the proposal that it be internationally accepted as a 'zone of peace' and showed a non-responsive reserve at the suggestion of a special relationship with India. Coinciding with the aerial dropping of supplies for the north-east Tamil Sri Lanka and the dispatch of the Indian Peace Keeping Force (IPKF) (1987), Nepal secretly ordered military equipment, including a few anti-aircraft guns, from China and requested that the equipment be supplied overland without traversing India. With India's continuing concern at the threat from China, there were strong political reactions at what was perceived as a deliberate circumvention of the spirit—indeed specifically the confidential letters exchanged at the time—of the 1950 Treaty. In March 1989, the Indo-Nepal Trade and Transit Treaties, which had governed their economic relations since 1978, were both allowed to lapse, and thereafter India purposefully truncated essential supplies to Nepal. This was seen as a punitive measure which even overlooked the hardship it could cause to the ordinary people, especially in the distant valleys. Nepal faced difficulties but arranged for expensive alternative supplies. For many in Nepal, the Indian actions revived the deep-down fears of India's coercive propensities.

The Janata government, which came to power in 1990, restored the previous arrangements but only on an ad hoc basis. The whole basis of the relationship including the Friendship Treaty of 1950 came to be debated on both sides. This deterioration of relations, in consequence and not by design, coincided and intensified the long-festering demand for the restoration of multiparty democracy under a new constitution in Nepal. During the defiant protests and in the run-up to the elections in Nepal, which were held in 1991, relations with India received constant mention. In India, there was obvious satisfaction at the prospect of the restoration of democracy after thirty years of Panchayati Raj which was considered a euphemism for the domination by the royal palace. India had not learnt the lesson of not allowing even a suspicion of partisanship and interference in the internal politics of the neighbour to arise. One Indian political faction sympathized transparently with the Nepali Congress and may well have adversely damaged the latter's electoral chances. It was ironical that the communist parties took strongly nationalistic postures and even criticized references to the development of rivers 'common' to Nepal and India. From this political gameplay, a major impediment amounting to a possible veto has now been created by inscribing in the new constitution of Nepal that agreements on natural resources must be ratified by a two-third majority of the elected Nepali Parliament. There were improved chances of more positive approaches between the Nepali Congress government and the new Congress government in India.[4] But the layers and layers of mistrust will need to be sensitively removed before the climate of relations becomes propitious for optimal cooperation, which would be not just beneficial but is essential for both countries.

The separate and shared interests of India and Nepal thus got subordinated to misconceived fears. Both countries turned a blind eye to national damage and national benefits and both overlooked the opportunity costs of delay. If constructive engagement is to be initiated, there must be an unabashed recognition that a grave economic crisis, including mounting disaffection and macro-ecological problems which confronts both countries, is in no small measure due to the inhibitions in pursuing patently obvious gains for both countries through riparian cooperation.

THE PARTITION TRAUMA ON THE GANGES

The problem of India and Bangladesh, where India is the upper riparian, has a somewhat different history, but here, too, the permanent interdependence has been obscured by the politics of suspicion and the insensitivity of diplomacy. For a quarter of a century, India's relations with the present Bangladesh (earlier East Pakistan) were a constituent part of the India-Pakistan cold war and its psychological legacy. Partition disrupted the water- borne communications of the Ganges delta, and almost cut off north-east India. It left East Pakistan with the near impossible task of restructuring its economy because the natural linkages with the surrounding neighbourhood were either diluted or deliberately severed. The central government of Pakistan did little beyond taking some flood-control measures to develop the water resources of East Pakistan. The Bangladesh of today, with a small area and meagre wealth of exploitable resources, has a greater concentration of want and poverty than any country in the world. Like Nepal, Bangladesh, too, has an abundance of water but not the same kind of mountains and gradients that have a potential for hydel generation. Notwithstanding the availability of natural gas, Bangladesh must import coal and oil for its needs. Being downstream in the Ganges, Brahmaputra and Barak basins, Bangladesh is at the mercy of India for moderating floods in the monsoon months (which jeopardize its agricultural productivity and its industrial development) and for regulating salinity from the tides and cyclones from the Bay of Bengal during the lean flow season.

The major riparian-related problem started when India proposed to implement a hundred-year-old proposal by Sir Henry Cotton, a British engineer, to divert a substantial part of the flow from the Ganges at Farakka for flushing the deteriorating port of Calcutta. India has plausible claims to the use of waters which are mostly generated in India. The hinterland of Calcutta port serves almost a third of India, encompassing thickly populated provinces and vital industrial and economic infrastructure, all of which have growing needs for fresh water. The climate of suspicion prevailing between India and Pakistan and the often protracted and frustrating negotiations on the division of the Indus system accelerated steps to establish rights of prior use on the Ganges and so hastened the Farakka project. The downstream economic needs and the long-term political consequences on relations in the area were not fully weighed. It is open to speculation whether the scope and timing of Farakka would have been the same if India had not been partitioned or the emergence of an independent Bangladesh had been foreseen. On the other side, Pakistan objected to the upstream diversions on the grounds that it would affect the traditional usage and needs of its eastern wing, but the objections also reflected the deep-seated adversarial attitudes and insufficient understanding of the importance of the Calcutta port.

The Farakka dispute had the features of a classic upper-lower riparian water-sharing conflict resembling in some respects the international disputes on the Colorado, Jordan, Tigris, Euphrates, etc. More to the point, it has some features of the unresolved problems between Karnataka and Tamil Nadu on the Cauvery, Madhya Pradesh and Gujarat on the Narmada, and Rajasthan and Punjab-Haryana on the waters of Beas-Sutlej, or indeed between Punjab, Sind and Baluchistan in Pakistan on the Indus. On the allocations from the Ganges within India itself, there may be a conflict in embryo between the increasing claims of the upper states of Uttar Pradesh and Bihar on the one hand and the downstream needs of West Bengal on the other. And thus West Bengal and Bangladesh may have parallel anxieties. While internal disputes can be consigned to a tribunal, the India-Bangladesh dispute can be resolved only by diplomatic negotiations. The crux of the problem is an old one—of optimal benefits between co-sharers of common resources. The Helsinki rules provide applicable guidelines but, whether a dispute is intra-federal or international, it is met with strong political resistance.

THE BIRTH OF BANGLADESH: HOPES AND REVERSALS

Beginning in 1960, many meetings took place between the experts and senior officials of India and Pakistan on Farakka, but these were largely dialogues of the deaf. However, in the wake of the establishment of Bangladesh, the changed political climate brought about the recognition that there were common stakes in the economic future of the two nations. Between 1972-5, the ministers and heads of government discussed the potential of riparian cooperation in a constructive spirit. A joint rivers commission was authorized to explore concrete projects and possibilities.

Farakka was nearing completion at a time when relations were exceptionally propitious between the two countries (1971-5). However, mutual sensitivities to the needs of the other country did not transform the negotiations into a will to compromise. Out of the statistically expected minimal flow of 55,000 cusecs during the leanest period, India claimed it required 40,000 cusecs to be diverted to the Hooghly. President Mujibur Rahman of Bangladesh, who had an obvious regard for and trust in Mrs Gandhi, would not initially concede even the right of India to make any diversion of the Ganges flow. Indeed, when the Indian government raised the matter in 1974-5, Mujibur Rahman did not want Farakka to be commissioned at all. Finally, on the basis of India's insistent pleas of its needs and friendship, he reluctantly conceded that only 15,000 cusecs would be diverted from Farakka and that too only for the year 1975-6.

After Sheikh Mujibur Rahman was assassinated in August 1975, relations between the two countries deteriorated sharply, and the negotiations in the summer of 1976 for future sharing ended in an ugly impasse. Forgetting the euphoria of liberation, public opinion in Bangaldesh was strongly aroused against India. Maulana Bhasani, a popular clerical leader, threatened to lead a march of hundreds of thousands across the India-Bangladesh boundary to demolish the Farakka dam. The government under Zia-ur-Rahman inscribed the item on the UN General Assembly agenda (1976). There was widespread international sympathy for Bangladesh. The internationalization of the dispute, however, carried the dangers of grave and protracted damage to Indo-Bangladesh relations. India urged continuing bilateral talks with the promise of a scaled-down demand in the lean season allocations. Because India had improved relations with Pakistan and initialled an agreement on the Salal, Pakistan helped in obtaining the withdrawal of the Farakka item from the UN agenda. Two rounds of talks followed while Mrs Gandhi was prime minister, which narrowed the differences. However, a five-year interim agreement was only reached in further rounds (April-October 1977) after the Janata government came to power. India scaled down its claims for the lean season allocations by another 1,500 cusecs below what was authorized by Mrs Gandhi's government. However, the Congress Party, which was in the opposition, bitterly denounced the agreement as a sacrifice of national interest, saying that the concession would endanger the Calcutta port. Nevertheless, in 1982, when the government was again led by Mrs Gandhi, the 1977 agreement was renewed without significant modification. So far, in the subsequent years, the exaggerated apprehensions by India for the Calcutta port or by Bangladesh for its economy from the upstream diversions have not come to pass.

The search for a long-term solution to augment the flow at Farakka, is, however, no nearer agreement. The alternative permanent solutions of building a water storage earmarked in Nepal for Farakka as proposed by Bangladesh or a giant canal from the Brahmaputra to the Ganges, cutting across north Bangladesh, as suggested by India, are not acceptable to the other country. It is not necessary here to recapitulate in detail the opposing arguments. Briefly, the position of India has been that the Ganges and Brahmaputra basin, taken together could satisfy the needs of both countries.

India has pointed to the heavier flow and the early monsoons in the north-east which through an inter-basin transfer could make available sufficient water to meet the needs of both countries. Moreover, by building dams in Arunachal on the tributaries of the Brahmaputra, the monsoon floods in Bangladesh could be moderated. Bangladesh on the other hand, has sought to restrict the proposal for augmentation to the Ganges system which includes many rich tributaries coming from Nepal, leaving the Brahmaputra to be treated as a separate system.

Discussions around these rival proposals have continued intermittently in the last decade and a half but with no substantial headway. A Memorandum of Understanding was signed by the two heads of government in 1985 at Nassau and a committee of experts was appointed with a new mandate. India also modified its earlier stand and agreed to a joint approach to Nepal, but Nepal questioned the benefits of facilitating India-Bangladesh riparian cooperation through earmarked storage in its own domain, which would have little lasting advantage, but instead would cause loss of land through submergence on its territory.

Meanwhile, the cost of no progress because of no solution is tangible in the mounting intensity of floods. The annual total damage may exceed Rs. 1,000 crore which probably exceeds the costs of ammunition and equipment losses in a conventional India-Pakistan war. In 1988, half of Bangladesh was submerged. Bangladesh is now preparing a national plan to moderate damage in one season and ensure greater availability in the lean months. It is noteworthy that while Bangladesh objected to inter-basin transfers in the discussions with India, the national plan envisages such transfers from the main rivers.

The fact is that such rationality in finding constructive compromises between the two countries has been subordinated by the psychological barriers of mistrust. Ever since Sheikh

Mujibur Rahman was killed, there is a feeling deep down in Bangladesh that India was not reconciled to the military governments that subsequently came to power. After a cold start, relations with the Zia-ur-Rahman government improved but only somewhat. The movement for the restoration of a multiparty democracy was suspected of being engineered by India when it was manifestly an internal political ferment. Eventually, the demand compelled the surrender of the regime of General Ershad and was widely acclaimed by the people regardless of their political affiliations. But in the elections of 1991, the old suspicion that India was politically partisan towards the Awami League was aroused and may well have been a factor in the triumph of Begum Khaleda Zia's Nationalist Party.

THE INHIBITING EXTRANEOUS LINKAGES

There are other constituents of the India-Bangladesh mistrust which have firmer basis in fact. The agreement on the Berubari-Teen Bigha exchange was reached between India and Pakistan in 1958. India took over half of Berubari but the corresponding obligation to lease Teen Bigha to connect with Dahagram and Angerpola has not been fulfilled. There was a protracted legal challenge to this 'alienation' of Indian territory, even though it was through an agreed exchange. The Supreme Court of India has finally dismissed the contention (1980) but India has not yet marshalled the political process to honour a solemn commitment. In the national memory of Bangladesh is also embedded the fact that after Sheikh Mujibur Rahman was killed, Tiger Siddiqui and the remnants of the Mukti Bahini were not only given refuge but also assisted in conducting raids into Bangladesh from the Garo Hills on the other side. The Chakmas of the Chittagong Hills suffered displacement because of the policies of Bangladesh and they have been agitating against the suffering and hardship inflicted on them. Bangladesh blames India for conniving in their protest which at times has taken violent shape. There is the more recent dispute on the maritime boundary to determine the ownership of New Moore, a delta island which has emerged near the coast in the Bay of Bengal. India has occupied the island. The reluctance to consign the question of ownership to international arbitration compounds fears that by its superior military capability, India is inclined to coerce and dominate Bangladesh and other small neighbours.

India pays a heavy price from this compendium of mistrust. The virtual isolation of India's north-east can be overcome only if the river transport and direct communication can be re-established through Bangladesh and so facilitate the development of the rich potential of Assam and the surrounding tribal states. Negatively, if an overpopulated Bangladesh cannot make dynamic progress—and, in this, controlling floods and improving the economic potential through riparian cooperation must be an important constituent—it is inevitable that migration from Bangladesh into the adjoining states of India will continue uncontrolled. Earlier, the fate of Hindus in East Pakistan/ Bangladesh evoked national concern in India but the migration of non-Hindus raises fears of a conspiracy to change the electoral arithmetic and the political complexion of India. The disaffection in Assam against 'foreigners' is only a foretaste of what may be more serious, both for domestic electoral politics in India and for neighbourly relations between the two countries. Illegal migration from a Bangladesh reeling under economic stagnation, as that from a desertified Nepal, cannot be contained by security vigilance and fences along the frontiers. This rumbling political-cum-economic earthquake cannot be quietened unless we muster the necessary political will to recognize that it is in India's national interest to so promote prosperity in the neighbours that this migrational tide is moderated.

THE CHALLENGE AND LESSONS FOR PURPOSEFUL NEGOTIATIONS

It is, of course, not easy for national leadership, which is often weak and vulnerable to populist sentiments and democratic opposition, to effect a political turnaround from past attitudes. But our own experience and lessons from the wider world suggest that such a change is not impossible; statesmanship and public opinion should be united to put the focus on the future. No progress is possible for any country if the legacy of past mistakes and misconceived political reservations towards other riparian partners are not corrected by deliberate policy. It is thus a challenge to diplomacy, which is after all the craft of negotiations for overcome the misperceptions between sovereign nations.

Through bureaucratic happenstance, as described elsewhere I was involved in the negotiations with Bangladesh, Nepal and Pakistan on problems directly or indirectly related to rivers. In each of them, the various governments in Delhi, when the broader implications were explained to them, allowed latitude beyond their previous positions to resolve the impasse that had persisted on Farakka for twenty years, on trade and transit with Nepal for nine years, and on the Salal project on the Chenab for seven years. The more enlightened political attitudes by India helped to modify the earlier rigidity and assuage the suspicions of the other side. Let me recall some specific points which have lessons for approaches and future negotiations:

i) The interim Farakka agreement was facilitated because, prior to the substantive negotiations, the harassing but transparently pointless raids into Bangladesh by the remnants of the Mukti Bahini from Indian territory were summarily stopped. The lesson is that as a curtain-raiser, and lubricant to any impending negotiations, the political climate must be improved by removing all possible prevailing irritants. The agenda may be specific but whether there is a will to compromise or not depends on the articulated or unexpressed political linkages.

ii) What one learnt from the negotiations on the trade and transit treaties was that the leverage and dangers from the omnibus treaty were minimal or hypothetical as compared to the Nepalese mindset that India denied respect to Nepal's independence. It was known that India had supported Afghanistan when the latter was claiming the right to transit across Pakistan after the latter had 'blockaded' the country on the Pakhtunistan demand. One treaty or two made very little substantive difference in controlling illegal trade into India. Smuggling, after all, is demand-driven and not just supplier induced. Smuggling from Dubai across the Arabian

Sea continues despite coastal patrols and a strong Indian customs regime and probably, if gold imports are included, the value exceeds what is brought in across the India-Nepal border. With an annual trade deficit of Rs. 300-500 crore between India and Nepal, 'smuggling' is an unorthodox method of correcting the rupee imbalance. Paradoxically, a customs regime along the India-Nepal frontier, of the kind that exists with Pakistan, would be even less effective, but it would economically and even politically alienate Nepal. By separating trade and transit, the fears of economic coercion of an India-locked small neighbour were temporarily removed and the political climate for Karnali negotiations was improved. Incidentally, the 'flirtation' with China and other powers was also somewhat moderated.

iii) In to the negotiations for a 690 megawatt power project at Salal in Kashmir on the Chenab, the difficulty was not just the background of the Indo-Pakistan suspicion, the dispute on Kashmir, and the provisions of the Indus Treaty, but the seated fear that India's purpose was not economic but a contingency preparation for a future India-Pakistan conflict. The entire political, bureaucratic, military and engineering establishment of Pakistan, by using provisions of the Indus Treaty, blocked consent to the run-of-the-river hydel project. After scores of meetings at different levels failed to obtain Pakistan's concurrence, India had all but decided to consign the dispute to international arbitration in accordance with the provisions of the treaty. The arbitration procedure—with each country choosing a nominee and the two together agreeing on a chairman—would necessarily have been time-consuming and the result could have been a less than optimal economic benefit for one or both countries. Meanwhile, public opinion in both countries would have exacerbated tensions and compelled greater political rigidity. In a high-level internal review, it was decided by Mrs Gandhi to make some technical concessions on the design of the dam, but in the negotiations what brought about a complete turnaround were calculations which demonstrated that damage to Pakistan from militarily abusing the storage facilities or

> obstructing military operations or truncating irrigation or causing downstream flood damage was minimal, indeed possibly non-existent. On the other hand, the penalty on India, from the loss of power, would be horrendously greater. The lesson was that data must be marshalled to assuage adversarial suspicions and not continue with the monologue on the possible gains or losses for one's own country. We agreed to slightly lower the height of the dam and block the bypass canal required for the construction, but the ultimate argument was that there was a limit to the extent to which India would cut its economic nose to politically or militarily spite Pakistan.

Incidentally it is worth mentioning in passing that since the Second World War, no existing irrigation or power project in a conflict area has ever been wilfully damaged. In India-Pakistan conflicts, the canal systems and major dams were never bombed. The Frelimo liberation movement against Portuguese Mozambique could have but never damaged the massive Cabora Bossa dam on the Zambezi which was financed by, and supplied massive power to the apartheid regime in South Africa. South Africa also did not intervene in a pre-emptive action to 'protect' the dam. This is relevant to the suspicions voiced in Nepal that Karnali, once built, could be appropriated by India disregarding Nepal's territorial integrity, and in India, that Nepal could switch off the surplus for India through internal malevolence or under influence of a hostile external counsel.

THE DIPLOMATIC CHALLENGE IN REORIENTING POLITICAL ATTITUDES

These stray examples must lead to the conclusion that when independence and cost-benefit stakes are so obviously high, sensitive efforts have to be marshalled through prophylactic diplomacy and in a sort of environmental engineering to change the political climate. When, for example, the national decision was taken on the integration of Sikkim into India, the rationale behind it should have been explained to Nepal and even Bhutan.

in advance. Nepal has from time to time accused India of overlooking the spirit of mutual consultations embodied in the 1950 Treaty of Friendship. If advance consultation or information sharing is for some reason not possible then quick damage-control diplomacy must try to preserve mutual trust and prevent unwarranted apprehensions. When the USSR intervened in Czechoslovakia (1968), the first country to be informed was the US, so that there was no suspicion that the Soviet Union would go on to move westwards after occupying the country.

Fostering a political climate which is conducive to compromise and concessions requires a conceptual approach which, in declaration and demonstration, envelopes all the countries in the region (Nepal, Bangladesh, Bhutan, Sri Lanka, Maldives and even Pakistan). India and China have the onerous problem of having more small neighbours than any other large country. Until the liberation of Bangladesh, by and large, India's relations with Nepal and Sri Lanka were unaffected by its adversarial relations with Pakistan. One cannot but recognize that in the 1960s and 1970s, there was a shared concern by all South Asian countries that India posed a threat to each and all of them. This unwarranted or exaggerated fear of the Indian hegemonistic ambition was unwittingly given credence by notions emanating from the US of the special role and responsibilities of regional gendarmes.

Experience should teach us to modify the old-fashioned notion of the use of coercive capability. The USSR with its military presence and ideological backing failed to establish an acceptable superintending domain in Eastern Europe. The US has not been able to make South America accept that the continent lies in its political sphere of influence. India obviously cannot shrink in size or power but every effort has to be made to revive the old faith that it respects other 'nationalisms' and does not rely on military might as the sanction behind diplomacy. On the other hand, both India and its neighbours can see that the large, and in many respects sophisticated, Indian economy is a mutual economic advantage. It provides a readily accessible and unsubstitutable market for the products of its neighbours and, should they want it, a source of credit and investment as well as appropriate and affordable technology for their own development. Not cutting off the economic nose to spite the neighbours' political face is a good adage for countries which are geographically contiguous partners.

When India voted differently from all South Asian nations on the Afghanistan issue (1980 onwards) and against Vietnam's attack and occupation of Kampuchea (1980), the security anxieties of India's neighbours deepened and found expression in the Bangladesh proposal to establish SAARC. However, the fact remains that the search for collective diplomatic strength and the small beginnings in regionalism did not arrest the debilitating trend towards increased militarization in their national policies. As it happens, old fears got strengthened. The air-dropping of food and civil supplies in north-east Sri Lanka in 1987, without previous clearance from the Sri Lankan government, was not seen as a humanitarian gesture but proof of disregarding national sovereignty. The dispatch of the IPKF, even though it had enabling or perhaps requested support from Sri Lanka, was seen by other neighbours as confirming their worst apprehensions that India would not desist from intervening militarily if it found it necessary in the pursuit of what it perceived as its own national compulsions. That the US all but approved of the dispatch of the IPKF did not make it less of a political mistake. In fact, there was an error in the military assessment of its success. The real tragedy is that the memory of the intervention may have long persisting adverse political consequences on India's relations with South Asia.

Extrapolating from these untoward and not necessarily unforeseeable consequences, what emerges is the validity of the mutual respect and equality of nations. Both as a normative principle of international law and behaviour and as a practical guide to policies in the twentieth century, nations must desist from coercion and subversion, and intervention in other nations. The days of figurative or actual gunboat diplomacy or stationing marines for years on end (as the US could do in Central America before the Second World War) are over. Notwithstanding the temporary exceptions in small islands like Grenada, coercing an independent country and more particularly a neighbour has proved costly and politically counterproductive. (Witness the US in Vietnam, the Soviet Union in Afghanistan, Egypt in Yemen, etc.) India, by calculated unilateral gestures, can restore confidence in its stated adherence to principles of equality and respect. While specific problems must be confined to bilateralism, the backdrop and impetus must be permeated with overall regional imperatives.

But India's neighbours must likewise become sensitive to India's national concerns on security and the important factor of Indian public opinion. Bhutan, which may have had some inward anxieties at the incorporation of Sikkim, showed shrewd non-provocative restraint and thus reaped enormous national gains for the country. The benefits of Chukha in obtaining vast amounts from the sale of the surplus power to India is a demonstration model in riparian cooperation which flowed from sophistication in diplomacy. On the other hand, Nepal's canvassing for being accepted as a 'zone of peace', which lacked substance and logic, predictably invited adverse reactions in India. Nepal, following a subcontinental variant of non-alignment by balancing aid and political relations with both her neighbours, made a mistake in allowing China to undertake projects in the Terai nearer the Indian border. It may be recalled that for over twenty years (1955-78), Afghanistan had coexisting aid relationships with both the USA and the USSR, but the former was not allowed to undertake projects north of the Hindukush, and the latter was not given permission for road construction south of Kabul. The arms acquisitions from China by Nepal amounted to a provocative statement risking revulsion in India and insignificant security gains for Nepal. For constructive approaches and a climate of trust, the small countries, no less than the big brother, must not take the others for granted and gratuitously imperil negotiations.

In all questions, such as major hydel or irrigation projects, beyond the feasibility studies and complex engineering designs, the effective negotiating leadership must be handled at the non-technical or foreign office level. Technical professionals get rigidly locked in irreducible minimums for maximum viability. But the policy decision and the negotiating approach must look to trade-offs between the optimal national gain and what is internationally feasible. Forty thousand cusecs were certified as the necessary minimum for effective flushing of the Hooghly, and an equal amount out of the available 55,000 cusecs in the leanest period was deemed essential by Bangladesh for controlling salinity and for economic needs. These irreconcilable minimums were part of the reason why negotiations became so bitter in 1975-7. It required an exceptionably able but also far-sighted and courageous minister like Jagjivan Ram to accept a compromise by prevailing over the technical advisers. The compromise on Farakka, reducing India's claim to 20,500 cusecs in the leanest period, proved fairly effective in improving draughts in Calcutta port and the corresponding reduction for Bangladesh has proved adequate. The controlling directions must come from the political leadership; the negotiating strategies must correspondingly be determined by those who can weigh the technical considerations with the diplomatic circumstances and margins. The 'generalist' is apt to be awed by the fat technical feasibility project reports. The military professional is almost duty-bound to prepare for worst-case scenarios based on future capabilities. There is no higher responsibility for a Foreign Office than to work to reduce the external threats, but there is no more important, even if difficult, challenge to a senior Foreign Service adviser than to have the courage to assess the likely as against the possible external dangers. The economic collapse of the USSR and the enfeeblement of the US are historical monuments of the economic and diplomatic professionals subordinating their responsibilities to 'Pentagon' orientation. China has improved its political standing in Nepal and Bangladesh not by brandishing its military prowess, but by sensitive and steady diplomacy. Just as war is considered too serious to be left entirely to the generals, the future of poverty eradication and economic progress cannot be left merely to engineers or dwarfed by soldiers. Realism about security is a precondition and the final lubricant to facilitate riparian and other trans-border cooperation.

Riparian relations are so vital to the future of the northern countries of South Asia that it would be expedient to establish subdivisions in the Foreign Offices to maintain steady interest in the negotiations and the implementation of riparian cooperation.

Compared to even disarmament and aid relationships, the importance of fresh-water diplomacy and the not unrelated international ecological threat deserves such an organizational improvement.

But, of course, in the final instance, directions can only come not from professionals but from political statesmanship which comprehends the gravity of the problem and the opportunity costs of delay. Only the political leadership can muster the will to find compromise solutions and embark on reorienting and educating its domestic political and public opinion. It is a slur on democracy and the comprehension of its citizens that even if all the implications are explained, they would acquiesce to greater degradation rather than support cooperation for future amelioration.

There are outside observers, some of them with genuine empathy for the subcontinent, who think nationalistic populism will never permit rational solutions. One adviser in Nepal, writing in the magazine *Himal* (May-June 1991) argued that Nepal could get power self-sufficiency without major projects like Karnali; so he asked why embark on projects to sell surplus power to India? But two can play the game of beggaring the neighbour. If selfish autarkism inhibits cooperation to help meet the power needs of India, then it would generate a retaliatory psychology and end in restrictions on 'foreigners' who are not born Indian citizens. That way lies national self-destruction. There can be no realistic alternative goal but to accept that the futures of these independent countries are all hostage to the prosperity of their riparian partners. It would be salutary to accept that no single country in the Ganges-Brahmaputra river basin is the sole master of its own destiny.

India has to play the critical catalytic role to bring about this transformation. It is also a challenge for SAARC. While specific problems must be consigned to bilateralism, the backdrop to all negotiations in the subcontinent must be permeated with the regional imperative. Within these constraints, after a collective decision of the Heads of Government, SAARC has been authorized to study the scope of regional economic cooperation. This must point to preferential tariffs within South Asia.

To transform the political climate and underscore the riparian interdependence of India, Nepal and Bangladesh (and also Bhutan), an autonomous South Asian Environmental Protection Authority should be established. It should have an equal number of official representatives from the participating countries and should also include non-official environmentalists and grass-roots developmental activists. This authority should be funded with an initial endowment and a pledged annual subvention by India, but constitutionally it should be made semi-independent of changes in governments. As a beginning, ten thousand young men and women should be given a year off (for which academic credit and 'brownie' points for subsequent employment could be promised as a reward) to work on wasteland reclamation in the upper catchment regions of both Nepal and India. A proposal like this would dramatically underline for public opinion that the nations have common stakes in Himalayan ecology and riparian cooperation. Such a project could be taken up under SAARC or outside SAARC, but once constituted, it should be largely autonomous. If such a lead is taken in ecological restitution on a regional basis, the creeping indifference of the international community towards South Asia could be arrested and even reversed.

It bears repetition that what is central and crucial is an enlightened political vision with the conviction that to fight the war against poverty, it is not the power of the gun or self-righteous national defiance that must be in command. Security and stability are now contingent on economic dynamism. The scientific, engineering and technological disciplines must send out one message, loud and clear: that it is an illusion that we can command the elements—the soil, the air, the water—for the nation's benefit as they simply defy territorial frontiers. Governments must be prepared to tell their people that riparian chauvinism is an invitation to a condemned national future. Cooperation amongst riparian partners is the only answer to treeless hills, a parched landscape and a burning stone in one season and turbulent, flowing, ocean-like rivers in another. It is also the only answer to hunger and thirst which gnaw at the entrails of millions and are putting all governments internally on the defensive. This region with an ancient heritage and God-given advantage must be inspired by a new faith, that national independence and progress go hand in hand with international interdependence and enlightened cooperation.

PART FOUR

Diplomacy between Unequal and Equal Neighbours

9

India and Nepal

Behind the current confrontation between Nepal and India, there seems to be an unspoken compact to take a worm's eye view of national futures. This at least is how the present crisis in India-Nepal relations will appear to a historian from either country ten years from now. The interdependence between India and Nepal is permanent because the high Himalayas run to the north of both countries which makes the Gangetic basin, to which Nepal also belongs, an integrated ecological system. The rivers flowing south are oblivious to sovereignty and frontiers, but over the millennia these life-giving waters brought about manifold cultural, religious, ethnic and economic linkages which got translated into a sense of kinship and common destiny binding Nepal and India.

Over the last forty years, the security scenarios and threat contingencies have remained unaltered: they are neither less nor more serious. But in the wake of decolonization, the rise of nationalism, the advances in technology, the information revolution, and the general diversification of relations among all nations, the political circumstances in the subcontinent and the world have changed wholly. But geography, which dictates that their separate and common interests can only be optimized in cooperation with each other, has not altered. The failure of diplomacy has been in not adjusting in style and form to what Burke called the changing 'empire of circumstances'. For outside observers, it is hard to detect the subjective factors like the chemistry of personal equations amongst decision makers. One cannot, however, help noting that the current positions have not

*Published in *Hindustan Times*, 28 May 1989. This was written soon after the Indo-Nepalese Trade and Transit Treaties, concluded in 1978, were allowed to lapse and so most points of entry and outlets between the two countries were closed.

seen even an oblique reference to the yardstick of long-term goals. While the present crisis may end with one country relenting, the other bending, or both compromising, it will leave a bitter residue of political alienation and there will be an even longer postponement in rediscovering the ultimate compulsions of their enmeshed futures.

The two Treaties of Friendship and of Trade, when signed in 1950, were predicated on the understanding that Nepal and India were indissolubly tied in security, commerce and unrestricted rights of movement and residence for citizens of both countries. They were concluded when India had become independent and the constituent assembly had committed itself to democracy, secularism and progressive social idealism. Nepal, however, was still under the Rana oligarchy. Partly by choice and partly by British imposition, Nepal had remained isolated from the rest of the world. It did not even have a motorable link with India; it had no foreign trade and no foreign exchange. The Ranas bought their Rolls Royces and Venetian chandeliers in Calcutta, and the British Government in India provided the sterling for the luxury needs of the senior members of the family. Nepal was independent internally, but externally it was a kind of satellite appendage of the British Indian Empire. With Indian independence on the one side and the triumph of communism in China and the threatened use of military to integrate Tibet on the other, the Rana oligarchy was apprehensive not just about the future of its own privileged dispensation but even of Nepal's separate existence. The conclusion of the treaty with the last Rana prime minister signified India's acceptance of Nepal's independent personality, but it also carried the implicit assurance that India would not subvert the internal regime, even if the regime was repugnant to its own ideals. The treaty actually disappointed the Nepali Congress leadership which expected India to make a parallel push for democratization in Nepal.

After the overthrow of the Rana regime and the transfer of authority to King Tribhuvan in 1951—India did not conspire with the king but helped the resolution of the crisis—India guided Nepal into the modern world by advice, not by dictation. (There were some incidents of pro-consular arrogance and high-handedness but these were not under Prime Minister Nehru's direction.) India built the motorable road link (the Tribhuvan Rajpath) and the airstrip in Kathmandu. Our assistance started Nepal on economic development and in drafting a democratic constitution which safeguarded the privileged position and the overriding discretion of the monarchy. By 1960, Nepal had a separate foreign exchange account, initially in the Reserve Bank of India and later in a Central Bank of their own.

It was Prime Minister Nehru who encouraged King Mahendra to come to Bandung in 1955 and introduced him to Chou-en-Lai. India welcomed the Nepal-China agreement which was, *mutatis mutandis*, modelled on our own 1954 agreement relating to the Tibet region. We endorsed the new diplomatic contacts promoted by Nepal. In 1955, India sponsored and canvassed for Nepal's entry into the UN (the Soviet Union incidentally did not endorse it). In brief, India was the guide, example and inspiration for Nepal's internal progress and development, and we also shepherded its entry into the arena of international politics.

Today, some criticize Pandit Nehru for awakening and unleashing Nepal and so encouraging it to international gamesmanship with other powers at the expense of India's interests. India's indulgence is unfavourably contrasted to the realpolitik and strategic rationale of China overwhelming the autonomy of Tibet. Tibet's position under international law is a separate question, but even after forty years the jury of international opinion is still out on whether China has best served its own ends by the methods it followed.

In any case, independent India was born with a different ethos. Our independence signified the end of colonialism and gave legitimacy to nationalism all over Asia and Africa. India rejected the arguments of orderly tutored guidance and controlled restraints in the involvement in world affairs. Nehru's initial approach to Nepal was prophetically in tune with the inevitability and march of time. The gallop of technology, especially of transportation and communication, was bound to repudiate some hoary old axioms like the impregnability of the Himalayas and the total dependence of the poor and small countries on the beneficent direction of the big powers. Modern media was bound to galvanize political awareness, and the sense of separate political identities of states even smaller or more handicapped than Nepal. The growth of population and increase of the educated were bound to raise demands for preference in domestic employment opportunities. Our small neighbours could not be quarantined from the twentieth-century exhilaration of independence especially when India was the spokesman and example of assertive nationalism. We should not have been surprised when we were flattered by imitation and Nepal got tempted to adopt a sub-continental variant of non-alignment between two powerful contending neighbours.

Let me briefly recall some of the twists and turns where diplomacy on both sides avoidably obscured or damaged the meaningful content of our bilateral relations. The first India-Nepal projects for flood control and irrigation on the Kosi and Gandak envisaged enormous benefits for India but provided for insufficient gains, and even some negative consequences, for Nepal. (At that time Nepal had no engineers to foresee these adverse effects.) Kosi and Gandak projects have cast a shadow on all subsequent negotiations for India-Nepal riparian cooperation. Having sponsored Nepal to the international arena, we were somewhat taken aback at Nepal's determination to demonstrate its independence from Indian tutelage. In 1956 itself, which was the very first UN session in which it participated, Nepal took up a position different from India's on Hungary. In 1959 it was the government headed by B.P. Koirala—an old freedom-fighter in the Indian struggle for independence—that adopted a neutral position when the Sino-Indian crisis erupted. When the democratic Constitution of Nepal was abrogated in 1960 by King Mahendra and the elected Koirala government was dismissed, Prime Minister Nehru spontaneously expressed his regret at the smothering of democracy in Nepal. For a while it would seem that even armed forays by Nepali Congress sympathizers from Indian soil were tolerated and connived at. India's reactions to the internal political development were denounced as interference in Nepal's domestic affairs. The episode is generally forgotten in India but frequently recalled in Nepal. It seized the moment of Sino-Indian tensions to play into the Chinese design which was to diplomatically isolate India. In the Sino-Nepal boundary talks, Nepal preferred not to recognize that the logic by which China claimed the whole of Arunachal—up to the edge of the plains—was consistent with the old Ching notion (and shown in some cartographic depictions) that Nepal and Bhutan and the northern half of Burma, Vietnam, etc., were old tributaries of China. On the other hand, the Indian case corroborated Nepal's own position that the southern border of the Tibet region ran along the Himalayan watershed. Indeed, the Nepalese contention implicitly confirmed that the MacMahon line had a traditional validity. Nepal's detachment in the Sino-Indian crisis became a milestone in the erosion of the spirit behind the 1950 treaty. To underline that it had come of age (or was it to win credit with China?) Nepal asked for the withdrawal of the Indian check posts along the northern border and the closure of the Indian military liaison mission in Kathmandu which was provided at Indian expense to modernize the Nepalese army.

From time to time, however, there was a return to the old pro-Indian tilt and implicit dependence on India. For example, during the Cultural Revolution in 1966 and onwards, when the Red Guards were demanding defiant militancy even in embassies abroad, the Nepalese government was offended that the Chinese mission even insulted the King and defied orders prohibiting demonstrations. The claim to Sagarmatha (Mt. Everest) and the incident of intrusion in Mustang—where Nepalese border guards were killed by Chinese patrols inside Nepal—evoked strong reactions. But China was quick to retrieve lost ground and wherever possible, seized opportunities to undermine India's standing in Nepal. In the 1970s, for example, China fully exploited the integration of Sikkim. Predictably it had created private anxieties in Bhutan but generated a public outcry in Nepal. The reactions in Sikkim led to several years of tepid relations between the two countries. The Soviet intervention in Afghanistan was another unintended setback to Indo-Nepal relations. Nepal sided with the non-aligned majority while India was more indulgent to the Soviet position. For Nepal, as it was for Bhutan, the vote was a kind of indirect protest against great powers overwhelming small neighbours.

Disappointments and complaints have been expressed time and again in India, that Nepal has shown no gratitude for the volume and diversity of our aid in the country's economic development. Our disappointment is not unlike reactions voiced in the US towards aid recipients. Donors/recipients generally show very grudging acknowledgement, indeed the donors often become a foil for the nationalism of the recipient.

If our judgement had kept abreast of modern realities, it should also have been obvious from the time it was admitted to the UN that Nepal would graduate to expect the rights of transit as for any landlocked country under international laws that were also incidentally affirmed in the declarations of the non-aligned, the G-7 and others.* India itself was sympathetic to Afghanistan in the 1950s, when in the wake of the agitation for Pakhtunistan, Pakistan denied the use of Karachi for Afghan exports and imports. We could not agree to Lesotho, which is surrounded by South Africa's racialist regime, being subjected to sanctions because it did not acquiesce in apartheid. All land-locked countries expect, as a right, the same transit privileges as the Swiss were accorded in peace and as were conceded even by belligerents during the two world wars. At this stage, it is unrealistic even to have transit rights of Nepal conditional on the end of smuggling, or in any way question Nepal's independent commerce. Nepal now has a road link to the north, and this crisis may become an inducement to build other roads up to and across Tibet, possibly linking them to the Karakoram highway to Karachi. Both the anti-communist Shah and fundamentalist Ayatollah of Iran made use of the highways through the USSR, even when relations with the northern neighbour were not good. Even if Nepal now accepts a single treaty for trade and transit, the psychological and political legacy will try to dilute the dependency on India in spite of economic costs to Nepal.

Even smuggling requires some deeper analysis. Because of the natural economic complimentarity with India, Nepal buys some Rs. 500 crore worth of goods from India every year. Beyond invisibles like Gurkha remittances and limited sales of agricultural

*For a detailed study see J.S. Mehta, *Negotiating for India*, New Delhi: Manohar, 2006, ch. 7.

products, there is very little possibility for Nepal to balance the Indian rupee trade. After its success in tourism, it has occasionally bought rupees with convertible exchange to meet its urgent payment obligations to India. India cannot offer loans every year to cover the vast deficit in trade. Over these decades, a part of the rupee trade gap was filled by India asking and Nepal supplying timber for sleepers for our railways. (We were thus, unthinkingly party to aggravating the floods in Bihar and eastern UP.) Smuggling in the final instance is the economic consequence of imbalanced trade and disparate economies. Seen in an unorthodox way, Nepal's foreign exchange earnings contribute to mopping up a part of the insatiable Indian demand for foreign goods.

India is apparently having great difficulty in controlling the smuggling of arms, drugs and gold even though the Indo-Pakistan border is heavily militarized. Similarly, despite the intervening Arabian Sea, the vigilance of our coastguard patrols and the long experience of our customs regime, smuggling from Dubai and the Gulf is greater in volume and value than through the open India-Nepal border. Needless to add, for moral as well as economic reasons, smuggling and unauthorized trade from any source must be plugged as earnestly as possible, but we must remember that economic coercion or even sanctions have seldom achieved the desired political or economic objectives. Nepal now has direct aerial links as far afield as Frankfurt, Singapore, Hong Kong, Bangkok, not to mention Karachi, Colombo and Dhaka. Millions cross the India-Nepal border both ways. The import policy of a semi-industrialized giant like India is bound to be different from that of Nepal. For all these reasons, the lure and scope of unauthorized trade cannot be effectively scotched whether there are one or two treaties. (It is no secret that a sizeable number of Indians are involved in this smuggling.) The costs of attempting a total control of unauthorized trade—by such means as electronic surveillance, deploying paramilitary forces or even building a wall along 800 miles—may far exceed the value of decades of smuggling and even then may not be effective. The US and Canada are moving towards a common market. We cannot emulate them but we must also not move in the opposite direction. The political and international consequences for the future of our relations by creating such a non-effective barrier with Nepal could be so far-reaching that responsible citizens on both sides should pause before from even speculating about them. In the final instance, smuggling across the Indo-Nepal border will only end at some distant date, when the people's expectations are nearer fulfilment and both countries prosper more or less in equal measure. We should encourage the industrial development of Nepal and give privileged access to the Nepalese manufactures into the Indian market. However, in the foreseeable future, smuggling will remain a pernicious proof of special geographic interdependence, and the disparities in the economic capacities of the two countries.

But Nepal, too, must recognize that nationalism is not a charter to slash its economic nose to spite India's political face. Most of Nepal's needs are readily available in India. Nepal simply cannot afford the opportunity costs of obtaining essential imports from other sources. With détente and perestroika, the aid fountains even for small countries like Nepal, both from the communist countries like China and the USSR and the consortia countries of the West, are going to stagnate or reduce in real value. Investment and even aid from India may still provide the only substantial source of investment for Nepal's development. Beyond the limited availability of trained Nepalese, because of language, religion, ethnic links and lower wage bill, suitable trained manpower and higher professionals for Nepal could best be found in India. Our ties are symbolized by the temples of Varanasi and of Pashupatinath. Any heroic efforts at distancing from India will only mean further impoverishment of the common man in Nepal and the country as a whole. Rejecting India and Indians would be like Uganda's Idi Amin's economic war. He started a process which put a potentially rich country into a regressive spiral from which even twelve years after Amin's fall, Uganda has not yet recovered. Such symbolic assertive nationalism like buying anti-aircraft guns from China adds nothing to Nepal's security but embarrasses whatever friends Nepal has in India.

The truth is, India and Nepal have got locked into a duel of self-destructive, self-righteous legalities because they have not husbanded and modernized their interdependence. Old special relations have not adjusted to new circumstances. There are still claims of special relations between the USA and the UK but no Englishman would now nonchalantly affirm that the fog in the Channel means Europe is isolated. The white Dominions still have a special affection for the Commonwealth but they do not now consign their strategic plans or even their nuclear policy to be decided by the Imperial General Staff in London. We are seeing a restructuring of the political relationship in the Warsaw Pact countries and in NATO, because of the need to adjust to defiant nationalism. China no doubt lured Nepal in the 1950s and 1960s, but it would seem that now it is Nepal which is playing the China card. The initiative for having arms from China, one suspects, came from Nepal. However, it is unrealistic to have expected that China—even if it was genuinely enthused by the prospect of improving Sino-Indian relations—would exercise a self-denying restraint and not respond positively to requests from Nepal or do so only after consulting India. China is now not in an expansionist or adventurous phase in its foreign policy but it has always had a longer perspective in its external relations. China was quick to score a point by readily endorsing the ambiguous notion of Nepal being accepted as the 'zone of peace'. One must, therefore assume that China must relish the irony of being looked upon with trust as the balancing protector of the Hindu Kingdom of Nepal.

Because of the current imbroglio, the greatest hardship must be on the poorest on both sides, but notably on those in Nepal who live outside the Kathmandu valley. There may be more than six million persons of Indian origin living in Nepal; a large number from Bihar and Orissa seek temporary employment in the Nepali terai at harvest time. On the other side, like the Central Americans who flock to the US, the Nepalese come down from the hills to seek jobs and opportunities in India. There must be over ten million persons of Nepalese origin long settled in the Indian provinces. There must be several scores of battalions in the Gorkha Regiments of the Indian Army and in the Assam Rifles who feel the ultimate identification with India. It would be a travesty to decry them as mercenaries but, still, it can be a grave risk to strain their loyalties by prolonged tensions with Nepal.

The hardship to Gorkha families in Nepal could affect the morale of the Gorkha soldiers in India. There could not be more than a few thousand Nepalese and Tibetans (mostly traders and muleteers) whose livelihood depends on good relations between China and Nepal; on the other hand, there must be some twenty million in India and Nepal who, in one way or the other, have a vested interest in harmonious and friction-free relations between these two countries. Notwithstanding its dilution in form, the effective 'dependence' and interdependence in India and Nepal must have increased a thousand-fold since the 1950 Treaty was signed. But this does not give either country capacity for one-sided blackmail.

The real Himalayan miscalculation lies not in any particular episode in the past but rather in not thinking of national futures. The hypothetical strategic scenario has not proved as menacing as many analysts argued. The security threat perception was being advanced by the intellectual second cousins of cold warriors but the parameters of the Cold War are being agonizingly reappraised everywhere. China's improved standing in Nepal has come about not by the threat of the use of force but by Chinese diplomacy. The undeniable, unchanging certainty is the tectonic rumbling of poverty and the vast population in Nepal and the adjoining Gangetic plains. If both India and Nepal raise their sights from the current fray, we could recognize there is no hope of India and Nepal repairing any dent to their macro-economic destiny without steady, unwavering trust and long term cooperation between the two countries. The facts are well known but they seemed to have been largely overlooked in the plethora of non-official comments. The natural resources of Nepal consist of forests and the waters which, unlike in the Indian plains, tumble down the Himalayan gradients. Simply by destroying the former and delaying the harnessing of the latter, Nepal has held to ransom the progress of the vast population belt of Bihar, Uttar Pradesh, and further downstream Bangladesh and West Bengal. On the other hand, the hydroelectric potential of Nepal (conservatively estimated at 85,000 megawatts) could, by development and sale of surplus power to India, transform the poverty of Nepal and, without fanciful exaggeration, ease the dire problems of the Gangetic provinces of India. It is a perfect fit of interdependence and the dream and challenge for development economists, engineers, and social scientists.

To move towards this feasible goal, the diplomacy of the two countries must navigate by a distant star and not get caught in the eddies and then turn them into storms as if national honour and prestige were in peril. The current crisis will look like a storm in a teacup in the future, but it will so vitiate the political atmosphere that progress on the well-identified joint projects like Karnali, Pancheshwar and Rapti may be postponed by years. The opportunity costs of this delay are not just that costs go up astronomically. For example, on the 4,500 megawatt project on the Karnali, which was identified twenty-five years ago, the estimates have probably mounted from, say, Rs. 300-500 crore in 1960s to perhaps Rs 6,000-8,000 crore at current prices. The foreign exchange we would have saved on imports of oil and petroleum products if the Karnali had come on-stream fifteen years ago may well have saved the desperate crunch we face today. More than this, each year, instead of selling surplus power, Nepal sends us the unrequired export of perhaps a billion tons of silt, which translates into an ever-increasing intensity of floods in the Gangetic plains. The annual damage in India from the Nepal share of silt may run into Rs. 1,000 crore.

Nepal must not pretend that it can comfortably do without preferential access to the Indian market. To depend on nothing more than the most favoured nation treatment in the trade with India is inviting cruel and needless hardship on the Nepalese people. India, of course, must recognize that even if it could barricade the India-Nepal border, it would be neither politically expedient nor legally justified to deny Nepal the right of transit, independent of the trade pattern. Statesmanship in India and Nepal must ensure, once and for all, that the two countries remain on a steady undeflected course of trust and friendship and move towards a common market. Professional diplomacy must anticipate and prevent, in good time, the outraging of the sensitive concern of the other country—if only because it will cause incremental damage in one's own nation.

Once again, a crisis in the subcontinent is likely to be regretted and would even embarrass the larger non-aligned fraternity and that too as we approach another summit in Belgrade. Our best friends will not want to see this crisis prolonged. What has transpired will be a more serious setback to SAARC than the presence of the IPKF in Sri Lanka. If the impasse is not resolved amicably, the new regional grouping may survive in form but will stall any substantive progress. The canard of Indian hegemonistic ambitions will get more grist for the propaganda mill, especially after the left-handed, if not deliberately mischievous, cover page story in an international magazine about India fancying itself as a potential superpower. In the interest of easing the hardship to the Nepalese people and reversing the damage to India's international standing, and, above all, to get a focus on the common ecological future, the two countries must forswear the present directions of policies.

Humiliated nations do not make pliable partners in progress. To make a new beginning we can again learn from Gorbachev who, with measured but enlightened unilateralism, has gone far to assuage deep-seated fears and moderate rigid national postures. Diplomacy in the twentieth century must reckon with small countries wielding the whiplash to inflict damage and sometimes defeat on big powers; indeed, new nationalism gets spurred by prestige into defiance, which takes masochistic satisfaction in disregarding the penalties of self-mortification. Therefore, the bigger country has to stoop not to conquer but to win trust and cooperation for larger benefits to both countries. India can set an example for North-South relations through this South-South crisis which has many parallel disparities. We could thus play a leadership role to reinforce the new international climate of economically and ecologically oriented priorities for peace.

Plate 7: 1959. Dalai Lama arriving in Birla House, Musoorie after escape from Lhasa. Author received him on behalf of GOI.

Plate 8: 1960. Palam tarmac before PM left to sign the Indus Treaty. Discussion was on my suggestion that while J&K may be disputed between India and Pakistan, the two countries could agree on the boundaries of pre-independence Kashmir. The suggestion was advanced by PM but was not followed up.

Plate 9: 1972 Dar-es-Salaam. President Julius Nyerere talking to Rama Mehta when author was High Commissioner.

Plate 10: April 1976. Taking over as Foreign Secretary from Kewal Singh. Others were secretaries and additional secretaries including future President, K.R. Narayanan.

Plate 11: April 1976. Mrs. Margaret Thatcher, then leader of the Opposition, being received by the author.

Plate 12: May 1977. 9 Kensington Palace Gardens. Dinner during Commonwealth Prime Ministers conference. British dignitaries present, including Harold Macmillan, etc. Lord Mountbatten and High Commissioner B.K. Nehru and author sitting on the floor.

Plate 13: 1977. British Prime Minister Callaghan and author in front of 10, Downing Street, London.

Plate 14: Kremlin October 1977. PM Morarji Desai with Brezhnev, Kosygin and members of the Politburo.

Plate 15: February 1978. Foreign Minister, A.B. Vajpayee and Gromyko with Ambassador Gujral and author standing behind.

Plate 16: Palam 1978. Phan Van Dong, the Prime Minister of Democratic Republic of Vietnam being received by Morarji Desai. Author in the background.

Plate 17: June 1978. White House, Washington. President Carter greeting the author.

Plate 18: June 1978. Connecticut, home of Chester Bowles. PM Morarji Desai called on Chester Bowles. Author and Sally Bowles present.

Plate 19: June 1978. Premier Kosygin shaking hands with author. The map of Asia is in the background.

Plate 20: Riyadh August 1978. Foreign Minister of Saudi Arabia talking to author prior to Non-aligned Foreign Ministers conference in Belgrade.

Plate 21: Patna 1978. Lok Nayak Jayaprakash Narayan talking to author.

Plate 22: Havana 1979. President Fidel Castro, Foreign Minister L.N. Mishra during the Non-aligned summit. Author in the background.

Plate 23: 1998. PM A.B. Vajpayee visited Udaipur and spoke at the Vidya Bhawan Institute of Local-Self Government.

Plate 24: 2002. Rastrapati Bhawan. President K.R. Narayanan conferred the award of Padmabhushan to the author.

Plate 25: 2002. Jeewan Niwas, Udaipur. Henry Kissinger called on the author.

Plate 26: 2002. Jeewan Niwas, Udaipur. Dr. Manmohan Singh called on the author when he was Leader of the Opposition.

Plate 1: 1950. The first Cultural Cooperation Agreement between USA and India. The signatories are PM J. Nehru and US Ambassador Loy Henderson. Sitting and looking on is Maulana Azad, the Education Minister. Standing, Dr . Tara Chand, Education Secr etary. Also in the pictur e ar e C.S. Jha, JS MEA, I.S. Chopra, DS MEA, and my wife Rama Mehta, then Under Secretary, Americas.

Plate 2: Burgenstock, Switzerland, 1953. Group of Indian Heads of Missions meet with PM Jawaharlal Nehru.

Plate 3: Burgenstock 1953. Series of photographs of J. Nehru taken by author overlooking Lake Lucern.

Plate 4: Engelberg 1953. Swiss Skiing Resort. Three PMs, present and future in a row (Jawaharlal Nehru, Indira Gandhi and Rajiv Gandhi). Sanjay with back towards camera and Ambassador and Mrs. Gundevia looking on.

Plate 5: Paro 1958. Prime Minister Nehru and His Majesty the King of Bhutan watching the national archery competition. Author behind the Prime Minister in Bhutanese dress.

Plate 6: 1958 French Embassy. J. Nehru shaking hands with Andre Malraux, French Minister for Culture.

10

India and Pakistan: We Know the Past; Must We Live in It?

It is a perversity of our times that diplomacy has become increasingly backward-looking. We expend our skills and energies on explanations, rationalizations, accusations, domestically oriented populism and external propaganda, and much less on understanding and persuasion between sovereign nations. Historical evidence is used selectively and becomes an oppression of worst-case scenarios. The irrelevance of history and the lessons we can learn escape us, and our problems are avoidably perpetuated.

The Indian subcontinent has a long history prior to British hegemony. Considering the circumstances of the partition, it was expected that post-independence relations between India and Pakistan would be difficult. During these decades there has been a running conflict between the independent dynamics of regional politics and the globalism of the superpowers. The superpowers alternated between indifference and conflict management, partisan involvement and exasperation, and the regional powers oscillated between dependence on and independence from outside powers. In varying measures, each country was guilty of inaccurate contemporaneous judgement, but this was compounded by the intertwining of the two dynamics. In South Asia, only the Soviet Union emerged with net political gains beyond what might have been anticipated at the end of the Second World War, and that too largely because windows of opportunity were opened to it. But after Afghanistan, even the USSR must have had agonizing regrets.

*Paper prepared for the Conference on Security of South Asia, University of Illinois at Urbana-Champaign, 1984.

1947-65: SOUTH ASIAN CONFLICT AND THE COLD WAR

Without recounting the entire history in detail, it is worth mentioning some milestones in this story of misperceptions.

It is well known that even before India and Pakistan could settle down to their independence, they became locked in a military and dramatic confrontation over Kashmir.[1] The expectation was that these two Dominions would remain economically dependent and politically pliant at least like the white Dominions in the Commonwealth. Pakistan's case concerning Kashmir and the Anglo-American attitude towards it were fundamentally an extrapolation of the pre-Independence rationale of religion determining the frontiers of the new Dominions. India argued that legally valid frontiers have the sanctity of international law against all forms of intervention. Despite a sense of disappointment with Anglo-American attitudes, India's relations with the West remained largely warm and trusting. In 1949, India decided to remain in the Commonwealth and Nehru expressed fulsome admiration for and gratitude to the American democracy during his first visit to the United States in the same year. Despite Nehru's open admiration for Soviet civilization and achievement, the Soviet Union extended an invitation in 1950 to Pakistani prime minister Liaquat Ali Khan, to visit the USSR and failed to extend such a courtesy to Nehru during the Stalin era.

It is often forgotten that the USSR adopted a neutral stand in the Kashmir debates in the Security Council during the 1948-53 period. It was detached on the resolutions constituting the UNCIP, the proposals made by General McNaughton (Canada), the selection of Sir Owen Dixon of Australia as mediator (1950) and indifferent to Commonwealth mediation (1951). The USSR criticized Anglo-American interference (which the British delegate described as fantasy), but even so, the Soviet Union never obstructed Western diplomacy during the period. When direct Indo-Pakistan talks were in progress during 1951-3, Nehru had warned the great powers to keep out of the problem. However, the West failed to anticipate that instead of the US-Pakistan mutual security arrangements (1953-4) doubling the pressure on

India, they would only provoke disenchantment and defiance and lead to the ending of discussions on the plebiscite modalities.

The endorsement of Kashmir's accession to India during the visit of Khrushchev and Bulganin only followed the Baghdad Pact and SEATO. The first Soviet veto was exercised in 1957, by which time even Ambassador Gunnar Jarring of Sweden had reported that the situation had materially changed. In brief, it was the intrusion of the Cold War that polarized and militarized South Asia. In India, the need to increase the military budget gathered momentum only after the India-China war of 1962.

China's relations with the subcontinent also contradicted the Cold War syndrome of global bipolarity. The US, the USSR, Pakistan, and indeed, China and India were taken aback when the Sino-Indian crisis of confidence erupted in the wake of the 1959 revolt in Tibet. During the 1959-62 period, the USSR oscillated between commitment to fraternal China and friendship for India. What is of interest is that at the end the Sino-Indian conflict (and the Cuban missile crisis) in 1962, the Soviet Union was not even alarmed at the rise of US influence.[2] There is no evidence that the Soviet Union did anything to frustrate the Averell Harriman-Duncan Sandys' shuttles between India and Pakistan. It may be open to speculation that, had Anglo-American diplomacy succeeded in bringing about pledges or peace and mutual respect and *de facto* acquiescence to existing lines of control, it would have been a sort of forerunner of Tashkent. The USSR may even have welcomed it.

Cemented only by their shared hostility to India and disregarding their communist-anti-communist leanings, China and Pakistan established bilateral relations. However, the United States was not even seriously concerned when, at the height of the Vietnam war (1967-9), China and later the Soviet Union supplied military hardware to Pakistan, which was still a US ally.

The next crisis in the subcontinent was the Indo-Pakistan war of 1965. Although the USSR had quietly acquiesced to American attempts at Indo-Pakistan rapprochement in 1962, the United States actually encouraged the Soviet role as mediator after the 1965 India-Pakistan conflict and expressed satisfaction at the success of Kosygin's diplomacy at Tashkent in 1966. This was the symbolic *obiter dictum* of the 125-year-old British policy of containing Russia and preventing it from gaining political access to the subcontinent and its limitrophic warm waters. It was not till 1979-80 that alarm was expressed but that was following the Soviet invasion of Afghanistan.

While professing to defend and promote democracy, the United States chose to establish relations with non-democratic governments in Pakistan. Similarly, the Soviet Union maintained relations with India's communist parties, but whenever there was a conflict between support for the established Central Government of India and their own ideological confreres, Moscow supported the former, often leaving the pro-Soviet parties in a state of dismay. The policies in South Asia of both superpowers have been ideologically agnostic; their propaganda and rhetoric have only caused confusion.

Notwithstanding the leverage of arms supply and economic aid, both superpowers have found that the regional powers were never wholly politically pliant, even on non-subcontinental issues. The United States never really controlled Pakistan's foreign policy. Pakistan's position on Israel was always critical of the United States; Pakistan befriended China and SEATO became all but defunct when China was most hostile and the United States was actively canvassing for political support on Vietnam. India was, no doubt, sensitive to the Soviet position on Hungary in 1956 and supported the USSR on some issues on the international agenda, but it remained detached and neutral on the Sino-Soviet rift, even when Sino-Indian relations were at their nadir. Later, India refused to endorse the Brezhnev doctrine for Asia and the notion of the non-aligned as 'the natural allies of the socialist bloc'.

What is common in all these cases is the deviation from the conventional wisdom that the bipolar Cold War syndrome dominated and determined the problems and politics of the subcontinent throughout these decades. It was the hypnosis created by East-West postures—taken too seriously both by protagonists and opponents—which culminated in the tragedy of the 1965 conflict.

Most of these fallacies could have been foreseen. Whatever

mutual assurances, public and confidential, were exchanged between the United States and Pakistan, the latter was not seriously committed to fight the communist states, and it was naïve to think the United States could ever be militarily involved against India. India could have been more diplomatically agile in forestalling the US-Pakistan security arrangements before 1953 and could have pre-empted the development of the China-Pakistan relationship in the early 1960s, which led to military supplies and a coordinated anti-Indian diplomacy. In general, various intellectual failures led to the exacerbation of regional problems by great power politics and this allowed the illusions to persist as long as they did. The resultant frustrations of all the powers in the quadrilateral were largely avoidable.

1965-80: THE REGION ON ITS OWN

The 1965 conflict was a dramatic jolt to the Cold War paradigm, and Tashkent was a turning point. It was really the end of a decade of East-West competitive globalism in the subcontinent. Contrary to the spirit of their military agreements, American weapons were used by Pakistan against India. Subsequently, the United States withdrew her military and economic aid to both India and Pakistan, causing much dismay, especially in Pakistan. While the two superpowers made coordinated efforts to defuse the 1965 conflict and subsequently muted their competition in the subcontinent, China turned blatantly partisan, and through frivolous but calculated ultimata, sought to influence the military outcome. But even China was not prepared to intervene directly in the conflict over Kashmir—which was only a Pakistani national purpose. Tashkent was a setback for China, but China persisted in cultivating Pakistan against what it perceived as India's double alliance with the United States and the USSR.

Some misperceptions that the East-West syndrome dominated regional politics in the 1970s are also worth recapitulating. After 1966, while nurturing its relations with India, the USSR sought to stymie China by developing parallel relations with Pakistan, and as stated earlier, for a while sought to increase its leverage through arms supplies to Pakistan. The US tilt in the 1971 conflict on the subcontinent was an aberration, primarily due to the US' pursuit of its globalist policies vis-à-vis the USSR. The Nixon-Kissinger policy reflected American enthusiasm at the prospect that Pakistan acted as an intermediary for the development of strategic relations with China against the Soviet Union.

During the early stages of the Bangladesh crisis, the attitude of both superpowers was similar. The Soviet Union did not encourage the dismemberment of Pakistan, but it was sagacious enough not to obstruct the inevitable emergence of Bangladesh, while the United States sought in vain to manage the conflict and put pressure on India. The Indo-Soviet Treaty was negotiated because of the fear, perhaps exaggerated, of the misconceived US tilt and China's hostility to Bangladesh's desire for independence. The dispatch of the carrier *Enterprise* became in the Indian mind a symbol of attempted American coercion, just as Pearl Harbor remains the image of perfidy, and Munich of appeasement.

However, after the emergence of Bangladesh there was no trace of the tilt or the US notion of a military or political parity between Pakistan and India. Even Kissinger (during his visit to Delhi in 1974) recognized the emergent pre-eminence of India in the subcontinent. President Carter went a step further and saw India as a regional power with a critical role in subcontinental security. (The other regional hegemons were to be Iran, Brazil, Nigeria and Egypt.) This notion of India as the regional dominant power produced resistance and did not facilitate subcontinental diplomacy.

Earlier, India and Pakistan had found, to their surprise, that both superpowers were united and earnest in their endeavour to ensure the adoption of the NPT (1968). However, both regional powers refused to sign it. After the passage of the US Non-proliferation Act (1978), the United States again found that both India and Pakistan were unwilling to surrender their nuclear option. As a result, aid was cut to Pakistan and, notwithstanding an existing bilateral agreement, fuel was delayed for the Tarapur reactor.

By the mid-1970s, and after nearly fourteen years of one-sided partiality for Pakistan, China adopted a more even-handed attitude towards India. In 1976, Sino-Indian relations were restored to the ambassadorial level, and following the visit of the Indian foreign minister to Peking in 1979, the strident Chinese commitment to Pakistan's position on Kashmir was muted, although not abandoned. The Sino-Indian territorial settlement remains unresolved, but if we set aside worst-case scenarios, Sino-Indian relations are more of a political than a security problem. Since then Sino-Indian relations have witnessed ups and downs, but these have been related to Afghanistan and Kampuchea and not to India-Pakistan or India-China problems.

By 1976, what was significant in the attitudes of the United States, the USSR and China was that, with differing rationales, all of them had moved away from the imposed either or commitment and partisanship for India or Pakistan. Of course, Washington, Moscow and Beijing remained vigilant that the subcontinent as a whole did not slip into the orbit of a rival power, but the trend towards a military non-alignment of the subcontinent caused no alarm in any of these capitals. The two levels of politics—global and regional—were decoupled. There was a quiet hope, if not positive encouragement, that the normalization of India-Pakistan relations would evolve through bilateral diplomacy. All the three great powers happily acquiesced (or positively welcomed) to the agreements reached between the countries of the subcontinent during the 1976-9 period.

This was a significant change, but it was slow and undramatic and went largely undetected by analysts and regional public opinion. The improvement in the political climate was not reversed in 1977 when the Janata government came to power in New Delhi or when Bhutto was replaced by a military regime in Islamabad. It was not even deflected by important events such as the Saur revolution in Afghanistan (April 1978) and the collapse of the Shah's regime and his exile (1979). The foreign policy approaches of the Democratic Socialist Republic of Afghanistan under Amin (on Iran, disarmament and other East-West issues) were wholeheartedly pro-Soviet, but this did not precipitate an improvement in US-Pakistan relations. The United States continued to reject Pakistan's requests for A-7 aircraft probably because India and Pakistan had maintained a dialogue and had more or less agreed that Afghanistan was an internal problem, and the United States did not want to complicate its relations with South Asia and fuel an arms race.

With the Soviet invasion of Afghanistan in late December 1979, ignoring the lessons of three decades, the two Cold Wars—global and regional—were re-enmeshed. What we have seen in the past five years is a telescoped re-enactment of the tragic story of South Asia after 1954. Not that it was impossible to perceive that there was no new or imminent threat to the subcontinent. Because of the hold of Cold War analysis and the fears and suspicions it embodied, instead of quarantining the conflict in Afghanistan, the regional and non-regional powers allowed tensions to revive and gave a dramatic spurt to what had been a flagging arms race. In the subcontinent Afghanistan provides another case study of the failure of contemporaneous judgements leading to tragic and ill-conceived delusions.

Afghanistan and Regional Stability

Having written elsewhere on Afghanistan, I will only briefly summarize my own understanding.[3] The 1978 revolution succeeded because of accidents and not because of external direction masterminded from Moscow. The Khalq was probably surprised to find itself in power as a dominant partner in the new 'Democratic Republic of Afghanistan'. However, the regime splintered within weeks and that too because of local dynamics. Overruling its coalition partner and disregarding its nationalist supporters, under Hafizullah Amin's leadership, it embarked on an over rapid transformation of a medieval religious tribal society into a socialist state. The Kremlin had naturally welcomed and extended unreserved support to Amin throughout 1978, but in due course, the Kremlin discovered that the forced advent of communism had alienated a country which had never been hostile to the USSR under the overthrown monarchy and the previous conservative oligarchy.

Having failed to moderate Amin—an obviously delicate task—the Kremlin planned, and fortuitously failed, in an attempt to eliminate Amin politically or physically in September 1979. Amin survived but was disillusioned that his loyalty to Moscow had paradoxically forfeited Soviet support. He turned nationalist and made concessional overtures, internally, to the tribal leaders and Mullahs and externally to Pakistan on Pakhtunistan. Amin may have hoped he could wriggle free of his dependence on the USSR and even make overtures to the United States. Instead, in an impetuous, defensive anxiety about the potential dangers from an alienated Afghanistan, the Soviet Union saw no alternative but to launch a massive invasion to remove their erstwhile friend, Amin, lest Afghanistan become a Soviet Nicaragua.

In retrospect, the Soviet Union, especially after Gorbachev came to power, realized the enormity of its military and political miscalculation. The Soviet action overlooked Russia's historical experience in Afghanistan and other more recent cases of outraged nationalism, such as Vietnam's intervention in Kampuchea. In fact, it proved to be an unexpected setback to Soviet policy in the entire Third World. However, Western scholars as well as the Carter administration interpreted the invasion of Afghanistan as the first step in a sweep towards the warm water ports, a threat to the oil flows of the Gulf, and linked it to the American hostages in Iran. Reflecting the entrenched hypotheses, the invasion was viewed as a menacing strategic manoeuvre against the West and proof of ideological expansionism. A local situation was thus transposed into an East-West problem.

None of these scenarios have come to pass, and we are left with unconvincing post hoc explanations justifying hollow fears. The Soviet expansion is deemed to have been halted because of prompt military reactions (the Rapid Deployment Force) as also the international boycott and alarm. In any case, it has been argued that Soviet capability for future military advances has improved, as if the Soviet Union has not always enjoyed a decisive military advantage in the whole area. It has been obvious for more than a decade—including when Soviet-Iraq relations were at their peak—that the USSR recognized that any provocation or direct threat to the oil carried the same hazard as the overrunning of West Berlin.

On the other hand, the exaggerated alarm of the United States and the subsequent involvement of the CIA has been conveniently used by the USSR as confirmation that the Soviet action was a necessary pre-emptive measure to prevent Afghanistan from becoming a Western satellite.

As in 1953-4, Pakistan was able to play upon Washington's alarm, inject warmth into the tepid relations with the United States, and obtain massive commitments of American arms and economic aid. American policy makers failed to recognize that Pakistan's most serious concern was not the Soviet threat (against which Pakistan is indefensible), but India. The nature of the weapons obtained and the location of the deployment confirmed that Pakistan's primary purpose was to bolster operational capabilities on its eastern rather than the northern or western fronts. The Pakistanis, however, showed greater diplomatic skill than India. Having used the developments in Afghanistan to consolidate relations with the Islamic world, assured of American assistance and in the meantime further strengthening their friendship with China, the Pakistanis were careful not to offend or provoke the USSR. Thus, it should have come as no surprise to anyone (but the Cold War warriors) that Pakistan rejected the Pentagon's plea for RDF bases on Pakistani soil and that it did not echo the hostile approach towards and apprehension of the Soviet Union. Pakistan's circumspection with respect to the Soviet Union notwithstanding, Pakistani leaders once again failed to anticipate the predictable Indian reactions.

India embarked on a massive programme of defence modernization with purchases from both the USSR and the West. These purchases more than matched Pakistan's military aid from the United States. In turn, Indo-Soviet relations were strengthened. The initial attitude of the Government of India (and to some extent, that of the United States) was complicated by the coincidence of the domestic general elections with the Soviet intervention, in Afghanistan. In the 1977 Indian elections (and even though elections were held in Pakistan also), no foreign policy issues were raised in the campaign. In 1979, international issues figured prominently during the pre-election debates. The initial reaction of the new Indian government to the Soviet intervention, as expressed in the speech of the Indian ambassador in the General Assembly debate on 11 January, gave credence to the official Soviet explanation that its forces were invited into the country. This view reflected the election theme that relations with the Soviets had been allowed to deteriorate in the 1977-9 period. The Indian position changed soon after the new government came to power. Within weeks, the Government of India publicly urged a Soviet withdrawal and a political solution. However, the consequences of the abstention on the crucial resolution before the UN could not be undone.

My own judgement is that if Mrs Gandhi had been re-elected in 1977 or if the Janata government had remained in office until 1982, the initial Indian reaction would have been different. India may well have anticipated that the United States would react with alarm and this would be used by Pakistan to obtain a resumption of military aid, in a way similar to that in 1954, and sought to prevent it. It is worth recalling that Mrs Gandhi had for years resisted the purchase of the Jaguar. It was the Janata government's decision to purchase squadrons of this subsonic deep-strike aircraft which provided the rationale for the supply of ultra sophisticated F-16 to Pakistan. The US administration's commitment to contain the 'evil' of communism and to re-establish military superiority which compounded the reenactment of the 1954 syndrome, but that came a year later. If the Indian approach to Pakistan in January 1980 had been similar to that of the foreign minister's speech in Karachi in June 1981, the subcontinental arms race may not have assumed its present dimensions. If India had anticipated the non-aligned vote on Afghanistan, it may have been better placed to play a more effective role in counselling Soviet withdrawal and rescuing Moscow from the Afghan quagmire. Afghanistan provided a unique opportunity to initiate steps towards an India-Pakistan rapprochement, an opportunity that was allowed to slip away. Paradoxically, the anti-American and anti-Pakistan hawks in India played into the hands of the Pentagon; the anti-Indian and anti-Russian militants in Pakistan must have provided grist to the Soviet military mill rather than to the prudent political strategists in the Politburo. Many efforts to find a solution to Afghanistan were proposed in 1980-1, but they all failed and were abandoned. My own proposal suggested in 1981 was 'From

Swedenization to Finlandization' to restore Afghanistan to its per-1978 non-alignment by a step-by-step regional initiative.*

THE INDIA-PAKISTAN CONFLICT

Whether the problem and solution of Afghanistan is distinct from or linked with that of South Asia, it should be recognized that its chief adverse fallout has been on India and Pakistan. The process of uncoupling South Asia from the Cold War that has been going on at least since 1971 if not 1966, has been reversed. Non-alignment, to which every country including Pakistan pays homage, has reverted to a balancing dependence on the competing superpowers rather than detachment from them. The future danger faced by both has become a convenient argument in East-West relations.

The repetition of the 1950s scenario did not stop with the negative consequences of the subcontinental arms race and revived tensions. The old lessons—that becoming an adjunct to superpower politics and strategies brought lesser security at higher costs—soon began to tug at policy makers. After commitments to a programme of massive militarization in the subcontinent, which may be to the tune of $20 billion, it has been realized that ultimately relations with one's neighbour are critical to the respective security futures of both states. Presumably, it was this logic that led Pakistan to reverse its earlier position and offer an unconditional no-war declaration with India. India hesitated but, with the unambiguous support of public opinion, responded with a counter-offer of an Indo-Pakistan Treaty of Peace and Friendship. In the same spirit, both India and Pakistan responded positively to the Bangladesh initiative for a South Asia forum for regional cooperation. Since then, there have been regular high-level visits between New Delhi and Islamabad. These unprecedented modalities may only be a beginning but neither country can casually back off in the future.

* For more on the subject see Jagat S. Mehta, *The March of Folly in Afghanistan 1978-2001*, New Delhi: Manohar, 2002.

The institutional motivations are of little more than potential importance if political attitudes remain inhibited. It cannot be denied that the Cold War cancer or suspicions, the chicken-and-egg accusations, and the subcontinental variant of a quest for parity and military superiority as a precondition to meaningful arms restraint have again come into play. It is an open question whether it is the pre-1965 situation (heading for a conflict) or the mid-1970s situation (with the prospect of a step-by-step easing of Indo-Pakistan tensions).

The answer, however, does not lie with the extra-regional powers. For all their separate or collective power and leverage, Washington, Moscow and Beijing cannot determine which way the region will turn—to war or to peace—or whether, when and how the arms they sell or supply will (or will not) be used. The decision rests squarely on Islamabad and New Delhi. Being neither a government spokesman nor officially informed, I can only speculate with the licence of no responsibility. I do know that the challenge to follow a constructive rather than a destructive path is not beyond the capability of Indian and Pakistani bilateral diplomacy.

The overriding impediment is the intellectual torpor of the Cold War. In the past, some national policy goals were misconceived, but the problem was compounded because the motives, power and capabilities of the other powers were misjudged. Before focusing on security futures, it would be useful to think of the fallacies that have been exposed in these decades.

The resilient old notion that India and Pakistan are not reconciled to each other's existence has all but died; it is realism to recognize that the Kashmir dispensation cannot be unscrambled without the hazard of a major conflict. The de jure confirmation of the present reality is a political problem (as the existing boundaries have to be accepted with a sense of finality). Other fears or illusions have been largely dispelled: that India and Pakistan could be surrogates of different superpowers, and that one or the other could be manipulated for competing superpower strategies; that Pakistan was truly anti-Soviet and pro-American, or that India was necessarily interested in undermining Western interests to subserve Soviet strategic goals, even where its own were not involved; that the benevolent commitment of one power would support or rescue its alleged 'client' in any regional conflict; that outside powers could prevent a regional conflict; and finally, that the superpowers would oppose (or even be able to obstruct) any regional settlement bilaterally reached if it was based on military neutrality in the superpower strategies.

Diplomacy also has its own Gresham's Law. The present political climate, however, does not reflect a confidence in bilateral diplomacy. A major intellectual effort would be required to muster the political will to prevent a slide into mutually reinforcing suspicion and actual conflict.

Both sides should remind themselves of the lesson furnished by the downfall of the Shah of Iran: national security in the twentieth century is multidimensional, a mix of internal and external factors, and it requires a combination of political responsiveness, social justice and economic growth, not just firepower. Political, governmental and non-official opinion must focus more than ever on the long-term internal consequences of Indo-Pakistan paranoia.

Except in unlikely contingencies, India has been secure against external imposition. However, it has to appraise the needs and expectations of a population which is expected to increase to one billion by the end of the century and to prevent internal disaffection from turning into violent disruption of its democracy. Pakistan has similar economic problems, but it should give priority to effect a transition to a representative form of government, and to find the equation between Islamic ideology, and the imperatives of modernization. Both India and Pakistan have had a foretaste of the serious regional problems that result from insufficiency and disparities in national economic growth. No outside power can cap these smouldering volcanoes.

Apart from water and ecology, there are more tangible gains to be realized from regional complementarities which could contribute to national development strategies—if only the region's economic interdependence were squarely recognized. SAARC promises only limited beginnings in this exploration. After meetings between unofficial economists, the Committee on the Study of Cooperation in South Asia has projected a fuller picture of the benefits in important sectors like energy, industrialization, transport, population control and technology sharing, which could only follow rational coordination within the region without compromise to any sovereignty. Such regional economic cooperation would no doubt depend on regional initiatives. The great powers could facilitate it with the promise of an imaginative response (such as the US response to Europe via the Marshall Plan), but it would be futile and indeed, counterproductive to imagine that they had the power or leverage to knock South Asian heads together.

Against these long-term problems and potential must be placed the opportunity costs of mutually-reinforcing fears and mounting defence outlays, the more so if these trends are extrapolated for the next decade and a half.[5] No one has ever projected what may have been the state of the Indian and Pakistani economies if only 50 per cent of the total military outlays expended by the two countries on efforts directed against each other had been available for developmental purposes. I was informed by the most eminent economic official in India—admittedly not on the basis of a detailed study—that both economies may have registered a minimum additional 3 per cent growth rate. If compounded, both countries may have attained a per capita income of over $1,000, double the present level, and presented the same picture as the ASEAN countries.

Finally, harsh realism must also recognize that for all the weight of reason and international consensus, a New International Order is not imminent. Even if the global economic recovery continues, détente is revived, and East-West arms restraints are underway (an unlikely prospect in the present scenario), international economic support for the Third World would range from meagre to dismal. This harsh reality itself demands the end of psychological dependence on the East or West, as a safeguard for security or as a source of economic rescue, or even as a scapegoat for domestic problems.

This odyssey of intellectual reappraisal points to a reversion by India and Pakistan to a diplomacy of beneficial bilateralism. The military or political involvement of the great powers can only be defied jointly. Regional trust and peace, and external economic indifference, can only be ameliorated by greater cooperation and optimized self-reliance.

Towards a Regional Political Settlement

What could be the modalities for a political breakthrough in Indo-Pakistan relations? Most of the models—the Tlatelolco Treaty, the Sinai Accords, the MBFR—are either not applicable or too premature for the subcontinent. If a parallel has to be found—and no parallel is exact—it is in the steps envisaged in the Helsinki-Belgrade confidence-building scenarios between Eastern and Western Europe. The aim should be to break out of the vicious grip of mutual suspicions. Successful diplomacy should start with an appreciation of the national psychology and legitimate vital interests of the adversary: a sensitivity to the nationalism of the other. This recipe for regional restraint and cooperation is not different from what the non-aligned countries have urged continuously on the superpowers: realistic limits to military vigilance and a vision of the economic costs in an interdependent world.

In relation to the six smaller neighbouring states of the subcontinent, India has a special problem which bears comparison with the United States in relation to the world. Just as the United States (barring Soviet military capability) is disproportionately more powerful than all countries in the world, India is not only larger but industrially and technologically superior in South Asia. On different scales, both India and the United States face the expectation of generosity, understanding and economic support from their 'neighbours', but both are treated, often unreasonably, as a foil rather than as a friend by the smaller and weaker nations. Indian diplomacy can no longer compartmentalize its relations with its neighbours. India's inability to dispel the historic fears in Pakistan could be overcome if simultaneously there was an improvement in relations with Bangladesh, Nepal, Sri Lanka and Bhutan. Contrariwise, tension with any one country has tended to create apprehension in all the other states of South Asia.

Although I do not minimize the role and responsibility of India in turning the situation around, Pakistan also has to make a critical decision. It cannot run with the hares of non-alignment and hunt with the hounds in the superpower game and still expect credibility with respect to its desire for peaceful and cooperative relations with India. India has the obvious advantage of defence in depth and is not likely to be blitzed into surrender. Even if New Delhi does not receive in per capita terms the kind of financial support that Pakistan is able to secure, an arms race would not prove an effective method for the economic attrition of India.

Both India and Pakistan should realize the inherent dangers and uncertainties of nuclear weapons as a method of defence or coercion. Any nuclear weapons capability, outside the full paraphernalia of mutually assured destruction and fail-safe as well as verification technology, would only lead to an illusion of deterrent or compellent capability. There can be no certainty that a threat or an actual nuclear exchange would be limited to the regional level, or that radiation hazards would be confined to the adversary's frontier. Furthermore, nuclear weapons cannot lead to the reduction or substitution of conventional armed capability. Morally and politically, the attempt to smother the nuclear option of either India or Pakistan by the United States, the USSR, or both, was unrealistic and politically counter productive. Whether Pakistan would now refrain from acquiring a weapons capability or whether it and India would be content with the prestige parity of a bomb in the basement would also depend upon their ability to develop a climate of mutual trust between them. If this goal proves elusive, they would only flatter the superpowers by imitation—in an unrestrained and spiralling arms race with a nuclear dimension.

Finally, the obvious truth must be stated: India has a vested interest in Pakistan's integrity and prosperity. At the same time, Pakistan must accept that the ultimate guarantor of an optimal future for independent Pakistan is a dynamic India, acting not as a regional hegemon but as a power which is central to the viability of South Asia. Neither the United States and the USSR nor China can be dependable allies or reliable patrons. Until the relations of the great powers undergo a sea change, none of them can serve independently as an effective mediator. But all of them—in varying measure—can be non-exclusive economic partners of South Asian countries. The awe and appeal of these great powers are exaggerated because of the failure to measure our own interests and capabilities. The only hope for Afghanistan—and South Asia as a whole—lies in regionalized non-alignment through regional diplomacy.

I remain persuaded that the countries of South Asia have the wisdom and the capacity to break out of the hypnosis of the past and the fashion a better security future. South Asia, which is the greatest open laboratory of development and modernization process, could play a critical role in bridging the North-South chasm. Moreover, if South Asia could disengage itself from the East-West strategic game, it may come as a relief and not as a loss to both Washington and Moscow. The superpower strategies of deterrence are essentially dependent on long-range missiles based in their homelands or under water in the oceans. A military presence or involvement outside their frontiers would create increasing political irritation, or even be a liability. They may also discover that the economic logic of arms control is undeniable. Stability in the regional subsystem may not jeopardize their interests or security. The real skill is to understand the role of nationalism in the region; the challenge is economic: how to be partners in the progress of a region involving one-fifth of the world's population. Similarly, if China envisages a revitalized role of leadership in the Third World, as is possible, it would prefer a parallel relationship with India and Pakistan where there is no demand for a partisan involvement on India-Pakistan issues. It might well be that all this could initiate a process by which the Third World—the new world of the twentieth century—through its own variant of the Monroe Doctrine and the Canning Declaration, could help rediscover its real strength and so redress the balance.

NOTES

1. See Sisir K. Gupta, *Kashmir: A Study in India-Pakistan Relations*, Bombay: Asia Publishing House, 1966.
2. John Kenneth Galbraith, *Ambassador's Journal,* New York: New American Library, 1970.

3. Jagat S. Mehta, 'Afghanistan: A Neutral Solution', *Foreign Policy,* Summer 1982; 'Solution in Afghanistan: From Swedenization to Finlandization', Kennan Institute for Advanced Russian Studies, Woodrow Wilson International Center for Scholars, Washington, DC.
4. Ibid.
5. These views are elaborated in the thematic essay, 'Third World Militarization,' in J.S. Mehta (ed.), *Third World Militarization: A Challenge to Third World Diplomacy,* Austin, Texas: LBJ School of Public Affairs, 1985.

11

Review of J.N. Dixit's 'War and Peace'

The title of J.N. Dixit's book on India and Pakistan echoes, in terms of its association and emphasis, Tolstoy's classic *War and Peace*, one of the greatest novels in world literature. *War and Peace* is the epic story of Napoleon's invasion of Russia and I suppose Dixit sees a parallel in the way the India-Pakistan problem has dominated subcontinental politics for over fifty years. As it happened, I started my service in the same week in 1947 when Pakistan came into existence. From my perch on the first floor of South Block as private secretary to the newly appointed Secretary General, I could have a look at the secret and top secret telegrams that passed through my desk. Like Dixit, I have also followed the tragic story of Indo-Pakistan relations, but respecting the constraints of space, I will confine my comments to periods when I was a close bystander to decision-making in Delhi. I cannot help feeling that Dixit's survey would have been more balanced in its perspective if some significant omissions could be corrected. There is a running thread of self-righteous accusations and pessimism, which shirks from introspective objectivity. It slurs over periods of Indo-Pak joint achievements and underplays the imperative of constructive diplomacy for the future.

BIPARTISANSHIP IN FOREIGN POLICY

I was appointed Foreign Secretary in April 1976 when Mrs Gandhi was prime minister, and continued in my post till November 1979. The year 1977 was the first time when there was change in the party complexion of the central government, so I had to 'manage' the transition and seek to preserve the respect

* See p. 286 for the text of Dixit's letter, suggesting that the review should be published as a monograph.

and independence of the professional cadre. Fortunately, Morarji Desai and Atal Behari Vajpayee demonstrated their own conviction that the continuity of non-alignment was the recipe for safeguarding and furthering India's national interests. Dixit minimizes the achievements of the Janata government, but what surprises me is that the book is less than just to Mrs Gandhi's tenure. The year 1976-7, in my view, diplomatically outmatches any other year since Independence in the positive harmonization of India-Pakistan relations. I will illustrate this in the following pages.

DIPLOMACY REQUIRES FORWARD-LOOKING VISION

Let me frankly acknowledge that professional diplomacy has not made its optimum contribution in the march towards India's tryst with destiny. The fault lies not entirely with the politicians. We, in the Foreign Service, with lifelong tenures, have failed many times in making sound judgements and in volunteering timely dissent. Dixit overlooks the seriousness of the failures of the professionals when they acquiesced to and even applauded mistakes, which had predictable serious consequences. The role of diplomacy goes beyond reporting and appraisals or even doing national public relations; it also involves crisis prevention, moderating aggravation and, more positively, conflict resolution. Diplomatic triumphs are greatest when sovereign misperceptions are overcome through persuasion, without causing subsequent recoil. The Foreign Service has a nobler and intellectually more challenging task than political historians or current affairs analysts.

HYPNOSIS OF THE COLD WAR: AN UNNOTICED FLAW

Let me quickly add that the future historians of international politics since the Second World War will pronounce that, despite the gallop of information, trade and technology, the record of diplomacy everywhere has been abysmal. The world was hypnotized by the ideological Cold War, with apprehensions that it would ignite into a global conflagration. The horrendous waste of resources has been greatly, though not wholly, responsible for the slow progress towards equity and social justice for peoples and nations. Among the few prophetic exceptions were the 'Marshall Plan' for the economic rehabilitation of Europe and the principles of non-alignment. Non-alignment was defiantly sagacious in urging ideological agnosticism in international relations: it demanded respect for responsible (not chauvinistic) nationalism, and focused on domestic economic strength with freedom to explore global economic complimentaries. Security hinged not so much on alliances and military might, but on the capacity of defence blended with development—in other words, a world made safe for political diversity freely permitting functional economic rationalization. However, when the principle of non-alignment was made a 'Movement',—I would detect it at the Algiers summit in 1973—it became a pale imitation of the military blocs, and the non-aligned started resorting to tactical gameplay, banking on the permanence of superpower competition. Not surprisingly, the non-aligned were almost taken aback when, after détente, their principles got universalized: the tragedy of the India-Pakistan cold/hot wars is that we got enmeshed in the big Cold War.

The posting in Peking (1963-6) was the most instructive in my professional education. Every day I waded through pages and pages of Sino-Soviet polemics and was aghast that right up to 1967, the USA was still convinced that it was fighting a monolithic communist bloc. In 1969 I shocked the Harvard academics in a paper entitled 'The Reluctant Coalition for Stability', which noted the emerging community of interest of nuclearized adversaries. But after the Suez crisis (1956), there was no greater mockery of the Cold War alliance system than the development of China-Pak relations (1962), which began even before the Sino-Indian war. The point to be acknowledged is that it took New Delhi, Washington and even Moscow by surprise.

From Peking, it also became evident that wherever possible, the USSR really wanted good relations with both India and Pakistan. We, however, preferred to rely on the half-truth that the Soviet Union was our best time-tested friend, little noting that while the Soviet Union always preferred India in any crunch situation, it really wanted a tension-free subcontinent. The

American ambassador, Galbraith, who was virtually the emperor of India at the time of the Sino-Indian conflict (1962), told me that Benedictov, his Soviet counterpart, instead of burning with anger and jealousy, quietly rejoiced in American-British attempts at India-Pakistan reconciliation. At the Security Council in 1965 and in Tashkent (1966), this purpose was evident; even in the first few months of 1971 (until Kissinger's secret visit to Peking), the Soviet Union did not want the dismemberment of Pakistan. I am not certain whether the provisions for mutual consultations on security in the Indo-Soviet treaty (August 1971) was at our or Soviet initiative but ever since, I have felt that while the provisions gave us psychological support, we needlessly compromised our non-alignment. Mrs Gandhi had already got the measure of Nixon's tilt, and as we saw, she was unperturbed by the *Enterprise* entering the Bay of Bengal. The revolt in East Pakistan exposed the flaws of the 'Two-Nation theory'. Bangladesh was not our conception: we only helped in the process of its delivery.

FATAL MISJUDGEMENT ON AFGHANISTAN

Afghanistan illustrated the fundamental dilemma of international relations in the Cold War years—what prevails in the conflict between ideology and national security. In April 1978, it was plain to me that the Soviet Union did not plan the Saur revolution as was widely suspected in the West, but of course it supported the revolution later with resources. However, when the ideological imposition of socialism on a conservative Islamic country by a pro-Soviet ideologue, Hafizullah Amin, seemed to endanger Soviet security, as became vivid in the Herat mutiny in March 1979, the USSR conspired for his elimination. When the Moscow-planned coup failed (14 September 1979), overruling a divided Politburo, President Brezhnev impetuously authorized the ill-conceived intervention. The White House should have recognized that the Soviet intervention was defensive in intent. It was the mindset conditioned by the Cold War that led India to be taken in by the rationalization that the CIA wanted to control Afghanistan. Dixit is inclined to cast slurs at the costly blunder of compromising non-aligned principles and abandoning Afghan nationalism in January 1980. It was predictable that it would lead to the remilitarization of Pakistan.

Our abstaining vote in the General Assembly debate on Afghanistan, in my view, has been a turning point. It led to the reversal in India-Pakistan relations and a slide in India's international standing. Though no longer carrying responsibility, I earnestly urged the continuation of the approach to keep our region away from great-power fallacies. Our vote sent shivers down the spines of our neighbours by its analogical application. The irony is that we would have been in a much better position to help the Soviet Union to extricate its forces from Afghanistan when, in 1986, Gorbachev made enquiries of our chargé d'affaires about India taking a hand in establishing stability in the country.

COMPREHENSIVE NORMALIZATION WITH PAKISTAN—MAY 1976: CONSEQUENTIAL CLIMATE CHANGE

Let me now come to some other specific points which were of nodal importance and led to the warmest period in India-Pakistan relations. Mrs Gandhi had remained adamant in Simla (1972) and thereafter that until Bhutto withdrew the complaint filed with the International Civil Aviation Organization (ICAO), India would not restore diplomatic relations. In March 1976 Bhutto notified the unilateral withdrawal of the five-year-old complaint, and Mrs Gandhi promptly got cabinet approval for the extensive normalization of relations. As Foreign Secretary, I was asked to lead a large delegation to Islamabad in May 1976.* The negotiations were not easy. Agha Shahi was my counterpart, but Prime Minister Bhutto himself sought to intercede by telephone calls from Gilgit. The agreement finally concluded was the most comprehensive ever reached with Pakistan; but it finds insufficient mention in Dixit's book. The agreement covered the restoration of full diplomatic relations, civil air overflights, the restoration of road and rail connection (broken since 1965) and state trading in specific commodities. I proposed that notwithstanding the complexity of the preliminaries, the entire process should be

* See J.S. Mehta, Chapter 4, *Negotiating for India*, New Delhi: Manohar, 2006.

completed within eight weeks. My colleagues were a bit stumped but we had no means of getting the authorization or refusing the deadline from headquarters, as there was no high commission and no cipher links. The two high commissioners did, in fact, present their credentials after eight weeks in exact synchronization. At the tail end of the three-day discussions, Agha Shahi, obviously for public record, mentioned Kashmir but I said the issue was not on the agenda. The discussion on Kashmir lasted barely thirty seconds.

On my return, G. Parthasarthy, then chairman of the Policy Planning Committee, politely mentioned that I had exceeded my brief by signing the memorandum in Islamabad. Mrs Gandhi, however, congratulated me fulsomely. Within hours felicitations from round the world started pouring in; the first, I remember, was from Moscow. These messages drowned the reservations about 'exceeding my brief'. The real diplomatic benefit was in the climate change not merely in official dealings but also in public opinion. I had hinted that as a follow-up, we could reopen consulates in Karachi and Bombay and this created an air of satisfaction in both countries. The positive fallout of improvement has either not been or just cursorily been observed by Dixit but to my mind it underscores the benefits of successful positive diplomacy.

IC 814: LESSONS FROM PREVIOUS HIGHJACKINGS

The hijacking of the IC 814 was not on my watch: Dixit's book has a detailed description. Two other hijacking incidents by Pakistan sympathizers could have been mentioned as providing some relevant lessons. In the 'Ganga' incident (1971), prior to the declaration of Independence of Bangladesh, the aircraft was destroyed on the tarmac after the passengers were released. India justifiably suspended overflight rights and, as mentioned, Pakistan filed a complaint with the ICAO. The second hijacking was in August 1976 when I was Foreign Secretary. Within fifteen minutes of the take off, Mrs Gandhi herself telephoned to me and the whole crisis management group assembled at Safdarjang in another twenty minutes. I persuaded Cabinet Secretary B.D.

Pande and the group that, notwithstanding the pro-Pak sentiments of the hijackers, we should ask the pilot to land in Lahore. I felt we would have much greater leverage in Lahore than in Dubai or Tripoli which were the alternative destinations suggested by the hijkackers. Thereafter I rushed back to the office, telephoned my Pakistani counterpart, Agha Shahi, and he in turn dispatched his number two, Shah Nawaz, to Lahore to handle the hijacking. The presence of the plane on Pakistani soil posed a dilemma for Pakistan which wished neither to own nor to disown the hijackers. During the day Shah Nawaz must have telephoned me thirty or forty times. He asked me what terms he should offer, whether, and if so, how near should the interlocutors approach the aircraft, etc. He was obviously nervous, if anything went wrong, wanted India also carry the blame. Finally, unknown to us, the Pakistani officials drugged the food that was sent to the hijackers and all the passengers were released in groups.

The decision from our side, which proved crucial, was to make Pakistan publicly responsible for our aircraft and passengers. Where diplomacy came in was that I hinted to Shah Nawaz that if they were not prepared to repatriate the hijackers, they should be seen to be taken into custody. (In my heart of heart, I really did not care if afterwards they were taken to a five-star hotel!) The hijackers were released in a few month's time and, for the record, we registered a formal protest.

The credit for the success must go to Mrs Gandhi for having authorized the comprehensive normalization in May 1976 and not stringing it out with diplomatic relations first and at three-monthly gaps thereafter if Pakistan 'behaved'. Had the climate not improved dramatically, we might have had a repetition of the 1971 incident. In the case of IC 814, we should have reacted faster to obstruct it from taking off from Amritsar, but once it had done so, we should have told the pilot to land in Lahore and stall there. Even in 2000, we had more leverage in Pakistan than with the Taliban in Kandahar.

BREAKING THE DEADLOCK ON SALAL

In the spring of 1976, following the obstinate refusal by Pakistan, to agree to our proposal for a hydel project. Mrs Gandhi approved the ministry's recommendation to refer the Salal dispute for arbitration under the Indus Treaty. When I took over and saw this, I was unhappy at the decision, as it could become another Kashmir—the internationalization of a bilateral problem. After the normalization in Islamabad, I recommended to the Prime Minister that she reverse her earlier orders. She readily agreed and allowed me to try further talks at the Foreign Secretary level. Dixit does not mention that the Salal project had been proposed in 1968; in the intervening years, seventeen meetings of Indus Commissioners and six between my two predecessor Foreign Secretaries had taken place but Pakistan had refused its concurrence, which was required under the Indus Treaty. (Incidentally the Indus Commission under the Treaty was established in 1960 and not afterwards as the book suggests.)

Salal is a microcosm of Indo-Pak relations and not dissimilar to the US-Soviet paranoia during the Cold War. Pakistan confidentially but confidently suspected that whatever India proposed, even when it was claimed it was for functional economic cooperation, there had to be a secret military purpose behind it. The Pakistan government and media had long been convinced that our real intention was to flood the Chenab if Pakistan was on the offensive and drown their advancing tanks, but what worried them even more was that India would dry the river bed by releasing all the stored waters from a run-of-the river project in advance of when India planned an attack to capture Sialkot!

Following the prime minister's authorization, I wrote to my counterpart asking for further discussions on Salal. Bhutto was planning an election and did not want to moderate his image of being an uncompromising hawk on India. It was only after two months of pleas and prodding that Agha Shahi finally agreed to a meeting in October 1976. It was Pakistan's turn to come to Delhi but a second, more crucial meeting followed soon afterwards in Islamabad. We marshalled evidence, never compiled before, that the unarticulated fears of the malevolent scope of the project were totally baseless: the damage apprehended was not only unlikely but was not even feasible. When I called on the Pakistan prime minister, I put it to him that if we embarked on drying the river bed, a great part (I forget the exact figure) would sink into the ground thirty miles from the dam site to the frontier. On the other hand, by stopping the turbines, 1,75,000 tube wells in India would be denied power, which would arouse the wrath of the Punjabi farmers and incidentally result in a loss of Rs. 10,000 crore in revenue in a week's interruption. The harm to India would thus be greater than to Pakistan. I concluded 'that there was a limit to the extent that India would cut its economic nose to spite and harm Pakistan'. Bhutto grimaced but Kokhar, the note taker at the time who later became high commissioner to India and is now the Foreign Secretary of Pakistan, confirmed that I said words to this effect. Bhutto asked me to postpone my departure, called a meeting of all civil and military chief engineers to check our calculations while I played golf! I will not summarize further interesting details but Bhutto finally authorized the initialling of the agreement and, as a quid pro quo, I volunteered the assurance that we would not publicize and embarrass him. The agreement was confirmed formally by Vajpayee and Agha Shahi in 1978 but exactly on the terms settled in October 1976.

Water and river basin experts have told me that power being supplied to a prospective adversary has no parallel. Canada has a dam on the Columbia, which helps in flood control and supplies power to the USA. Even so, the USA pays $250 million annually to Canada. No functional linkages have ever been established between Siberia and Alaska. The 690 megawatt from Salal dam feeding into the north Indian grid from a point in a 'disputed' or claimed territory (Kashmir) must be lighting bulbs in Delhi! (In contrast, we do not get a single megawatt from Nepal, which has a 85,000-150,000 MW potential.) The credit again should be attributed to Mrs Gandhi, who was then the presiding head of the government. Salal would never have been settled except for the goodwill generated by the comprehensive normalization in May 1976. I do not know how many hundreds of thousand crore we lost by the avoidable delay of eight years.

Let me mention another fact which so far has been discreetly kept out of the public domain. The differences on diversion of waters from the Ganges at Farakka into the Hooghly to ease the siltation of the Kolkata port had erupted in 1960: they continued even after Bangladesh came into existence. In 1975 the barrage was completed but in discussions in April, Sheikh Mujibur himself expressed strong reservations and finally agreed to release 15,000 cusecs for one year only. After Sheikh Mujibur was assassinated in August, the differences became more acute and in 1976 Bangladesh put the item on the General Assembly agenda. G. Parthasarthy, who had much experience as Representative to the UN, was expected to handle the item, but he regretted his inability to go to New York; so the responsibility devolved on me. After intense lobbying, we managed to persuade Bangladesh to withdraw the item. (I am told this is the only case where a sponsoring nation has withdrawn an item before voting after the item had been inscribed on the agenda.) Let it now be revealed that Pakistan helped India by persuading Bangladesh to fall in line with the Indian request. For this too the credit must go to the normalization of Indo-Pakistan relations in May 1976.

WITHDRAWAL OF POLEMICAL PAMPHLETS

What has also not been revealed so far but must be on our record that by discreet prophylactic diplomatic initiative in January-February 1977, we managed to prevent the publication and distribution of two polemical pamphlets proposed by Bhutto—one on Kashmir and the other on Indo-Pak relations—to give additional mileage to his election campaign. As it happened, in 1977 neither in the Indian nor the Pakistani elections was there any significant focus on foreign policy issues. (In this respect, our elections in 1979 proved a tragic, needless departure as it made no difference to the election result but created a lasting setback.)

KASHMIR-KARGIL

The deterioration in Kashmir and the consequential ignition of insurgency have several reasons. I have no first-hand knowledge of the 1990s except as an itinerant member of the National Security Advisory Group in 1998-9. The decline of democracy during 1983-9, after Sheikh Sahib died, the break up of the National Conference, the removal of Farooq Abdullah, the resignation of Governor B.K. Nehru, the reappointment of Farooq Abdullah by Rajiv Gandhi as the head of an imposed coalition, and the blatantly rigged elections of 1987 (in contrast to the fair elections of 1977) created conditions which precipitated the insurgency in 1989. The ISI jumped in later with infiltration, military support and terror. (The return of democracy after the 2002 elections may reopen positive possibilities, damaged in 1983.) Kargil was the culmination of the folly that began in the 1980s. The book omits that mention—which is relevant from the foreign policy viewpoint—that the intruders included Arabs and Afghan veterans who had fought the Soviet forces with the Mujahideen. They were originally brought in by the CIA but after the Soviet forces withdrew, India continued to be seen as an ally of the communist 'infidels', and we became second only to American imperialists as the targets of the militant jehadis.

The book mentions that apart from Pakistan army units, there were 'mercenaries' and the Taliban in Kargil. It is misleading to describe Afghan and non-Pak jehadis as 'mercenaries'. The jehadis were no doubt misguided but the motivation was not monetary. For my part, I have speculated that had we voted with the non-aligned in the General Assembly on the issue of the Soviet invasion of Afghanistan there might not have been a Kargil, or at least there would not have been any non-Pak volunteers in any infiltration or intrusive operations. I cannot hypothetically prove my point, nor can it be disproved, but our betrayal of our own principles indubitably provided the provocation, when for the first time foreign militants became associates of Pakistan operations in Kashmir.

LINE OF CONTROL

Perhaps the most important point on which there is extraordinary convenient amnesia in the book is that between 1976 and 1979, there was no infiltration across the Line of Control. Pakistan de facto respected the LOC as if it were an international frontier. What was not done on paper at Simla was obtained de facto in those years. In fact, the hawks in India and Pakistan are together in this conspiracy of silence—lest the idea is resurrected to the embarrassment of Pakistan, and to justify our adversarial postures. It should be recalled that the restraint shown by Pakistan started in Mrs Gandhi's time but was continued in the Janata period. More than once I told Prime Minister Morarji Desai and Foreign Minister A.B. Vajpayee that the Kashmir problem was on the way to solution but I requested that this should not be mentioned publicly as it would invite retraction and disturb a promising process. Unfortunately the quadrilateral of misperceptions (of the two superpowers and India and Pakistan) after the Soviet invasion of Afghanistan shattered what I believe was the most propitious moment for rationalizing India-Pak relations and confirming the LOC in Kashmir.

VAJPAYEE'S SUCCESSFUL VISIT TO PAKISTAN

Coming to the Janata period, Dixit acknowledges that Vajpayee's visit to Islamabad in 1978 is looked upon even in Pakistan as the high point in India-Pak relations but he does not fully underscore the significance of the talks with Zia-ul Haq and, more so, the first ever open press conference by an Indian leader in Islamabad. Vajpayee started by recounting his own anti-Pakistan past and thus successfully disarmed the entrenched suspicions of the assembled journalists. He seemed to have somehow carried conviction with the broader public opinion in the country when he declared he wished Pakistan well. The Lahore press had been very critical at a member of the Jan Sangh being allowed to come to Pakistan. It was an act of great political courage for Vajpayee to have gone at all in the face of such public hostility. The visit has been compared to Sadaat going to Jerusalem, but Sadaat had not publicly crusaded against Israel as Vajpayee had done against Pakistan all through his political life. No one at home or abroad expected such a turnaround. (The impact lasted longer than Vajpayee's speech in Nishan-e-Pakistan in 1999 as Kargil followed soon after his bus journey.) In 1978, both the USSR and the USA as well as the Muslim nations felicitated India: they were fully persuaded by the claim of the continuity of non-alignment. One commentator half-seriously and privately called Vajpayee the new Qaide-Azam!

Dixit's book implies that Pakistan began giving malevolent encouragement to the Sikh militants in 1978-80. To my knowledge, this is not correct. The number of Sikhs going to Pakistan may have increased but there was no evidence of Pakistan sowing seeds of disaffection in 1978. During the Janata period, it was the Congress in opposition which was bolstering up Bhindranwala in his extreme demands. The latitude of toleration continued even after Mrs Gandhi was re-elected in 1980 unfortunately for too long. It finally led to the Blue Star operatrion in June 1984 and the assassination of Mrs Gandhi in October 1984. The Pakistan exploitation of the Khalistan agitation was in the 1980s and not in the 1970s.

In his reference to the visit of Vajpayee to China, Dixit mentions that there was not much substantive result from it. I again suspect that his research assistant has not factored in the background and the real accomplishment from the visit. In 1979, when Vajpayee went, the Sino-Soviet polemics had continued with revived intensity. Moscow was deeply worried that the Indian foreign minister would be charmed by Peking and that relations with the Soviet Union would be correspondingly downgraded. I had done my best to assure the Russians in advance that beneficial bilateralism did not amount to risking the dilution of old friendships, but I was still worried that China could deliberately embarrass us. Deng-Hsiao Ping had toured the US just prior to Vajpayee's visit and on every occasion he had denounced the Soviet Union. Deliberate anti-Sovietism seemed like a planned method of cultivating the USA at the time. On arriving in Peking, even prior to the banquet, I called on Vice Minister Han-nien-Lung and told him that in the speech to be delivered that evening, we did not want any criticism of Russia. It was an anticipatory precaution but proved a wise one. This was the only Chinese speech in those months without any criticism of the USSR.

Vajpayee's visit to China was also fruitful for many specific reasons, the details of which seem to have escaped Dixit's attention: (a) China stopped referring to Kashmir as it had been doing in the past to please Pakistan; (b) until our relations diverged on Afghanistan in 1980, China stopped making a separate mention of Sikkim in its statements, underlining non-recognition of its constitutional integration with India; (c) the Chinese confirmed that in the future they would not give arms to any insurgents in the north-east of India. In other words, on all live controversial questions, there was definite progress.

CONCRETE IMPROVEMENTS FROM CHINA VISIT

I would like to add that we had agreed in advance that the territorial question would not be discussed in Peking. A full *de jure* territorial settlement poses a political problem for any government, especially in a coalition on how to get a constitutional amendment ceding Aksai Chin as part of the formula of mutual accommodation. The 1962 war was essentially for political and not territorial gains, as was confirmed by the withdrawal from NEFA (Arunachal) in November 1962. In 1965, I went on record affirming that if we did not give China any serious provocation, there was unlikely to be a major conflict with that country or a tilt in favour of Pakistan.

I will not dwell on some small inaccuracies in the book. Some Indian critics (not the Soviets) needlessly saw the Chinese attack on Vietnam when Vajpayee was in the tourist part of the visit as a deliberate insult to India. It would suffice to mention that Indo-Soviet relations remained wholly undamaged. The proof was the visit of Kosygin to Delhi in the next month (March 1979). Only twenty months after the first official visit of Morarji Desai, Brezhnev—not Kosygin, his counterpart—asked the Indian prime minister not to transit but to spend some days in discussions and attend functions in Moscow in June 1979.

JUNE 1979: A HIGH POINT IN FOREIGN POLICY BIPARTISANSHIP

In my view, the month of June 1979, when Morarji-Vajpayee returned after their second visit to Moscow and eastern Europe, was the highest point in our foreign policy. The late Emily Macfarquahar of the *Economist* acknowledged this. (I cannot think of any other period when India was totally free of international criticism or malevolence from any part of the world.) Mid-1955 has been often considered the high point of international respect for India. In that year Churchill called Nehru the 'Light of Asia', but by 1955 Pakistan had already joined the Baghdad Pact and SEATO. In June 1979, Washington, Moscow, Peking, Islamabad, the Arabs and the Third World—and also London, Paris, Bonn, Cairo, Riyadh, etc.—respected India; at least none misunderstood our country. We had only one unresolved major problem baffling us—continued fuel supply for the Tarapur reactor. However, Morarji and Carter had similar values and principles. (The two, to the surprise of assembled guests, escaped unnoticed from a White House banquet to visit the Lincoln and Jefferson memorials in Washington!) Even when India and the US disagreed or became hugely embarrassed by a super sensitive microphone picking up Carter's whisper to Cyrus Vance, the Secretary of State, to write a 'rude and blunt letter' on non-proliferation, there was dissent without giving way to public anger. The year 1979, in my view, was the culmination of diplomacy which had the unspoken backing of bipartisanship and national consensus. Alas, the Janata government disintegrated in July 1979.

STRATEGY FOR INDIAN DIPLOMACY

The period I have described, which Dixit sidesteps or misinterprets, happened more than twenty years ago. There are, however, lessons of abiding validity for the future. Let me dwell on what I think should remain the broad definition of the ends and role of diplomacy as a means of India's foreign policy. These *mutatis mutandis* must also permeate the approach to India-Pakistan relations. For me, India's strength as a non-expansionist, instinctively non-militaristic nation with a unique pluralist heritage and a flawed but functioning democracy, lies in its faith in purposeful diplomacy. Notwithstanding Nehru's many misjudgements, the distilled legacy in my view remains in greater reliance on enlightened internationalism. I also cannot help feeling that even in this violent, strife-torn world, the Gandhian obiter *dictum*, of showing sensitivity and understanding to the merits of the adversary, provides the path to diplomatic problem resolution. From Gandhi we can also learn that self-righteousness is not real patriotism; indeed it can be counterproductive. Further, arrogance, suspected or real, is not a good lubricant to diplomatic persuasion. Nehru himself rejected total disarmament and non-violence. (I have written to Perkovich, the author of the book entitled *India's Nuclear Bomb*, expressing my disagreement with his contention that Nehru would have approved of India going nuclear—but anyway, the nuclear eggs cannot now be unscrambled. We hope ours will not be Saddamized.) The application of the Nehru heritage to diplomacy signifies the courage to limit militarization to 'sufficiency' (a Schevernadze, the Soviet Foreign Minister, phrase in a General Assembly speech) and being on guard against competitive and imitative condign power. Extrapolating from the principles of non-alignment means maximizing the latitude to gallop economically and socially, keeping as the benchmark a target of an eight, preferably ten per cent growth rate as essential to our long-term political stability and security. A militarized India which remains comparatively poor will continue to be misunderstood by its neighbours and only lose in international respect. Unlike the defence establishment, which must go by the capability calculus, a foreign office must have the courage to identify the 'probable' rather than the 'possible' external threat including the menace of terrorism. I am conscious of the memory of the defeat against China, but to my mind, apart from the military failure, it was a diplomatic misjudgement, first in not understanding China's proud nationalism and then not recognizing its ambition to be pre-eminent in Asia. In the probability scale, the threat of terror is far higher; though much of it is from the Pakistan border, there is also desperation within the country from poor governance and socio-economic stagnation.

Obviously, finding an appropriate blend between guns and butter is forbiddingly hazardous, and all but a real statesman would shirk from making a choice. Anyway, I cannot think of Nehru echoing Bhutto that India's future lay in affirming the 'we will eat grass', etc., approach. That is a recipe for a failed state as nearly happened with Pakistan and was evident in the confused and contradictory responses to terrorism and militancy. India is better placed in its adherence to its own heritage and principles.

India's ultimate strength and destiny rest in showing that democracy within a civil society, even in a poor country, can deliver social justice and economic growth and yet remain a stalwart of principled internationalism. (China has run away with our clothes —economic strength through a mixed economy and higher international standing.) The geography and the unity prescribed by monsoons, even failed ones, will not change and must be consciously respected. Therefore, our most formidable foreign policy challenge remains winning and keeping the trust of our neighbours. Our failures can be seen in allowing our exaggerated fears to take root. Even if not wholly justified, these apprehensions have inflicted intangible penalties in the opportunity costs for us. The upstream deforestation in Nepal has led to heavy siltation, downstream floods and the inability to harness renewable power for India. Maoism in Nepal is in part traceable to India's diplomatic shortsightedness. The suspicions create fertile ground for Pakistan's diplomatic mischief and spread this virus of allegations of hegemonism of India.

Perhaps it was only by happenstance that I was entrusted with the leadership for negotiations with four of our neighbours and was given latitude for initiatives in four other hard diplomatic challenges. I am confident that even in difficult problems, some in stalemate for many years, patient and sensitive diplomacy can overcome rigidities to arrive at agreements which enhance national interests. Let me, however, repeat that successful negotiations hinge on the backing of an enlightened government but professionals must see it as their duty to offer unsolicited constructive advice. If by chance, negotiating responsibilities fall on one's shoulders, what makes the difference is whether one brings to the task the long-held distant vision of true national destiny. Professionals must at least never be content with gaining short-term populist brownie points for domestic applause.

There are many thoughtful analysts in India today who have a sort of intellectual schizophrenia: they are against the manifestations of communalism within the country but hesitant or even opposed to the goal of improving India-Pakistan relations. For me it was heartening that the cycle of the Godhra-Gujarat violence was reversed in the Akshardham temple in Gandhinagar.

In the long run, there has to be consistency in domestic and foreign policy, especially where ethnicity and minorities are affected. If there are militant communal incidents, then the broad support of good relations with Pakistan is bound to have even less appeal and coherence. I for one have long believed that it is in India's narrow interest to enusre that Pakistan and all our neighbours are stable and prosperous. Hopefully they will work their own way towards democracy at home. Pakistan, on the other side, must learn to rejoice, at least privately, in secularism in India and abandon the frustration of holding on to the ghosts of the two-nation theory. Therefore, with my old respect for Dixit, I would disagree with the concluding judgement that we must approach Pakistan with 'abundant caution'.

Appendix

J.N. DIXIT
Indian Foreign Service (Retd.)

Former Foreign Secretary
to the Government of India

House No. AJM 102A
Arjun Marg
DLF Qutab Enclave Phase-I
Gurgaon-122002

Tel. : 91-6351800 (From Delhi)
Fax: 91-6351555 (From Delhi)
STD: 0124-6351800, 0124-6351555
ISO: 0091-0124-6351800,
0091-124-6351555
E-mail: jndixit@hotmail.com

November 27, 2002

Dear Sir,

I have received your letter of 14th of November along with the long communication commenting on my book: 'India and Pakistan in War and Peace'.

I am grateful to you for having spent so much time reading the book in such detail. Your letter is full of additional information and valuable comments.

The question of my rejecting your critical evaluation just cannot arise. It is also true that some of the details of India's relations with Pakistan and China between 1977 and 1979 have not been mentioned in my book in detail as you have stated in your long letter.

Thank you for providing additional perspective, or a different perspective to the book which I wrote.

I do hope that your letter could be published as a Monograph or a commentary on my book.

With regards and respects,

Yours sincerely,
(J.N. Dixit)

Shri Jagat Singh Mehta
Jeewan Niwas
Udaipur – 313001
RAJASTHAN

12

Resolving Kashmir in the Perspective of the 1990s

Kashmir in the 1990s must be seen against the backdrop of the about-face in world politics and the tribulations confronting both India and Pakistan after four-and-a-half decades of Independence. The Cold War edifice, based on little substance and more paranoia, conditioned the whole world to the paradigms of strategic globalism. While some analysts of 'great power' politics acknowledge the past fallacies, others continue to justify them with post-hoc rationalizations and fail to recognize that the Cold War might well have been needlessly debilitating. At all events, a revolutionary reversal and restructuring of adversary relationship is now underway. The Third World, which had got accustomed to the leverage or fears from the great-power competition, has not yet fully grasped the implications of this change in world politics. A more objective history of discarding intellectual vested interests should help to liberate the mindsets bequeathed by these decades.

PARTITION WAS NOT THE LESSER EVIL

From whichever national angle one may look at Kashmir, it has bled India and Pakistan through tensions, frustrations and wars. India and Pakistan will regain the constructive confidence necessary to redeem the pledges of national freedom only if they, after an introspective scrutiny, are prepared to effect a catharsis by acknowledging the penalties of past misjudgements. Significant opinions in both countries are veering towards acknowledging

*Originally published in Raju G.C. Thomas (ed.), *Perspectives of Kashmir: The Roots of Conflict in South Asia*, Boulder: Westview, 1992.

that Partition was not the unavoidable lesser evil, as had been made out by most earlier analysts and associated decision-makers. Partition did not solve the problem of the Muslim minority in old India. Pakistan did not achieve a national cohesion around a shared faith which, transcending geography, could weld sub-identities and sub-ethnicities. The co-religionists in East Pakistan ultimately revolted against the domination by West Pakistan. In the western half, religion has not subsumed the minority apprehensions of the Sindhis, Baluchis and Pathans or prevented strife between the different sects of Islam. More significantly, those who migrated from India with a conviction in the two-nation theory are still looked upon as foreigners (Muhajirs).

India's 110 million Muslims remain on the defensive. They were saved from further degradation and condemnation as second-class citizens only because India's secular democratic constitution gave them a bargaining political leverage in the electoral arithmetic. Even so, the Muslims remain hostage to the majority's suspicions of their loyalty to the country of their domicile. But having been deserted by a large proportion of the elite with education, wealth, and administrative experience, they remain economically handicapped. The Indian National Congress, in its exasperation at the perceived delay in gaining independence, overlooked the long-term economic and ecological consequences of a transparently artificial division of the country. There was a vague hope in India of an early reunification of the country. But in the meanwhile, the Congress leaders welcomed the incidental gain in the prospect of being able to establish a strong, purposeful, modern democratic and secular federal government. (This, of course, is now being questioned for both its design and its execution.)

The third party to Partition, the British government, was so enfeebled from an exhausting war that it did not have the capability to hold the ring and manage the suspicion-riddled politics of India. But it was exasperation, not statesmanship, which determined the way the British decided to divide and quit.

Some recent research, including that by Pakistani scholars (for instance, Ayesha Jalal), suggests that even while crusading for a separate Muslim majority state, Jinnah's original purpose was only to bargain for a balancing weightage in the Central Government of undivided India. When Pakistan looked like becoming a reality, Jinnah, on the question of how to safeguard the future rights of the Muslim minority left behind in India, could only bank on the balance of hostages—the Hindu and Sikh minorities in the new state of Pakistan as against the Muslims in Hindu majority India. Jinnah hoped Pakistan would give full protection to the minority community.[1]

In any event, none of the three contending political parties—the Congress, the Muslim League, and the British Government—foresaw the holocaust killings of half a million and the cross-border migrations that exceeded, in total, seventeen million Muslims from eastern Punjab and northern India to Pakistan and of Hindus and Sikhs from the whole of West Pakistan eastward across the new frontier. In retrospect, when looking at the consequences of Partition, it could plausibly be contended that persisting with a loose federal structure, initially on the lines of the British Cabinet Mission proposal (1946), with residuary powers with the states, would have been less pregnant with disaster.

One recalls all this not to contemplate the unscrambling of the present political frontiers but to underline that optimal progress by the countries will come only with the unabashed recognition of the enmeshed plurality and interdependence of the subcontinent. The patchwork of religious and cultural multiplicity—which was the somewhat unique feature of the 'Indian' civilization—cannot be scissored along any rational seam in the fabric. Instead of stability in the separated parts, the divisions have increased the propensity towards social tensions and internal political violence and have compounded the temptation to turn to outside dependence. This acknowledgement means that improvisations in response to a particular crisis (as at present in Kashmir) must not offend the eventual possibility of functional cooperation between nations of the subcontinent where the monsoon and the rivers determine their permanent interdependence.

CONFOUNDING FALLACIES OF THE COLD WAR

The 'original sin' of Partition was compounded by the fallacious premises of the Cold War which enveloped the subcontinent in the great-power ideological and strategic competition and, in the process, militarized these poor nations, retarded their development, and exacerbated tensions between them. The story of how Pakistan became a Western ally in the Baghdad Pact (later CENTO) and SEATO and, as a balance, how India turned to the Soviet Union for military aid and political support has been variously described. In this context, it need only be mentioned that the implicit premise of advantages from the respective linkages with the great powers were frequently exposed as fallacious but, in the entrenched suspicions of the great powers at one level and in the subcontinent at the other, they were never fully digested even by sophisticated analysts. India did not anticipate, or at least took no effective steps to forestall the alliance between the US and the military regime in Pakistan in 1953-4 because it truly took seriously its belief that the USA would not arm a country against the largest functioning democracy in the Third World. Later, India also did not foresee that Pakistan would repudiate its anti-communist commitment and bring about a China-Pakistan rapprochement, which, in the spring of 1962, led to the provisional ceding of some territory to China out of what were considered the inherited frontiers of the state of Jammu and Kashmir.

Likewise, Pakistan was taken aback when in the 1965 Indo-Pakistan conflict, the US did not support its 'ally' Pakistan. In fact, the US stopped military aid to Pakistan after the latter launched its efforts to wrest Kashmir. The governments of neither India nor Pakistan anticipated that Washington and Moscow would work together and not at cross purposes in the UN Security Council to bring about a ceasefire. At Tashkent, the USSR was impartial, with no tilt towards India and, as the Lyndon Johnson papers in the Presidential Library show, the US was fully supportive of Kosygin's mediatory effort. When the Soviet Union sold substantial arms to Pakistan in 1968, the purpose was to balance the influence of China in Pakistan, not to subvert a US ally nor to encourage Pakistan's belligerence against India.

The Soviet Union has stood by India in vetoing resolutions when Pakistan insisted on bringing the Kashmir dispute to the UN Security Council. However, since Tashkent, except for the later stages of the Bangladesh crisis in 1971—that is, after Pakistan arranged for the secret visit of Kissinger to Peking (July), the Indo-Soviet Treaty (August), and the attempted gunboat diplomacy of the *USS Enterprise* (December)—both superpowers, though coming from different past positions, have had parallel and not antagonistic approaches to the India-Pakistan relations. The point to note is that, in general, India and Pakistan should have understood that neither the US nor the USSR was wholly identified with partisan affiliations on regional issues—notwithstanding the Cold War—transfer of aid and arms, and humouring the loyalty of their 'client' and not gratuitously disabusing their hopes. Both superpowers wanted to see a regional détente fructify in South Asia. After the Bangladesh war, while they were hesitant to take the initiative, both the US and the USSR indirectly gave every encouragement and support to the success of Indo-Pakistan bilateral normalization (1976) and Salal negotiations (1976).

When the Soviet Union intervened in Afghanistan, the subcontinental adversaries succumbed to the erroneous analyses and policies of the superpowers, and as a consequence the fallacious 1954 scenario was re-enacted. In intervening directly in Afghanistan the Soviet Union had acted impetuously, but it was with a defensive psychology, to eliminate a disillusioned pro-Soviet ideologue. The justification by Moscow that the US was planning to establish itself in the soft belly of the USSR was, to my mind, a transparent public posture and rationalization. On the other side, it was equally patent that the Carter White House and American establishment were mistaken in their fear that the real aim of the USSR was to sever the oil artery to the West. India and Pakistan should have separately and jointly stood aloof from these great-power war fallacies and misjudgements. But the intellectual surrender to the great-power propaganda or ill-grounded fears led to the rude and disastrous reversal of the process of steady improvement in India-Pakistan relations, underway since 1976. The misperceptions finally became plain (and took Washington, New Delhi and Islamabad by surprise) with the unilateral withdrawal of the Soviet forces. Indeed, the pro-Soviet ideologically 'progressive' government of Najibullah itself was taken aback at being abandoned when it faced continued insurrection from diverse fundamentalist and anti-Soviet nationalists. Now the insurgent groups are baffled that lobbies in Washington are retracting aid and support for their anti-communist crusade! In the context of Afghanistan, I have argued in print for the last decade[2] that the horrendous penalties of misjudgements on all sides could have been avoided if the Cold War postures had not been taken at their face value by the countries of the subcontinent.

Since the 1960s it has been my persuasion[3] that notwithstanding defensive vigilance, political competition and occasional initiatives to seize targets of opportunity, both superpowers have had an overriding community of interest in non-conflict and stability. In fact, despite the occasional one step forward as part of the war-game habits of defensive vigilance, in general, they have been retreating from partisan involvement in Third World conflicts. The process has now culminated in the dramatic repudiations of friends and allies. Even the pretensions of shared ideological or strategic interests have been jettisoned. Examples are Vietnam, Ethiopia, Cuba, Somalia and Mozambique. One implication of this sea change in the superpower relations is that the problem of Kashmir must now be seen as reverting to the crucibles of the domestic politics of India and Pakistan. All hopes for creating the conditions for resolutions hinge on the sensitive sagacity of their bilateral diplomacy and internal reorientation of priorities.

THE CRUDE, CONFIDENTIAL REALITIES OF THE KASHMIR PROBLEM

After forty-four years of a tension-riddled story, the crude political reality about Kashmir remains that no government in Delhi could peacefully acquiesce in the detachment of the state of Jammu and Kashmir, or any further part outside Azad Kashmir, from the Indian Union. On the other side, no government in Islamabad could appear half-hearted in helping to detach the Valley from

Indian control. But behind this impasse, there had developed an unspoken common ground. Ritual reaffirmation notwithstanding, at least since Simla 1972 and possibly Tashkent 1966, Pakistan was content to let the Kashmir question recede into the limbo of half-forgotten unresolved international problems. Indeed for some years, one could privately observe that Kashmir as an India-Pakistan problem had been solved with a de facto division along the ceasefire line. (If, however, such an affirmation was brazenly trumpeted, it would invite a 'firm' denial.) The situation was somewhat similar to the unresolved Sino-Indian boundary problem but with the fundamental difference that there were no Tibetans, Ladakhis or Kashmiris inhabiting the barren Aksai Chin plateau.

When, however, the present disaffection erupted in the Valley in 1989-90, the central governments in Islamabad and Delhi reacted in predictable fidelity to their old public postures and not their prudent silence. Benazir Bhutto and the Pakistan Peoples Party (PPP) had put no emphasis on Kashmir in the electoral campaign in 1988, but when in 1989, the PPP came under criticism from the opposition, led by Nawaz Sharif, at the indifference to the strident liberation struggle in the Valley, Benazir could not risk appearing to be indifferent to the efforts of the Kashmiri people to break out of Indian control. Not to be outdone by the opposition in expression of sympathy and support, she echoed her father's pledge to fight India for a thousand years over Kashmir. Yielding to populist sentiments, combined with the pressure from sections of the Army General Staff and the powerful Inter-services Intelligence Agency, she acquiesced in authorizing support to the Kashmir 'freedom fighters'.

The newly constituted coalition government of V.P. Singh in India, also sensitive to populist pressures, could not appear weak-kneed at the revived threat to national integrity, and so, transposing cause and consequences, yielded to the old line that Pakistan was the primary factor behind the violent disaffection in the Valley. While lip service was paid to an eventual political solution, the immediate thrust of policy was to authorize stronger steps at counter-insurgency. As the situation in the Valley continued to deteriorate, the decibels of mutually reinforcing rhetoric were correspondingly raised in both countries. It resulted in creating, at least for a while, the atmospherics of an impending India-Pakistan war even though in cold reason, neither government wanted to see it precipitated.

ORIGIN OF THE PRESENT DISAFFECTION

It may be recalled that in 1947 and 1965, the initiative for the armed infiltration into the valley had come from Pakistan. The people in the Valley, however, showed no heart to join in a jehad against Indian domination or in their own 'liberation'. Eventually, the national armies of the two countries became locked in combat, but when the ceasefire agreements, sponsored by the UN Commission in 1948-9 and the Security Council in 1965, came into effect, tensions got quickly defused. The current crisis is the culmination of years of perverse politics in the state, especially following the death of Sheikh Abdullah in 1982. For all the vicissitudes of its long political record, the National Conference has continued to command a substantial following amongst the Kashmiris including some non-Muslims in the Valley. Farooq Abdullah inherited the mantle of the Sheikh and the support of the party. Even when he consorted with the National Front—a coalition of parties opposed to the central government under Mrs Gandhi and the Congress Party—he did not lose his popular support, but it provoked the anger of the authorities in Delhi. In consequence, Farooq Abdullah's government was superseded and a Congress-supported coalition with defectors from the National Conference was installed under G.M. Shah. The governor (B.K. Nehru), who opposed this travesty of parliamentary democracy, resigned and was finally transferred. After a period out of office, Farooq Abdullah changed his political affiliations and made a compact with Rajiv Gandhi's government and the Congress Party and was reinstated as the chief minister. The 1987 state elections held following this unprincipled coalition are generally believed to have been riddled with serious malpractices. In the process of these political somersaults, Farooq Abdullah lost a great deal of his own political standing and damaged the National Conference in the eyes of the Kashmiris.

During these years of imposed or unprincipled politics, corruption became rampant; socio-economic development got even more sluggish, and all this fanned disenchantment, especially amongst the growing numbers of the educated unemployed youth. The resentment got crystallised into a will for defiant disaffection against the Indian connection. The winds of fundamentalism and the stories of 'heroic terrorist' round the world provided the inspiration and the spur to turn the latent dissatisfaction into militancy. With funds from the illicit drug trade and arms readily pilfered or easily bought from the Afghan Mujahidin in Pakistan, the insurgency took the shape of a classic liberation struggle. This 'liberation' movement—divided in many respects but united against India—received not just political encouragement from diverse anti-Indian elements in Pakistan but also sophisticated arms, material support, training and guidance from the official Pakistan agencies. Infiltration across the porous border became easier than it had been when there was not the same kind of popular dissatisfaction. The origins of the present people's disaffection can be traced to maladministration and political manipulation jointly and separately by authorities in Delhi and Srinagar, but it has been aggravated by official, semi-official, and religious support from Pakistan. But managing the crisis is beyond Pakistan alone; it must reckon with the people committed to independent defiance disregarding the destruction of their own homeland.

INTERNATIONAL EXASPERATION AND DETACHMENT

The international media has publicized the sullen and militant alienation of the people, the breakdown of civil authority and the repression and violation of human rights by the security forces in the Valley. This gives encouragement to the militants and raises their hopes of international intervention. These insurgents have resorted to misinformation to inflame international opinion against India. Impartial observers have, however, publicized that the insurgents are also indulging in brutal killings of innocent civilians and needless disruption of the economic life of the Valley. But censorship and official control of information have increased the bitterness and complaints and the general suspicion that the Indian authorities are concealing a policy of brutal suppression.

Even in the face of all these reports of violence and clashes between security forces and the militants, the reactions of the international community have ranged from indifference to exasperation. Even if not convinced by the official Indian viewpoint—that the Kashmir disaffection comes only from Pakistan's connivance and support—international opinion, including that of the great powers, is unsympathetic to the idea of unscrambling the existing dispensation and demarcations in Kashmir. Countries with past interests in the subcontinent, when approached, have responded with pleas for peace and direct parleys between the governments of India and Pakistan. The great powers have shown no heart for an active separate or joint initiative. The Gates Mission from the US, which visited Delhi and Islamabad in the spring of 1990, was deliberately low key, with the limited purpose of averting a war by miscalculation, and more specifically by warning Pakistan against the use of nuclear weapons. Subsequently, the US in a significant departure from its earlier position has officially stated that it no longer favours a plebiscite in fulfilment of the old UN resolutions. There may even be a quiet recognition amongst responsible or interested governments that, while the revival of outside initiatives cannot prove fruitful, any resurrection of the old UN resolutions or a new attempt at international mediation may actually ignite the explosive situation. One can safely predict that every attempt will be made to discourage the revival of the Kashmir question for formal consideration before the UN Security Council.

THE DILEMMAS FOR INDIA AND PAKISTAN

This benign advocacy for a 'peaceful resolution by the parties' comes close to the Indian position that the Simla Agreement, which envisaged bilateral negotiations provided the modality for a final settlement of the question. However, the present international attitude reflects detachment and not partisanship. When the governments in power in India and Pakistan are transparently weak, and political parties are posturing before or after their national elections, a bilateral meeting on Kashmir, even at the summit level, could at best only initiate confidence-building measures. It is unlikely to end in a substantive resolution of the problem. As at present, any Pakistan government, be it led by Benazir Bhutto's or Nawaz Sharif's, would find it politically suicidal to accept the Line of Control as an international frontier. In fact, the Pakistan government can no longer conceal that despite religious affinity, there is growing dissatisfaction in the Pakistan-occupied part with the heavy-handed control and denial of democratic freedoms.

Pakistan, of course, takes a malevolent satisfaction in the revived headlining of the Kashmir problem, but one suspects it cannot be easy to reach a consensus in Islamabad on what should be the actual steps to be pursued to take advantage of the situation. Various elements in Pakistan—the officer corps, the intelligence agencies—would like to avenge the defeat in Bangladesh and may be tempted to give more supportive bolstering to the insurgents and so paralyse and then sever the Indian control of and connection with the Valley. But those holding ultimate governmental responsibility cannot be unaware that escalating the militancy could trigger a war with India with unpredictable consequences and without realization of the national goal of accession of the state to Pakistan.

Drawing their subjective lessons from the Gulf scenario, the extreme pro-American fringe and the anti-Indian elements in Pakistan might hope that if an India-Pakistan war should break out, another US-led international coalition would intervene and, like Kuwait, Kashmir would be 'liberated' and a UN regime established which would permit 'self-determination' for the state. However, it must be realized that such direct intervention even in the post-Cold War convergence of the great powers is unlikely. Kashmir does not have the strategic importance of oil from the Gulf. Moreover, Kashmir is legally a part of India, not a separate sovereign state and India is not a brutal dictatorship. There could be no illusion that India would resist such an intervention even against a multinational coalition constituted with UN approval. As in 1965, the field of conflict is not likely to be restricted to Kashmir, nor would ground operations end in a hundred hours.

Moreover, Pakistan's relations with the US are now bedevilled with suspicions of nuclear proliferation and even the budgeted aid allocations for the current financial year have not been released.

In the unlikely event of an India-Pakistan war, what is likely is again a resort to the UN Security where the US, Russia and others would marshal their combined efforts for a ceasefire ending in a new 'Tashkent', this time more likely at 'Camp David' and under American tutelage. When both countries are near bankruptcy, the stick wielded by the State Department and the World Bank would be telling and could bring about the end of a conflict even if such pressures were insufficient to compel a final settlement. The present international consensus seems to be that even if the Kashmir Valley simmers, it will not ignite. Most countries feel that it is a tragedy that this beautiful valley should be in a ferment which economically debilitates two important countries in Asia, pre-empts tourism, and politically erodes their respective standing. As hinted earlier, the threshold of tolerance, or call it exasperation, of Third World conflicts is much higher than when every problem was seen as a piece in the global strategic chessboard.

This nonchalant detachment may cause Pakistan some anxiety, but it does not warrant comfort or complacency in India. Kashmir is a grave internal threat to India as it compounds the centrifugal strains in national politics, when India faces simultaneously violent disaffection in the Punjab, Assam, Telengana and similar incipient protests elsewhere. Kashmir is also one out of the many situations in which the armed forces are dragged in support of civil power and in general this strains its morale. Kashmir vitiates the internal politics in both countries as the opposition has ammunition to criticize the government, while those in power are baffled by the choice between unsuccessful or dangerous options. Those in India directly responsible for policy directions on Kashmir privately concede that counter-insurgency operations have not, so far, proved effective. They are also not unaware that security operations often lead to needless brutalities which, in turn, swell the number of recruits for fearless militancy. It is conceded that the pacification of the Valley and recapturing the shattered trust of the Kashmiris is a political challenge and an urgent one for the Indian Union.

THE RATIONALE OF DÉTENTE BETWEEN ADVERSARIES

Facing this vicious politico-economic internal security and foreign policy problem obviously requires sagacity and sophistication. India and Pakistan cannot run away from it like the rest of the world. Ready lessons can, however, be distilled from the dramatic change in the nature and compulsions governing relations between the erstwhile adversarial East-West blocs. In many respects, India-Pakistan relations are a mirror image of the decades of US-Soviet confrontation. In both cases, mutually reinforcing suspicions led to protracted over-militarization and self-inflicted economic emasculation. Following introspective objectivity and a succession of measured unilateral concessions, Gorbachev managed to assuage the fears and suspicions of public opinion in the West. In turn, the cry for détente became a political pressure on Western governments to change course and make positive responses towards détente. The drive for strategic outreach has already halted: indeed many old bases will slowly if not dramatically be closed in the future. Gorbachev has acknowledged that the desperate economic situation in which the Soviet Union finds itself negates the utility of its military power and even undermines it as a sanction for diplomacy. The peoples of Eastern Europe have, in turn, demonstrated that the Berlin Wall of ideology and security was based on hollow fallacies. The Bush administration is still enjoying the political dividends of the Gulf victory, but thoughtful minds in the US are not unaware that all too soon and even in the next presidential elections the domestic economic situation may again come to the fore. Even in the face of the demonstration of the utility of sophisticated military hardware, a reduction in defence outlays and a slowing down on the manufacturing of new weapon systems may have to be brought about to effect the restructuring of the American economy, spur technological modernization and regain the self-reliant competitive edge for commerce.

Each one of these considerations applies mutatis mutandis to India and Pakistan. Indeed, in comparison with the area, resources and infrastructure of the US and the Soviet Union, the magnitude of the economic problems for both countries is immeasurably greater. But far from seeing the handwriting on the wall, India and Pakistan are under populist pressure to 'stiffen the sinews' and prepare for a war. The Warsaw Pact has been wound up and NATO powers are cutting defence expenditure by 20-30 per cent. China is reported to have cut back its army by half a million. However, no steps have been initiated in South Asia so far to reduce forces, negotiate arms control agreements and shift priority attention to economic restructuring. The social opportunity costs of unrealistic threat perceptions must now be brought into the calculus when defining national interests. Like the Soviet Union, 'sufficient' and not overkill militarization can help meet people's strident expectations and overcome or at least moderate the eruptions that undermine the integrity and security of India and Pakistan. Both have to recognize that the multiple threat within is far greater than the hypothetical external dangers that have blinded the countries for the last three decades.

THE CHANGED CLIMATE FOR INTERNATIONAL AID

There are more direct consequences for the Third World from the transformation of East-West relations. For the West, the rehabilitation of Eastern Europe, with its ethnic and cultural pulls will have higher claim than even the basic needs of the poor nations. US military aid to Pakistan is already problematic and the Indian rupee payment for Soviet military hardware may likewise end. Most of the surplus of Soviet resources will go for internal rejuvenation and making perestroika work. With the shrinking availability of surplus resources from both blocs, India and Pakistan may find themselves jostling in the same queues as the former communist countries when looking for soft aid in convertible currencies. Even for commercial credits and investments by multinational corporations, the subcontinent countries with their declining credit rating may get a lower priority than former or even presently 'communist' countries. Paying for the Gulf War and the scores of billions required for reconstruction will also reduce the availability of external resources from the Arab states even for Pakistan. The leadership in India and Pakistan has not so far taken serious steps to educate their domestic opinion at this changed international climate, but however politically embarrassing it may be, the sooner they do so and spell out the implications the better.

THE WORLDWIDE PHENOMENON OF SUB-NATIONALISM

In their parochial fixation on Kashmir, India and Pakistan often overlook the fact that Kashmir is not the only case of frustrated aspirations of a minority and a sub-identity. At least analysts and informal academics and back-bench supporters of the governments should be tutored to bring out the fact that there is a worldwide phenomenon of sub-nationalism resembling Kashmir within well-established countries. The information revolution has raised political awareness around sub-national personalities. Sometimes fired by religion, sometimes ethnicity, language, or culture, or simply tribal solidarity, such protest movements have surfaced around the world and in many cases have taken violent and terrorist dimensions. Such sub-national disaffection, with its own special characteristics, bedevils the USSR (in the Baltic, Central Asia, Georgia and even the Ukraine), China (in Tibet and Sinkiang), the UK (in Ireland, Scotland and even Wales), Canada (in Quebec), and all over tribal Africa. Long-lasting civil wars in Sudan, Somalia, Angola, Mozambique and Ethiopia have precipitated famines, cost millions of lives, and are taking some countries back to the stone age. Yugoslavia, hovering on the brink of disintegration, provides a negative object lesson of the penalties of uncompromising militant subnationalism. India and Pakistan, however, must note that with a pluralist population complexion, it is better to loosen federalism than persist with the old conviction that a modern state must be unitary with a strong central government. On the other hand, India's own experience in Nagaland and Mizoram has showed that moderating political defiance and overcoming terrorist propensities require time, economic resources, socially sensitive programmes of development, and an unwavering commitment to democracy.

These factors—the change in the international climate, the world phenomenon of militant subnationalism, insurgency flowing from economic stagnation—must be understood by governments and articulated by non-official opinion to reorient the citizenry in India and Pakistan so that Kashmir can be seen in a constructive perspective.

THE PACIFICATION OF THE VALLEY

It would, however, be wishful to pretend that only enlightened perspectives and distant parallels would have an immediate telling impact on the insurgents already embattled in the Valley. The alienation in Kashmir has a long history of justified grievances and has created deep feelings of mistrust. It does not matter to those in the Valley that two to three million Kashmiris may be holding to ransom the future of a billion people in India and Pakistan and that nearly two-fifths of them, like many in Kashmir, are subsisting below the poverty level.

It is both a positive and a negative reality that the anti-Indian disaffection is not a united movement with an undisputed leadership and a coherent definition of goals and modalities. The Jammu and Kashmir Liberation Movement demands democracy and independence, but is strongly opposed to the state becoming a part of Pakistan. The fate of democracy in Azad Kashmir provides no attraction to them as an improvement to the connection with India. The Hizbe-Nizami and Hizbe-Mujahideen and some other groups are blatantly fired by a religious zest for Islamic solidarity and demand accession to Pakistan. As in dealing with the Afghan Mujahideen, Pakistan, through pressure and inducement, tries to create a unified coalition, but the preferential treatment of some fundamentalists only alienates the other groups. In fact, rivalries and even occasional conflicts highlight the differences between Pakistan's aims and the distinct features of the traditional Kashmiri personality with its affiliation to Sufism and religious catholicity. As in Afghanistan, Pakistan's purpose would be to enlarge the domains of its control and influence but it has to reckon with Kashmiri's aspirations for its traditional autonomous character.

THE POLICY CHALLENGE FOR INDIA

The challenge for India is to restore faith, at least for the more responsibly motivated, in a democratic political order which would permit the preservation of the distinct personality of Kashmir. This difficult task falls first and foremost on the Government of India and the governor, but its implementation rests with the officialdom down the line in the state machinery and the agencies of the central government functioning in Kashmir. There can be no let up in the responsibility to scotch insurgency, plug infiltration, ferret out the terrorists and persuade the law-abiding citizenry not to aid and comfort the militants. To quarantine Kashmir against militancy, until a political solution is reached, a ten-kilometre belt could be created running on both sides of the Line of Control from which all non-residents would be debarred and all residents required to carry laminated identity cards.

But when much of the population is alienated, what is required is simultaneous and not sequential steps to launch a credible political initiative and combine it with socio-economic developmental initiatives which are striking for their differences with the past. We can learn from the negative experiences of the US in Vietnam and El Salvador, the Soviet Union in Afghanistan, France in Algeria and the positive one of British counter-insurgency operations in Malay (in the 1950s). The lesson is that firepower and security operations alone are never effective unless there is the parallel track of a policy to regain the confidence of the broad mass of the people.

Conceding that the present deterioration started with sins of omissions and commissions in New Delhi and Srinagar, a whole gamut of measures have to be taken in order to create a new image of the civil government. Many thoughtful observers have worked in detailing steps which could wean the people away from their sullen disenchantment and conniving at violent disruption. To make a dramatic impact and assuage the feeling that Indian federalism has no respect or room for Kashmir's autonomous personality, a national policy of constitutional decentralization for the whole of India could be announced as a long-term goal. The demand to delete Article 370 of the constitution should be deflected in a policy of loosening over-centralization all over India. Secondly, repressive brutalities by security forces must be demonstratively punished; arbitrarily arrested persons against whom no charges are framed should be released; and the channels for redress of public grievances should be resurrected. In other words, the ugly memories of perverting democracy must be erased by restoring the legal processes.

Much needs to and can be done to revitalize the development of the state. Kashmir requires greater availability of electric power and improved communications within the valley. There should be a commitment to establish larger industrial units, beyond that there must be a greater impetus to handicrafts and small-scale industries. There should be greater support to agriculture and horticulture, and massive efforts by governmental and voluntary oragnizations at reforestation. All such economic policies must have a localized focus and should be planned to increase employment opportunities for the professionally trained youth. This would require freer availability of venture capital, and the reinduction of banking and financial institutions. Kashmir's economy depends overwhelmingly on tourism, which is transparently sensitive to the image of stability. An effective revival of tourism could go some way in separating the militants from those with established commitments to normalcy in towns and tourist centres. Everywhere, the credibility of a new approach will depend on whether the old corrupt leakage in the trickle down of the development process can be plugged demonstratively.

The new pacification and development approach must go hand in hand with an honest revival of democratic liberties including the right of peaceful protest, non-violent demonstration, the restoration of freedom to the local press to report and articulate criticism, and more autonomy in the programmes of the local television station. The present policies of media control and restrictive access to the foreign press have been counterproductive and should be reversed. Ultimately, credibility in the government's intent to restore democracy will come by a bold announcement to hold new provincial elections—as was done, despite the Khalistan insurgency, by the Chandrashekhar government for Punjab. One might recall that it was the free and fair elections of 1977 in the state of Jammu and Kashmir that demonstrated the working reality of the Indian democracy and revived faith in the Indian connection amongst the Kashmiri people.

A side consequence and a foretaste of the communal fallout is the displacement of 200,000 Hindus from the Valley into the cities of north India. Their bitterness is understandable and deserves sympathy and generous support for their temporary rehabilitation. They are victims of a long-tragic story, but their resentment should not be allowed to veto the political approaches to restore normalcy (and incidentally their return to their homes) any more than the Valley of Kashmir should continue to damage the future of both India and Pakistan.

The Jammu and Ladakh subdivisions, with their identities distinct from the Valley, have their own apprehensions about the political goals of the militants and even the notions of a looser autonomy for the state. But the answer eventually lies in the promise of general decentralization and not in the special vivisection of the old state of Jammu and Kashmir.

FURTHER POLITICAL UNSCRAMBLING WOULD REPEAT THE FOLLY OF PARTITION

But, and here is the rub, if permitting greater autonomy and decentralization is to be effective and peaceful, it must realistically stop short of the option of secession of Kashmir from the Indian Union. Again, lessons can be drawn from the wider world. It was prophetically wise of the Organization of African Unity (OAU) to decide that, regardless of the demographic, tribal and religious illogicality of the inherited imperialist frontiers, the old established boundaries of Nigeria would not be altered. Not just the OAU, both the superpowers and international consensus (with the exception of France, China and a few others) stood by the federal structure of Nigeria, and eventually Biafra capitulated and the meaningful unity of Nigeria was restored which has not thereafter been seriously strained.

Pakistan, in its self-interest, must not risk arousing, much less provoking, the monsters of secession and communalism in India. With three million unassimilated Afghans, Pakistan cannot accommodate another massive wave of refugees. Unlike Israel, which still keeps itself open as a homeland for the flood of Jews from Eastern Europe and elsewhere, neither Pakistan nor the fifteen other Muslim majority nations are likely to receive the co-religionists wanting to migrate to their countries. Beyond the issues of communalism and enforced migrations, it would be irresponsible to underestimate the hardship from a long-lasting civil conflict creating chaotic disruption of the normal life in Kashmir. It would be well to recall that Vietnam had a worthy cause, but it has still not recovered economically after its successful liberation struggle. As mentioned earlier, many Third World countries (like Lebanon and Nicaragua) and Afghanistan are vivid monuments of destructive civil conflicts. Kuwait, Iraq and Iran, even with their oil surpluses, may take decades to fully rebuild their economies.

Carrying the economic logic a step further, there must be a principled restraint in all policies whose primary justification is to beggar the neighbour. Those who advocate India retaliating against Pakistan for abetting the insurgency in Kashmir by fuelling the Sind disaffection against the Muhajirs are also guilty of another Cold War fallacy; viz., that outside fostering of internal problems for a potential adversary is a decisive national security gain. In fact, as a rule, such actions strengthen non-representative governments and perpetuate non-enlightened policies. If an India-Pakistan détente is the ultimate goal and India wants Pakistan to deny support to the Kashmir militants, then the support for the Najibullah government in Afghanistan must not be motivated by the enemy's enemy rationale. However long and difficult, self-denying restraint has a psychological importance, far exceeding the nuisance value of irritants.

THE BASIC QUESTION

This brings one to the basic intellectual conundrum in both India and Pakistan in the assessment and approach to the resolution of the Kashmir problem: is Kashmir the cause and the root of India-Pakistan tensions or is it its perverse result? Nobody would dispute that the cause and consequences get viciously entangled. But in India, and more so in Pakistan, there is a strongly held view that Kashmir must be settled first and only then can normalization of ties follow or be facilitated. The obverse of the same argument is that if Pakistan does not keep its hands off Kashmir, India has no alternative but to be prepared for thousand years of struggle and defence, for if Kashmir goes, then, as it is argued, secularism, democracy, Punjab, all north-eastern states, and possibly the southern states, could aspire to detach from the Indian Union. As a part of electoral rhetoric in 1991—perhaps no more than that—a senior politician threatened that as a protest against the domination by the central government of the Gangetic heartland, his own state could contemplate seceding from India. One might recall that in 1947, not just the Nizam but some other medium-sized princely states contemplated full independence after the lapse of paramountcy. There is a very strong and justifiable national consensus against the dismemberment of India even if it means economic penalties and another India-Pakistan conflict. Even disaffected states seem to take for granted the economic linkages and infrastructural dependence on the whole of the Indian market. Incidentally, a splintered India would also set a bad example for Pakistan. Both countries must take decentralization more seriously, but both have an enlightened interest in the federal unity of the other country. It is also worth recalling that when relations between India and Pakistan were free of active friction (as during the period 1966-70 and 1976-80), even though the Kashmir problem was not officially settled, the economy of Kashmir was comparatively on the ascendant.

A LARGER VISION AND A LONGER PERSPECTIVE

A responsible approach to the Kashmir question must be for the long term and in line with the larger vision for the subcontinent as a whole. The endeavour must be to recapture the unique pluralist, tolerant and assimilative features of the Indian civilization. The imperatives of restoring democracy, of defusing and not adding to communalism in the national body politic, of promoting greater confidence in the Muslim minority in India, of not precipitating displacements within the country and migrations abroad, of developmental progress through functional cooperation where it is economically beneficial, are all in keeping with the new thrust of world politics and economics.

Both countries must strive to rediscover in their self-interest that the lesser evil is to work towards a climate of bilateral relations which afford scope for the plurality of religions and autonomy in Kashmir. India-controlled Kashmir and Pakistan-occupied Kashmir could not be quarantined from contacts across the ceasefire line. To ensure a cooperative approach, Pakistan cannot for ever be excluded from a non-political role and links with Kashmir. But to include Pakistan in a constructive involvement, the precondition as stated is the chemistry of mutual trust. Pakistan must begin by acknowledging that India and Pakistan cannot prosper in suspicion or hostility. India has to demonstrate, by deeds and not by declarations alone, that it has sympathy and, where feasible, stake in assisting in the resolution of Pakistan's own economic problems. Small but significant unilateral restraints, as followed by Gorbachev's diplomacy, could have disproportionate psychological benefits while running minimal security risks. After the Saur revolution in Afghanistan in April 1978, India made a telling impact by unilaterally assuring Pakistan that it would not take advantage of any tensions which may develop between the Democratic Republic of Afghanistan and Islamic Pakistan. Since the US was simultaneously informed of this assurance, Pakistan's request for A7 aircraft was actually refused by Washington in May 1978. This nurtured trust was shattered after the divergent reactions to the Soviet intervention in Afghanistan in January 1980.

My negotiating experience with Pakistan, Bangladesh and Nepal convinced me that the demonstration of sensitive respect for the anxieties, however exaggerated, of our South Asian neighbours can help dilute if not disarm entrenched suspicions. It has never been noted, for example, that following the normalization of relations with Pakistan and the resolution of the deadlocked negotiations on the Salal dam on the Chenab, it was Pakistan's helpful neutrality which facilitated the withdrawal, before voting, of the Farakka item inscribed by Bangladesh in the General Assembly agenda of 1976. If the item had been voted upon, no interim agreement on the lean season division of the Ganges flow at Farakka would have been reached in 1977. Indeed, like the item on South Asia nuclear free zone, Farakka would have become a hardy annual international embarrassment for India and an additional irritant to India-Bangladesh and India-Pakistan bilateral relations.

Diplomacy between unequal neighbours in the twentieth century cannot rely on the power of coercion from size or superior military capability; it must reckon with the strength of nationalism which gives grit and bravado to defiance. If the false fears of Indian hegemonism have to be assuaged, India must go beyond the compartmentalized resolution of specific problems with different countries in its neighbourhood. India has to stoop not to conquer but to catalyse cooperation. But Pakistan too must, by now, become more confident of its identity, independent of the Indian bogey. Pakistan's foreign policy must not revolve around the fear of India or a political crusade against it.

Today, nation-states have to manage two powerful contrary forces. On the one side they have to deal with the centripetal politics of nationalism and on the other, they must improve the capability of earning international exchange, promoting trans-national trade and forging links for wider functional cooperation. Kashmir wants independent fulfilment but it endangers the beneficial functional linkages between India and Pakistan and the wider international world.

On the eve of the twenty-first century Kashmir does not have the luxury of a long period for introverted consolidation nor the resources to develop into an Asian Switzerland. It required some seven hundred years to make a multicultural Switzerland, universally accepted as 'neutral', which then led all countries to find it as a special haven of investment and prosperity. But even Switzerland now wants to economically integrate with the broadened community of Europe. It is also too late for Kashmir to bank on being able to play non-alignment between neighbours, as Nepal tried to do. Pakistan may not find it politically possible to openly modify its old commitment on Kashmir, but it must consider that such an ambition could be the enemy of the feasible. Pakistan and India must recognize a vested interest in the success of SAARC as a viable regional organization. To facilitate this, it would be in their common interest to ensure that the Kashmir problem slides off the headlines and again recedes into the limbo of officially unresolved problems—as it was between 1972 and 1989.

In his seminal work published in 1966, *Kashmir: A Study in India-Pakistan Relations*, the late Sisir Gupta dwelt on the issues and prospects in Kashmir.[4] In some detail, he weighed the pros and cons of various suggested solutions to the problem. He examined inter alia the idea of a plebiscite, a confederation of India and Pakistan, a condominium over the state, sub-partitions separating Ladakh, Jammu and Azad Kashmir with the former two acceding to India and the latter to Pakistan; and finally independence for the whole of the pre-Partition state of Jammu and Kashmir. He concluded that much as the Indians and Pakistanis may object legally and morally to the other's 'occupation', the de facto partition around the existing ceasefire line was the only feasible solution to the difficult problem. The 'final settlement' which Bhutto tentatively promised in the confidential discussions at Simla in 1972 was also on the lines of integrating Azad Kashmir with Pakistan, which could be followed by the acceptance of the rest of the state as part of the Indian Union. But Bhutto argued that in the wake of the military defeat and the dismemberment of Pakistan, he could not immediately commit himself in writing to this solution. Afterwards, he either changed his mind or never felt politically strong enough to go through with the first step of the envisaged solution. Such a solution itself discounted the resilient Kashmiri nationalism which would not acquiesce to a permanent division, with one part subsumed in Islamic Pakistan and the other in secular India. But in reality even then, it was presumed as the feasible lesser evil.

A *de jure* partition along the Line of Control is sometimes now argued satisfactory to Pakistan or acceptable to the Kashmiris on both sides of the line. Taking past history and present international realities into account, a more realistic approach, which avoids the risk of war, must see Jammu and Kashmir as no longer a divisive bone of contention but as a potential catalyst towards South Asian cooperation. While unscrambling the established division could be explosive, democracy, internal decentralization and restoration of autonomous Kashmiriyat must be considered as absolute imperatives. The answer may be to turn the Line of Control into a soft border permitting free movement and facilitating economic exchanges where for decades these have been prohibited. For an agreed period, the full legality of Kashmir's accession to India and the illegality of Pakistan's occupation and the opposite view held by Pakistan can be kept in cold freeze with neither country abdicating its position. But the Line of Control could be immediately demilitarized to a depth of five to ten miles on either side and a mutually agreed method laid down to verify its compliance. Thereafter, there could be genuinely free democratic elections in the India-controlled and Pakistan-controlled parts of Kashmir; the subsequent elected governments of the two halves should be permitted to contact each other and promote cultural and economic exchanges between these parts of old Kashmir. With such step-by-step approaches, it is possible that some rigid old attitudes could mellow and tensions ease. Even within the present political linkages, the psychological barriers might be lifted and prospects of the restoration of the Kashmiriyat identity may hold some promise. Such development could simultaneously catalyse mutual confidence between India and Pakistan. The proposal would not be wholly to the liking of either India or Pakistan, but permitting it could ease internal disaffection and rescue both from their respective dilemmas. Without abdicating their formal position or letting go their security vigilance, such acquiescence by India and Pakistan would keep the problem within the South Asian ambit. But continuing insistence on internationalization with partial or state-wide plebiscite under imposed peace-keeping, even under the UN auspices, would be firmly rejected by India.

THE NEED FOR MASSIVE RE-EDUCATION

There have been other specific and plausible suggestions to break the gridlocked impasse in Kashmir. What in any case is essential is to accept that the situation for India and Pakistan has greatly deteriorated and the hopes of obtaining partisan and balancing support from outside is now only hypnosis from the past. A massive effort at political re-education and re-orientation is called for to get out of this military, political and intellectual bog, where each of the contending parties is sinking deeper because they lack the vision and courage to reflect and retreat. If the national leaders in India and Pakistan want political longevity and an honourable place in the history of their respective countries, then a new approach, a new perspective, and a new diplomatic strategy must imbue their postures on Kashmir and towards each other. If they do, some day, hopefully not far off, a joint Nobel Peace prize awaits a leader each from India and Pakistan.

At the moment of writing, there is, side by side, rampant militancy and repeated instances of innocents suffering and dying in the crossfire. There is also a certain weariness at the hardship from the disruption of the daily lives of the people. The man in the street in Karachi and Chennai, as also in Lahore and Lucknow, is more concerned with inflation and social disabilities than India-Pakistan tensions. Both governments have parallel compelling problems: debt traps and threats to their national cohesion. If India and Pakistan go to war again over Kashmir, this vast subcontinent will make the wreck of Afghanistan and Lebanon seem like a pale shadow. The world will express some sympathy but is unlikely to energetically rescue the countries from chaos. It will be a humiliation for our many cherished faiths and mockery of the ancient civilization that inspires both countries. The end of the Cold War means that the burden of independence and shaping the future now rests squarely on our disciplined sagacity. Only if India and Pakistan come to terms with contemporaneous realities in their external relations and decide to address themselves to their internal problems, can Kashmir be pacified, democratized, and be made to move towards meaningful autonomy. This would be a giant step to catalyse the delayed invigoration of South Asia.

NOTES

1. Ayesha Jalal, *The Sole Spokesman: Jinnah, The Muslim League, and the Demand for Pakistan*, Cambridge: Cambridge University Press, 1985.
2. See Jagat S. Mehta, 'Deja vu on South Afghanistan', *New York Times*, March 1981.

   Afghanistan: from Swedenization to Finlandization: Kennan Institute Wilson Centre 1981 in *The March of Folly in Afghanistan*, Manohar, 2000.

   Neutral Solution & Afghanistan: Foreign Policy Summer 1982.

3. Unpublished monograph deposited in the Center for International Affairs, Harvard, 1970, titled 'The reluctant coalition for stability'.
4. Sisir Gupta, *Kashmir: A Study in India-Pakistan Relations*, Bombay: Asia Publishing House, 1966.

13

India-China Relations: A Review and Prognosis

There exist divergent explanations on the ups and downs in India-China relations in the last four decades. This has inevitably led to differing prognoses on the future prospects. Some analyses appear still unadjusted to the exposed fallacies of the Cold War; indeed, even while homage is paid to the new dynamics, much of it is derivative of the strategic globalism of alliance politics and antagonistic ideological confrontation. India, like Pakistan and indeed the non-aligned and the Third World, generally did not anticipate the end of the superpower competition. There followed a barely concealed anxiety at the loss of not only political leverage but also partisan protection. The new international environment coincides with the economic recession and the world resource crunch. The Third World was unprepared for the dramatic change in which the developed world domesticated foreign policies and subordinated its external relations to the imperatives of national economic needs. There is patent indifference to poverty and developmental problems, especially in relation to Asia and Africa. The old problem of India-China relations must be reviewed in the background of this radical disorientation. However, this is also the moment to reappraise the much cherished analysis with a conscious effort to reject old mindsets. It is only thus—confessing to past misjudgement and factoring in the new international attitudes—that we can make a careful prognosis for the future.

* Paper prepared for the Centre of Policy Research, New Delhi, 1992.

DIVERGENT ANALYSES AND APPROACHES

There are five principal strands of analysis of the present state of India-China relations.

First, with the anxiety at the loss of the time-tested friendship of the Soviet Union, one Indian view is that the residue of hostility and reserve towards China should be fully buried and a new India-China axis contemplated as the nucleus of a bloc to embrace all Asian developing nations. This axis might later even include Japan. The purpose would be to neutralize the US which is perceived as the remaining superpower embarked on dominating and hectoring the poor nations of Asia and Africa.

Second, an opposite approach focuses on the combined pressure from all five nuclear powers to control the development of independent nuclear weapons capability of India. Along with that of Pakistan the abiding threat of China's nuclear armoury and its continuing increase of missiles and warheads, which are still being tested for sophistication, and especially with their deployment on the Tibetan plateau, it would not be prudent—so it is argued—to go too far in the restoration of India-China friendship. Consistent with this logic, it is urged that India must guard against the repetition of hypnotic security complacency which put faith in a India-China fraternal friendship as was feted by the two governments in the 1950s. A full-throated revival of the India-China friendship, according to this reasoning, would relegate India to a permanent second-grade power position.

Third, a variant of the security-determined approach argues that a restored Sino-Indian friendship would dilute the thirty-year-old Sino-Pakistani friendship which, after all, started in the early 1960s with a parallel hostility of the two neighbours against India. A resurrected India-China friendship would reduce the possibility of another military adventure by Pakistan. By the same logic, it is suggested, that China would be more forthcoming towards India's own concerns if India could politically quarantine the Dalai Lama or even persuade him to shift his base elsewhere or persuade him to return to his homeland unconditionally. Accordingly, it was tactically prudent for India to endorse China's objection to the criticism of the denial of human rights in Tibet as nefarious interference in China's internal affairs.

Fourth, the opposite view suggests that India's interest is served by moral and diplomatic support to the resilient aspirations of the Tibetan people because it coincides with the national security rationale of India. If Tibet was autonomous or independent, it would once again become a kind of buffer against China's military and territorial ambitions in the subcontinent.

Finally, some analysts strongly reflect a sense of guilt that India needlessly allowed the friendship with China to be disrupted by provocation on the border and remained for long reluctant to repair the damaged relations. Consistent with this line of thought, there is an impatience to settle the border dispute by accepting the principle, long put forward by China, of 'mutual accommodation' which would, in effect, amount to the legal surrender of a part of Aksai Chin and a de jure confirmation of the line of present effective control and even give up Tawang.

When the Indian prime minister, Rajiv Gandhi, went to China in 1988 and more recently when the Chinese premier, Lei Peng, came to India in 1991, there was a general affirmation that a new chapter was being opened and old hurdles like the boundary question, even if so far unresolved, would be settled through more enlightened political directions. Even from those not so optimistic, there was widespread support to 'settle the border', though there was no consensus on the framework for such a resolution.

The prognosis for the future flows from one or other interpretation of the decades of Sino-Indian relations. Space does not permit a discussion of the strengths and flaws in the approaches crudely summarized in the foregoing paragraphs. But after the cataclysmic changes in world politics (and new decision-makers on the scene), as a preliminary, it should be easier to acknowledge that grave errors of judgement were made in managing Sino-Indian relations over the past four decades. The hypnosis of the Cold War was certainly part of the reason, but more relevant was the failure to anticipate that the dynamics of Sino-Indian developments were outside the superpower relationship.

NEHRU'S FAILURE WITH CHINA

In a paper prepared for a conference around the Nehru centenary,[1] I sought to set forth my own understanding of the roots of the ups and downs in India-China relations. In my view, the conceptual framework of India's China policy has to be traced to Nehru's intellectual genealogy. Not only was Nehru committed to nationalism against all manifestations of imperialism, but having been influenced in the 1930s by the Fabian philosophy, he also believed in democratic-socialism against a rampant-free market philosophy. This developed into a deep faith that the priority of socialism was always to build an egalitarian and socially just society. This required peace, and so Nehru concluded that there was no likelihood of socialist Russia or communist China turning belligerent or expansionist. Nehru's attitude to China also reflected his conviction that relations between independent countries in Asia would be harmonious and peaceful once European imperialism had been compelled to withdraw. This half-reason and half-hope was not shaken even when China showed a Stalinist suspicion of non-aligned (but democratic) India's continued ties to the West, or when China moved into Tibet with not even a courteous diplomatic intimation to India. Since the flowering of India-China friendship in the years 1954-8 coincided with the high-water mark of Nehru's international standing, a feeling also developed that China truly understood and prized the friendship with non-aligned India.

The downturn in Sino-Indian relations started in 1959. The deterioration came in the wake of the revolt in Tibet and some border incidents. Even when the political climate had changed sharply, more so after the Forward Policy (1961 and 1962) right up to September 1962, Nehru, like Krishna Menon, did not expect a massive conflict with socialist China.

Seen in hindsight from 1992, Nehru's international perspectives were not wholly naïve. His vision of the priority of national economic development and social justice, the faith in internal democracy, and the caution against not only alliances but also militarism have now overtrumped the paradigm of the unending ideological incompatibility of blocs, justifying priority for adversarial competition across the global arena. Non-alignment and nationally determined socio-economic philosophy have become the universal conventional wisdom; economic dynamism is now the determinant of national foreign policies. While Nehru may have been mistaken in believing that socialism was the irreversible wave of the future and appropriate for India's developmental strategy, he was not far wrong in underlining the importance of economic and social development for national cohesion and security. He was needlessly alarmed by the rhetoric and propaganda of the Cold War and the likelihood of every regional conflict leading to a world war with the superpowers joining in as partisans. With his firm opposition to imperialism and his lifelong call to allow national fulfilment through independence, Nehru also did not foresee that nationalism in the Third World could turn into chauvinism and lead to conflicts with other newly emancipated countries.

Given his intellectual conditioning, traceable to a period before India's independence, Nehru was sympathetic to China which was facing the Western policy of ostracizing the country from the international community and militarily containing it. Nehru did not foresee that China could act militarily against a consistently friendly non-aligned India. This wishfulness, flowing from Nehru's long-held credo, provides an insight into the tragedy of Sino-Indian relations. Without recapitulating the well-trodden chronology of bilateral relations, some analytical conclusions can be distilled from the historical experience. Generally, they provide an insight into the many misjudgements that have frequently escaped attention; moreover, they have a bearing on any attempt to shape future relations between the two countries.

OSCILLATIONS IN SINO-INDIAN RELATIONS

A review of the oscillations in the India-China relationship would show that they were not brought about by bilateral problems between the two countries. India was prompt in recognizing the People's Republic and became a vigorous spokesman for its seating in the UN. Because of China's ideological predilections, which were then parallel to the reserve of Stalin's Russia, bilateral relations between India and China remained tepid and in some ways hostile. Relations warmed up after India's independent role in international politics, especially on Korea and in the Indo-China Conference in Geneva (1954), but it should be noted that such rapprochement was not because of the progress on or resolution of the inherited bilateral problems. The 1954 agreement, by which India recognized Tibet as a region of China and gave up the right to station Indian army units in Yatung and Gyantse, rationalized the arrangements for border trade and pilgrimages and surrendered Indian control over the post and telegraph administration of Tibet. The agreement was signed on 29 April 1954 when relations had already eased significantly. It was in this agreement that the five principles of coexistence were embodied, but they got their international boost when soon afterwards Chou-en-Lai came to India on his way back from the Geneva Conference on Indo-China.

The years 1954-8 were of mutual affirmation of the indestructible friendship between the two countries symbolized by the slogan '*Hindi-Chini Bhai-Bhai*' (Indians and Chinese are brothers). Notwithstanding the ideological divergence and the known differences on the notions of their common border, relations were positive and harmonious between the two central governments with emphasis on similar approaches to international politics. Nehru, with his faith in post-imperial Asian harmony, was the spokesman for the new China, notably at the Non-Aligned Conference at Bandung (1955). However, even during this period there were difficulties on the border and in the implementation of the Tibet Agreement, but consistent with the cherished overall logic of good relations, the problems were minimized or suppressed.

The crisis in the relations in 1959 was not anticipated by either sides. Indian public opinion had not been aroused much at the reports of the Khampa revolt underway since 1956, but it became stridently sympathetic after the Dalai Lama's escape and the reports on the plight of the Tibetans streaming into India. The reactions in India reflected the working of a parliamentary democracy in an open society. China's accusations that the disaffection in Tibet was due to subversion by Indian bourgeois-reactionaries, flattered the capabilities of the Indian Intelligence agencies to ignite and sustain such a revolt deep inside Tibet. Whether the civilian government in India and Nehru personally were fully aware of the CIA-Taiwan involvement in the air-dropping of arms to help the anti-China elements is uncertain, but it is now known that the CIA activities started in 1956, that is, during the period of Sino-Indian friendship.

The Tibetan disaffection was due to the failure of China's minority policy; the disaffection still persists though now China accuses neither the CIA nor India of fomenting it. The propagandist defence at the exposed failure was compounded by China bracketing Nehru by name in an authoritative article printed in May 1959 in the *Peking Review* entitled 'The revolt in Tibet and Nehru's philosophy'. Knowing that Nehru was held with great affection in India and that he had risked Western displeasure in urging the people of India to have faith in friendship with China, China made a thoughtless mistake by smearing him. During the friendly years, the Chinese knew that India had registered its objections on border violations, and that India had refrained from advertising the less than satisfactory response from the Chinese government. In the face of deep Western suspicions, India was crusading for non-alignment and was reluctant, but not wholly effective, in winning the conviction of communist China. (This was part of the reason why India did not wish to alienate the USSR on the insurrection in Hungary.) India did not even release Nehru's letters to the Chinese premier in December 1958 and March 1959 on the border question. Incidentally, even Chou-en-Lai's first reply to Nehru in January 1959 did not specify China's own notions of the common boundary.

The two governments had divergent rationales for fostering the psychological and concrete manifestation of their friendly relations. For their respective reasons, each was reluctant to probe and thus risk exposing the ambiguities in their respective understandings. At all events, neither government foresaw the explosive potential of the divergence in their respective notions of their common boundary, but neither did any Indian academic or Western scholar realize this fact. Post-hoc analysts and some latter-day politicians who make accusations of failures of judgement on the Indian side in not settling the border dispute in the Chou-Nehru meeting (April 1960) overlook the complete transformation of the political climate in India by April-May 1959. After May 1959, for the first time in his tenure as prime minister, Nehru became aware that public opinion was outraged against China and he became defensive in his foreign policy. His primary concern thereafter was not to be cornered into abandoning non-alignment as the basic tenet of his international approach.

From the long-term perspective, the failure to anticipate a Sino-Pakistan rapprochement was even more serious than the failure to foresee the political bombshell of the sharp differences with China and the possibility of a major military conflict. Here too, Nehru's intellectual conditioning provides a plausible explanation. In 1959, after the deteroriation in India-China relations, Nehru had dismissed President Ayub's offer of a policy of joint defence against China. He assumed that a country allied to the West in CENTO and SEATO and committed to containing the two communist giants would never be befriended by China. Although from 1962 to 1976, China and Pakistan coordinated their policy of political hostility against India, Sino-Pakistan relations were also complicated by inner unarticulated differences between the two countries. Under Bhutto's persuasion, the Pakistan government of Field Marshal Ayub Khan was carried away by the hope that China would risk military involvement against India to help realize Pakistan's national purpose of wrenching Kashmir from India. This expectation was no small part of the calculus behind the preparation for Operation Gibraltar and the Indo-Pakistan conflict of 1965. Even at the time, when, as head of our embassy in Peking, I was given the two ultimata on 16 and 19 September, containing ominous threats around some frivolous demands of returning sheep and yaks and demolishing bunkers, my own view was that Pakistan was naïve in thinking that China would actually start hostilities in order to support Pakistan to victory or rescue it from defeat. The point to note is also that China did not seize the opportunity of the India-Pakistan war to enlarge its control in the disputed areas. It merely lived up to its commitment to Ayub by appearing to enliven the frontier in

Sikkim as a means of helping to protect East Pakistan and creating in the Indian mind serious apprehensions of a two-front war. While China did not turn belligerent, it did cement its friendship with Pakistan, which, to this day, even with all the changes of governments on both sides, remains firm and provides a baffling challenge to Indian diplomacy.

The 1962 India-China War provided China the opportunity to demonstrate its military superiority over India which had presumed to politically defy the People's Republic. Having proved that India could not hold China's forces, the latter called for a unilateral ceasefire. China in effect broadcast the message to adversaries and admirers alike that it was fearless both of the superpowers and of the Western and Eastern blocs. The unilateral ceasefire and withdrawal halted the adverse political fallout of China's military action on a two-thousand-mile front. The summary defeat of the Indian army greatly enhanced China's military and political standing. But correspondingly, during and after the conflict, there was prompt and genuine sympathy for India in the Western bloc. This manifested itself in offers from the USA and, to a lesser extent, the UK, to help India's defence capability to contain China's aggression. The urgency, however, was dissipated with the sudden end of the conflict. In Western non-official opinion, there was also a kind of Schadenfreude at the exposed failure of India's faith in non-alignment. In the Third World, instead of universal condemnation at the massive attack, China's standing suffered little lasting damage. China must have had the satisfaction of having achieved its political goals. In India, the fear took root that such a massive attack would be repeated, especially since India was unreconciled to the humiliating loss of territory. Senior members of the government even gave me precise dates when a new attack could be expected. My own view was that there was no likelihood of China taking action to forcibly control the claimed territory beyond what it had already occupied. In the last three decades, there has not been any substantial increase in Chinese military deployment along the border beyond the force levels that were reached after the India-China War. Indeed, there has really been no serious border clash on the Sino-Indian boundary, at least not one that has had the potential of a major conflict. The 1967 firing across Nathu La was a by-product of the Cultural Revolution, where the local commanders (like some heads of Chinese diplomatic missions) tried to demonstrate their political militancy and so earn credibility with the Red Guards. The incident in Sumdorong-cho in 1986 at the time of a small dip in India-China relations was precipitated by an Indian commander in a disputed pocket where there could be conflicting interpretations of the watershed delineation. Seen in the perspective of 1992, the old apprehensions of another war with China have come down in the probability scale in the judgement of even the most alarmist sections of the Indian establishment.

The revival in political relations between the two countries can be dated to 1976—a year or so after China finally recognized Bangladesh. This step towards normalization came not because of the resolution of the long-pending bilateral problems but as a by-product of the changed international situation. The mutual desire to normalize relations was extraneous to the subsisting differences. The Parliamentary resolution of 1962 passed in the wake of the India-China war implied that relations would not be normalized until control of all Indian territory was won back and for this reason, the diplomatic missions had remained headed by a chargé d'affairs. Even though there was no move towards the fulfilment of the resolution, the reappointment of an ambassador to China in 1976 was not opposed by any party in India. China perceived that India had emerged politically self-confident and economically resilient after the Bangladesh crisis even in the face of the US-China tilt towards Pakistan. Sino-Soviet relations had continued to be under strain, and China sensed the possibility of being able to wean India away from its friendship with the USSR. Moreover, the political dispensation within China after the fall of the Gang of Four was in a constructive mood after a decade of turbulence during the Cultural Revolution.

Foreign Minister Atal Behari Vajpayee's discussions in Beijing in 1979—three years after diplomatic normalization—were satisfactory on all live issues between the two countries. (It had been agreed in advance that the border question would not be discussed as it was quiescent anyway.) Following the visit, China did not unilaterally focus on Kashmir or make statements, as it had done in the previous four years, to signify the non-recognition of the integration of Sikkim with India. Subsequent to the visit, there was no evidence of the continued supply of arms to Nagas and Mizos. In general, the hostile propaganda against India was quietly muted. In fact, in the Vajpayee discussions there was an understanding that the unresolved boundary question would not stand in the way of improved functional cooperation between the two countries. The results of the visit were positive, notwithstanding efforts by the pro-Soviet opposition to decry the visit by needlessly projecting China's attack on Vietnam, while Vajpayee was still in a provincial city, as a deliberate insult to India. Sino-Indian relations, however, again suffered a setback in 1980 and this was because of India's indulgent support of Soviet intervention in Afghanistan and, more so, after the Indian recognition of the Heng Samrin government in Kampuchea. The latter action led to the cancellation of the visit of the Chinese Foreign Minister fixed for August 1980. What must be noted is that this deterioration after diplomatic normalization did not occur because of any new Sino-Indian bilateral problem.

THE BORDER QUESTION: IS IT CENTRAL TO FUTURE INDIA-CHINA RELATIONS?*

At this stage, it may be worth reviewing the actual significance of the territorial dispute. When India became independent, it was aware, even if imprecisely, that China's notions of the common border, the legality of the Simla Agreement and the MacMahon Line were different from India's. When PRC troops entered Tibet in 1950, the issue was raised in the Indian Parliament and in public discussions. Nehru then declared, in effect, that notwithstanding Chinese maps and claims, India's border corresponded to the MacMahon Line. Subsequently, Nehru took the initiative to raise the question of Chinese maps in the Chou en-Lai–Nehru talks in 1956-7. (These maps showed large areas south of the Himalayan borders as part of China.) However, the boundary question remained in the background until after the

* See also J.S. Mehta, *Negotiating for India*, New Delhi: Manohar, 2006, Chapter 2.

Tibetan crisis when the Dalai Lama took refuge in India. It came to the forefront of bilateral diplomacy only in the Nehru-Zhou meetings of 1960. To the surprise of none, at least not anyone in the Indian government (even after seven conversations with only one interpreter from each side present), the two prime ministers could not agree on a settlement of the problem.

Attributing central importance to the border question for the future improvement of relations came about as a by-product of the secretary level meetings that started in 1980. When such high-level discussions were taking place outside permanent diplomatic channels, it was inevitable that there would be public expectation of progress on the resolution of the dispute. After the experience of the 1950s, such official level contacts could not be kept shrouded in secrecy. Placing critical focus on the boundary question was in some part due to the functioning of the parliamentary system in India. The responses to questions asked on the eve of India-China meetings about the territorial question boxed the Indian government and the designated senior officers to affirm its importance, probably knowing that no substantial progress could possibly be made. A moment's reflection would have made it plain that the government of the day in India must obtain a prior national consensus within and even outside Parliament before officials could discuss territorial accommodation. This inevitably must involve the possible surrender of claims to some territory to which independent India had asserted its title. The Supreme Court judgement on Beru Bari in 1959 stated that the alienation of any part of the country, deemed to be part of India when the Constitution was promulgated in 1950, would require a constitutional amendment even if it was in an advantageous exchange.

The constitutional requirement underscores the political rather than the territorial aspect of Sino-Indian relations. It is not far-fetched to presume that the Sinkiang Highway and consequently the eastern part of Aksai Chin must be considered as vital non-negotiable interests for China. Correspondingly, China must also know that India cannot surrender Arunachal even at the peril of another war. The very fact that Chinese forces withdrew in 1962 from much of the area claimed by China in the Eastern sector would suggest that the persisting claim to Arunachal was essentially a bargaining tool towards a final settlement in order to obtain a de jure acceptance of Chinese control of Aksai Chin. In this gridlock, the official-level talks could only be confined to exploratory probing around the substantive issue and at best discussing appropriate negotiating processes. The repeated assertion in India that the talks were towards a settlement of the dispute was simply for public relations, but it carried the hazards of disappointment at the lack of progress after repeated meetings. Meanwhile, it should have caused no surprise that China would challenge any political or legal encroachment which appeared to dismiss China's claim to Arunachal as a non-serious bargaining counter. It was to be expected that, for purposes of record, China would protest when Arunachal was constitutionally integrated into the Indian Union and given the same administrative status as other states.

It was reported that the idea of sector-by-sector talks was proposed during the secretary-level discussion. This idea of sector-wise negotiations starting in the East was examined by me in as early as 1978. If sector-by-sector negotiations had started with the Eastern sector, it would have led to partial legtimization of the Indian official claim and so could be presented domestically as a diplomatic success. But when I first examined this possibility, I concluded that China was unlikely to agree to such a half settlement which would jeopardize or delay recognition of Chinese control in the Western sector. From what has been stated above, the final resolution of the boundary question hinges not on diplomacy but on the domestic politics in India.

HISTORICAL EVIDENCE CONDITIONED BY THE POLITICAL PRISM

If we go by the yardstick of historical consistency and impeccable legal validity, flaws can be found in the evidence officially furnished by both sides. The ultimate permanent reality of the Sino-Indian border is geography: the divide traverses the high Himalayas with even the passes at altitudes of between 12,000 and 16,000 feet, and at this altitude there is no permanent habitation. Over the centuries, ethnicity, religious faiths and administrative control straddled and blended across a high mountain border. The ruling powers exercised authority in limited ways and that too in small habitats. The idea of a firm line of control came as a by-product of the great game of rival European empires in the nineteenth century. The British were looking at ways to safeguard the outer defensive parameter and determine the appropriate minimal pattern of administration along the peripheries of the empire in India. The various lines considered and proposed by the British Indian authorities—the Ardagh line of 1877, the MacCartney-MacDonald line of 1899 (or for that matter of a frontier along the Sela Pass south of Tawang in the Eastern sector)—followed the surveys but were permeated by political and security considerations. The internal discussions in Whitehall and Delhi perceived Afghanistan, Central Asia, Sinkiang and Tibet as necessary strategic outreaches for the protection of the Indian empire. China's effective control of the claimed area was historically even more dubious. China's relations with Tibet were characterized by the extension of the former's control and authority at one time and complete withdrawal from superintendence over the theocratic dispensation at others. The arguments about 'imperialist expansion', be it British or Chinese, are based on the selective use of evidence from history in order to reinforce convenient contemporary political attitudes.

After Independence, the historical background was first examined in the 1950s by the Historical Division of the Ministry of External Affairs under Dr K. Zachariah, the first director. He recalled the various lines proposed by the British government. The government was then chiefly concerned with the Eastern sector where there was a sizeable tribal population. In the Western sector, the government decided not on the extreme Ardagh line but a compromise line which had some plausibility. The primary concern was the reluctance to prematurely precipitate a threat to the developing bilateral relations with China. It was a similar political logic which overruled the plea by Sir G.S. Bajpai, the former secretary-general of the ministry, to raise the boundary question in the Tibet talks in 1953-4. But it should be recalled that notwithstanding these hesitations, China would have been aware of India's contention on the border. Apart from Nehru's statement in Parliament on the MacMahon Line, made in 1950, India had embodied its concept of the border in the first official Indian map issued in 1954.

George Patterson, a Tibetologist, who had lived in Darjeeling, writing about the dramatic downturn in Sino-Indian relations in 1959, is one of the few who captured the political trauma in India. He was not always friendly to India, but in his book, *Revolt in Tibet*,[2] he describes how the propaganda attacks on India increased Indian public sympathy for Tibet and the Dalai Lama. He confirms that Nehru had to bow before public opinion, which was overwhelmingly sympathetic to the Tibetan plight. There were a few Indian officials who wanted the Dalai Lama to be thrown back into Tibet in order not to jeopardize Sino-Indian relations. Nehru, with his sensitive political antenna and genuine sympathy for the plight of the Dalai Lama and Tibet, never seriously considered such an option.

No scholars, Indian or foreign, examined the relative worth of the respective border cases until after India was catapulted into a political commitment to the 1954 delineation. Indeed, most academic analyses started only some time after the officials' report, which was issued in 1961. These researchers have missed the point that the officials of the two governments were asked by the two prime ministers in 1960 only to bring forth evidence 'to support the stand of the two Governments'. In effect, the exercise gave no scope for give and take. While ostensibly the officials were entrusted with a factual and historical compilation job, in essence the report was a diplomatic document with the officials as advocates. The brief joint communiqué after the prime ministerial talks had in effect prescribed in advance the end conclusion. After April 1959, the political dynamics had developed in a way not foreseen by either country. For India, where the government was responsible to an elected Parliament—even though under a powerful leader like Nehru—there never was any negotiating margin on the basis of the results of the report.

In order to understand the unusual structure of the officials' report, one must mention that in 1960 neither India nor China wanted that relations should deteriorate further. The Chinese were caught in a dilemma—the essence of the Chinese case was that, in the absence of a formal delimitation agreement covering the common border, there could be no valid boundary. In the light of the prime ministerial injunction, the Chinese delegation wavered between quoting Nehru's statements in India on the vagueness of the boundary and furnishing whatever positive evidence they could marshal. The Indian purpose—conditioned by the political commitments made in and outside Parliament—was to prove that the traditional boundary was known and corresponded with its own cartographic delineation. The concluding chapter of the Indian report which is a summary of our positive evidence carried veiled political overtones. The chapter contrasted the comparative strength of the Indian evidence with the paucity of Chinese positive evidence to substantiate the Chinese claim. Our chapter even stretched the argument that bits of Chinese evidence strung together actually substantiated the Indian case. The fact is that the two official teams were at cross purposes in their goals: China wanted to establish that there was no violation as there was no agreed border; on the other hand, India asserted that it had openly and officially notified its territorial frontiers which had a traditional validity and so the occupation south or west of the 'Line' was an illegal intrusion.

DEFINING THE STATUS OF TIBET

Let me give one specific example to illustrate how the political overhang determined and inhibited the logical use of historical evidence in the advocacy. The Chinese case on the area south of the watershed in the Eastern sector was based on the connection of the Tibetan theocratic reach to Lamaist monasteries, notably of Tawang and Walong. Some of these monasteries had exacted monetary and non-monetary collections from the resident believers, and this was interpreted as revenue/tax collection and thus adduced as proof of China's claim to what is now the Indian state of Arunachal Pradesh. (Incidentally such evidence covered only small pockets in the north, with no item covering the total area claimed which extended up to the edge of the Brahmaputra river plains). The interesting point arising from the Chinese argument was that such evidence was purely from Tibetan, as distinct from Chinese, sources. The items tabled by the Chinese team should have invited the riposte that this evidence itself suggested that Tibet had the attributes of sovereignty in international contacts and thus made irrelevant the argument that because the Chinese government had not ratified the Simla Agreement of 1914, the agreement had no validity. It also clearly implied that China did not dispute the right of bilateral dealings between Tibet and the Government of India.

In this context, a reference might be made, as a digression, to the recent book of Alistair Lamb[3] in which he argues that Tibet had acted autonomously even in its defiance of China's power and interests. For example, in the face of the Anthony Eden Memorandum of 1943 and the strong pressure of both the British and American governments, the Tibetan authorities did not agree to the transit of arms to Kuomintang during the Second World War when Japan was the common enemy. The Lamb study marshals hitherto unpublished evidence on the running differences between the British Indian and Whitehall attitudes on Tibet. The British Indian view, persistently argued by Olaf Caroe of the External Affairs Department of the Government of India and supported by Gould who was Political Officer in Gangtok, was to preserve Outer Tibet as a buffer for India. In effect, the argument was that the British-Indian special relationship with Lhasa and Tibet as a de facto buffer must be preserved and China should be kept out of even a parallel relationship with Tibet. To give this approach the sanction of international law, it was even sought to refine the definition of suzerainty. In contradistinction to the view from India, Whitehall always had greater sensitivity to good relations with the central government of China. Anyway, the efforts to exclude China from Tibet failed if only because the US remained firmly committed to Kuomintang's claim and never endorsed the idea of even de facto autonomy for Tibet.

On the Indian side, we were fully cognizant of the British Indian archives. Our dilemma was a political one: how not to get out of line with the logic of independent India's foreign policy. Consistent with the goal of friendship with China and the rejection of the

British imperial strategic considerations, the Government of Independent India had formally accepted Tibet as a region of China in 1954. In keeping with this policy, in the officials' discussions, we had to avoid defining the international status of Tibet during the period 1911-50. To get around the contradiction between India's affirmed attitude on the status of Tibet ('suzerainty of China, subject to the autonomy of Tibet') and the need to bring telling evidence to support our stand in the Eastern sector, we, in the official discussions, confined ourselves to asserting that the evidence volunteered by China was itself a clear acknowledgement that Tibet had treaty-making rights during the period. This in effect gave legality to the Simla Agreement and the MacMahon Line.

This position enabled us to remain consistent with the overall rationale of the Indian case that geography and specifically the water parting was reinforced by the traditional de facto separation of Tibet from the adjoining parts of India. We also argued that contrary to what was urged by China, all over the world, natural frontiers had come to be accepted even before confirmation by formal delimitation. Modern treaties with maps or detailed description were negotiated only in the nineteenth and twentieth centuries and which, unless transgressed by conquest, tended to confirm natural borders. The MacMahon Line, which both in the Eastern sector of India and in north Burma coincided with the watershed, confirmed the validity and practical sense that the high Himalayas were the divide between the plateau in Tibet and the subcontinent to the south. The Sino-Burmese and Sino-Nepalese treaties, negotiated in 1960 after the Sino-Indian crisis, both acknowledged that the watershed corresponded to the traditional boundaries.

THE OFFICIALS' REPORT: AFFIRMATION OF DIFFERENCES BUT AVOIDING AGGRAVATION

In the communiqué authorizing the officials' discussion issued in April 1960 the two prime ministers laid down that they expected a single report within a specified period to enable future consideration of the problem. The scheduled pace of meetings—

every alternate day—was observed scrupulously with only one requested postponement. (This should be contrasted with many years of the intermittent US-China, Geneva/Warsaw meetings which were only dialogues of the deaf.) The divergent purposes and political dynamics militated against one report; as stated, in the second half of 1960, both sides were anxious not to be vulnerable to the charge of aggravating the problem. This was overcome by the transparent subterfuge of having the two separate Indian and Chinese monographs introduced by a common forwarding preface signed by the leaders and deputy leaders of both sides. In writing the respective reports, each side was left to summarize its own version of the positive evidence and the refutation of the adversarial arguments. The draft chapters written by one side were given to the other side to judge that they were faithful to the presentation made in the original discussions. This scrutiny of the other side's report and its acceptance was tortuous and could easily have ended with no common report to the two prime ministers. Here, I would like to pay tribute to the skill and sagacity of the late Chang-wen-Chin, leader of the Chinese team, for agreeing to many semantic compromises to facilitate the presentation of a 'single' report. It was noteworthy that these agreed summaries by each side of its own verbal presentation, compiled into one report, came to six hundred printed pages. It was drafted, scrutinized and signed within less than six months of the first meeting. (The verbatim record of the discussions is about ten times longer than the published report.) The report, signed in December 1960, was printed and submitted to Parliament in February 1961.

The story of the subsequent Forward Policy (1961-2) and the eventual conflict has been chronicled by other publications. The very democratic openness of India led to analysts finding flaws, gaps and weaknesses in Indian decision-making. One has no more than vague hunches of the decision-making processes on the Chinese side. The tragedy was that the antennae on the Indian side were dead to the possibility of an India-China war. In the very circumstance of how the crisis developed, there could have been no compromise settlement: the most one could claim for the officials' discussions is that despite the sensitivity of the problem, the diplomatic marathon of facts and arguments was conducted in an amicable way, and that during the six months there was a freeze in military deployments and propaganda decibels were significantly moderated.

MISSED OPPORTUNITIES FOR A BORDER SETTLEMENT

The suggestion that the exchange of Aksai Chin for Arunachal could have been negotiated in 1959-60 overlooks the political circumstances and their unforeseen evolution in the 1950s. If either India or China had possessed better crystal balls, a settlement with mutual accommodation might have been possible in 1955-7 when mutually cherished trust and friendship prevailed between the two countries. Instead of ambivalence and hesitation, China should have come clean with its own notions of the border in the conversations between Chou-en-Lai and Nehru. Had that been done, the subsequent crisis in the relations might have been averted. Nehru might well have seen the logic of China's need for the Aksai Chin highway. He was politically strong enough to persuade Parliament and, if necessary, to pilot a constitutional amendment to concede territory in the Western sector in exchange for the recognition of the legitimate Indian presence in NEFA (Arunachal). If China had been restrained in its criticism of India over the Dalai Lama's flight and desisted from accusing Nehru, it is possible the deterioration in relations would have been short-lived. As events transpired, after May 1959, this might have been possible only if India, like China, had a non-democratic, non-parliamentary system of government.

The failure to comprehend more incisively the rationale of the relations towards the other country can only be traced to misperceptions on both sides. Vertzberger,[4] inspired, as he says, by the trauma of a national earthquake for Israel in the Yom Kippur war, undertook to study the misperceptions in foreign policy-making as illustrated by the Sino-Indian conflict. He recaptures probably better than others the subjective perceptions in India-China relations prior to the 1962 war. Steven Hoffmann,[5] who published his meticulously researched study after interviewing most of the senior Indian officials involved over a period of almost twenty years, also dwells on the psychological setting that enveloped the Indian decision-making process. These studies, however, cannot be wholly complete as the authors had no access to Nehru and the then senior political leaders of the Indian government. In any case, there is no access to the personnel or processes on the Chinese side, who or which alone can make an objective and balanced appraisal possible.

After the end of the period of political attrition and following the diplomatic normalization in 1976, the old attitudes were moderated and fresh opportunities opened up for legally resolving the Sino-Indian boundary question. The coalition Janata government was not strong enough to grasp the nettle and deliberately kept the boundary question aside. However, following the general elections of 1980 when Mrs Gandhi came back to power, the accommodation process could have been initiated. In 1983, when China was somewhat isolated internationally, there was another propitious moment, but the Indian government was too preoccupied with serious internal problems. In 1985, the Congress Party under Rajiv Gandhi had commanded a three-fourths majority in Parliament and that was, in my view, the best opportunity after 1957 to reach a settlement. Rajiv Gandhi had come with an unprecedented political and psychological advantage. But the initiative was not seized and soon his political charisma was eroded by other problems. When finally Rajiv Gandhi went to China in 1988, he succeeded in creating a striking improvement in the climate for better functional relations. But he was then looking ahead to new elections and was reluctant to risk mustering an adverse political consensus to settle the border and so he merely pledged to give a political push towards a settlement. In 1989, the parliamentary equations changed so radically that there could be no movement on the boundary question.

The government of P.V. Narasimha Rao had less than a comfortable majority in Parliament. In 1991, with political courage Rao could conceivably have overcome the pockets of hesitation in the opposition and authorize substantive negotiations to get a de jure settlement of the boundary question. Such an authorization to the officials was inhibited by serious domestic, economic and political problems. However, preliminary steps to marshal an internal consensus could still have been taken by confidentially sounding out all the political parties and then allowing the officials to probe for a substantive settlement. But such political clearing of the decks should have been done discreetly and well in advance of the high-level visits.

Beijing could also facilitate the political passage of a settlement in the Indian Parliament and help assuage public opinion in India. China could demonstrate its goodwill by hinting to the Indian government its offer to withdraw from the two thousand odd miles of area overrun in the 1962 conflict, which is neither politically nor strategically vital for China. It could make such accommodation even easier if, corresponding to some old maps, the control of the Chang Chenmo valley up to Lanak La were not ruled out in substantive confidential negotiations. (It would still not endanger the security of the Sinkiang highway.) The Chumbi valley, to which the Sikkim kingdom had some historical claim, has often been suggested as a sweetener to a settlement. My own guess is that the Chinese are likely to be more rigid about the Chumbi valley. The claim was, in effect, abandoned in the British Indian negotiations in 1890, when the boundary of north Sikkim was formally agreed upon. (Incidentally, this is the one segment of the boundary that would satisfy the Chinese definition of formal delimitation.)

Even with some territorial withdrawal by the Chinese, it is patent that a feasible boundary settlement would only be a variant of the line of control established since 1962. While China would have to accept India's position and presence in Arunachal and the Middle sector, India in turn would have to legally concede China's control in Eastern Aksai Chin. In private conversation, there is a broader consensus amongst the political cognoscenti in India in favour of a settlement around this de facto position but no political party in India has come forward to suggest it publicly.

REALISTIC PROGNOSIS ON INDIA-CHINA RELATIONS

How then can, constructive relations free from sharp tensions and grave apprehensions, be established between these two great Asian powers? How can the relations be managed to mutual advantage and reciprocal deference without the dramatic oscillations of the past. The two countries have their own civilizational ethos and values. India has had an assimilative pluralist civilization. Even though India suffered frequent invasions, it has no nostalgia for dominion beyond its natural and cultural frontiers. China, which was geographically remote from the cross-flows of other cultures, developed the concept of the Middle Kingdom and had a distinct sense of purity and superiority woven into its history and civilizational personality. Its traditional attitude on its limits was derived from the concept that a territory where once China had extended its language and civilization should not be given back to the 'barbarians'. In his book on the frontiers of China, Francis Watson suggests that in regard to natural features as a basis for frontier settlement, the historic Chinese preference was for a frontier carried down to the further slopes of a dividing mountain range.[6] This notion illuminates how the Ching dynasty looked upon Nepal, Bhutan, North Burma, Laos and Annam (Vietnam) as tributaries of the Chinese Empire. Even though for a while schoolbooks published a map suggesting the old notions, this concept of the tributaries along the peripheries has not been articulated by the People's Republic. Indeed, it was abandoned in the border treaties with Nepal and Burma. India, on the other hand, has a traditional sense of the high Himalayas being part of the source and sanctity of India's religion and culture. China has recognized this in agreeing to the pilgrimages to Kailash and Mansarovar in the 1954 agreement. However, in the present revival of the pilgrimages, China insists the parties should be controlled by escorts, but this does show sensitivity to the Indian sentiments.

When China adopted politically belligerent postures—as, for example, against both superpowers during the Vietnam war—it was militarily prudent and non-provocative. But China has not hesitated to use its forces when threatened as when the American forces crossed the 38th Parallel into North Korea and on a smaller scale against the Soviet Union in establishing its claim to the Damanski island in the Ussuri river (1969). Against Vietnam China used its armed forces aggressively in 1979 in order to politically discipline a neighbour and a historical subordinate. The action was in sharp contrast to its position when China had affirmed a permanent 'lip and teeth' friendship with Vietnam. But China seemed to have embarked on this punitive action as a reaction to the Soviet-Vietnam Treaty and the Vietnamese intervention in Kampuchea. The recent military occupation of the Spratley Islands is also an ominous sign of China's greater military assertiveness. The continuing programme of nuclear weapons sophistication and rapid militarization also cannot be justified on the grounds of deterring only the old superpowers.

Considering these examples that are indicative of China's capacity to use its force, even without defensive compulsions, how is one to assess the likelihood of a repetition of the 1962 military action? Even if India did not correctly judge China's political purpose in 1961-2, it would more readily be accepted that India did not really conspire to uproot China from Tibet. China can be fairly confident that weighing regional and international configuration, there is not the remotest likelihood of India embarking on a provocative intrusion into Tibet in the future. In spite of the grave hazards of such a prophecy, I have challenged the contention argued from time to time by diverse scholars, analysts and even the higher echelons of the government that there is a likelihood of China attacking India again across the long frontier. Diplomatic professionalism must have from the courage to assess the likely threat and cannot yield to the lure of analysis based on the calculus of military 'capability'. If there is any lesson to be learnt from the Cold War, it is that military paranoia can emasculate a great nation (the USSR) and enfeeble a superpower (the US). There are more hazards to national growth, stability and security if the external danger is overpainted on the basis of historical parallels discounting the consequences of economic bankruptcy, political turmoil and social disintegration. After appraising China's present priorities, I would reaffirm that unless diplomacy blunders again, there is no likely danger of Chinese militarism against India around the subsisting territorial dispute. Moreover, all military observers recognize that the Indian army, which is better trained and deployed, will not crumple as it did in 1962.

As mentioned earlier, the *de jure* settlement on the boundary question is essentially a problem of political management. It should be noted that even without a border settlement, the relations between the two countries have improved significantly, especially after meetings at the higher levels. They could be further optimized economically, functionally and culturally even without a territorial settlement.

An objective review of the relationship in the past decades, however, also reveals that differences can recur and relations deteriorate on issues unconnected with any tension on the border. For example, while the Government of India is disinclined to let Tibet's internal situation cast a shadow on its relations with China, there is public sympathy within India for the Dalai Lama and Tibet's aspiration to meaningful religious and cultural autonomy. Indeed, in the Indian democracy, at the non-official level, there is bound to be a stronger instinctive echoing of concern at serious violations of the human rights of the Tibetans. Even at the governmental level, there may be divergent attitudes between India and China on the brutal suppression of liberties and democratic forces in Burma (now Myanmar). There are reasons for suspecting that China was a party to the diversion of the heroin trade across Burma from southern China towards India. For two decades China was behind the Khmer Rouge while India supported the Vietnam-backed government in Kampuchea. Even now India is more categorically supportive of UN peacekeeping in Kampuchea than is China. There are other examples of present or potential differences on non-bilateral problems. The climate of good relations between the two countries will be specially vulnerable to the divergence of interests and policies of India and China towards the countries of South Asia. It would be prudent to understand them objectively, as South Asia will remain the critical heart and core of the success and failure of India's foreign policy and indeed of its international standing.

INDIA, CHINA AND SOUTH ASIA

China's military triumph against India both frightened and impressed India's neighbours. Its military prowess will always be of ominous significance, but China's past thrust as well as future purposes in other countries of South Asia have not been and will not be dominated by its coercive capabilities but by its soft diplomatic sophistication. In the years of Sino-India friendship, India had sought to assuage fears of China in Nepal and Burma. China, however, always pursued the quest for independent and parallel relations with the countries of the subcontinent. It has been forthcoming in economic aid and is politically agile in taking advantage of situations of strain between India and its neighbours. It has provided significant military hardware to Bangladesh. When following a request China despatched a few anti-aircraft guns to Nepal through Tibet, it did not warrant a security alarm in India but signified that China placed a rather low premium on the reactions in India when an opportunity for a diplomatic advantage presented itself. India has been more concerned about China-Pakistan relations after the ideologically unprincipled rapprochement and blatant threatening belligerency in the 1960s. For three decades China has steadily consolidated the relations with Pakistan and substantially augmented the latter's military muscle and potential. This level of nuclear cooperation, including support to Pakistan's missile capabilities, cannot be slurred over merely as a legacy of the past when the two countries were jointly as well as separately hostile to India.

But all these less-than-friendly actions of China pose a diplomatic challenge rather than a military threat or an aggressive anti-India conspiracy. The realistic threat perception should, of course, be continuously reviewed. For the present, it should spur efforts to improve relations simultaneously with China and with India's other neighbours. China is not likely to obstruct India-Pakistan normalization once it realizes that China-Pakistan bilateral relations will not be seriously diluted as the obverse of improved India-China relations.

The overriding fact remains that in the nature of the permanent economic, riparian, and ecological interdependence, India cannot be substituted by China in South Asia. All the countries have greater and more vital stakes in finding the chemistry of good relations with India, if only because the ethnic, economic and ecological links with India alone can find answers to their own horrendous problems of poverty. We would be justified in expecting that China's relations with India's neighbours do not go beyond commercial and beneficial economic cooperation.

When China deliberately becomes party to undermining India's position, it cannot but be considered as proof of insensitivity to India's vital interest and so bring reserve in accepting China's profession of friendship with India. Given a careful husbanding of the present climate, China can be restrained from such complications. In the recent past, China has refrained from pronouncing on the internal problems of India such as Punjab or even Kashmir. Sino-Pakistan relations are not likely to result in a coordinated adventure to serve Pakistan's national goals in Kashmir. However, in this diplomatic game, while it would be prudent to anticipate that China will show sympathy with India's smaller neighbours and echo their fears of hegemonism, the negative attitudes can only be effectively assuaged by sensitive and generous good neighbourly policies on the part of India. My experience as Foreign Secretary in the period 1976-9, when several successful negotiations took place, convinces me that China does not—perhaps it cannot—hinder our purposeful and cooperative diplomacy. However, it would be wishful to expect that China could help our purposes beyond detachment.

In the very nature of international politics and bilateral relations between India and China, the diplomatic game that both are bound to play will always be a mix of rivalry and common approaches. A country like China has an advantage in that its time-perspective is for a long diplomatic marathon, while a democratic country like India (or for that matter the US) with populist compulsions runs into sprints and sudden exhaustion, leading to momentary euphoria and deep disappointments. In these decades, India all too frequently forgot the balancing advantage of an old pluralistic civilization and the ethos of its own independence. It should have remained transparently committed to respecting and supporting the fulfilment of independent nationalisms everywhere including its own neighbourhood. Such political pluralism and assertive nationalism, as indeed the sub-nationalism of the weak, is reflective of the power of the powerless in the twentieth century.

Ultimate stability and mutual respect between China and India will hinge on how, with their own chosen strategies, the two countries can find the right mix for nation building and dynamism at home but with flexibility adjusted to a new globalism in external relations. The importance of this assessment points to a digression into China's domestic achievement and future problems.

CHINA'S PRESENT PRIORITIES AND POLICIES

The long-term international goals of China, one must assume, are to rival and outstrip other great powers. The present priority is the four modernization drives undertaken in the fields of agriculture, industry, defence and science and technology, and to that end, attracting and imbibing imported technological and managerial know-how and of uninhibited economic liberalization. The eastern seaboard of China is already the fastest-growing economy in the world, where under the Communist Party's political licence, the Hong Kong model of rampant free enterprise is being transplanted. It would be safe to assume that in the foreseeable future, China's relations with the major technological powers and investors—Japan, Europe, the US, South Korea and of course, investors in Taiwan—will have the highest priority and will not be jeopardized because of any ideological inhibitions.

Long ago, China abandoned the old policy of tempting and inducing modern technology commanded by Japan and the West to be brought to China's doorstep. Like Japan after the Meiji restoration, China after the Cultural Revolution started sending hundreds of thousands of students, scientists, engineers and future managers abroad to study, observe and actually work as interns in the advanced industrialized countries. One assumes China was not oblivious to the danger that when the technological elite and the managerial executives came in contact with innovative freedoms, they would be contaminated by the democratic political urges. After the Tiananmen explosion in 1989, there is a more careful political check on the selection of those sent out, as there is, more determined vigilance exercised against Glasnost and democratization. But notwithstanding the risk of politically motivated or economically lured defections and the brain drain of trained personnel, China is not shutting itself into the old self-imposed professional and technological isolation. Under Deng Hsiao-Ping's direction, ratified by the People's Congress, growth targets have such overriding priority that even demeaning compromises are quietly accepted. In the US-China talks on 'Article 301', after an initial rejection of American demands to open China to American goods, the PRC stooped to make the concessions in order not to damage the thrust of the present external economic relations. Without accepting the legal contractual system and patent rights of the West, China wants to be accepted on trust as a good commercial partner in global economics.

The clear fact is that the policy initiated by Deng only fourteen years ago has been a spectacular success. The per capita income has doubled; consumer satisfaction enthuses the people. 'One state and two systems' has worked so well internally that China hopes that Hong Kong (and later even Taiwan) will rejoice to peacefully reunite with the mother country. In fact, overseas Chinese capitalists, whetted as they are by the success in investment in China, seem to be inclined to agree that political democracy should not be allowed to impede the integration.

In its impressive economic achievement, China has buttressed modern nationalism by drawing on the Confucian civilizational axioms that translate into disciplined work ethics. (Russia, after all, was part of the European heritage even if somewhat separated from the West by the Orthodox Church and modern theory of communism.)

In international politics, China has come a long way from the time when it was against détente, favoured revolution in Africa, the Che Guevera strategy in Latin America, the Naxalites in India, and supported OPEC on the oil price hikes to enfeeble the industrialized countries. The grand strategy then was of the three developing continents of Asia, Africa and Latin America ('the villages of the world') surrounding and smothering North America and Europe ('the cities'). China has not and will not openly abandon the role of being the spokesman and leader of the developing countries. Wherever possible, as, for example, on global warming, China will articulate Third World concerns. But in the final instance, Deng's China will not risk jeopardizing the reputation, which it has already established, of a consensual member of the 'Directoire de Cinq' of the permanent members of the Security Council.

Riding these two horses—of being against the developed powers and their domination on the one hand and acting as a partner of the great powers on the other—will from time to time pose difficult problems for China. During the Iraq-Kuwait crisis China initially showed sympathy for Saddam Hussain's government but eventually went along with the UN Security Council in endorsing the US-led military intervention. In the medium term at least, China will not go beyond the rhetoric to marshal the 'have-not' world to confront the 'have' world.

China also carries the germs of another antagonistic contradiction—how to blend political authoritarianism with economic liberalization. With the reach of the information revolution leading to the universal rise of political awareness, the urge and demand for democratic freedoms and institutions will not forever be effectively suppressed even in Confucian/ Maoist China. The urge for democracy has shaken totalitarian states around the world. As Hong Kong approaches British withdrawal, there is a foretaste of the conflict between the economic advantage of rampant capitalism and the democratic urge for political liberties.

When China becomes an economic giant and a political superpower, it may also face diverse kinds of international problems. There would be sharpened commercial rivalry with the Far Eastern 'tigers'. With Japan, the conflict of policies will not be just for markets and supplies, but also for political influence. Moreover, China has more small neighbours than India and most of them have historical memories of China's domination and could become alarmed again. In particular, China will face a delicate but formidable challenge in South-East Asia. The nationalism of a region now economically strong will have to be assuaged without resorting to coercive postures or repeating punitive adventures as with Vietnam in 1979.

INGREDIENTS FOR FUTURE INDIA-CHINA RELATIONS

India and China were perceived as two pacesetters of the decolonized post-War world. Both belonged to the non-Caucasian Third World and faced similar problems of development. After almost half a century of friendship and hostility, although they still have common interests and attitudes such as on North-South problems and their own development accelerating global warming, these two large nations are different in history, values and national personalities and will remain commercial and political rivals. As of now, India is no longer considered in the same international league as China. Indeed India may have a great deal to learn from China in managing liberalization after recognizing that the publicly controlled commanding heights have in many respects asphyxiated the dynamism in the economy. But it must be acknowledged that India will not accept the position of being a junior partner to China.

China and India must get used to the idea that mere common approaches on the same problems cannot fructify into a strategic or political alliance and identical long-term thrust to international political relations. The idea of an India-China axis amounts to felicitating the exposed fallacy of bloc politics. But rejecting such an axis should not impede a purposeful and sagacious effort to improve relations on the basis of an equation of mutual respect. To obtain such a basis, India must match China's economic strength. This would depend overwhelmingly on our domestic discipline and capacity to manage our modernization in our own way with the goal of satisfying the basic needs of our people.

The international standing of both India and China will hinge on whether, in their different routes to progress, they can live down the fears they evoke as regional powers. As large countries with small neighbours, both have advantages of proximity to markets, but for both this is also a complex political and diplomatic handicap. Much will depend on which country is seen to be abjuring the propensity to coerce and coming to terms with the new strength of nationalisms.

In the politics of the twentieth century, the final advantage will rest with a country which can combine domestic economic dynamism with institutionalized democracy, affording scope for diversity in religion, culture and ethnicity. The subcontinent, before it was splintered, was a rare example of established pluralism. It could have provided an example of functional regionalism if the post-Partition Constitution of India had not taken the path of over-centralization. For India, the great handicap, for which there is no parallel in China— certainly not Taiwan—has been the pall cast by Partition. Thereafter, India got trapped into taking more seriously the superimposition of the Western strategy of containment and competition than the real burden of independence, which is social progress through domestic mobilization. After the Sino-Soviet rift, China wriggled free from the ideological and military discipline of the Soviet-led bloc. India, like Pakistan, has yet to shake off the hypnotic hold of the fallacies learnt from the East-West policies, that 'beggaring the neighbour' is a justified national imperative. India will have to discard the old hypothesis that military capacity is the final ingredient of national power. The process of centralization was alien to India and has to be constitutionally reversed. But having grounded parliamentary democracy as a political safety valve, India has institutionalized a process which exposes governmental and bureaucratic abuses of power and failures of policies. This gives India an advantage over China. Even conceding the grave problems of internal sub-nationalism in India, China with its tradition of Han domination has a more difficult problem in adjusting to the resilient demands of its small but dispersed minorities in Tibet, Sinkiang and Mongolia.

THE CHALLENGE TO SOPHISTICATED DIPLOMACY

Both India and China have to comprehend and adjust to the political and economic disorder of the post-Cold War world. The way towards stable India-China relations requires mature diplomacy. It warrants neither euphoria nor pessimism; neither guilt at the past nor paranoiac fears about the future. At present, China looks like the hare which is racing ahead economically, but the world may be making a misjudgement in writing off the Indian democratic tortoise. India has somewhat forgotten that its original strength was moral; its highest standing was when it demanded the fulfilment of nationalism through worldwide decolonization and, thereafter, the respect for equality of all nations in the society of nations. If India can gallop ahead economically, accommodate sub-nationalism domestically, resist communalism, ensure social justice and citizens' rights democratically, and also catalyse functional cooperation in South Asia, it could dramatically regain international political stature.

India-China relations have now returned to the ambit of beneficial bilateralism. There will be no damage to this potential of mutual respect if the rhetoric does not claim total identity on international problems. Once India has regained internal strength and regional deference, India and China may well vindicate once again the five principles of friendly neighbourliness which were affirmed in the 1950s and which, in two-sided misperceptions, were compromised by both. Both India and China are necessary as independent pillars for a stable international system.

NOTES

1. Paper presented at a seminar in Toronto in 1989, and published in Milton Israel (ed.), *Nehru and the Twentieth Century*, Toronto: University of Toronto, Centre for South Asian Studies, South Asian Studies papers, Number 4, 1991.
2. George N. Patterson, *Peking vs. Delhi*, New York: Praeger, 1964.
3. Alistair Lamb, *Tibet, China, and India 1914-1950: A History of Imperial Diplomacy*, Hertfordshire: Roxford, 1989.
4. Yaacov Y.I. Vertzberger, *Misperception in Foreign Policymaking: The Sino-Indian Conflict, 1959-1962*, Boulder: Westview, 1984.
5. Steven Hoffmann, *India and the China Crisis*, Berkeley: University of California Press, 1990.
6. Francis Watson, *The Frontiers of China*, London: Chatto and Windus, 1966.

PART FIVE

Looking Ahead: Globally and Regionally

14

Can Non-Alignment Survive its Universalization?

The story of non-alignment has been a kind of philosophical paradox. There was incisive foresight when, in the face of pressure and prejudice, the principle of dissent and nonconformity was asserted against ideological and military globalism. The philosophy was vindicated with a rapidity unforeseen even by its proponents. Premier Khrushchev and President John F. Kennedy (in his inaugural address) applauded the right of non-alignment, which had been denounced with contempt by their predecessors only a few years earlier. Within two decades the UN itself came to be dominated by the non-aligned. But the Movement, which came into existence at the non-aligned summit in 1973 at Algiers as the custodian of the principles, was inevitably overtaken by the search for unity and consensus. Not surprisingly, it is riddled with deep differences which cannot be concealed by the proclaimed adherence to a common allegiance.

This triumph and disarray were inherent in the contradiction between the fundamental right of dissent in sovereign states and the organizational compulsion for conformity—a philosophical conflict between the faith and the church it created. The result is that the abiding validity of non-aligned principles faces the danger of being mocked by convenient compromises, nonchalant defiance, or irreconcilable differences among its own votaries.

The birth and growth of non-alignment as well as its decline and loss of cohesion can be traced to the confluence of two independent developments in the post-war scene: the

* Article written in 1983 to coincide with the summit in Delhi. First published in the *Mainstream* and *Seminar*.

decolonization of the empires in Asia and Africa on the one hand, and the regrouping of the old world of Europe and North America into two monolithic blocs in global confrontation and competition on the other.

The Cold War injected ideology and the concept of secular universalism into the relationship of sovereign nations. Survival, it was argued, demanded the harmonization of economic, social and foreign policies among like-minded nations superseding the traditional rationale of national interest. Both NATO and the Warsaw Pact (and the latter's extension in the Sino-Soviet treaty) were formed on the assumption that the democratic and the communist worlds were locked in a life-and-death struggle. Each feared the malevolence and compulsive expansion of the other, and so the adversary group had to be militarily 'contained', 'rolled back', or 'buried', and at least economically ostracized with all means at the disposal of the State.

The formation of these blocs arrested and reversed the process of demobilization and the return to peacetime normalcy within two years of the end of the exhausting world war; it turned former allies into adversaries and defeated enemies into friends and future comrades-in-arms. It so vitiated the international environment that notions of neutrality outside the bipolar block system were looked upon as morally reprehensible and militarily suicidal. It was against this international background that decolonization got underway. More than a hundred countries which had been ruled by and tied to the European system came to join the international community. The new nations were throbbing with the aspiration to exercise the show and substance of independence. They looked forward to refashioning their own socio-economic domestic structures and determine their own pattern of functional international relations. The two processes of the Cold War and decolonization were inherently in conflict: one required conformity and was centripetal, and the other was centrifugal, diverse and divisive.

Decolonization did not have to coincide with the Cold War. The US wrested its independence in the eighteenth century; the Spanish and Portuguese empires wound up in South America in the nineteenth century. India could have been given the substance of power before 1939. The world war hastened decolonization in Asia and Africa, but in the end the process was inevitable. Imposed isolation and insulation had kept Asia and Africa outside the pale of international politics, but with modern communications the urge for self-government could not but reach all the colonial dependencies.

The war brought defeat and the occupation of France, the Netherlands and Belgium. Many of their colonies were overrun by the Axis powers. After the war, imperialist nostalgia tried to regain its old hold in Indochina, the Dutch East Indies and North Africa, but the attempts only invited frustration and failure. Britain was not defeated but was enfeebled by its exertions. In any case, the illusion of permanence and the invincibility of European hegemony was shattered by the war and the US and the Soviet Union emerged as the two world powers.

The process of decolonization, let it be added, was not precipitated by the advent of communism or the establishment of socialism in the Soviet Union or even the constitution of the communist bloc. The USSR banked on proletarian internationalism and, at least initially, thought decolonization was a charade and the new nations were not necessarily free to develop meaningful relations with the socialist system.

Although the decisions leading to the two events arose from independent and separate processes, the year 1947 was critical for both the advent of the Cold War and the beginning of post-war decolonization. Britain under a Labour Government started the process of decolonization by the transfer of power to India and its Asian colonies. The Truman doctrine of global containment of communism and the transfer of power (and Partition) in the subcontinent happened to synchronize but their interaction and international consequences were not perceived at the time.

Non-alignment was born in defiance of the global bipolarity, which started with the policies of containment. The Cold War beleaguered new countries in the wake of their independence. Their nationalism baulked at the demand for conformity. The new countries refused to accept the 'either/or' choice of socio-economic systems. Nor were they prepared to accept that a military alliance with one or the other of the contending blocs was the only guarantee for preserving national independence.

The earliest definition of non-alignment, no doubt vague but nonetheless incisive, is found in the writings and speeches of Nehru, enunciated even before he became head of the government of independent India. In his first broadcast as vice-president of the Interim Government in September 1946, Nehru had said: 'We propose as far as possible to keep away from power policies of groups, aligned against one another which in the past have led to world wars and which may lead to disaster, even on a bigger scale in the future.' Nehru's approach was more significant as his pronouncement against joining alliances was made even before the wartime allies and adversaries had regrouped into military blocs.

The elements that constitute non-alignment have never been embodied in a clear Charter of Principles. In fact, non-alignment has been defined by the same country in different ways at different times to fit in conveniently with its prevailing national policies and circumstances (contrast Indonesia's Sukarno's attitude with that of Suharto's, Ethiopia's approach under Emperor Haile Selassie and now under Mengistu). However, the essential core and consensus of the non-aligned principles can be extrapolated, distilled and broadly defined as follows:

i) Non-alignment implicitly stood for plurality and democratic equality within the international community. It affirmed faith in self-determination and the total end of colonialism. It opposed all forms of pressures and outside interventions in the internal politics of a nation. While opposed to disciplined bloc conformity, non-alignment was predicated on the freedom—indeed imperative—of international cooperation and beneficial functional relationships in an increasingly interdependent world.

ii) Non-alignment, in its essential thrust, stood for all fundamental human rights. More particularly, it challenged racialism and apartheid. It also supported the right of individual political liberties and the demand for economic and social justice.

iii) Non-alignment, which asserted ideological agnosticism in determining international relationships, also stood for freedom of nations to democratically determine their internal socio-political philosophies. It did not reject the validity of different and opposing socio-economic concepts, but denied the right of imposition of an external ideology or system. In effect, it argued that a nation must have the right to evolve from its own civilizational roots and economic circumstances. Any or all ideologies could compete in the national political arena, but they had to be grounded in the soil of the country.

iv) Non-alignment was based on the premise that national security—internal and external—was a function of the totality of national strength. In effect, this implied that neither morally nor pragmatically should internal legitimacy be based solely on military power. Even less prudent was the surrender to outsider protection. The key to national modernization and security was development and social justice.

v) Non-alignment asserted that for the fulfilment of national aspirations and the exercise of sovereign independence, international peace was an overriding precondition. Non-alignment, therefore, pleaded for peaceful co-existence and the avoidance of such confrontation which would lead to international conflicts. This was all the more vital in the face of weapons of mass destruction and the moral and military implications of a nuclear war. With unprecedented dangers from international conflicts, especially between the great powers, the non-aligned placed emphasis on the peaceful resolution of all disputes.

Put together, the axioms of non-alignment were independence, development and peaceful coexistence in an interdependent world. These principles added up to a protest against any form of imposed globalism: militaristic, economic, ideological or political. It was a plea for a balance between pluralistic internationalism and the persisting reality of nationalism in the nation-state system. These principles, it may be repeated, were never formulated in this form but there was an implicit broad consensus around them amongst the early mentors of the movement.

The non-aligned approach was initially advanced during what was perceived as the most serious crisis in world history. Dean Acheson, while urging the adoption of the Truman Doctrine, had declared that never since Rome faced Carthage was the world confronted with such a division and challenge. John Foster Dulles, as we know, denounced notions of neutrality as immoral. It required the fire of deep conviction to challenge the prevailing counsels of the powerful nations of the world.

Initially, India was almost alone or, at least, the most defiant against the conventional wisdom that emanated from the great powers. India led and persisted for decades in urging that the UN should be a universal, non-ideological organization of states, and so communist China should be admitted to its membership. India transmitted the warning to the Western powers against enlarging the Korean war by US troops advancing north of the 38th Parallel. It played a key behind-the-scene role in the Geneva Conference on Indochina (1954). Yugoslavia became a pioneer when it broke away from Stalin's demand for ideological conformity in the socialist commonwealth. The refusal of Egypt under Nasser to be cowed down by the summary withdrawal of promised aid for the Aswan Dam was the first assertion against economic aid being politically conditioned. Egypt survived the conspiratorial aggression by the British, the French and Israel to re-establish control over the Suez Canal. However, while Yugoslavia and Egypt had shown the courage of defiance against great powers, they did so only on national problems. India's stand was on international problems affecting world peace.

India can, therefore, legitimately claim some credit for asserting the kind of independent judgement that gave courage and appeal to non-alignment. In the 1950s there was no multilateral strength. The moral standing of India's non-alignment itself was admittedly diluted when New Delhi shirked from raising its voice against intervention at the time of the Hungarian crisis of 1956. However, the point to note is that the non-aligned approach achieved its notable successes on major international problems when the aligned blocs were both strong and intolerant of any dissent, before a collective forum of the non-aligned had emerged. One could almost go so far as to assert that the greatest glory and achievement of the non-aligned approach occurred before the founding of the Non-Aligned Movement (NAM).

By the end of the 1950s, the process of decolonization was well underway. The important colonies in Asia became independent in the 1940s (India, Pakistan, Burma, Ceylon and Indonesia). Most, but not all of them, were initially inclined to adopt non-alignment as their foreign policy. By 1960, the winds of change were blowing across Africa, and Britain, France and Belgium were in the process of transferring the substance of political power to their respective colonies in the continent. The Organization of African Unity (OAU), formed in 1960, inscribed in its founding charter a commitment to non-alignment. Since then, non-alignment has swept the international checkerboard.

At the last non-aligned summit (1979) held in Havana, the membership of the NAM had reached ninety-five without counting observer and guest members. Country after country made it plain that they prized their national independence through detachment from the two major alliance systems. Many countries which initially chose to belong to the blocs have since repudiated their commitments and turned to join the fraternity of the non-aligned nations. Iraq renounced its membership in the Baghdad Pact after its revolution and Iran did so after the fall of the Shah. Pakistan finally applied to join the non-aligned in the late 1970s.

What is more significant is that countries which are still tied militarily to the blocs are showing a kind of independence from the superpowers' leadership, which is associated with the approach of non-alignment. France and Rumania, even in the 1960s, started asserting that their national interests did not fully coincide with the discipline implicit in the collective foreign-policy approach of their respective blocs.

Looking back on these three decades, the approach of non-alignment—of independence and coexistence rather than a disciplined conformity and preparation for an inevitable war—has been prophetically vindicated. The old bipolarity is dead and the international system has become polycentralized. The rationale of total Iron Curtain adversary relations between different socio-economic systems is all but repudiated. The possibility of a major conventional or nuclear conflict is now considered unlikely. After the defection of Yugoslavia and the Sino-Soviet split, ideology has ceased to be a cementing force for their political relationships. Even where the same ideology is professed, as in the Soviet bloc, socio-economic policies have been nationally domesticated.

The quest for alliance relationship has indeed led to curious aberrations and contradictions. The US rejoiced in the independence of communist Yugoslavia and has found itself buttressing military, fascist and blatantly undemocratic regimes. The USSR bloc and the communist countries have all too often befriended countries which outlawed communism at home.

The great achievement of non-alignment was to have anticipated and contributed to the restoration of the traditional sovereign discretion to independent nations, and if given internal strength, nations can once again, more or less, fearlessly determine their relations with each other on the basis of their perceived political, economic and security interests. Left to themselves, most countries now recoil from peacetime military commitments outside their own direct security concerns. At all events, they reject the notion that the threat to one country must be automatically perceived as a threat to all nations. Nationalism against imperialism and peace and coexistence against confrontation and conflict are no longer questioned as morally reprehensible or defensively suicidal. In brief, today non-alignment is no longer at bay. It is the US and its allies and the USSR and its voluntary or involuntary followers who find themselves in a minority and often in opposition in international councils.

And yet, despite the vindication of the non-aligned philosophy and the growing universal appeal of its principles, NAM is transparently in disarray—enfeebled from within and, notwithstanding verbal homage and ulterior purposes, disregarded from without.

It is worth reviewing how this paradoxical degeneration came about. The struggle between the original principles and the obsessive search for demonstrable unity was evident throughout as non-alignment went on from one meeting to the next. It became more difficult as the numbers grew and activist delegations, overlooking the essential spirit of non-alignment, sought to bend the consensus of the movement to their own national perspectives. The movement, as a whole, did not see how non-alignment was slowly but steadily departing from its spirit of safeguarding dissent and diversity in the international system. Unwittingly, it was being reduced to flattering the philosophy of the aligned—of multilateral conformity and subordinating the inherent differences of national interests.

The spirit of non-alignment came out best at the Bandung Conference in 1955, which was not a meeting of the non-aligned at all even though it was restricted to the countries of Asia and Africa. The deliberations saw a debate between the concept of peaceful co-existence between different social systems and the notion of security through external military dependence and the perceived threat of communist expansionism. The majority came out on the side of detachment from the Cold War confrontation. but, it was more than a negative affirmation against conformity. Even with Chou en-Lai there, representing communist China, the declaration demanded the right of new countries to choose their economic partners according to their own discretion and needs. It called on the International Bank for Reconstruction—The World Bank—to provide assistance to the developing countries according to their developmental needs. Bandung was the first summit-level meeting of the leaders of Africa and Asia, and was thus historic in symbolizing the end of European domination of international diplomacy.

By 1961, when twenty-five nations met in Belgrade at the first Non-aligned Conference, peaceful coexistence had ceased to be morally retrograde or politically reprehensible. Racialism persisted in South Africa; but only Portugal was vaunting justification for its colonies. The French were on the way to withdrawing from Algeria. Only in Vietnam was the fulfilment of nationalism being resisted and this was the legacy of the Cold War syndrome of the 1950s. Meanwhile, following the launch of *Sputnik* and the Soviet Union mastering the technique of making a thermonuclear bomb, there was a growing recognition of the dangers of the nuclear arms race and the threat from continuing atmospheric explosions.

In Belgrade itself, there was a conflict between two views on international priorities: whether to focus on peace, disarmament, coexistence and positive cooperation across the ideological divide or to continue confrontation with the old imperialism of which the USA was then seen as a latter-day leader and protector. Sukarno became the spokesperson for the confrontationist lobby while Nehru advanced his vision for peace and cooperation, and spoke of the dangers of nuclear war and testing. He urged positive enlightened internationalism to make the world safe for diversity and independence. The Belgrade Declaration was a compromise document but has remained the point of reference on principles, priorities and qualifications for membership of the movement. The conference was on guard against institutionalizing an anti-bloc bloc and never even considered holding a subsequent summit.

The second summit of the non-aligned held in Cairo in 1964, was called mainly to pre-empt the proposal to hold a second Bandung. The confrontationist concept had, in the meanwhile, gathered momentum, especially following the Sino-Soviet rift. China had launched a call for revolution and solidarity of the Third World against the 'cities of the world', which included both the Western bloc and Soviet-led Eastern Europe.

The Sino-Indian dispute, which had erupted in 1959, had culminated in a short but massive war in 1962, and cast its shadow on non-aligned cohesion. It was a clear case of the use of force against an established or, at least, an openly claimed frontier. The interim mediatory proposals by Ceylon (now Sri Lanka) and other non-aligned countries in 1962-3 failed as China rejected the proposal for withdrawal to create a non-administered no-man's-land even from the territory overrun during the 1962 conflict. It was the first major challenge to whether the non-aligned, as a movement, were going to face squarely the problems of the use of force which affected one of their members. As we know, the conference evaded the India-China issue. This has been the bane of the movement ever since—that intra-Third World problems, when they could not be attributed to Western imperialism, were to be played down in the quest for consensus and unity.

Holding of the Cairo Conference before the second Bandung did, however, enable the non-aligned to survive as a movement. Had the second Afro-Asian Conference been held before the Cairo Conference, there might have been efforts to hold a tri-continental conference, then proposed to be hosted by Cuba. Since Belgrade, Sino-Soviet competition had overtaken even the East-West confrontation as the major dilemma before the Third World. Specifically, the difference in approach was on whether or not the USSR was to be accepted as an Asian power and in its true significance, whether non-alignment was to be on the side of peace, détente, cooperation with different blocs or was it to take sides with China in the confrontational approach to international politics.

The second Afro-Asian Conference was originally scheduled to take place in Algiers in April 1965; it was postponed at the last minute because of the fall of Ben Bella. By November 1965, when it assembled, Sukarno had also been displaced. When, at the pre-conference meeting, it appeared that the broad majority was not in favour of keeping the USSR out, the conference itself was abandoned and the idea of another Bandung has never since been seriously revived. It illustrated and highlighted the trend of wanting to use multilateral fora to subserve the particular goal of some powers, rather than a constructive endeavour to support peace and resolve serious international problems.

Even after the Cairo Conference, no decision was taken to hold a third summit of the non-aligned. The next summit was held after a gap of six years in Lusaka in 1970. While rejecting any formal commitment to institutionalize the movement, it was decided there that a non-aligned summit would take place every three years. The membership of the movement had already increased to fifty-four. Unconsciously, the trend was to imitate the practices and procedures of the established international institutions like the UN. Aside from the declarations, fourteen separate resolutions were passed at the conference, pertaining mostly to Africa and to racialism but also to Vietnam and East-West issues.

The fourth non-aligned summit was notable as Algeria, the host country, showed great determination in exercising its leadership over the movement. It proposed and secured the creation of a Bureau for inter-summit coordination under the chairmanship of the host country. The Algiers declaration, in keeping with Algeria's own radical approach, veered away significantly from neutrality between the blocs. A consensus was claimed at the conclusion of the conference but it was at variance with the internal and external policies of a vast number of countries represented at the meeting.

Incidentally, before the fourth summit, OPEC had already come into existence. The oil weapon was projected as a telling leverage against the West and its continuing 'neo-colonialist' hold over the former colonies, with multinational corporations (MNCs) acting as the instruments of such exploitation. The Third World, as a whole, vaguely hoped that the oil weapon could be used not just to get an equitable price for the exporters of a depleting resource but also for parallel advantages for the commodity exports of the other developing countries with mono-economic cultures. The Algiers Conference endorsed the right to use raw material as a weapon for confrontation with the affluent world, but shirked from contemplating the foreseeable consequences of oil price hikes on the fraternal members of the movement.

The fifth conference in Colombo (1976) corrected the balance somewhat against the radical twist given at Algiers. However, the trend to overlap and duplicate the UN agenda became even more pronounced. In the wake of the energy crisis, there was great elaboration on the economic problems in the developing world but, in deference to OPEC members, the serious concern of the non-aligned oil importers was not allowed to be raised and embodied in the recommendations.

The Colombo Conference was also memorable for the gargantuan diplomatic efforts of the Democratic Peoples Republic of Korea (with a several-hundred-strong delegation, most of whom were staying on board a ship berthed in Colombo harbour) to obtain non-aligned backing for its own position on the reunification of the two Koreas. Even though it ended in failure, it was symptomatic of the effort to use non-alignment for purely national interests. In contrast, the presence of the Vietnam delegation, led by Premier Pham-Van Dong, after having defeated the mighty US, vindicated the validity and strength of nationalism.

The Vietnamese delegation commanded immense respect by refraining from victory polemics or ulterior manoeuvres; it won a seat on the Non-Aligned Bureau with ease.

The sixth summit conference in Havana in 1979 saw the revival of the sharp debate between the moderate, hitherto quiescent majority and the radical active confrontationists, on the purpose and direction of the movement. Cuba sought to give non-alignment a slant which was in keeping with its own national perspectives and policies. Castro had no hesitation in denouncing Yankee imperialism and its old and new allies. (The most important new ally was, of course, China, which up to 1965 had been a firm friend of Cuba.) Castro did not conceal the fact that he saw the socialist bloc, led by the USSR, as the natural ally of the NAM.

Using the administrative advantage of being the host country, Cuba sought to exclude the delegation of the Pol Pot regime in Kampuchea, which had represented the country at the previous conferences and still held the Kampuchean seat in the UN. The other issue that cast its shadow on the conference was whether Sadat's Egypt, having recognized and compromised with Israel, should be condemned by the movement as a whole.

The important question that surfaced was whether the NAM was to function democratically or be slanted to reflect the views of an activist host. President Tito's call to the conference to remain the conscience of humankind and refrain from a partisan twist was generally acclaimed but the spirit of the conference was far removed from that concept. Burma highlighted the problem when, even though being an original member and loyal in letter and spirit to its policies, it withdrew after calling for a faithful adherence to non-aligned principles. In fact, the meeting ended with a feeling of impending crisis rather than unity.

The serious division in the Movement was highlighted when, three months after the Cuba Conference, the USSR intervened in Afghanistan. As Cuba's own position was at variance with that of the majority, the movement as a whole refrained from taking any initiative. As a consequence, the Cuban chairmanship and indeed the movement as a whole remained virtually paralysed during the next three years. The crisis was once again dramatized when the venue of the next summit, under preparation for years at a cost of hundreds of millions of dollars, had to be shifted from Baghdad to Delhi. The proposed host was involved in a long-lasting conflict with Iran, another non-aligned country. Each was accusing the other of territorial aggression, violation of human rights, unjustified intervention, and professing outrage against the principles of non-alignment. The mediatory effort of the non-aligned proved infructuous and, in the process, the movement itself suffered a serious loss of credibility and all round embarrassment.

At the Delhi Summit, the membership crossed the hundred mark. The summit was an impressive organizational feat, particularly as it was done at only a few months' notice. The professional competence of our officials was once again demonstrated. Mrs Gandhi's stewardship commanded universal admiration, and the threat of the movement becoming ideologically tilted was laid to rest. Her leadership prevailed against the actual disruption by controversial issues like the representation of Kampuchea. But the problems of Kampuchea and Afghanistan remain; and it is possible that when the General Assembly meets, a majority of the non-aligned will repudiate the Delhi consensus. Since the conference, or as a result of it, none of the ongoing problems have been resolved or even eased on the basis of the appeal of the heads of governments. The Iraq-Iran conflict has continued with the familiar ferocity and unreason. Indeed, the two have refused to cooperate even to tackle the oil slick in the Gulf which could spell disaster for them and affect all the nations bordering that almost enclosed, critically important international sea.

In Kampuchea, since the conference, the conflict nearly spread to Thailand, and in Afghanistan the insurgency has intensified. There is little prospect of agreement on a conference to restructure the international monetary system. By asking for universal participation, the declaration may embarrass the USSR and provide an excuse for the Western nations' continued indifference. The prospect of global negotiations, a meaningful launching of a common fund to stabilize commodity prices, and support for the universal committee for International Development Strategy are previous recommendations bedevilled by old and familiar resistance. What is welcome in the declaration is its programme for greater focus on South-South cooperation and its call for self-reliance and regional and intra-regional cooperation.

The Delhi Declaration in fact has two contradictory strands running through it which illustrate the problem of the near universalization of the movement. On the one hand, aside from old issues like Israeli aggression and expansionism, Namibia and apartheid, there is a call for a new kind of globalism—against superpowers, imperialism, racialism and for a new global economic order. But this avoids issues born out of the differences that involve the non-aligned themselves. On the other hand, is the call for disciplined development and cooperation at the national and regional levels and the implicit recognition that diversity in the international system cannot be overcome by global prescriptions. It is a conflict between globalism, which is an intellectual legacy of the Cold War, and internationalism which must recognize the compulsions of interdependence and marshal solutions acknowledging the reality of independence and diversity while demanding enlightened accommodation amongst nation-states. The non-aligned are in a position to assert that globalism has failed and the building blocs for international stability must start with national self-reliance, regional cooperation and the practice of non-aligned principles by the non-aligned and the aligned alike.

An analysis of the world's inequitous economic balance supported by a sense of shared grievance, is insufficient to obtain results or establish the credibility of the movement. These contradictions are the manifestation of the conflict between the principles of independence and diversity on the one hand and the movement's preoccupation with a show of unity and solidarity on the other. The problem has not ended with the affirmations of a declaration. Indeed, it will bedevil and burden India as we go through a succession of conferences, meetings and committees and find that little headway is being made in solving political or economic problems. Should China eventually seek to join the non-aligned movement? There can be no technical objection to its doing so as the Sino-Soviet Treaty has lapsed. The movement may then hark back to the 1961-5 period when the debate was between anti-superpower confrontationist globalism and international cooperation based on diversity. Anyway, the cause of peace and cooperation is unlikely to have been effectively advanced by the conference process.

What can one conclude from this brief survey of twenty-one years of the non-aligned movement? The membership has steadily increased to a comfortable and permanent majority in the UN. The principles are no longer condemned as immoral and are barely challenged by the aligned. Nationalism is securely resilient. With grassroots strength, it could defeat (as in Vietnam) the most powerful superpower, and against all military odds, it could defy the other superpower (as in Afghanistan). The policy of enveloping developing nations into military alliances, as in SEATO and CENTO, has proved a dismal failure. The international system has become pluralist; coexistence has become the declared goal of the aligned and non-aligned alike.

However, since 1961 the scorecard of successes—which can be directly attributed to the non-aligned—is almost blank. The movement has, at best, been a pressure group supplementing initiatives in the UN or other international bodies. Nothing like the special or exclusive role in Korea, the Geneva Conference and the Indo-China commissions, or the decisive lead emanating from Belgrade to call a halt to nuclear testing, can be claimed. The movement had consistently focused on decolonization in Africa but finally the Portuguese empire collapsed in Lisbon and the Zimbabwe settlement was reached in the Commonwealth Conference in London. South Africa alone is still not relenting on apartheid and Namibia.

On the other hand, except for the arms race of the superpowers, every other major problem that erupted has involved conflicts between or outrage against the national integrity of the non-aligned nations. The Israeli aggression in Lebanon, its consolidation of its hold on the left bank of the Jordan and the unresolved Middle-East problem, the Iraq-Iran war, Afghanistan, Kampuchea, Chad, El Salvador and Central America are all challenges to non-alignment. NAM has been unwilling or unable to tackle them. It has ignored innumerable violations of non-aligned principles by its own members, including the interventions and long-term presence of foreign troops in non-aligned countries. Terrorism and subversion have not been brought to book. Unable to discipline or even condemn such dereliction, the broad umbrella of non-alignment has come to shield or tolerate every deviation from the original spirit. The movement, as a principled guardian of peace and diversity, thus stands enfeebled and exposed, and the consensus documents can scarcely conceal the divisions and disarray.

What are the reasons for the present loss of effective vigilance by the movement, when the principles for which it stood stand vindicated? It is true that the attempt to hijack the movement as a natural ally of one bloc or the other, has not succeeded. The only running thread in all declarations has been the momentum of anti-imperialism and what has later come to be described as neo-colonialism. Colonialism and the Cold War had given birth to the idea of non-alignment, but they became both a kind of foil and a fixation for its continuing momentum.

The focus on anti-imperialism had understandably given non-alignment its original anti-West tilt. As South Africa, the home of professed racialism, was allied to and for long condoned by NATO, it reinforced the anti-West direction. But colonialism was in retreat before the first non-aligned summit, and even in 1961, Nehru did not see that the collective effort of flogging a dying phenomenon was important. There was reluctance to criticize the outrages by the other bloc or by the non-aligned themselves.

Indeed, hypnotized by past history and perceptions, the non-aligned were inhibited in any objective recognition of the changes in the world situation and the new problems of the post-colonial world. Collectively, they never quite saw that the non-aligned principles were no longer being questioned and challenged. Even when the blocs splintered and confrontation eased to vigilant competition, the non-aligned continued to base their analyses on imperialism and the Cold War. A kind of intellectual vested interest had taken root in the presumed permanence of the Cold War. Thus, the posture of the movement fell short of valid contemporary attitudes.

The rapid development of long-range missiles which could be

targeted from home bases and submerged submarines, and the capacity of satellite and electronic surveillance reduced the importance of countries which earlier were deemed essential for the ring of containment. The superpower hotline, the agreement on a partial ban on nuclear testing, the strategic arms limitation talks and the creeping recognition of common interests between the superpowers, even as adversaries, made the non-aligned strategically less important. The process of change was gradual and even suffered reversals but the non-aligned did not grasp, at least not fully or in time, the implications of détente between the blocs, even though that détente was the fulfilment of their own proclaimed goals.

There was a similar imperceptible change affecting the economic relations of the non-aligned with the developed world. The Cold War competition had brought the bounty of massive economic aid from the affluent nations. Parallel with inter-bloc dialogue and détente was the development in which the donor nations of both blocs became more selective and restrained in offering aid to the developing world. Domestic lobbies started pointing out that frequently foreign aid was wasted or diverted to prestige projects or helped to buttress the positions of the established civil or military elites.

In any case, the aid process did not obtain either the expected economic growth or secure allegiance and gratitude in the manner hoped for by the donor nations. It was the obverse consequence of the congruence of Cold War competition and decolonization—too much early involvement and tutelage in the affairs of newly independent countries was followed by a peremptory withdrawal and the disenchantment syndrome. (There were, of course, exceptions but these were for special reasons or as residuary legacies of the past.) The wrong rationale—security rather than international economic justice and the wrong development strategies for helping established elites rather than basic needs—had all too frequently been endorsed by aid-givers.

Let it be acknowledged that, on the side of the recipient nations, the foreign-aid process had, in any case, softened the determination for optimal efforts towards economic development even in such fields as food sufficiency, rural development and basic infrastructure. In many countries, nationalism was not marshalled for economic discipline and social justice, as had been pledged in demanding independence. While verbal homage was paid to cooperation with fellow developing countries, the habit of seaborne trade and continued dependency on the old metropolitan countries was abetted and even intensified. The potential of regional economic cooperation was not seriously explored. In fact, where such regional institutions had been inherited, as in the East African community, they were allowed to disintegrate for short-sighted political reasons, discounting permanent geographic and economic compulsions. The attempt to establish tripartite cooperation between Yugoslavia, Egypt and India was hurriedly conceived without seriously considering that the economic complimentary between them had limited scope and doubtful potential.

As stated earlier, the OPEC cartel at one time looked as if it had picked up a uniquely powerful weapon against the modern industrial State. A substantial part of international liquidity flowed to a few developing countries, which held the promise of compelling an imaginative rationale for equitable world development. The non-aligned, however, hesitated to demand enlightened consideration from the fraternal ranks of the oil-affluent countries. The paradoxical result has been that the major oil exporters—all of them non-aligned—have become the conduit for the scarce and hard-earned resources of the poorer importers finding their way into the coffers of the already affluent world!

When, after the energy crisis, the blueprint of a New International Economic Order was formulated and endorsed by the non-aligned, the Western developed nations were able to point to the world economic recession brought about by the sudden oil price hikes, the OPEC nations turned a deaf ear, albeit with expressions of sympathy and vague promises for the future. The indifference of the Eastern bloc further weakened the leverage of the Third World. The present agony of the Third World—of a growing economic chasm and barriers to trade and resources—was compounded by the aid weariness of the North, insufficient efforts at self-reliance of the developing nations and the South-South energy crisis. NAM has remained silent on how much the present economic malaise is due to the non-aligned nations themselves.

The commitment to disarmament, nuclear and conventional, and the plea for diversion of resources to international economic development has also been the constant refrain of the non-aligned. However, the Third World has generally shirked from the introspective examination of its own militarization. It was an article of faith of the non-aligned that development and social justice provided a firmer basis for internal stability and external security than grandiose militarism and external dependence. The wisdom of the faith has been proven time and again, most dramatically in Iran. But few countries—very few indeed—can claim to uphold the principle in their own internal policies. No doubt the origin of the Third World military build-up was in part due to the great power policies and the commercial salesmanship of arms manufacturers. But it would be a travesty of the truth and a self-confessed slur on their sovereign discretion not to recognize that the excessive militarism has been because of the voluntary militaristic policies of most governments of the non-aligned themselves. The present problems of the non-aligned, if analytically scrutinized, can be traced to both a change in the international environment and myopia in their own policies and appraisals.

Historical reasons aside, the basic fact is that the enfeeblement of the movement was almost inherent in the process of institutionalizing non-alignment. Non-alignment slid, no doubt unawares, into the pitfalls that beset most multilateral diplomacy. The positive thrust, envisaged by Nehru, unavoidably gave way to the lowest common denominator that covered up differences. The search for consensus led to a concentration on outdated issues of a negative nature or on unrealistic approaches. The whole process and measure of achievement got caught in drafting gamesmanship rather than problem resolution.

To reach agreed declarations, NAM conferences split up into committees, subcommittees, regional group meetings, drafting caucuses—all in imitation of UN procedures and practices. Every meeting became a tortuous non-stop drafting exercise, at times going on for eighteen to twenty hours in the day. Even professional diplomats when weary and bleary-eyed are apt to yield on substance and lose sight of the wood for the trees. The show of verbal solidarity—transparently divorced from reality—became an all-consuming preoccupation before or at the conferences.

A recent compilation of non-aligned documents shows that the Belgrade Declaration has only eight pages; the Cairo Declaration after the second summit stretches to fourteen pages; the Lusaka Declaration and resolutions into eighteen pages; for Algiers, there are thirty pages; in Colombo it jumps to sixty-two pages and the Havana document is spread to over ninety-four pages. The Delhi Declaration with its annexures runs to almost 160 pages. The international impact of these conference declarations has been almost in inverse ratio to the length of the recommendations. The political and economic declarations reiterated old and known positions—agreed at the UN or other agencies. The non-aligned have made recommendations on practically every problem of functional international cooperation covered by international agencies including insurance, sports, fisheries and Antarctica.

While the conference documents became longer, they also became distorted in their emphasis. While there is extensive elaboration on non-controversial issues like racialism or virtually defunct ones like imperialism, current serious issues elicited only brief and bland mentions. The Declaration at the last Foreign Ministers Conference in Delhi contained ten pages on Africa (prepared no doubt by the African group) but only a brief paragraph on Afghanistan, two on South-East Asia including Kampuchea, and nothing substantial on the ongoing war between Iran and Iraq. There is a similar imbalance in the seventh summit declaration.

It would be safe to surmise that hardly any member of a delegation is able to scrutinize carefully the entire documentation for possible contradictions, in word or spirit, before the final endorsement. Not more than half a dozen delegations (India invariably being one of them) have the personnel or expertise to take an active interest in all subjects and all the drafting committees. Most delegations confine their scrutiny to a few paragraphs of sensitive interest to their own country. It is doubtful if any head of a government could even cursorily glance through the totality of documents or even the political declarations to which, by adoption, they would stand committed.

Like the growing length of non-aligned documents, the diplomatic process has continued to mount and become more exacting. A nucleus of a small secretariat has had to be created in the UN delegation of the current chairman of the movement. Apart from the meeting of the Foreign Ministers at the time of the UN General Assembly, every year there is at least one annual meeting of the Bureau at the level of Foreign Ministers. In addition, a meeting of all the Foreign Ministers takes place between summits in one of the non-aligned capitals. Every important meeting of the Bureau and the Ministers, and more so before the summit, requires pre-conference consultations through the visits of officials to many, if not all, the capitals. There is even the practice of sending formal invitations through special envoys instead of using the established diplomatic channels.

The conference arrangements generally require years of preparation and may cost hundreds of millions of dollars which often eat into the scarce resources.

The cost-effectiveness of such multilateral diplomacy cannot, of course, be measured in monetary terms. No doubt for a week or so, the host country can rejoice in being the focus of world attention with international publicity for the country and its leadership. The professional diplomats can meet with their opposite numbers. Sometimes the summit provides an opportunity for a more discreet meeting between heads of governments when bilateral visits may be politically premature or arouse excessive expectations. In the process, a breakthrough might be achieved on some subsisting difficult problems.

But even allowing for these incidental side benefits, can the vast assembly of thousands including one hundred heads of government, and their ministers, obtain real progress on the problems on which the consensus documents make elaborate declarations at least in principle? Can the non-aligned afford the diplomatic effort and financial outlay consumed when the actual results are predictably minimal or even negative? Like the UN itself, the non-aligned conferences are apt to be used as platforms for international polemics and explanations for failures rather than for constructive focus on the items on the international agenda. Needless to say, although adopted non-aligned declarations are adduced where convenient, they are not treated as mandatory any more than the resolutions of the UN. The declaration have been flouted, in letter and spirit, with impunity by the non-aligned themselves.

The problem for NAM is, of course, not untypical of all multilateral diplomacy. Conference diplomacy involving sovereign nations inherently carries the compulsions for compromise and evasions with sleight of hand drafting. The hazard is greater when the agenda is political or open-ended, and not specific or technical.

The OAU has confronted the same kind of differences and difficulties in reaching consensus and enforcing its charter principles. In the case of NAM, however, the search for consensus unwittingly grooved it into a process which was necessarily going to negate the fundamentals of its principles—to safeguard peace through dissent and defiance of imposed globalism on a priori situations in the international system. Some nations, including India, have long been on guard against institutionalizing the movement by creating a permanent secretariat.

The process, however, inevitably got underway with the decision to have summit conferences every three years and other regular periodic meetings. The Belgrade and Cairo summits never decided on a subsequent gathering. It would have been far wiser to have preserved the practice of deciding on high-level meetings only when the international situation or a particular problem required the focus of concentrated attention. The war in Vietnam could have been an appropriate subject for a non-aligned initiative in the late 1960s. Even today, conferences on Namibia or Afghanistan, Indo-China or Central America could address themselves to the challenge of reversing interventions and restoring non-alignment through the collective weight of their counsels.

However, if drawing attention to interventions or their threat is to serve this purpose, it cannot be done selectively. If all cases of foreign pressure or presence are to be raised in one or more conferences, the same differences and divisions will be exposed. A fixed timetable with a comprehensive agenda was, in any case, bound to degenerate into little more than semantic diplomacy, 'full of sound and fury' but signifying little.

As stated earlier, the non-aligned now command the UN with an unshakeable majority. Except for the veto of the permanent members in the Security Council, there is no substantive recommendation which may be adopted by the non-aligned which cannot also be pressed through the world body. True, the UN itself, including the Security Council, is becoming ineffective or irrelevant on most difficult issues. But the UN, enfeebled as it is, cannot be abolished. Indeed, the smaller nations must be vigilant that the big powers do not withhold their contributions because they object to a UN approved programme. The established UN procedures at least permit issues to be raised in a less inhibited and hesitant way than do the non-aligned forums.

The non-aligned do not even have the same options for sanctions and enforcement as are provided in the UN charter. The UN has laid down methods of checking credentials. In the present situation, the non-aligned can at best make duplicate echoes covering the same ground as the UN, the GATT, the World Bank, the IMF, etc. It would have been a different story if the pooled resources—financial and managerial—of the non-aligned had created a separate energy affiliate to boost world economy and so benefit the OPEC, the developed and the developing countries.

Should then NAM keep going mechanically, from conference to conference, with a grand jamboree of a galaxy of presidents, prime ministers and potentates every third year? Should not the movement be wound up now with the satisfaction of a mission accomplished: that the international system will remain diverse and differentiated against uniformity and conformity? Do the current problems of the world, which violate the non-aligned principles, straddle the old blocs or are they within the non-aligned fraternity itself? Realistically speaking, if excessive rearmament (often for chauvinistic or ulterior ambitions) continues in the Third World, the counsel to the major powers against their bigger arms race will only invite nonchalant indifference.

The non-aligned umbrella comprehends the full spectrum of the differences on foreign and economic policies. It ranges from pseudo-alliance or treaty relationships for military contingencies with one or the other superpower to deep suspicion and hostility towards the other. The economic interests of the non-aligned nations are vastly divergent and on many issues permanently so; in fact, the diversity is greater than that between the respective interests of the non-aligned and the aligned. For instance, the semi-industrialized nations like the developed nations of both blocs do not want prices of minerals and commodities to be raised, while primary producers cannot but want that market forces should not be allowed to depress their export earnings. The Lome Convention signatories want not just privileged access to the developed world but preferential advantage vis-à-vis other developing (non-aligned) countries. If the energy and economic problems within the Third World could not be resolved on the principle of enlightened internationalism, what hope is there for an urgent meaningful two-way dialogue between all-the-rich on one side and all-the-developing ones on the other? Is it not better to recognize that the challenge now is too great and the non-aligned ranks are too divided (and this is an achievement not wholly to be decried)? Is there any advantage in persisting with an effort which must pretend to a complete and comprehensive unity of purpose but show up as redundant in recommendation or/and ineffective in impact?

It will, no doubt, be argued that the magnitude of the subsisting problems justifies the existence and collective efforts of the non-aligned on some major issues like disarmament and world economic relations. Indeed, it is true that in the last few years, specially since the Reagan administration took office, the politics and polemics of the Cold War have revived and the pace of the arms race between the powers has quickened. Economic disparities have increased and the logic of interdependence and survival is being callously ignored. But even so, the process of poly-centralization and diversity has got accelerated within the blocs and outside them. The game is now not of compulsive bipolarity. International communism cannot be denounced when democracies hope to play the China card.

The communist countries have become increasingly dependent for trade, technology, food and financial credits on the adversary group of powers. Far from burying the capitalist system, they are adopting managerial independence and features of the market economies. Coexistence and cooperation cannot for long be thwarted by the retrograde approach of any power. When Western Europe defied the USA on the Siberian pipeline it was acting according to non-aligned principles of safeguarding national interests through non-ideological international cooperation. The American sale of grain is scarcely consistent with its administration's professed strategic containment policies.

Unless the superpowers belatedly arrest and reverse their mad arms race, predicated on the scenario of pre-emptive nuclear wars, they will get more and more isolated from the rest of the world, including their own allies. One notable liberal scholar, Prof. John Kenneth Galbraith, has already called for a requiem for the superpowers! The strategy of a possible and winnable nuclear war is being challenged by a tidal peace movement which cannot be dammed and will not be diverted. The non-aligned, as representatives of the international conscience, should have been in the vanguard of the cry of 'Halt!' and a demand to turn back and forswear these foolish nuclear strategies. But we would be making the old mistake if the non-aligned denounced the 'new cold war'—while they themselves voluntarily keep fuelling and feeding the global arsenal of destruction and even cherish nuclear ambitions. At all events, neither for idealistic nor for realistic reasons is there any need to hitch the non-aligned wagon to a failed hypothesis and an analytically doomed aberration which is the present Cold War.

The implication is not that there are no national, regional or international problems. Indeed they are increasingly grim and the prevailing perverse international attitudes are monstrously aggravating them. The world ecological threat can only be averted if all nations across the ideological divisions become alive to the common danger. International economic and scientific cooperation has a vast agenda for functional multilateral diplomacy. But there is little scope for tri-continental non-aligned cohesion. It will either merely echo the recommendations by other established international agencies or veer towards a kind of anti-superpower globalism. The last trend goes against the spirit of non-alignment which was to safeguard diversity and urge functional and economic cooperation on a non-military basis.

The solution or the best tribute the non-aligned could have paid to their faith would have been to reaffirm in a charter the distilled essence of their all but forgotten principles. The Delhi Declaration, like Panchsheel (but unlike previous non-aligned declarations), could have been a simple affirmation of the abiding principles of independence, peaceful coexistence and international cooperation. Temporary problems could have been eschewed. The validity of the principles would have been highlighted. Without being bogged down in controversy, all instances of the suppression of nationalism, direct and indirect interventions and militaristic ambitions would have stood impartially condemned by implication in those principles. Every nation that claimed to subscribe to non-alignment could have been left to live up to its principles.

The experience of the last three decades amply proves that, whether they were big powers or small, disregarding these principles only worked to their long-term disadvantage. It is clear that nations will not surrender for long their discretion to a monolith again, not even to NAM. Neither would any custodians of non-alignment, especially if their faith is half-hearted or their commitments selective and ulterior, command any moral authority to enforce correctives against the violation of these principles. India with its historic commitment as the originator and mentor of non-alignment could thus have rescued the principle of diversity from the dreary desert sands of multilateral diplomatic habits. Though world circumstances are wholly altered, Mrs Gandhi could have lifted our eyes again to the lodestar of principles, above the fray of controversy and confrontation—just as Pandit Nehru had sought to do in Belgrade. The charge that even under India's tutelage, non-alignment was split between the professed principles and an ineffective movement could have been avoided. The assembled dignitaries could have decided that the fixed calendar of conferences and the practice of issuing consensus documents could now be abandoned.

This is not to write the obituary of non-alignment, but to save India, as chairman, from the embarrassment of appeals and recommendations being flouted, from the ignominy of the consensus being ignored. The imperceptible, unwitting slide into a compulsion of conformity and consensus which neither conceals the differences nor develops a special sanction for correcting violations of professed principles, would have been reversed. Informal liaison on specific or general issues like the seabed exploitation could continue in and around the UN or other appropriate international fora with no embarrassment to the principles of non-alignment. (Such a liaison can be between all or some of the non-aligned and include like-minded aligned or neutrals as well.) Without having to reach comprehensive paper agreements, the agreed positions could be determined more democratically and commitments be made more sincere.

Even if a few countries do not live up to the injunctions and wisdom of the non-aligned principles, the intrinsic rationale of those principles will not die. Great powers may delay but they cannot gainsay the imperative of peace, cooperation and coexistence. The superpowers can destroy the planet but they cannot establish world hegemony. Non-aligned nations, once relieved of the tortuous burden of periodically welding consensus and evolving semantic compromises between countries with patently divergent interests, could in their homelands concentrate on the problems of their own and their respective regions and continents. One can be confident that if the ritual and routine which developed after the movement started the practice of periodic meetings is ended, the untrammelled soul of non-alignment—its principles—will like John Brown's soul, go marching on!

15

Cooperative Security: The North-South Dimension

To design a cooperative security system for the twenty-first century on the collapsed edifice of the Cold War, more particularly in the North-South context, one must start by not shirking from recognizing that these decades may well have been the grossest example in history of what Barbara Tuchman in her famous book described as the 'March of Folly'. Overlooking contemporaneously available evidence, nations went on acting contrary to their own enlightened long-term interest, leaving behind a world redundantly militarized, with a greater chasm between the rich and the poor, with the poor countries hopelessly in debt and rampant in disaffection and violence.

Only a future historian who came to maturity after 1989, wholly uncontaminated by the atmospherics of four decades, will be able to assess the full opportunity costs of the Cold War. For two generations, the most powerful nations, commanding the best minds and technology, remained on an odyssey of self-inflicted enfeeblement. It took a Robert MacNamara to confess that decision-makers were trapped by 'misinformation, misjudgements and miscalculations'.[1] It is also worth reminding ourselves how resilient these entrenched misperceptions have been. Decades after peace had become stable under the balance of terror, the multi-billion dollar Space Defence Initiative (SDI) was launched. After Gorbachev unilaterally stopped nuclear tests, offered to withdraw intermediate range weapons from Europe, and end Soviet involvement in Afghanistan, the first statement of the Bush White House (on 21 January 1989) warned against glibly believing that the Cold War was over! Within only a few

* Paper written for the M.I.T., Department of Political Philosophy, Cambridge 1995.

months, the Berlin Wall came down, and in quick succession, the communist dominoes fell, the Soviet Union splintered and NATO had to begin a search for a political *raison d'être* for its continuance. The biggest challenge in reordering the world is the mindsets, which have been conditioned by the 'decades of folly', and which resist becoming contemporaneous.

THIRD WORLD UNPREPAREDNESS FOR THE UNIVERSALIZATION OF NON-ALIGNMENT

While the decision-makers in the North, overcoming entrenched vested interests, are trying to manage a transition from over-militarization to new priorities, governments and public opinion in the South remain intellectually caught in the grip of Cold War fallacies. The non-aligned, while asserting independent judgement with a focus on peace and development, had come to bank on the permanence of the ideological divide and relished the artificial importance that flowed from the East-West confrontation. They were quite unprepared for the political earthquake in which the aligned jettisoned strategic globalism, disengaged from extended military and political commitments, domesticated their foreign policies, adopted eclectic liberal socio-economic models, and, disregarding ideology, felt free to choose their trading partners. It is now honestly affirmed that national security hinged more on economic and technological dynamism than on conventional firepower or nuclear arsenals. The non-aligned had got predicated on the persistence of hostility from the power blocs and were quite unprepared to find that their original gospel was being embraced by the aligned and had become universalized!

In my view, the penalties of the protracted Cold War were not unavoidable. This conviction came to me when I found myself as the head of the Indian embassy in Peking in the years 1963-6. The seeds and compulsions of détente were planted when within a few months of the Cuban missile crisis, the 1963 Partial Test Ban Treaty (PTBT) was signed. This ignited vicious open polemics between China and the Soviet Union and started the systematic splitting of the international communist movement. It was obvious then that ideology was irrelevant to international relations. But for the hypnosis of the Cold War, Vietnam could not have been seen as the battleground between the search for US-USSR détente (as desired by the USSR) and its denunciation by China as the makings of a duopoly. Under the then domination of China, the Democratic Republic of Vietnam also refused to sign the PTBT, and Khrushchev, fearing nuclear escalation, actually stopped aid to the socialist country fighting the arch-imperialist enemy—America. Soviet arms aid was resumed by Kosygin primarily to outbalance the influence of China and thus facilitate a negotiated solution to the conflict. The communist side of the Vietnam war has not been sufficiently researched, but even the study of the open comments of Tass, Hsinua agencies and of the Lao Dong party from Hanoi might have avoided the tragedy and trauma of Vietnam if the bipolar fallacies had not been so entrenched.

My own understanding of the non-ideological rationale of international relations was set forth not just in reports to my government but in an academic monograph written in 1969-70, as a Fellow of the Centre of International Affairs at Harvard, under the heading 'The New Bipolarity'. I argued that an amorphous 'Syndicate of Stability', consisting of the governments of the superpowers and the developed nations, would have to face a transnational 'Fraternity of the Frustrated' consisting of some irresponsible governments and non-governmental factions seething with dissatisfaction with a propensity for defiant violence and terrorist disruption. There must be many flaws in my non-scholarly thesis, especially in not identifying the hollowness of the socio-economic progress in the communist countries, but even after twenty-three years I am not embarrassed by my basic analysis. It invited polite incredulity from my academic friends and diplomatic colleagues of the West, but the point of this personal digression is that when I thought I was arguing a thesis consistent with an independent non-aligned perspective, the non-aligned decision-makers and my professional peers were dubious and more inclined to take seriously the ritual Cold War affirmations from Washington and Moscow. The subsequent developments—the reversing of bloc connections by Ethiopia and Somalia (1975-6), the crises in Angola and Mozambique (1975-6), Nicaragua, Granada and Afghanistan (1978-9), etc.—were considered proof of a new Cold War when, in fact, they were no more than defensive reflexes born out of the programmed paranoia.

THE OVERLAP OF THE COLD WAR AND DECOLONIZATION: THE CONSEQUENCES

The present economic and security disarray in the Third World can be traced largely to the fortuitous coincidence of decolonization and the Cold War. The former ended empires and made international society multi-continental, multiracial, multi-religious and diverse; the latter negated plurality by demanding ideological conformity and strategic subordination. The two processes were antithetical to each other. Decolonization was centrifugal and the Cold War thrust was centripetal. If the transfer of power in India had taken place to near Dominion status on the basis of the 1935 Act and the decolonization process initiated before the Second World War, not only would the tragic Partition of old India have been pre-empted but responsible nationalism under Gandhi's leadership would have retained a stronger vigilance against militarism and a greater zest for economic self-reliance. The Cold War, no doubt, accelerated the transfer of power in the European empires, but it also vitiated the positive dynamics of self-determination and blurred, for a while, the lasting diversity of international and human society. The competitive quest of both blocs to win friends and allies by forging military pacts, thrusting military hardware and showering economic aid on newly independent countries insidiously weakened their resolve to democracy and national discipline.

THE PSYCHOLOGICAL LEGACY OF THE COLD WAR

After a century or more of exploitative foreign rule, most old colonies lacked the infrastructure for handling the burdens of self-government. There was thus a strong merit in the call for enlightened internationalism to bridge the chasm between the industrialized North and the developing South. The irrefutable logic was endorsed in blue-ribbon recommendations of the

Pearson, Brandt and Palme Commissions, the Brundtland Report, and the declaration of the New International Economic Order the UN, the non-aligned and others. In all but a few analyses, the rationale was implicitly hooked, openly or discreetly, to the East-West ideological and security competition. The taxpayer in the democracies was asked to accept the burden and sacrifice as a contribution to safeguard his own liberty and not as an investment in a common peace and participatory prosperity in the shrunken world.

The recipient nations welcomed the assistance without necessarily endorsing the threat perceptions and ideologies of the donors. The Third World countries, however, convinced themselves that the self-interest of the donors guaranteed unending economic support and rescue, and in this complacency the developing countries actually got co-opted into a debilitating dependency. Third World leaders, mostly from the middle class, were intellectually convinced that socialism was the only way to distributive justice and the wave of the future. While criticizing the West, they overlooked that political independence had given them a margin for self-regarding discretion and discipline. Most countries insidiously got accustomed to outside help even when it carried damaging donor strings. They never anticipated that the Cold War would end and the dependent nations would be abandoned and saddled with debts and inadequate earning capacities. The South is now groping to adjust to the unfamiliar international landscape of superpower détente. The protracted world recession makes it even more painful. But to help shepherd the developing countries towards a new cooperative world order, one must identify, as a preliminary, some of the intellectual fallacies that have been bequeathed and imbibed from the Cold War decades.

Dependence on the Military as Aid to Civil Power

First, social progress as a vital ingredient to national security—a basic element in non-alignment—has been almost forgotten in practice. While paying lip service to economic development, military security has become central to the national agenda of even the social democratic countries. Some Western donors went to the extent of defining the military as the most reliable engine of modernization of traditional societies. The armed forces have become the protectors of the governments at home, and this has become as important a priority as being the guardians of the frontiers. The officer cadre, with large numbers trained abroad, has become a part of the international rotary of professional soldiers, defence scientists and strategists with a shared allegiance to a weapon culture which has spread a fascination for exotic sophistication of military hardware.

The National Security State

At the height of the Cold War, the Third World used to be in the vanguard of the call for disarmament, arguing the logic of turning swords into ploughshares. Now, when the North itself wants to strengthen domestic economies by cutting back on defence, the Third World is muting its own thesis. In fact, with rampant unemployment, internal disaffection, manifestations of terrorism, and frequency of assassinations, even the non-aligned have become 'national security states'. The right to individual protection for lesser members of the government, the leading legislators, including members of the opposition, senior bureaucrats—in all totalling several hundred—has become a status symbol. It is not surprising, that there is an unspoken consensus for more security rather than reliance on political management of civil administration.

Legacy of Soft Economic Priorities

Third, the Cold War interaction and the flow of aid has made most Third World countries 'soft' economies, with little reserve to resist debt traps. In many countries, notably in Africa, development was financed almost wholly by outside help, with a negligible share from domestic savings. Even then, aid was not harnessed to improve economic productivity; indeed, a great part was squandered on prestige purposes. For example, the Third World capitals are dotted with sophisticated conference complexes funded by foreign aid, which cannot now be maintained and exist as monuments to ill-conceived glory and glamour priorities. A large number of institutions were established with insufficient foresight about their utility and efficacy. The foreign aid connection has also tended to encourage imports and inappropriate technology. The construction of the TANZAM railway, which connects the Tanzanian port with the copper belt in Zambia was for the Chinese not East African gauge. The preference to import is the origin of the Swiss Bank account corruption. One could argue that but for the Cold War, many countries in the Third World would have resisted dependency and not gone into the present economic freefall.

The Habit of 'Scapegoating'

Fourth, in imitation of the politics of the great powers, 'scapegoatitis' has become a standard part of the craft of governance. Never before in peacetime have domestic failures been habitually deflected by the projection of imminent external threats or malevolence. The perceived menace of international communism led to the McCarthyistic anti-communism witch-hunt; the Soviet Union justified the brutal suppression of Hungary by pointing to the diabolical design and unreconciled hostility of imperialism and capitalism. Trillions of dollars were expended on propaganda, intelligence, covert subversion, disinformation and counter-insurgency. There is very little to show lasting positive gains from these massive outlays. Flattering these examples by imitation, the smaller countries also established their own intelligence set-ups which were allowed vast non-accountable funds to defeat subversive external threats. These set-ups too became extra-governmental nuclei of power and policies like the CIA and KGB. When governments floundered at home or protest became articulate or militant, the bogey of the foreign danger was used to whip up populist support and to brand dissent as traitorously disloyal to national interests. In the process, fledgling democracies were jeopardized.

In the old power blocs of East and West, scapegoatism has now been virtually jettisoned. Gorbachev never blamed the CIA for the revolt in the Baltic states; instead, he confessed to the domestic need for Perestroika and Glasnost. However, the Third World has yet to give up use of the phrase 'foreign hand'.

The Double-Edged Information Revolution

The Cold War connection also led to a false faith in the power of modern technology to marshal and maintain people's confidence. The information and communication revolutions and the new military innovations led, no doubt, to enormous accretion of power in central governments. In one-party states, these instruments fostered the Orwellian illusion of being able to condition or coerce the people to obedience. As it transpired, these same instruments politicized and empowered the people and actually challenged the authority of the most powerful states. The information revolution thus became the vehicle of disbelief in the information ministries!

The revolution also went on to arouse ethnic, tribal, sub-national and fanatical sectoral identities. Where there is a well-established democratic safety valve, such demands for autonomy and independence (e.g. Quebec and Scotland) are being negotiated, but in most of the Third World violent centrifugality poses a serious threat to the national establishment. The disintegration of the USSR and Yugoslavia illustrates the process. In response to this challenge, instead of accommodation national governments have often resorted to brutal suppression. But the capacity of the state to suppress and coerce has been over-trumped by the power of defiance and terrorism. The hijacking of aircraft, thanks to the media, has become an instrument of propaganda of freedom fighters and disaffected minorities. For our purpose, it would suffice to note that nervous governments challenged from within are more likely to be hesitant about a cooperative global order, as such an action is bound to imply reduction of the means to suppress counter-insurgency and dissidence.

Economic Dependence and Sovereignty Sensitivities

The physical debris of wasted years is scattered round the world. The forgotten defoliated fields and forests in Vietnam, the ten million unexploded mines embedded in the pathways of Afghanistan, Kampuchea and Angola, and the astronomical costs and difficulties of safely defusing 30-40,000 nuclear warheads are symbolic of these decades. But quarrelling with history is distracting and debilitating. Surplus resources for repair do not exist in the world or at least cannot be politically marshalled. The mindsets conditioned by militarism, economic extravagance and populist scapegoatism will have to be exorcised or reoriented. As stated earlier, the tragic superimposition of the Cold War on the process of decolonization debased nationalism, undermined constitutionalism and deadened enlightened internationalism.

In contemplating a global cooperative security we have to reckon with this legacy, which manifests itself in parallel but contrary attitudes. In the face of deficits and urgency of economic development or coping with disasters, there is no alternative for the Third World but to look to outside rescue. The appeal for help when made is urged on the grounds of enlightened internationalism in an interdependent world. But when it comes to the application of international political principles such as the Universal Human Rights and arresting ethnic genocide, the old resistance against intervention in internal affairs gets triggered. The ambivalent attitude crystallises around the way the Third World countries look at the US. On the one hand, the US is recognized as the respondent of the last resort for economic assistance and disaster relief (and, as in Somalia, even acceptance of the induction of the armed force), while on the other hand America, the 'sole superpower', is frequently seen as a threat to national sovereignty and must therefore be kept out. This nervous sensitivity about sovereignty is part of the legacy of the Cold War.

SLOW, GRADUATED STEPS TO A COOPERATIVE INTERNATIONAL ORDER

The compulsion and reward for a peace dividend has not yet developed for itself a strong constituency where it should be most insistent—that is, in the developing countries. There is still reluctance to recognize that far from competitive or protective godfathers, powerful nations have turned indifferent and can no longer be frightened into generosity and friendship. After decades of persuasion and dragooning to keep in step, the world has reverted to plurality. But this withdrawal syndrome actually signifies aid weariness and, at times, even callous revulsion. While poor nations must continue to lobby against this regression, they must also shake off complacency, dilute their expectations and be prepared to marshal their people to disciplined austerity. The imperative and framework for a cooperative global order can be reactivated by enlightened intellectuals in the West. However, there should be no illusions that the acceptance of such a new order can be forced to trickle down from above: it will have strength only if it is built up from below—in other words, starting with the people and governments of the Third World.

Reorienting National Public Opinion

The first task is to make governments and public opinion aware of contemporary realities, that the presumed free ride of the Cold War is over. There must be recognition that the greater dangers are internal and not international. Governments should note (with due deference to Mao-Tse-tung) that power does not flow only from the barrel of the gun; that the people are informed and aware and do not get fooled or for long remain quiescent. When political rights to the economic and social dividend are denied, people could put the most powerful governments on the defensive. People will follow examples of austerity and of moral purposefulness, but bloated bureaucracies are forfeiting credibility and losing legitimacy. Scapegoatism has diminishing returns; self-righteous hyper-nationalism becomes a liability and does not command respect or response, internally or internationally. With commercial considerations on the ascendant, the flow of investment and technology will come with proof of internal stability and for economic returns, and less and less for political or strategic considerations.

Projecting these non-populist lessons after decades of delusions may well appear politically suicidal. But beating the drums of callous international forces will not yield results or overcome their indifference. This is all too evident in the attitude of the West towards so many countries. Africa is being assessed journalistically in the West as sliding out of history and is being dismissed as beyond rehabilitation. An enlightened government could encourage backbenchers to lead the reorientation chorus. If this is combined with rigorous discipline—as some East

Europeans are attempting—it could evoke greater sympathy, aid and even indulgence. Special responsibilities rest with Third World academics to become more self-critical and warn against ostrich-like chauvinism. Nations have to realize that by reversing militarized redundancy, long-term national interests and even security may actually be better safeguarded.

Defusing Internal Strife and Disaffection

Second to moulding domestic public opinion is the crucial need to find negotiated solutions to internal civil strife. There is some progress in ending long-lasting civil wars in Mozambique and Angola; a striking revulsion at militarism is evident in Eritrea's return to peace after twenty years and in the mutual trust being re-established between Christians and Muslims in Lebanon. But on the other hand, in many countries such as Kurdistan and Sudan bitter conflicts which are entirely internal continue. There is obviously no will to reconciliation and national reconstruction in Afghanistan; there is no retreat from personalized corruption in Zaire, neither is there an end to fratricide in Kampuchea. The world looks on at such ferocities with horror and with superior contempt. For every case of suffering that has drawn international concern, there are many more on which the world has turned its back.

Most countries in the world, not just those in the Third World, need to reverse the practice of centralization of power and embark on a deliberate policy of constitutional devolution. Federalism and democracy, rather than repressive unitary governments, will succeed in assuaging the rise of ethnic politicization.

The Third World must also confront the deep sociological problems arising from modernization and the impact of Western culture and values in traditional societies. Unemployed youth is being caught up in drug peddling and narco-violence, with the television giving it an exotic fascination. The backlash of religious fundamentalism has internal and international ramifications. The moderation of such extreme manifestations requires a moral legitimacy in governments but cannot be managed from the outside.

THE CHALLENGE OF REGIONAL DIPLOMACY

It was a basic error to see all interstate conflicts as proxy wars of the superpowers. Intra-Third World conflicts have generally had a regional dimension which got submerged or exacerbated by the false globalism or half-truths of the Cold War. Almost all tension-riddled areas—South Asia, South-East Asia, the Middle East, Korea and the Far East, West Asia, East and Central Africa, the Central American area—have historically a local ethnic or regional dimension. Even though ASEAN may have achieved limited success in regionalizing trade and development, it has spectacularly succeeded in moderating old bilateral and regional political tensions. (It should be recalled that ASEAN was born in South-East Asia, it was not induced and brokered by the West.) The Arab-Israel problem, like the dismantling of apartheid in South Africa, is at last inching towards negotiations because in both cases the anti-communist strategic argument has patently lost its force. But there is not yet full recognition that the hope of alleviating poverty in South Asia (with 500 million below the poverty line) rests on functional cooperation in the subcontinent, notably around international rivers and the region's economic and ecological interdependence. But even after a late start, SAARC is still bedevilled by old bilateral problems, almost unmindful of the sea change in the world. The critical factor is the lack of political will to cooperate regionally.

REGIONAL GENDARMES WILL BE SUSPECT

What must also be lived down is the false concept conceived in Washington that regional hegemons like the Shah's Iran, India, Egypt and Nigeria have special responsibilities for regional security. The stronger regional powers can promote confidence only by offering economic opportunities, but they too, like the superpowers, will be frustrated if they arouse the suspicion, even if unwarranted, that they are coercing their smaller neighbours. India's intervention in East Pakistan in 1971 was to support Bangladesh's clearly established demand for independence and produced no immediate backlash because it lasted only one hundred days. However, India faced frustration in Sri Lanka, despite the deployment of substantial military capability, because it offended Sri Lankan nationalism and was simultaneously opposed by the LTTE militancy.

THE UN AND GLOBAL SECURITY

What has been urged so far is that the quest for international peace must be secured first from within the countries and regions. But legitimacy for intervention beyond regional management must have UN sanction and not be outside it. With the end of the Cold War and, hopefully, the lifting of the paralysis of the veto, the UN can start afresh, nearer the 1944 Dumbarton Oaks vision of collective response for international conflict resolution and peace-making. A prophylactic role for the Secretary-General and the Military Staff Committee should be reactivated and peacekeeping responsibilities should be planned. Within three years, the UN commitment to peacekeeping, envisaged at the planning stage, has already stretched to fourteen countries including the enabling approval for the operation in the Gulf and a $2 billion deployment in Kampuchea. While there is now wider support for intervention under UN auspices, in practice, the effective role has still to overcome many impediments. Financing such operations by an organization already too bloated and tethering at the prospect of bankruptcy is only one of them.

The more difficult problem is how an intervention can be projected as principled peacekeeping. The protracted hesitation to intervene against religious intolerance and ethnically motivated barbarism in Yugoslavia in the 1990s, when NATO forces were readily available, has damaged the moral prerogative of the North to intervene in cases of genocidal tribalism in the South. Iraq's invasion of Kuwait—where there was the global interest of oil—may not be duplicated. The US then carried the major share of the operational responsibility, but reflecting the US' changed economic capacity, even it had to seek contributions to share the financial burden.

In the future, any UN sanctioned force must be a mix which more or less reflects the racial, religious and cultural diversity of the organization. But such operations would still have to rely on sophisticated logistics and verification capability which is commanded only by the US, Western Europe and possibly Russia. The great powers should assure this infrastructural support on an impartial basis, if the UN role is to be made credible.

To give the UN a moral authority aimed at non-violent defusion of conflicts and ending internal barbarism, the organization's capacity to act independently and promptly should be built up. It seems to me that it is time to discuss the idea of a directly recruited standing foreign legion of, say, three independent brigades of blue helmets solely under the discipline of the UN only. Such a force could provide the trained nucleus for expansion according to the particular requirements of a crisis. Some new method of independent revenue for the UN (for example, a small tax on international tourism which, after all, is dependent on international stability) could also be envisaged.

The crunch is—how can we square the international justification to intervene without offending the principle of domestic sovereignty? A careful case law should be developed so that any outrage to international law and morality or humanitarian disaster would warrant effective action by the UN or a regional body. There is great sensitivity in the South but even so they will be acquiescence to pressure to restore peace and provide relief (as in Somalia and Kampuchea) ameliorate gross tragedies. But the UN must retain the image of independence and impartiality and ensure that interventions do not appear to subserve the interest of the Group of Seven (G7) industrialized nations. The new internationalism through the electronic media will be able to provide sanction and support for principled peacekeeping and disaster relief if there is no suspicion of selfish selectivity.

ARMS TRANSFERS AND SALES REGISTRY

It is vital that the reduction in military budgets by the former members of the alliances should not spur the intensification of competitive arms trade abroad, which, in effect, means the export of militarization to the impoverished South. For too long, Third World economists have conveniently argued that arms transfers were wholly supplier induced; in other words, such transfers promoted the political or commercial interests of the exporters. However, actually, even in the Cold War years, arms transfers were at requests and often tailored to the security perceptions of the requesting or receiving states. After the oil price hikes, the OPEC nations went on an arms purchasing spree and the arms producers responded with alacrity by selling overpriced over-sophisticated weapons as an easy method of recycling petro-dollars. Even in the face of opposition from both prospective buyers and sellers, the collective international NGOs should urge that there should be a requirement under UN auspices for the compulsory registration of arms sales and transfers. There have been an unknown number of Irangates of arms sales for profit. Paying commission with or without governmental connivance will continue with the increase in Third World conflicts and transnational and internal violence, but international public opinion can be built up against this 'arms bazaar'. We need to replicate the Amnesty International on surreptitious sales of arms, nuclear material and technology.

Ultimately, arms control will make progress only with regional confidence-building. The old Conventional Arms Control Talks, summarily terminated by the US in Mexico in 1978, must be resumed on a multilateral basis with the requirement that its progress be reported annually to the UN General Assembly. But long ago, I argued that Third World militarization is first and foremost a challenge to Third World diplomacy.[2]

The problem of nuclear proliferation also exemplifies the confusion between old and new definitions of security and how domestic politics and prestige considerations complicate them. It would now be broadly conceded that Hiroshima was an original sin; not persisting in consigning atomic weapons and technology to the UN under the Baruch Plan was the second mistake. Thereafter, the British, by retaining the nuclear option for which, as an ally of the US, there was no plausible military justification, made nuclear weapons a symbol of political prestige. Finally, some forty years later, the collapse of the Soviet Union has, in my view, demonstrated that a nuclear arsenal by itself neither gives prestige nor helps to preserve the integrity of a State. In this confusion, in which every country with nuclear capacity projects a subjective rationale, any progress towards non-proliferation hinges on all nations, especially those in the nuclear game, quietly recognizing that possessing such weapons carries more penalties than rewards. It produces more psychological nervousness than national self-confidence. On the other hand, non-possession of nuclear weapons has not prevented Japan from becoming a superpower, capable of brazen disagreement with the US (which is not only Japan's protector but also its biggest trading partner) or defying its nuclear neighbours (Russia and China). Hypothetically, Sweden and Switzerland, Mexico and Cuba, Libya and Syria, Vietnam, Afghanistan, Bangladesh and Nepal, Croatia and Serbia, and others could one day make crude bombs. Further, even a terrorist organization could deposit or deliver such a device in a vehicle or find a suicidal human bomb carrier to do so. Non-proliferation is another example of a problem where progress will come only when international principles are observed and adopted without selective exceptions. The problem of cooperative global security is how to get from here to there.

THE NORTH IN RELATION TO THE SOUTH

While arguing that the promotion of stability and security must be built brick by brick from below, it would be unrealistic to deny that the ultimate success depends on the carrot and the stick wielded by the G7, specifically the US. However, the arrogant assertion that the G7 must police the world, with the UN Security Council in tow, reflects an error in comprehending the dynamics of the nationalism of the weak but sensitive South. The asset of the G7 is that they can promise economic and humanitarian relief also. Ultimately, outside socio-economic help provides the chemotherapy against the spreading cancer of violence. But the G7 countries, having lost their respective global enemy, should see their role as guardians of principled internationalism. The hesitation in the G7 comes because in wielding the stick they do not want to risk retaliatory bruises and bloodshed. It is a false fear to look at every operation as if it were Vietnam all over again. This can paralyse deterrence, the authority of the G7, but also the credibility of UN sanctions and peacekeeping.

There is a welcome spur to internationalism in the issues involving ecology and human rights. Distant starvation now intrudes into our living rooms. The US, because of its history and power, is still looked upon as having a deeper concern for the world. Therefore, the world accepts US leadership when it crusades against brutality and armed aggression. But the US would have to exercise restraint on its own arms exports. Giving priority to rescuing Russia and Eastern Europe commands understanding, but if the old Cold Warriors now see the civilizational unity of Europe and North America against the Islamic fundamentalism or politico-economic co-prosperity Axis of China/Japan and the Far East, then there will be no chance to scale down the present levels of conventional or nuclear arms programmes.

CONCLUSION: CHALLENGE TO DIPLOMACY

The immediate prospects for cooperative security in the South are not bright. There has been too much paranoiac militarization, turbulence, violence, criminalization and corruption in politics. There is too much ethnic and tribal disaffection—pandemonium, according to Daniel Patrick Moynihan—which threatens the integrity and viability of states. The defeat of communism has given a sense of triumph to liberal democracy and market economy but it is not the end of history. Even Francis Fukuyama acknowledges that in the same world, history will continue side by side with liberal post-history.[3] The Kantian concern for peace in an interdependent world has still a long road ahead.

A liveable, safer, freer world requires a corrective both in the North and in the South. Exasperation in the North and the old suspicion in the South are part of the dregs of the Cold War. The process of reorienting domestic priorities has begun in the North but a disregard for opportunity costs—the old March of Folly—persists in the South. But one must caution against exasperation and pitching in prematurely in conflict resolution. The cry of neocolonialism still has a catchy appeal. However, the constituency for 'Restoring Hope'—as the intervention in Somalia was named—is growing faster than could have been foreseen in 1990.

Finally, the world must go back to restore faith in diplomacy. For all the sinews of interdependence, we still live in a world of selfish sovereignties; rogue nationalism holds sway over many parts of the world. Over these Cold War decades, diplomacy was reduced to the craft of complaints and accusations, rhetoric and semantic jugglery. The diplomacy of the twenty-first century must be constructive, if only because big 'wars must not be fought and cannot be won'. It must reckon with the novel consequences of the information revolution. Nations have a new sense of equality and are confident in their independent nationalisms even though they are different from each other in terms of their size, economic capacity, technological base, work ethics and military capability. Constructive diplomacy will require comprehending the sensitivities and misperceptions between sovereign negotiating partners, each with its own politicized public opinion. In fact, people's reaction, as much as governmental calculus, now determine the negotiating latitudes. The challenge in the post-Cold War world is to find non-offending compromises. Gorbachev achieved a miraculous turnaround of entrenched suspicions by unilateral concessions. This is wholly different from the traditional method of professional diplomacy which was based on hard reciprocal bargains, negotiated in total secrecy. The present challenge to diplomacy is to carry the conviction that the common interest is in cooperative peace and progress for the whole world rather than a world dominated by the three hubs of North America, Europe and China-Japan.

The hopes of such a cooperative world order will depend on example set by the North of elevating principles of international law and morality above and against coercive abuse of power. They must not give way to callous indifference to poverty and suffering and selfishly disregard global ecological interdependence. All nations must act as if they have a joint stake and a shared responsibility in the common future.

NOTES

1. See Robert MacNamara, *In Retrospect: The Tragedy and Lessons of Vietnam*, Random House, 1995.

2. J.S. Mehta (ed.), *Third World Militarization: A Challenge to Third World Diplomacy*, Austin: LBJ School, University of Texas, 1984.
3. Francis Fukuyama, *The End of History and the Last Man*, New York: Free Press, 1992.

16

The Challenge for Democratic Statesmanship in South Asia

SOUTH ASIA'S DECLINE FROM POLITICAL FRONTRUNNER TO ECONOMIC AND SOCIAL STRAGGLER

The transfer of power to countries in South Asia (India, Pakistan, Ceylon and Burma) in 1947-8 was a turning point in world history. It signalled the end of European empires and triggered the era of decolonization and the universalization of the international community. Today, South Asia and sub-Sahara Africa are looked upon as the basket cases of social and economic stagnation. Nowhere else as in South Asia was the struggle for self-government as long, as determined, and as intellectually sophisticated. Political defiance was largely elevated to constitutionality debates, and the 'ends' of political freedom were subordinated to the right 'means' of non-violent non-cooperation. In December 1946, on the eve of talks in London between Attlee, Nehru, Jinnah and Sardar Baldev Singh, even Dean Acheson—no particular Asiaphile—stated publicly that the peace of the world would be determined by the independence of India. Today, this region with one quarter of the world's population and an exceptional reservoir of scientific, managerial and technological talent stands marginalized in international trade and politics. In Africa, in the 1950s, even a progressive leader like Nyerere thought it would be soon enough if effective power came to Tanganyika by the 1970s; in India, however, political reformists, cultural revivalists and Europeanized intellectuals had started arguing for self-government in the nineteenth century. After the First World War, President Wilson was persuaded by the European

* Paper presented at a conference on the subject in Dhaka sponsored by the Bangladesh Institute for International Strategic Studies (BIISS), in 1994.

allies to exclude India from the application of the Fourteen Points with the right of self-determination. The end of the empires finally came because Britain was exhausted in the Second World War and France, the Netherlands, Italy and Belgium suffered defeats and lost control over their overseas colonies.

In hindsight, it is better to recognize that in delaying decolonization there were penalties for the rulers and not just for the ruled. The technology of print and surface communications, if not then of airwaves, was already stimulating the aspirations for self-rule. (The information revolution was underway even though it was not described as such in the first half of the century.) The message from the French Revolution, from the struggles of Mazzini and Cavour, and from the philosophies of Locke, Rousseau, John Stuart Mill and Kant was fermenting the minds of men and demanding democratic legitimacy. The exposure to the working of the parliamentary system in England had inexorably consolidated into the nationalist urge for transplanting the system in India. Marxian philosophy reinforced the quest for independence with the appeal and demand for social justice and the rights for the working 'proletariat'. Britain did initiate steps towards progressive self-government in India in the first decade of this century, but right up to the Second World War, diehard imperialists and European Herrenvolk continued to believe that the art of governance, economic dynamism, industrial growth, scientific enquiry—all these elements of modernization—were the bequeathed monopoly of European ethnicity.

In retrospect, it would have been wiser to have accepted the historical inevitability of decolonization after the First World War by conceding at least Dominion status to India. As it happened, the postponement doomed the process because decolonization and its centrifugal diffusion of international management, coincided with the centripetal fallacies implicit in the confrontational bipolarity of the Cold War. The ideological dimension—the promotion of democracy or socialism—was only the propaganda face of paranoiac strategic anxieties. There was not the deep-down enlightened and abiding concern for the development of liberated countries, as was claimed by the rival protagonists of the Cold War. More to the point, the liberated countries forgot, except in declarations, the national responsibility for national futures and the need for the continuous nurturing of the moral underpinning that characterized the struggle for self-government.

In South Asia at least, there had been a confident articulation that freedom would lead to a gallop in people's welfare and poverty alleviation. It had been firmly asserted that national handicaps of resources, the indifference or malevolence of the great powers would be defied or mastered by the mobilized national will under the leadership of nationally responsive patriots. As it transpired, by taking the professions of the great powers seriously, the idealism and determination to shape our future in our chosen mould was slowly corroded both by the weakening of the native resolution and by the ulterior motives behind the international pressures.

THE IMPACT OF THE COLD WAR AND ITS PSYCHOLOGICAL LEGACY

What, if any, were the common features that led all South Asian countries to fall short of their aspirations in nation-building? Were there avoidable misperceptions? Or was it that intra-regional suspicions obscured the pledges to their own people? And now that all or almost all South Asian nations have democratically elected governments, are there better chances for these nations to resume their march towards the original hopes of national self-determination and social progress? Or will populism drag them from constructive dynamism? As a corrective, can they project the opportunity costs of a continuing drift and so to raise their sights, stretch their muscles and retighten their sinews? Or is democracy, which has to be punctuated by elections every four or five years, incapable of looking ahead as it is condemned to the lowest common denominator around temporary problems, and has only a worm's eye perspective on the future? Can foreign policies be remoulded by the touchstone of national development, resisting the mindsets that gave an overriding emphasis to external security and that were tempted by the lure of borrowed strength, surrender to dependency and excessive expectations from the great powers?

In this rather restricted purpose, I would avoid well-trodden ground and not refer to the familiar specific problems between South Asian nations. There is broad consensus that good intentions and declarations notwithstanding, most intra-regional problems in the South Asia region remain gridlocked and are hurdles to economic optimization.

I am aware there are divergent views on the genealogy of the division of India in 1947 and the subdivision in 1971. Whether or not Partition and sub-partition were the lesser evil for the parent nation and/or the breakaway political identities, for my purpose here, I stand firmly with the premise that existing political sovereignties cannot and should not be unscrambled. Even so, one cannot close ones eyes to the abiding ethnic, linguistic, religious and cultural pluralities as an irrevocable part of the South Asian demographic and political profile. It is a legacy from what throughout history was called the Indian civilization. All countries in South Asia have sizeable numbers of minorities, forced migrants and voluntary refugees either originating in or having special kinship in other countries of the subcontinent. Aside from the domestic administrative burdens of managing their protection and affirmative action, such as reservations for the under-representated communities, this straddling ethnicity develops populist foreign policy dimensions. It is not fortuitous that all South Asian countries have pockets of violence and serious disaffection. These are no doubt in part local but they spill over (or are deliberately supported from) across the border and end up in exacerbating regional tensions.

On the other hand, on the positive side, wittingly or unconsciously, we tend to overlook that no other mainland region of the world had such a natural economic interdependence as the monsoon-dependent sub-Himalayan subcontinent, creating an exceptional advantage for development and ecological restitution. While accepting the political vivisection that has taken place, we must, sooner or later, re-establish functional cooperation between sovereign neighbours to optimize our social progress. There can be no economically viable alternative to these natural complementarities; indeed this may be the only recipe for preserving national unity and self-confidence. My contention is that conflict resolution in South Asia will follow only if the linkages between the separate national problems are factored into the perspective of the shared common destiny. Without having experience of the political marketplace, it seems to me that there is more political longevity in adherence to a distant vision of stability and growth, based on the permanence of geography, than in continuing confrontationist postures and impetuous improvisations as concessions to populism and continuously reviving historical animosities.

The end of the Cold War is the right time to draw up an incisive balance sheet of the number of odds against nation-building, which were imposed on us by the great powers, and the measure of negative and avoidable flaws of national judgements within the parameters of national decision-making. We also fall into the trap of the great Cold War malady of scapegoatism—covering up domestic dilemmas by blowing up the image of an enemy at the gate or external malevolence subverting the national body politic. The subcontinent also gave external security a higher priority over domestic imperatives. It is by now patent that the focus on the enemy factor has proved to be the undoing of the USSR. Even for the USA, it has been a four-decade-long journey in self-enfeeblement. It is my persuasion that if our independence had not been caught in the vortex of Cold War politics, South Asia, with its unique advantages, would not have been deflected from its original priorities of national reconstruction and social progress. Beyond all plausible reasons, our failures were of intellectual surrender and moral degeneration. The challenge for statesmanship is to rise above explanations, accusations and public relations and make courageous attempts to draw from the lessons to reshape the futures of billion plus people of South Asia.

As a beginning let me try to encapsulate some of the factors where, I believe, the impact of the Cold War enfeebled us psychologically. No doubt the weightage varies in importance from country to country but in some measure they characterize all the countries in our region.

i) Lord Mountbatten was confident that his shock therapy of accepting Partition and advancing the date of the transfer of power from June 1948 to August 1947 would reverse the mounting communal tensions. Mountbatten's judgement was belied but it should be noted that except for Mahatma Gandhi, the future leadership of India and Pakistan failed to foresee the killings of hundreds of thousands and the uprooting and migration of millions that transpired during Partition. The rehabilitation on both sides was generally rapid and administratively creditable, but the memory of the South Asian holocaust has remained a shadow on the national psyche and on sober decision-making in the subcontinent. As in Bosnia, the metaphysics of peace and development have been vitiated by the periodic recurdling of historical memories, thereby steeling intransigence and inhibiting compromises. The memory of the holocaust nightmare may or may not have been politically essential for the cohesion of Israel, but in the demography and cultural pluralism of the subcontinent, it has become a populist trump card which some day will have to be wrenched from our own pathology.

ii) The death, not infrequently by assassination, of the first generation of leaders was a tragic blow for statesmanship in South Asia. The personality and dedication of those who had struggled and suffered imprisonment or privations naturally emerged with a towering standing prior to obtaining political power. In a sense, the lead of those who were present at the creation—to use Dean Acheson's phrase—(Mahatma Gandhi, Jinnah, Liaquat Ali Khan, Sheikh Mujib, King Tribhuvan, Dudley Senanayaka, Jawaharlal Nehru, etc.) could not be replicated. Political courage was, in any case, essential in leading nations with inherent handicaps and having to cope with complex international pressures. Not surprisingly, but not necessarily unavoidably, the quality of public life degenerated, which in turn produced cynicism and fed disenchantment.

iii) The imposition of the heavy hand, and tempting bribes on the subcontinent from the competing superpowers, became a deleterious factor. Relations between these surgically separated twins—India and Pakistan—would have been difficult anyway. It is, however, worth remembering that the early vision (1947-53) in both India and Pakistan was for detachment from the East-West politics. With hindsight it should be acknowledged that it was a great mistake for India and Pakistan to have ranged themselves on the opposite side of the global gameplay. It gave South Asian countries illusions of great and permanent 'strategic' importance but it overlooked the available evidence that relations with the superpowers were necessarily non-reciprocal and temporary. The lure of military supply arrangements and economic gains was compounded with intelligence linkages and hypocritical ideological pretensions. It ended in a kind of psychological tutelage and surrogate attitudes in international politics.

The worst example of the abdication of objectivity in South Asia was the way India and Pakistan reacted to the intervention and civil war in Afghanistan. In a world of long-range nuclear missiles and well-established balance of terror, we should have dismissed as fictitious the view that the Soviet intervention was a revived quest for warm-water ports and that Armageddon would be risked to throttle vital oil supplies. Instead of prophylactic diplomacy, we were drawn into the superpower paranoia. This intellectual subordination has proved catastrophic for the subcontinent. Both countries, in their respective long-term interests, should have been detached and united in the call for deference for Afghanistan's integrity and non-alignment. There was never any doubt in my mind that, however misconceived the Soviet intervention may have been, there was no likelihood of a threat to the Gulf or to Pakistan. Arms to Pakistan was a *déjà vu* mistake by the Reagan administration as in 1953-4 when the regional India-Pakistan problems were submerged by global strategic anxieties. As a by-product of the rival misjudgements of the USA and the West, India and Pakistan became partisan and so accelerated their own arms race. Neither India nor Pakistan anticipated that the USSR and the USA would turn their backs on Afghanistan and leave behind a country in anarchy, with millions of anti-personnel mines embedded in the pathways. The refugees are a lasting menace for Pakistan, but in the bargain, South Asia has become over-militarized and economically crippled.

The other case where we forgot our own principles of non-intervention was in succumbing to intervention in Sri Lanka in 1987. Again, I had little doubt—and said so openly within days of the start of the involvement—that whatever may be the success of the military operation, it was going to be a political disaster for bilateral and regional relations. The point to note is that our interests and principles were needlessly surrendered to the hypnosis traceable to the Cold War.

iv) The flow of military and economic aid including PL480 funds from the US led to the atrophy of the will to economic self-reliance in the newly independent countries through the pursuit of their own developmental strategy. External aid was welcomed with the high logic that it was the wages of imperialism, the catalyst to interdependence and an essential investment for the New International Economic Order. In claiming aid as a right, we jettisoned our own commitment to sacrifice and austerity. No doubt South Asian countries made better use of external resources than Africa but not as well as the countries of the Far East. We also became party to our own underdevelopment and turned our countries into very soft economies. India's democratic polity was comparatively more vigilant in limiting abuse of incoming resources, but, in general, aid flows have led to excessive bureaucratization, non-economic prestige projects, and downgrading of social priorities. In comparison with sub-Sahara Africa, South Asia has had a remarkably high rate of savings which have been ploughed into national development, but the mega-development plans financed by external resources have generally pampered the middle class and focused on urban and industrial growth and neglected the rural poor.

v) Nehru, in enunciating the approach of non-alignment, had urged concentration on development as an essential component for political stability and national security. The

> major powers are now sharply cutting back on overstretched military outlays and recognize the sagacity of that blend which puts higher priority on economic dynamism. However, South Asia's own defence expenditures have shown a steady increase over the decades (1960-90). In contrast to the developed countries, our region has even started boasting of military capability, showing a nonchalant indifference to the unfulfilled agenda of people's basic needs.

There are other political maladies that have corroded the body politic of South Asian countries—rampant corruption, both real and suspected, a creeping distrust of politicians who are being perceived as moneymaking professionals and not as those engaged in public-spirited service. Historically, the people of South Asia have strong law-abiding instincts but there is a tangible devaluation of the respect for authority and the laws of governance. This new cynicism leads to an aggressive assertion of tribal, communal, caste, linguistic and cultural sub-identities and, in turn, becomes a threat to civil society and rational progress. Some of these factors are, no doubt, part of a global phenomenon and are not necessarily due to the sociology of poverty and the misjudgements of new independence—there is corruption in Japan and sub-national demands in Quebec and Scotland. But all these factors have compounded the insidious impact of the Cold War and the portfolio of populism. Among the salutary lessons that governments have to register is that even when all the modern media was marshalled to internal propaganda, the State was not able to recondition the people's minds to unthinking docility. In today's world there should be no reliance on the ability to fool even a lot of people all the time.

Put together, we have to come to terms with the recognition that there is no alternative to rebuilding internally the decimated confidence to the long haul of participatory nation-building. That calls for bold leadership qualities.

SOUTH ASIA'S SHAME IN THE HUMAN DEVELOPMENT INDEX

The comparative poor performance of South Asian countries (barring Sri Lanka) comes out dramatically in the statistical aggregates compiled in the Human Development Reports of the UN. Along with the disaster-riddled African countries, South Asian nations find themselves bunched in the low third of the Human Development Index. The SAARC Report on Poverty Alleviation also confirms this embarrassing record.

But when one looks at the absolute and percentage figures on military expenditure, South Asia almost tops the scale and Sri Lanka no longer remains an exception. The last UN Human Development Report (1993) defines the five new pillars of a people-centred world order: (i) a new concept of human security; (ii) new models of sustainable human development; (iii) new partnership between the State and the markets; (iv) new patterns of national and global governance; and (v) new forms of international cooperation. The report underlines forcefully that human development hinges on people's participation and a democratic system. The Third World can scarcely criticize this definition for a new order as these were the fundamentals in their struggles for independence. It was a mistake to put security in a separate privileged non-plan compartment, disregarding its economic consequences and its impact on the nation-building agenda. Should we not confess that we are part of both the problem and the solution in the design for a world order?

The logic of the Human Development Reports is telling but it verges on an old delusion. Over the decades, such reports by Partnership for Progress, the UN Declaration on the New International Economic order, the Brandt Commission, the Palme Commission on Common Security, Bruntland on *Our Common Future*, and the RIO Summit on Environment and Sustainable Development, all imply, with persuasive statistics, that the right global vision projected on the international stage will necessarily lead to corrected global reorientation. The latest Human Development Report raises expectations for the Social Summit scheduled for 1995. The well-documented and well-argued blue ribbon reports did serve the purpose of educating international opinion in the meaning and obligations of the global village but they all discounted the extent to which the world, while becoming enmeshed, remains subject to the gameplay of self-regarding sovereignties. While always sensitive to encroachment into our domestic jurisdiction, the decolonized world came to bank excessively on the enlightened internationalism embodied in such reports. In the process, we became inured to international realities and were not alert to the abuse of aid, etc. The right to aid today is questioned by the taxpayers because of the wrong justification—strategic security was given as the reason and not the more worthy and permanently valid goal of international social justice and all-round stimulus to trade through higher purchasing power. We must accept that with the end of the East-West competition, the lobby for resource transfer has become attenuated and we have to live with the old grim truth that the 'ought' does not determine the 'is'.

The transition to new economic priorities—as part of the new definition of national security—is painful for the rich countries but the paradigm of withdrawal from economic and political concern for the global village and plundered planet looks irreversible. Aid is getting smaller and more selective. Except for the Scandinavian countries and the Netherlands, the target of one per cent of GNP set forth in the 1970s is mocked by progressive reduction. The USA now gives higher priority to its erstwhile adversaries, and selectively for some regional commitments or special political preferences like Israel but not for equitable economic development for the underdeveloped world in general where live two-thirds of the world population. More aid goes to El Salvador with a population of five million than to Bangladesh with a hundred and twenty million!

The era of godfathers is over. The hope of outside rescue has to be exorcised. We should recognize that the great powers were never as benign as they pretended and we expected them to be; neither are they as powerful as once feared or even as malevolent as is conveniently or sincerely dreaded. With the downgrading of strategic importance, the overriding rational of external relations will be commercial. Dramatic disasters, horrendous suffering and starvation on television screens do evoke a burst of sympathy and spontaneous relief does come from the US and, to a smaller extent, from Western Europe and Japan, but the attention span even for human suffering is short, especially when widely separated crises and disasters follow in quick succession and compete for sympathy and support.

With these factors, the decision-making for national problems has reverted more than at any time since Independence to the national political fora, posing a challenge to national statesmanship. Many brutal truths follow. Scapegoatism and blaming the outsider, or threatening to defect to the other bloc, etc., are played out. Population and unemployment remain the greatest problems for developing countries. Nations will have to overcome the old populist resistance which inhibited effective family planning. There has to be more than rhetoric about gender equality and literacy, especially for the girl child. The ecological threat has certainly sunk into public consciousness but its gravity is not yet wholly manageable nationally. It was regional myopia that caused both India and Bangladesh to complacently overlook the havoc that logging and soil erosion in Nepal would cause downstream by flood damage, costing thousands of crores annually. With the lowering of ground water tables, a menacing shortage of water is now on the horizon and, of what is available, eighty per cent is not potable. Only ten per cent of the people have access to water closets and perhaps three-fourths of the urban dwellers live on open sewers. The health costs are astronomical but what is relevant to remember is that epidemics are bound to spread to and come from the neighbours. All these factors add to the danger of internal disaffection and destabilizing violence, and this is more certain than the projected external threats.

The conclusion emerges that the long-term solutions for national economic and social problems and the maintenance of cohesion and consensus in civil society in South Asian countries depend not just on enlightened domestic governance, but on the reorientation of regional foreign policies and effective success (not mere plans and intentions) in regional cooperation. Intra-regional cooperation and national viability are not parallel alternatives: they are integrally interactive and mutually reinforcing and, if neglected, collectively destructive. The lesson from ASEAN is that the conflict of national egos and even divergence of interests must and can be brought into an orchestrated harmony. The Indonesia-Malaysia hostility of the Sukarno period was buried, enabling ASEAN to get underway.

The EEC only took off because the centuries-old French-German hostility was ended by the deliberate statesmanship of Monnet, Schumann, de Gaulle and Konrad Adenauer. No doubt what spurred them was the perceived threat from the East but the lesson remains valid: countries in regional propinquity must make a purposeful effort to advance together. The challenge for political leadership in South Asia is to see the enemy as the future. We have to come to terms with the contemporaneous consensus, that economic dynamism thrives with regional harmony. The burying of the old mindsets of historical suspicions is vital for national stability and meaningful independence.

DEMOCRATIC POPULISM VERSUS THE IMPERATIVES OF THE FUTURE

It used to be argued that once all countries in the region turned democratic and had representative governments, and correspondingly military regimes were superseded or the exclusive powers of the monarchy constitutionally limited, then the fog of artificial hostility among the South Asian neighbours would slowly be lifted and beneficial functional cooperation would take off. I have always believed that the relevance of ideology as a distinct factor, to catalyse economic or political relations, was grossly overplayed during the Cold War. The Sino-Soviet split should long ago have opened our eyes to the fallacy that communism smoothes differences between states and subsumes nationalism. A socialist China even made a so-called punitive attack on a socialist Vietnam. We also know, only too well, that democracies steadily cherished the friendship of non-democratic countries for strategic reasons. By now, we recognize that economic complimentarity has a stronger logic than political ideology or systems of government, but democracy does give space to peacefully argue the case for compromise and cooperation for the greater national benefit.

The success in attempts to promote functional regionalism under the auspices of SAARC has so far been minimal. Such arrangements as have been agreed on have as yet made no impact on the common or separate poverty agenda, much less served as a catalytic intermediate for the chemistry of trust. Political perspectives remain hesitant, showing continued disregard for the economic opportunity costs of gridlocked suspicions and the consequential dangers of aggravating internal disaffection.

It is, of course, obvious that political parties and the leadership in a democracy cannot get too far out of step with the perceived predilections of the electorate. On external relations, there is always an extra dimension of sensitivity and stronger propensity for national self-righteousness. The days are over when foreign policy remained more or less consigned to secret diplomacy, left to be handled by professionals or personal envoys of the executive heads of governments. To assess the latitude that may be permitted by public opinion is now an essential ingredient in preparing the negotiating briefs. Indeed democratic politics yield, only too readily, to the temptation to exploit or bend popular emotions. All too often great and mature nations have evoked images from the past in order to furbish convenient arguments in the present. During the Cold War, recalling Munich as a symbol of appeasement or Pearl Harbor as signifying perfidy was a standard gimmick to have the Pentagon and defence budgets passed through the respective legislatures. In India, the 1962 China war became a reminder of complacency or deception and the despatch of the USS *Enterprise* to the Bay of Bengal became the symbol of modern-day gunboat diplomacy and was recalled whenever anti-Americanism was in the air.

In the circumstances confronting South Asia, statesmanship has to reject historical horror stories and boldly don the mantle of prophets and project enlightened perspectives to reorient public opinion. The advantage of the democratic system is that dissent and detached opinion can command attention when trumpeting for a change of policies. Even when governments are inhibited by fears of a political backlash, they can encourage their own backbench supporters in the legislatures to float trial balloons for new policies. More importantly, non-governmental organizations these days have become the cheerleaders for unselfish internationalism and people-oriented priorities. Indeed, in the West, environmentalists and peace and human rights activists are effectively out-trumping the powerful old security strategists and stick-in-the-mud conservatives. In 1989, after Gorbachev had heaped unilateral concessions on the West, it was public opinion which pressed the Bush administration and West European governments into accepting the logic of détente. Permanent civil servants in the parliamentary system can be a force to delay if not to resist populist improvizations and urge holding on to long-term priorities. One might add in parenthesis that the professional soldier, whose training, responsibility, and schooling in military history teach him to prepare for the worst-case scenario, is not so much to blame if he advances military needs, disregarding their political and social consequences. It is democratic civil authorities who must make the courageous choices between populist extravagance on the one side and disciplined investment in the future on the other. It is interesting that in the West it was often the civilian strategist who crusaded for the nuclear overkill, and a person like President General Eisenhower warned against resources being appropriated by the military-industrial complex to the detriment of national welfare.

Under the hypnosis of the Cold War literature from the West, many Third World economists and political scientists, instead of raising warning signals against chauvinistic bravado, came to be in the vanguard of national self-righteousness. Few anticipated the flaws of the East-West paradigm, much less than what we would see articulated as the end of history with the triumph of liberal democracy. Our progressive economists failed to pay sufficient attention to the quiet, balanced example of Japan which, while paying lip service to and echoing US security arguments, never allowed its own non-productive expenditure to go beyond one per cent of the GNP.

On regional relations, it is very important for the print media not to fan national chauvinism. Senior journalists with their weekly columns and regular editorials often shape public opinion, especially on foreign policy. Newspapers could also lead the way in correcting past errors of policy without the same embarrassment that politicians face.

Considerable blame for past mistakes and not effecting a redefinition of national security and national interest falls on professional diplomacy. It is our responsibility as representatives stationed abroad to accurately understand the political realities behind the facades of foreign countries and identify the misperceptions of adversaries and neighbours and thus help to define the margin of political compromises.

Finally, as a means to policy change, measured unilateralism may be the way to reorient domestic public opinion and also assuage entrenched suspicions abroad and thus give diplomacy a chance to effectively serve development and people's welfare. Democratic civil governments aided by responsible professional diplomacy can learn a great deal from the steady even if at times agonizing reappraisal underway in East and West Europe and North America. In barely four years, the four-decade-long military mindsets have been unscrambled to kick off the groping towards people-centered security and functional economic cooperation.

THE PRELIMINARIES TO THE CHEMISTRY OF TRUST

After all these generalities, let me not shirk from being more specific about the challenges for India and other countries in the region.

I would straightaway accept that the success or failure South Asia's attempt to redeem its tryst with destiny rests overwhelmingly with India which neighbours all the countries in the subcontinent. India alone is in a position to orchestrate a turnaround from a climate of mistrust to one of positive underpinnings of cooperation. Only China has more neighbours than India, but not all of China's neighbours are comparatively as small and poor. And unlike China, historically India was not considered expansionist or domineering. Indeed, like the US India at one time was looked upon as the inspiration for other nationalisms. In the last three decades, even leaving aside Pakistan as a special case, there have been ups and downs—sometimes dramatic ones as in Bangladesh—in India's relations with South Asia. Now India has unwittingly become the foil for most South Asian nationalisms. But even so, like the US in relation with its own neighbours—summarized in an old Mexican adage, 'Too far from God and too near the United States', India is also privately perceived as the crucial source for ready economic support. India has a ready potential for capital transfers, technical and managerial skills and provides a market for non-internationally competitive domestic products. For millions in neighbouring countries India is the convenient haven for migration. Pakistan fancies that with its Islamic affinities, West Asia can provide substitute linkages and so it can turn its back on India and the rest of South Asia. Even if the common civilizational umbrella, the religious traditions and linkages, and the cultural and ethnic connections with India are discounted, the geographical interdependence is indestructible. Pakistan can never escape being a lower riparian to India, just as India cannot be indifferent to deforestation and resource damage in Nepal and poverty in Bangladesh. For all countries, the economic costs of blocking natural trade and denying the logic of transport savings amounts to political myopia. For any country in South Asia, denying dependency on neighbours is the supreme example of populism.

There is admittedly a difficult but not insuperable challenge to Indian diplomacy to resist irritation and exasperation at the seeming ingratitude of neighbours. We have to accept the inherent odds of size differentials in a politically aware and equal world. Just as we in India expect from the US, we will have to sharpen our understanding of the contradictions that are manifest in presumed economic dependence and expectations of non-reciprocal concessions on the one hand, and unreasoned political hostility from our South Asian neighbours on the other. India has to guard against the suspicions that it is treating South Asia as a captive market; instead, with sensitive persuasion and concrete generosity, we have to demonstrate that self-interest on all sides is served by regional growth, especially when external support will inevitably decline in relation to our enormous economic and ecological needs. Trade concessions were urged by SAARC at the last summit in the South Asia Preferential Trade Agreement (SAPTA), but that has not yet fired the political imagination and significantly stimulated regional commerce. One warning should be registered—good relations must be consistent in their approach to all neighbours and resist acquiescence in planned exceptionalism. Regional diplomacy has to be more than the sum total of bilateral relations if the hegemonistic falsehoods have to be dissipated.

Having conceded the crucial role of India, the neighbouring countries must recognize that they have a responsible and perhaps even more desperate self-interest in not provoking Indian public opinion. Elections in Bangladesh, Nepal and Sri Lanka has not been above the temptation of wanting to score anti-Indian brownie points. The approach to India must not be constantly hedged by unrealistic conditionalities. India-baiting only strengthens the hawks who despair of friendship with neighbours. The suspicion, sometimes almost openly manifested, of ganging up against India is more self-destructive than effective.

The conflict resolution paradigms of the Cold War, in my view, have marginal relevance in South Asia. In the US-USSR eyeball to nuclear eyeball confrontation, the spur was to avoid war by inadvertence as it could give no victory but risk destruction of humankind. For years the East-West confidence building measures (CBMs) focused on technical fail-safe controls, quick or advance warnings, permissible verifications of capabilities, acceptable aerial reconnaissance, etc. It must now be assumed that though India and Pakistan have nuclear weapons capabilities, they do not pose the threat of igniting the global inferno. The risk of a regional nuclear war in 1990 was, in my view, exaggerated; and acknowledging each other's nuclear capability is not really a CBM. From time to time India and Pakistan have also agreed on various CBMs, such as hotline connections, prior notice on manoeuvres, pledges not to strike at each other's nuclear installations, etc., but such CBMs have not catalysed the political will to lower the decibels of suspicions or competitive beggaring of the neighbour.

I am conscious that this whole thesis would invite derision as being pathetically unrealistic, a kind of idealism which borders on political imbecility. I do not share the view of many commentators and political scientists that there is no political longevity except floating with the populist mainstream and that diplomacy in South Asia can be little more than political cosmetics at least for some decades to come. What is required of a statesman is to not to shirk from the honest projection that the wages of no-change are nothing short of misery for millions and a mockery of independence. One should take pride that South Asian countries are not just heirs to a great civilization; they were torch-bearers in political courage. As a region, they can boast that they are now all, in their different ways, consolidating democracy, even if imperfectly and tortuously.

I have not hesitated to acknowledge India's critical role and responsibility to bring about a regional turnaround, but let me now illustrate my point about the potential of statesmanship with some recent examples from my country where principles and integrity have overtrumped populism.

Manmohan Singh, the finance minister, had a long-established reputation for his ability but, like many of his generational peers of economists, he too urged state-directed economic policies for development. When he was inducted in the government in 1991, he had no political base whatsoever. Notwithstanding his earlier professional inclinations, he mapped a strategy of economic reform for India which was designed to liberate what *The Economist* years ago had called 'the Caged Tiger'. He obviously could not start without the encouragement and unreserved support of Prime Minister P.V. Narasimha Rao, but one cannot recall a comparable example with a kind of intellectual *mea culpa*. No doubt there was an urgency with the looming prospect of foreign exchange default when he started but it was nevertheless intellectual courage with which, like the legendary Samson, he shook the entrenched political and bureaucratic conventional wisdom of import substitution and regulated management of the economy. In two years, the policy has shown considerable but not yet spectacular success: deficits and inflation still dog his economic projections. But it was his established reputation of integrity that facilitated the change of course and won indulgence for the new economic policies. His stature was enhanced when after his ministry was held partly responsible by the Parliamentary Committee for a major bank scam, he promptly tendered his resignation. He thus upheld the almost discarded tradition of ministers accepting constructive responsibility for official wrongdoing or negligence of public interest under their charge. Even though his economic policies continued to be challenged, especially the unpopular steps taken to reduce subsidies and scale down unprofitable public sector enterprises, his surprise resignation seemed to release the nation's suppressed quest for higher values and probity in public life. The demand that he should be persuaded to stay on was echoed across the political spectrum. Overnight, from just a successful finance minister he became a statesman and guardian of India's economic destiny, and possibly the most popular person holding political office. The point to underline here is that he has acquired a standing which would give him the licence for greater long-term correctives in public policy simply because he shunned or at least did not succumb to populism and the suspicion of clutching to the lure of office.

Another example can be seen in the growing backing for the Chief Election Commissioner, T.N. Seshan who seems launched on a single-handed crusade to plug loopholes and abuses and purify the democratic election process. He has been criticized and opposed in and out of Parliament by political parties across the board, but Seshan obviously understands his responsibilities under the democratic constitution and the electoral laws. Far from being cowed by political criticism, he persists with his exposures and correctives. The result is a snow-balling consensus to give him more power. It is surprising and unprecedented that a civil servant is looked upon as the saviour of democratic rectitude and the imperatives of higher morality in political life. He could bring about a lasting cleansing effect and reduce disenchantment and cynicism. Any attempt to clip his administrative wings could actually be politically counterproductive.

What both these recent instances demonstrate is that principled perspectives and policy audacity are not politically suicidal. 'Statesmen' can overnight command people's enthusiastic acceptance and backing. It proves that the ultimate strength of democracy is that Churchill's figurative call to 'blood and sweat, toil and tears' could be made even in peace-time by leaders of proven integrity showing transparent concern for the people and the future.

There are now innumerable studies on the benefits from regional cooperation in South Asia. Even the idea of a Customs

Union of South Asia on the model of the EEC has been statistically examined and not dismissed as wholly premature. However, one recent study by the Asia Pacific Development Centre found that the current picture, even after SAARC was founded, is of further disintegration rather than of progressive increase in functionally beneficial cooperation and regional trade. The horrendous costs of the failure of all countries (India, Bangladesh, Nepal and even Bhutan) to adopt a comprehensive Rivers of Hope approach on the eastern rivers have been tabulated frequently but it is still inhibited by competitive and narrow perspectives. To highlight the ecological interdependence, I put forward the idea of establishing an official-cum-non-official Environmental Protection Authority for South Asia. It envisaged that youth in joint brigades from countries affected by eco-destruction and floods spend a year in camps to rehabilitate the forests in the Nepalese and Indian Himalayas. I thought that this kind of regional public service would dramatically increase regional interdependence and such work could be counted towards subsequent employment. For all the talk of environmental restitution, the idea has evoked no interest or enthusiasm in the prevailing political climate. Without regional cooperation, the mega-environmental damage control cannot even get started.

The fact is that mutually reinforcing paranoia permeates policy approaches in South Asia. Our region is still caught in the war-minded mindset that coexistence is only for rhetoric and not worth the risks in realistic goals for state policy. SAARC is still debarred from discussing bilateral problems and this reflects the institutionalized inhibition on all sides. Therefore, the notions of negotiation, mediation, arbitration, the Helsinki or other models, etc., even if mentioned in speeches, essays, conferences, and communiqués, lack the oxygen of sincerity.

It bears repetition that the relationship of trust and cooperation requires, above all, a faith in the positive value of friendship rising above the economic costs of continuing suspicions and drift. It would be honest to acknowledge that even the Kashmir problem cannot be allowed to vitiate the future of a billion people. Pakistan has to recognize its interest is in not straining the Indian government's capacity to protect the Muslim minority in India.

The protracted indifference to the genocide of Muslims in Herzegovinia, next door to NATO must also be seen as an eye-opener on the lack of will and capacity for international intervention. Correctives have to start from within the country and be publicly acknowledged as national interest, and then go on to reach the geographical neighbourhood. And this means shunning accusatory populism.

The conclusion then needs to be trumpeted that we in South Asia have a stake in our separate and enmeshed futures. The alternative could be Balkanization, Somalization, Angolaization, Ethiopization, Kampuchization—all of which illustrate and have relevance to aspects of the current problems of India, Pakistan, Bangladesh, Nepal, Sri Lanka and Bhutan. We are all sitting on a combined big volcano. Democratic statesmanship must resist complacency; it must shepherd countries from continued political if not physical bloodletting which could hurtle us towards the precipice of disintegration and terrible human suffering.

Finally, a small personal note. Because of the turn of the bureaucratic roulette, by accident rather than merit, I was involved in six negotiations with India's neighbours—all on hard, long-smouldering unresolved problems. Agreements were reached after eluding us for eight to fifteen years. My experience gives me an untypical but resilient faith that political statesmanship can give (or be persuaded to give) space and direction for enlightened professional diplomacy. The credit belongs overwhelmingly to the political leaders, but we as professionals must never abdicate our duty to give honest advice for our national futures.

We have seen people rejoice at the fall of the statues of Lenin and Stalin. Mao, who was acclaimed as the sun in Chinese hearts, remains ritually on the pedestal but his party no longer really proclaims that China, much less the East, to be Red. History rejected them and their *obiter dicta* because they were callous or insensitive to people's political, economic and social aspirations. They became too intoxicated with what Henry Kissinger called 'the aphrodisiac of power'. We have also seen old fighter politicians like Arafat and Rabin, Nelson Mandela and de Klerk burying the hatchet and turning into democratic statesmen. It is now the turn of the leaders of South Asia to jointly win the Nobel Prize and have familiar faces from India, Pakistan, Bangladesh, Sri Lanka and Nepal on the cover pages as regional peacemakers. We were the first to be free; future generations of our respective nations will not forgive us if we are the last to be friendly, constructive and cooperative.

17

Nuclear Non-Proliferation

PART I

The prescribed five-yearly review is to take place in 1985 in Geneva on the Nuclear Non-Proliferation Treaty of 1968. The United Nations General Assembly will also, no doubt, have a lively debate. The nuclear weapons powers have all but forgotten their obligations under the Treaty to move purposefully towards nuclear disarmament. Notwithstanding the resumption of arms control negotiations at Geneva, which seem so far not to have gone beyond political postures and public relations razzle-dazzle, the superpowers are relentlessly bending technology to militarize beyond the horizons into outer space. Some lobbies, it is suspected, want to defer or deflect the review altogether. Thoughtful opinions, not just of governments but of citizens round the world, would want to look back on the tragic story of nuclear weapons and the dangers from their relentless sophistication and, in turn, the imitative proliferation of nuclear weapons capability.

The advent of the split atoms has, throughout, posed the choice of the lesser evil and, in retrospect, one cannot help but feel that almost invariably the wrong choice was made. The plea for using nuclear energy exclusively for peaceful purposes was obscured by the wartime compulsion to pre-empt the possibility of a German technological breakthrough in nuclear fission, which could have turned the tables on the Allies. The question whether in the future nuclear weapons would be essential for national defence in order to resist coercion or even enforce compulsion was not weighed against the capability of potential adversaries to nullify the advantage. At every stage in the development of nuclear weapons—the MIRV, the ABM, the SS-9, the SS-20, the cruise missiles and now laser-based systems—the consequential spur to negate the lead was incorrectly assessed. What compounded the problem was that the international fallout was ignored until, on the one hand, the superpower balance of terror became patent, and on the other, the dangers from proliferation of nuclear weapons nations loomed as an equally dangerous contingency.

When Second World War in Europe ended, the choice as perceived by the United States was whether to use the atom bomb or face the possibility of a million American casualties in a landing and conventional operations to defeat Japan. The consensus now is that Japan had little staying power left and would have surrendered within a few months with a fraction of the anticipated losses without the use of the atomic bomb. Hiroshima and Nagasaki destroyed the moral and political restraint against a weapon whose military use has proved dubious but which imperils civilization and humankind. There was still a choice of consigning all forms of nuclear energy to international control. This was proposed in the Baruch Plan. But in the exaggerated alarm at Soviet intentions and capability, the United States yielded to the illusion of keeping a long-term nuclear monopoly as a protection against Soviet conventional superiority. Even some statesmen like Dean Acheson—not noted for a soft attitude to the USSR—argued strongly for immediate international control. It is not possible to conclude whether Moscow, with its historic sense of insecurity and suspicion of the UN as a Western tool, would or would not have built its own nuclear arsenal anyway. Whether the USSR would have used nuclear weapons or threatened to do so anymore than the USA did when it had the monopoly also cannot be argued conclusively either way. But this does not gainsay that unilateral or agreed restraint might have had a better chance of arresting vertical and horizontal proliferation at a more manageable level than when, two decades later, the two superpowers came around to urge it jointly. As it happened, the USSR reached a more or less matching assured destructive capacity much faster than was foreseen in the West.

The United Kingdom developed its own nuclear weapon capability, not so much with the confidence of an independent defence capability, but to preserve its claim towards a great power status. The Attlee decision was taken in great secrecy, bypassing normal parliamentary practice and the convention of cabinet responsibility.[1] British nuclear warheads on US missile launchers ensure neither independence nor defence. The British decision inevitably provoked de Gaulle to have for France its own symbolic claim to 'greatness'. The justification of the British and French nuclear capability gave weight to the strongest argument for proliferators, viz., that no nation could trust another and risk nuclear destruction. The logic of the British and French nuclear strategy is in effect, that a war involving their countries must ensure the simultaneous mutual annihilation of the superpowers and the rest of the world. This is scarcely a plausible defence strategy or a national consolation of continued importance in international politics. What Britain and France did was to give nuclear weapons a prestige symbolism. It was bound to tempt other nations, with far fewer attributes of all-round power and economic strength to acquire nuclear weapon capability, not as a realistic requirement for defence but as a hallmark of greatness and independence.

Coming to the next stage, one cannot help wondering whether, on balance, the USA, USSR and UK were not ill-advised not to have concluded a comprehensive rather than a Partial Test Ban Treaty in 1963. It might or might not have restrained China and France from the atmospheric tests, but a Comprehensive Test Ban Treaty (CTBT), immediately followed by the Non-Proliferation Treaty, would have avoided the suspicion that the five permanent members of the UN Security Council claimed a privileged licence for unrestrained increase in the quantity and quality of nuclear destructive capacity. The expectation of the charter, that they could or would act in concert to preserve international peace, had already been falsified. The problem of nuclear proliferation became intractable because the weapons powers were perceived as seeking to impose a regime which, by implication, amounted to a claim to the permanent moral as well as military superiority of five nations. The international community of the twentieth century was not going to acquiesce in this assumed arrogance where their precepts were being outraged by their own example.

Since the Non-Proliferation Treaty of 1968, the two

superpowers, in their mutual paranoia, have faced the dilemma of an unending race between patent deterrence and military superiority on the one hand and apprehended danger for them, if not for the world, from the spread of nuclear weapons capability to 'less responsible nations' on the other. It is the old dilemma of one nation's pursuit of its defence and strategic advantage overlooking the consequential alarm it provokes amongst the adversaries which in the end, only brings new hazards for its own security and, in the process, jeopardizes the enlightened goals of international stability.

The USSR has been comparatively less ambivalent than the USA in its policy on non-proliferation. The governments in power in Eastern Europe were ideological allies, but Moscow has not encouraged them; rather it has effectively prevented them from any attempts to develop their own nuclear weapons capability. The nuclear cooperation programme between the Soviet Union and China barely lasted a year and a half (1957-9). In fact, the breach with China started because the Soviet Union was not prepared to allow its own nuclear capability to be used as a provocative threat to Taiwan and the USA during the Quemoy-Matsu crisis in 1958. Moscow then went on to repudiate its agreement on nuclear cooperation and refused to help China develop its own bomb. This precipitated the Sino-Soviet rift and the loss for the Soviet Union of its unchallenged leadership of the Socialist bloc. The Soviet Union has refused to transfer any destructive technology, weapon-grade fuel, or heavy water to any country without insisting on the safeguards laid down by the International Atomic Energy Authority (IAEA). The United States was less principled, or at least less vigilant, when Israel was able, with or without the US government's connivance, to pilfer technology and fuel from the United States. Israel does not deny, in fact probably wants the world to believe, that it has developed the bomb, even if it has not tested it. Because of domestic compulsions, the USA has been inhibited from any punitive measures or sanctions against Israel. Israel's pre-emptive strike against Iraq's nuclear installations had to be condoned with a regretful shrug but without any political or economic reactions. In the circumstances, how far and for how long can the logic of non-proliferation be sold to or enforced on Syria, Iran, Iraq, Egypt, Jordan, Libya, or some combination of Arab or Islamic countries, when they remain apprehensive of or at odds with Israel? Similarly, the awe at South Africa's bomb will not compel the African nations to accept the moral justification for legalized racialism or defuse the internal struggle against apartheid.

But notwithstanding these aberrations, one must acknowledge that both the superpowers are probably truly concerned and are earnest in trying to restrain the further proliferation of nuclear weapons capability. Since the Cuban Missile Crisis, they have invariably retreated from the brink of confrontation with each other. Knowing better than others the destructive potential of such weapons, although with different arguments and rhetoric, they both argue that nuclear wars should never be started and could never be won. But they shirk from the honest acknowledgement that they have an overriding community of interests of a kind never known in history between adversaries. The hypocrisy is in suppressing the merit in their policy and advertising their defiance of their own and international consensus on the non-positive utility of nuclear weapons. In fact, their policy ambivalence, year by year, increases the danger of war by inadvertence. Continued vertical proliferation by the superpowers and shortened reaction time makes the threat of a nuclear holocaust as serious as from horizontal proliferation and the possible impetuous use of nuclear weapons in a regional conflict. The overwhelming consensus of war-game theorists is that there can be no advance guarantee that a regional nuclear exchange will not cross the strategic threshold and lead to a full-scale nuclear war and, therefore, be suicidal for the country that uses nuclear weapons in a regional conflict. These regional powers can, at best, have only a psychological confidence of deterrence from their small nuclear armouries. Much of the world is unconvinced that the security of the superpowers demanded the successive breed of weapons that are already deployed, much less the need and viability of space defence systems that are now being planned. Having ceaselessly ignored their own commitment under Article VI of the Non-Proliferation Treaty to reduce their own nuclear armouries, the nuclear weapons powers have all but forfeited their right to urge non-proliferation on other nations and arrest such regional nuclear arms development.

However, one must note and commend even the flawed attempts to arrest proliferation. France was persuaded by the USA to cancel its contract to build a reprocessing plant for Pakistan. The London Suppliers Club, with a membership straddling the ideological spectrum, was remarkable in its constitution and, up to a point, effective in controlling the flow of sensitive technology and material which could be used in nuclear weapons development. It may well have delayed some programmes which envisaged developing the weapons option. But, as is evident from the way Pakistan was able to surreptitiously smuggle designs and equipment for its centrifuge plant, the club failed to prevent critical leakage. Similarly, the international nuclear fuel cycle regime, conceived by the Carter administration, died in its tracks and, in any case, has been abandoned by the present US administration.

When the picture presented by the superpowers and other weapon powers is one of continuing sophistication of their own military capability beyond persuasive reason, it should have been obvious that, following their example, other nations would look upon nuclear weapons as the final arbiters for national security. Israel, which has the protection of a superpower, was the first to pursue the logic that no outside protection can be dependable. Brazil and Argentina seemed to be engaged in a regional competition with a mixed-up motivation of military superiority and political prestige. And this is the heart of the problem in the Indian subcontinent.

Indian nationalism was not prepared to accept the symbolic significance implicit in the Non-Proliferation Treaty, that the independent development of nuclear research was to remain the privilege of the five great powers. Earlier, it may be recalled, India under Nehru was second to none in its enthusiastic support of the Partial Test Ban Treaty. Nehru wanted the Indian envoys to be among the first to subscribe to the Treaty when it was opened for signature in Washington, Moscow and London. The 1974 underground explosion in Pokharan was no breach of any treaty commitment, but a protest against 'nuclear apartheid' and a demonstration that technology cannot remain the exclusive monopoly of a few nations. India's explosion was not secret. Even though a decade has passed, it is generally accepted that India has not made and stored bombs in the basement. India still has a revulsion for nuclear weapons and many thoughtful observers understand the dangers to world peace from the spread of nuclear weapons capability.

But for its own regional security imperatives and international standing, India too faces the dilemma of choosing the lesser evil. As leader of the non-aligned movement, notwithstanding some compromises, India's approach has been against national policies which, in pursuit of security, endanger international stability. India was entirely justified in refusing to accept the unilateral modification of the 1962 US-India agreement because a US domestic legislation passed in 1978 laid down retroactive conditions for the continued supply of fuel for the Tarapur reactor on the grounds of controlling nuclear proliferation. The unanswered problem for India is on the question of the principle of non-proliferation. There was, perhaps, a premature confidence in India that nuclear explosive capability could be used for peaceful purposes. But India never took the position that China did, that until there is total nuclear disarmament, every country which can, has the right to make its own nuclear weapons.

Indian opinion was no doubt alarmed when China tested its own bomb at Lop Nor in October 1964, only two years after the India-China conflict and when relations between the two countries had deteriorated sharply. But India did not rush to match China's threat and nuclear capability. China, by now, has a substantial nuclear armoury and a lead which is virtually impossible for India to match and overtake. Moreover, China has a critical advantage of strategic asymmetry because short-range missiles deployed in Tibet could pose a threat to the population and industrial centres in the whole of northern India. This would have to be countered with intermediate-range missiles with a 2,000-2,500-mile reach or long-range bombers in order to achieve a parity with China in mutually destructive capability as a deterence.

It is the assessment of Pakistan's nuclear programme and

intentions—not China's nuclear arsenal—that will determine India's policies on exercising the nuclear option. India's concern today is because it is variously reported that Pakistan is galloping towards nuclear weapons capability. There is, indeed, the self-confessed evidence of Z.A. Bhutto in his statement at the trial prior to his execution, that he contemplated the manufacture of an 'Islamic Bomb' and the nuclear processing plant even before the Indian PNE in 1974. Nevertheless, the Pokharan explosion has provided Pakistan with imitative arguments and justification for its own nuclear programme. Even though most observers agree that the uranium-enriching method pursued by Pakistan is geared specifically to weapons production, Pakistan continues to affirm that its programme is only to meet its long-term energy needs. Like India, it claims its intentions are only for peaceful and scientific purposes. The dilemma for India is to choose between the possibility of a regional nuclear arms race, compounding and not slowing down the conventional arms build-up, or to accept a common verifiable nuclear discipline for the subcontinent as a whole. India has so far sagaciously refrained from exercising the weapons option. But any government in India, responsible to a democratically elected Parliament will come under compelling pressure to start a weapons programme, when it is confirmed that Pakistan has put together a nuclear device, and particularly if Pakistan goes in for an explosion. The process then is unlikely to stop with the parity of symbolic 'peaceful nuclear explosions'. It is not too far-fetched to fear that on a small scale but with even more economically disastrous consequences than in the mutually reinforcing weapons programme of the US and the USSR, a vicious momentum of a nuclear arms build-up could develop in the subcontinent. As with the superpower programme, there would be higher and higher costs and commitment to numbers and sophistication in nuclear weaponry but with less and less security. The most that could be hoped for—and this is being optimistic—is that in the subcontinent the process would halt with one or two or at the most only a few non-usable bombs on the racks. It would nevertheless be embarrassing for India and Pakistan to take positions on disarmament when they are out of tune with a majority of the non-aligned and in the company of South Africa and Israel.

The question is posed, what can be done by outside powers to prevent a nuclear race from developing in the subcontinent? The short answer is, not much positively but a great deal more negatively. As argued earlier, it is naive and wishful to expect that non-proliferation can be imposed by those who pursue forms of proliferation themselves. This requires, as a precondition, a faith in the imperative of a political turnaround in their deeply entrenched mutual suspicions. The outside powers could be more persuasive if they could discard the mindset that every local or regional problem is, in origin and its consequences, merely part and parcel of the East/West conflict. While Afghanistan continues to be destroyed in a simmering unresolved conflict, the vital interests of both blocs, even after five years, are neither more nor less secure. In India, it was always considered naïve to believe that the supply of conventional military hardware to Pakistan, justified on the grounds of a direct military threat from the USSR in Afghanistan, would stop Pakistan's uranium enriching nuclear programme in its tracks. In fact, the recent flow of arms has only exacerbated tensions and increased the likelihood of nuclear weapons capability being developed in the subcontinent. The arms flows have interrupted or delayed the hesitant process of improving relations through Indo-Pakistan bilateral diplomacy. Both the Soviet intervention in Afghanistan and US military aid to Pakistan have proved to be examples of mistaken impetuosity and exaggerated alarm and, in the process, have eroded their capability—what little there was—of arresting proliferation. As with the Iraq-Iran conflict, arms supplies have not given the leverage to recipient nations to prevent a regional war. In fact, in Pakistan and India, the expectation persists that in the event of such a conflict, the other superpower might get involved. What is likely is that neither superpower would in fact, support or rescue the client or friend from defeat or serious destruction. But the superpowers could have avoided these contingency dilemmas, and could even now minimize the dangers, if they had persisted with the negotiations on conventional arms transfers which had made not unpromising beginnings in 1977-8. The dangers and dilemmas will increase enormously, not just for the subcontinent but for the superpowers as well if primitive nuclear capability is acquired by Pakistan and then India follows suit. On the other hand, restraint in involvement, militarily and politically, in the subcontinent could improve the chances for subcontinental diplomacy and regional cooperation. What is relevant here is that the detachment of the outside powers from an essentially regional problem would put the dilemma of the pros and cons of nuclear weapons squarely where it belongs—with Pakistan and India.

Notwithstanding the double standards and implicit arrogance embodied in the Non-Proliferation Treaty, no one concerned with the threat of nuclear war and radiation can minimize the dangers from the proliferation—vertical or horizontal—of nuclear weapons capability. A Princeton undergraduate, by putting together the design for a nuclear bomb on the basis of published scientific and technological literature, has vividly highlighted that in time and with determination anyone can make the bomb. The story of Israel, South Africa, Pakistan, Argentina, Brazil and possibly India could go on with fifteen or twenty nuclear weapons powers by the end of the century. The war-games scenarios get correspondingly more complicated, and the possibility of a nuclear war would multiply.

Are we, then, to reconcile ourselves to unrestrained proliferation with increasing probability of a nuclear bomb being despatched by a madman or as a reaction to a false alarm, triggering a war which could escalate into a nuclear Armageddon? What can the conference achieve at the quinquennial review scheduled for later this year? Not much would be the answer of most realists and the diverse nationalists. But the hazards are too great for the internationalists and those concerned for the future of the planet and humankind, including all nations—big and small. We cannot be content with resignation or despair. We must persist in trying to turn back and forswear our foolish ways.

The superpowers have to recognize that their interests, their security, and world peace stand threatened first and foremost by their paranoia about each other but also by provoking the emulation of their false logic. Their competition and the mirage of military superiority as a means to effective deterrence has only undermined their endeavours to contain the proliferation of weapon capability. Pakistan could not be bribed to stall its programmes. New Zealand has decided to exclude US weapons, even at the risk of punitive economic measures. It may be only a matter of time before the people's movement in Western Europe demanding a nuclear freeze and removal of nuclear bases spreads to Eastern Europe. The superpowers could, at least confidentially, acknowledge that they would be able to maintain their leadership within their respective alliances by arms control agreements and political détente rather than by the quest for redundant military superiority of their destructive capabilities. Without any real jeopardy to their own security, they may be well advised to openly affirm their commitment to automatic measures against all countries, including their respective friends, who openly or surreptitiously embark on a weapons programme. The five permanent members of the Security Council are pledged to act together in the event of nuclear use or threat, but with their continuing suspicions and the revived Cold War rhetoric, this commitment has lost every semblance of credibility. Arresting the dangers of proliferation or even drawing the line at the present level of nuclear weapons capability can be facilitated by the reversal of programmes that are being developed by the nuclear powers. At this juncture, when star wars and space-based systems are considered a viable defensive necessity, that is expecting too much, at least from the superpowers. In that case, the international community, when it debates the issues, must collectively bypass the superpowers and other present and potential proliferators and reaffirm that outer space must not be militarized, except for verification. The non-nuclear powers could draft and open for signature a Comprehensive Test Ban Treaty and defy the protracted ambivalence of the superpowers. This may not change the policies of the weapons powers but would morally corner them even more at the bar of international opinion.

The Third World countries must recognize that regardless of the adamant persistence of the superpower arms race, they have their own stakes in and compulsions for taking a more purposeful interest in nuclear non-proliferation. It is important, indeed essential, to discard the notion that nuclear and conventional arms restraint and demilitarization hinge wholly on the role, actions, consent and blessings of the superpowers. The origins of most conflicts and the roots of militarism were never entirely, and now even less so, due to the manipulation of the superpowers. Arms trade and supplies to the Third World are as much demand-driven as it is induced from the supply side. Pressures for commercial benefit or political advantage for the manufacturing nations are often in an unspoken conspiracy with the importing governments. The threat of proliferation in the subcontinent, the Middle East, and Africa has its origins in regional politics which has only been compounded by the superpowers. In South America it was simply regional rivalry and not the interplay of superpower competition that started programmes in which the nuclear weapons option was not excluded. Just as the international consensus demands restraint in vertical proliferation by the superpowers, the smaller nations in different, fairly well-defined areas must collectively urge for nuclear weapons restraint and political solution in their respective regions. The superpowers should not find it impossible, either by parallel or unilateral declarations, or preferably through joint approaches, to encourage nuclear-free zones and peace-in-parts.

The only sanction behind such forlorn hopes is the self-regarding concern of nations for themselves and the endangered planet. It is time to recognize that the North-South dialogue has stalled, and the New Economic Order only preoccupies international conferences and well-intentioned public pleas. The disarmament debate must focus on the opportunity costs, not just of the superpower arms race, but for the Third World itself. The ideal of nuclear disarmament by existing weapons powers must not become the cover for rampant militarization by the Third World itself.

In other words, nuclear proliferation is too dangerous to wait upon the dawn of sagacity in the superpowers. The experience of these decades has exploded the myth that a great power role and influence depends principally on nuclear or even conventional military capability. It is the non-nuclear powers like Japan and Germany that have advanced through economic growth and trade in the ladder of international prestige. Even if the Japan-US security alliance did not exist or had lapsed, an economically powerful non-nuclear Japan, even in close proximity to the USSR and China, would be more secure than, say, neutral Sweden. When the choice is between defence at the expense of social progress and adequate but not absolute security which does not obscure the desperate urgency of development, the lesser evil, in every case but especially for the Third World, may be a little more butter rather than the hazards in the possession of and the suicidal dangers in the use of nuclear guns!

PART II

NON-PROLIFERATION (2005)

The foregoing paper was written in 1985. Another quinquennial review of the Non-Proliferation Treaty (NPT) is to take place in 2005. When last renewed in 1995, the NPT had no specified time limit. The UN Security Council by its Resolution 1540 reaffirmed support for the NPT; in 1996 the World Court judged that nuclear weapons were 'generally contrary to the principles of International Law'. In these twenty years many other important developments have occurred. The ABM treaty has been diluted by the US; the CTBT has not been approved by the US Congress. On the other hand, further sophistication of technology and research has continued in nuclear blockbusters, battlefield tactical nuclear weapons, renewal of the Star Wars project and, of course, nuclear tests conducted by India and Pakistan in May 1998 followed by both nations declaring themselves unilaterally as 'nuclear weapon powers'. In some cases, horizontal proliferation has been reversed, but my guarded hopes have not been fulfilled. Without modifying a single word of the original paper, there are new dangers on the horizon which demand that analysis on nuclear proliferation must be made contemporaneous.

The overriding reality is that even though humiliating defeats and setbacks were suffered by the nuclear weapons powers, there has been no 'use' of nuclear weapons since Nagasaki. Resorting to nuclear weapons was not contemplated when, in 1989, the Berlin Wall was dismantled or when the Cold War ended and the USSR disintegrated into seventeen successor states. The Soviet Union was obliged to retreat from Afghanistan, and for the past ten years it is being challenged in Chechnya. In 2003 the US won a spectacular military victory in Iraq within weeks, but it continues to be bogged down by the willful defiance of Iraqi nationalists. These 'nuclear' decades may go down as one of the most embarrassing politico-military disasters suffered by great powers. The nuclear weapons, which for over sixty years were known to be monstrously destructive, stand exposed as irrelevant and unimportant as instruments for the protection or pursuit of national interests.

In fact, the nature of conflict in the twenty-first century may itself have changed radically, thus further mocking the nuclear arsenals. Conflicts will now be in the form of terror. Emboldened by the information revolution, the enemy will comprise non-uniformed, desperate, disaffected people. Nuclear weapons may well remain permanently ready for launch in the silos or basements of governments, but they could be best referred to as technological 'dinosaurs'. However, having made such heavy investments in them, countries will keep clutching to the theories of strategic nuclear deterrence, overlooking that they may in fact be actually aggravating internal insecurity. One suspects the 'guns or butter' debate is being deliberately discouraged by the conditioned mindsets of the respective decision-makers.

A vast number of books on nuclear weapons and their future have been published in these years. Most are coloured by the Cold War paradigm and its fascination round the world. I would like to list only six publications representing different viewpoints which I found useful as reference: (i) *Danger and Survival in the First 50 Years* by McGeorge Bundy, (ii) *India's 'Nuclear Bomb'* by Perkovich, (iii) *Nuclear Weapons and Indian Security* by Bharat Karnad, (iv) *Engaging India* by Strobe Talbott (v) *The Gift of Time* by Jonathan Schell, and (vi) Amaratya Sen's Dorothy Hodgkin lecture in August 2000 to the Pugwash assembly at Cambridge entitled *India and the Bomb.*

The prospects ahead for the non-proliferation of nuclear weapons are mixed. The search for weapons of mass destruction (WMD) was the justification (or was it the excuse for the control of Iraqi oil?) for the pre-emptive attack on Iraq; none were found to confirm the 'intelligence' if it was so, given by different agencies. On the other hand, during these twenty years following Sweden's example, South Africa (that too the apartheid regime), Brazil and Argentina decided to wind up their nuclear weapons programmes. At the end of 2003, Libya, in a complete policy somersault, gave up its nuclear weapon programme and in the process revealed that oil worth four billion was supplied free to Pakistan in exchange for nuclear knowhow. Libya has now opened all its nuclear installations for inspection by the IAEA. Israel is continuing with its secret weapons programme, but is doing so without undertaking any tests. A year or so after the nuclear explosions in the subcontinent, India made public its nuclear doctrine of minimum deterrent capacity but pledging 'no first use' (NFU) and asserting that its ultimate goal to have the triad of nuclear capability. Meanwhile, the Agni and Prithvi missiles are being sophisticated. Pakistan with Chinese and North Korean cooperation has been developing the Haft and Ghauri missiles, which could carry nuclear warheads. The American anxiety about horizontal proliferation is now concentrated on Iran and North Korea. The European countries think they can succeed in dissuading Iran from developing nuclear weapons capability, but the talks with North Korea in which the US, South Korea, China, Japan and Russia are participating have not made any significant headway.

After 9/11, international attention has shifted and is now focused on the war against terror. The baffling anxiety, deliberately underplayed, is that the next time non-state actors may embark on using nuclear fissionable material. As a result of the succession of poor contemporaneous political judgement, a new bipolarity has taken shape with anti-Americanism enveloping the Islamic world on the one side and Islamophobia on the other not just in the US but throughout the Caucasian Christian world including Russia. These irrationalities could dominate the new century just as the ideological Cold War determined international politics in the second half of the twentieth century.

In the first part of this essay, I had noted the sheer lack of anticipation of the consequences of Hiroshima. Now twenty-five years after I retired, I can reveal my own views as urged in 1967-8 when the NPT was on the anvil.

For me, whether or not India should subscribe to the NPT raised the fundamental question of the vision and values of India's foreign policy. India's unique strength was that it had stood for the principle of independence and equality of all nations, regardless of their race, size or military capability. Our civilization alone was traditionally based on plurality and toleration. This implied as far as possible supporting internationalism, collective security, adherence to international law and respect for other 'nationalisms'. It was the pursuit of 'principles' that had given India a leadership role in voicing concern against imperialism, racialism, denial of human rights, etc. These principles meant that our national interests lay in setting examples for other countries to adopt. On the NPT, we had to resist or risk jettisoning our moral heritage of internationalism. Our position was strikingly distinct from that of China (at the time not in the UN), which argued that all countries which with their own resources would make the bomb had the right to do so. We had favoured nuclear disarmament. Some, perhaps many in India, were of the opinion that we should be one of the few to belong to the exclusive club with the right to nuclear weapons capability.

I was aware that idealism had to adjust to the world around us, especially when it impinged directly on our security but I believed that, in view of our broader vision, even the compromises to be made must not depart too far from the North Star of non-ulterior enlightened approaches. The promise of plebiscite to ascertain people's will was consistent with the concept of self-determination but it was deflected by the Security Council gameplay; we resiled from our pledge after the extension of military alliances to our neighbourhood. Decolonization was a principled commitment and so was the pledge of a non-military approach to the liberation of Goa, as mentioned by Nehru to President Kennedy; but to have resorted to military operations was a departure and, in my view, a needless one. There was certainly a wishful idealism and failure of professionalism in underestimating China's nationalism. It caused a fatal shock to Nehru and the present normalization process is a vindication of the goal of peaceful coexistence. I was in Europe in 1962, but in 1965 when I was in Peking, even after receiving the ultimata from the People's Republic, I asserted in writing that China was not likely to enforce by military action its cartographic territorial claims and, in effect, our socio-economic goals, if jettisoned, would only compound the defeat. While experience and prudence required strengthening the border conventionally (the border had earlier been left effectively unguarded), it need not have swung to the extreme of preparing for a repeat of massive operations or the likelihood of nuclear blackmail by China. I felt then, and have done so ever since, that diplomacy must not be swayed by the capability calculus but must identify the *likely* threat. China's Lob Nor explosion and its nuclear programme did not warrant that India abandon its goal of nuclear disarmament. In other words, I was worried that the consequences of exceptionalism as it would damage our principled internationalism and not give us 'prestige'.

While our opposition to the NPT on the grounds of containing discriminatory provisions had to be affirmed, standing aloof from the Treaty was bound to lead to suspicions that we too like Israel had the intention of making nuclear weapons. Our posture alienated us from our international constituency. I might add that even in 1967, I did not believe that nuclear weapons were a security imperative or by themselves gave additional political clout.

To my mind, the issue was different from Kashmir, Goa and the disappointment with China which had strong national imperatives. I wrote a Policy Planning paper and urged my viewpoint on Rajeswar Dayal, who had taken over as Foreign Secretary. I had heard that L.K. Jha, principal secretary to the prime minister and foreign secretary C.S. Jha, his predecessor, when looking at nuclear protection guarantees after the Chinese explosion in 1964, had been told by Kosygin that 'it was unthinkable that India would not sign the Non-Proliferation Treaty'. Dayal did not disagree with me but in the cabinet meeting he urged further examination of the implications of the treaty. Mrs Gandhi and the cabinet were, however, fired with nationalist sentiments and expressed our reservations about the discriminatory nature of the Treaty. The NPT was the first occasion when a stand was taken by India, striking forth an attitude which was different from the vast majority of nations on an issue concerning all nations.

Disarmament, especially arresting the development of nuclear weapons, was at the heart of Nehru's internationalism. He was the first statesman in the world to raise his voice against the danger of nuclear wars and radiation. I have the feeling that if Nehru had lived, he would have signed even the flawed NPT. After all, even the Partial Test Ban Treaty (PTBT) was not perfect, but he was greatly enthusiastic about it. The opposite view has, however, been gathering increasing support. Those who wanted India to go nuclear have sought to suggest by selecting his out-of-context quotes, that Nehru was himself a closet supporter of India making the bomb. K. Subramaniam, Bharat Karnad and several others have argued and Perkovich in his monumental work completed after fifteen years of research, endorsed the contention that Nehru favoured nuclear capability for India's security. I feel such a view amounts almost to accusing him of hypocrisy. Perkovich had kindly endorsed a copy of his book to me and after reading it, I wrote disagreeing with his opinion.

The lobby for India becoming a nuclear power became stronger after China's Lob Nor explosion, coming as it did only two years after the massive attack on India. Bhabha claimed that India had the capability and the infrastructure to go nuclear, and a small device would cost only an additional 12 lakh. Bhabha died in an air crash in 1966, but other scientist colleagues and many senior officers in the government echoed his persuasion to keep open the option and did not weigh its larger implications for our foreign policy. Eventually it led to the underground nuclear explosion in 1974, which we claimed it to be only a PNE (peaceful nuclear explosion). International cognoscenti thought that there was no real difference between a so-called PNE and the bomb.

Let me now supplement the first part of the essay by describing my peripheral involvement after the 1974 test. Our ministry, indeed most of the cabinet and governmental hierarchy, were in the dark about the Pokharan explosion except Prof. P.N. Dhar, the principal secretary to the prime minister and of course, the concerned officers of the Atomic Energy Commission. The explosion occurred within a month of my joining the ministry after having served as High Commissioner in Tanzania. I remember Prof. Dhar walking into room, disregarding the conventional hierarchical protocol as I was only an additional secretary dealing with administration. He was an old friend and asked me how to contain the international political fallout. Foreign Secretary Kewal Singh and other secretaries had been marshalled to provide 'explanations' to the accredited diplomats, and were told to emphasize that we had not violated the PTBT and our continuing commitment to non-proliferation of weapon capacity. My advice to Prof. Dhar was that we should do everything feasible to fortify our assertions that the experiment was peaceful and that we intended to use it for constructive developmental purposes like building harbours or mining gas. If in fact there was no radiational leak (and our scientists had taken good care to ensure this) we could minimize the adverse reactions by immediately inviting all members of the Geneva-based Nuclear Disarmament Committee to come and see for themselves and accept our claim of not giving way to weapons development, but my suggestion was not pursued.

The debate whether India's interest lay in reaffirming its old revulsion for nuclear weapons or demonstrating its developing weapons capability continued for the next twenty-four years. Rajiv Gandhi as prime minister, around 1987-8, apparently authorized the Atomic Energy Department and the Defence Research and Development Organization (DRDO) to prepare for another underground explosion to reaffirm our weapons capability. As it happened, about the same time he also put forward a proposal before the UN General Assembly for a step-by-step programme for nuclear disarmament to be completed by 2010. Though there was some interest in the Third World, we had suffered damage to our moral credibility after the 1974 explosion, and there was little international enthusiasm for the proposal. We stood isolated on the issue even amongst the non-aligned.

In 1989-90, India-Pakistan tensions increased along the LOC and the US suspected that it might precipitate a conflict, which could turn nuclear. President Bush sent Bill Gates to defuse the possibility. We again contemplated explosions during the period when Narasimha Rao was prime minister, but this too was detected by the CIA and we were dissuaded from going ahead. Finally, in the 1996-8 general elections, the BJP in its election manifesto specifically included a commitment to develop nuclear weapons capability. Within weeks of the Vajpayee government assuming office on 11 and 13 May 1998 the Pokhran-II explosions took place. There was widespread condemnation in most countries. Sanctions were imposed and aid promised or in the pipeline was reduced. For different reasons, the reactions were the sharpest in the USA, China and Japan. Adverse reactions were more or less expected, but within the country there was widespread euphoria, much greater than in 1974. Only a small though significant group of intellectuals and Gandhian idealists articulated their dissent on moral or practical security grounds. The USA tried to dissuade Pakistan from following suit by exploding its own devices but domestic opinion in Pakistan was so strong that Nawaz Shariff gave in and conducted three explosions at Chagai in Baluchistan. It was a blow to the NPT and the goal of arresting further proliferation.

My own view is that by declaring itself as a weapons power, India has minimized not enhanced its international position. I had given my reasons for holding this view as a member of the first Strategic Advisory Committee. There were some others who seemed to share the logic of my stand, but in general, I was in a minority. I sincerely believe that there is no likely nuclear threat to India and we remain hostage to the apprehended malevolence of our nuclear neighbours; we are not strengthening but debilitating our diplomacy. Pokhran-II may have demonstrated our technological capacity, but by triggering Pakistan's devices, it has blurred the fact that Pakistan was the first in the subcontinent to embark on a weapons programme. Our explosion has infact neutralized India's multifaceted military advantage over Pakistan. The subcontinent became the subject of trenchant criticism for nuclear irresponsibility. I do not share the Western alarm but I do feel it has compounded the lowering of India's principled leadership role in international forums.

By 1998, as a result of reforms started in1991, India's economy was gathering momentum. After the final end of the Cold War (which I always thought was only mutually reinforced paranoia),

India commanded corresponding increase in strategic importance. The Talbott-Jaswant Singh talks were tortuous but friendly, and at one stage, there was some hope that an agreement might be reached by India signing the Comprehensive Test Ban Treaty (CTBT). In the end the talks failed. In any case, the US Congress did not approve the CTBT and this took the wind out of Talbott's sails. The sanctions have gradually eased and Indo-US relations improved, enabling a five-day visit of President Clinton to India with only five hours in Pakistan.

After 9/11, the entire scenario changed. Nuclear weapons capacity is now challenged by the defiant reality of terrorism and the suicidal fearlessness against militarily powerful nations. Much literature has followed after 9/11 and the emerging contradictions of our times have been brought to the forefront.

As stated, except in subjective psychology, nuclear weapons have shown less and less deterrent utility; but they have absorbed more and more of the scarce financial and scientific resources. There are many reasons for the sluggishness of social progress, but insufficient funding is a principal one. The UN Charter, virtually written in stone in 1945, gave the five powers (P5) the veto authority and the NPT subsequently gave them the privileged licence of retaining and developing nuclear weapons. The NPT also expected sincere commitment from the P5 to regulate disarmament and manage international peace. In this, they have failed, and not surprisingly, they command diminishing respect. Anyway, 9/11 showed that nuclear weapons have not deterred the small and poor countries from motivated defiance. The US in Iraq is a case in point, and India's problem with its neighbours is not dissimilar. However, notwithstanding these anomalies, the possessors of nuclear weapons (and those aspiring to them and supported by nuclear hawks and scientific and technological enclaves) still believe in outdated unproven strategic concepts like massive retaliation, flexible response, launch on warning, Mutual Assured Destruction (MAD), etc. If a small part of resources absorbed by nuclear strategy had been applied towards societal renovation, it may have been possible to moderate insurgencies, genocide and terror and even possibly prevent them in many parts of the world, notably in Africa and Asia.

The inherent danger of nuclear weapons going into

irresponsible hands, or what the West calls 'rogue nations', has come to the surface. A.Q. Khan, the father of Pakistan's bomb, with the probable connivance of the Pakistan army, had been personally earning millions of dollars by private export of nuclear centrifuges and technology to Iran, North Korea and Libya. As it was predicated on the judgement that India-Pakistan hostility was permanent and irreversible, and this naturally caused alarm. Contrary to the spirit of the NPT, China also gave technical support to Pakistan's nuclear programme. The international configuration however had changed so dramatically that Pakistan abandoned the Taliban and again dutifully joined the American war on terror. A.Q. Khan, known for fundamentalist bias, has now been stripped of his authority and immunity and stricter controls have been imposed on Pakistan's nuclear installations. Apparently, over the years fissionable material and nuclear technology was leaked deliberately or through lax controls from the USA, Germany, the Netherlands and Switzerland. There has been some suspicion that in the wake of the disintegration of the USSR, there might have been pilferage of enriched uranium from reactors originally under Russian surveillance. The USA had showed indulgence towards Pakistan (when both were assisting the Mujahideen against the Soviet intervention in Afghanistan) by not enforcing the 'Glenn Amendment' (which required stoppage of aid to countries with nuclear ambitions) and approved false certification to waive the requirement under the Pressler amendment.

In the attack on the World Trade Center and the Pentagon on 11 September 2001, hijacked American Boeings were used like missiles by a handful of disaffected fundamentalists. The preparations for this attack, it has been revealed in the Congressional report on 9/11, had been going on for four years. It would be naïve not to anticipate that such non-state actors would not use stolen or make available fissionable material in any future 9/11. It is plain that if nuclear weapons fall in their hands, they could, even more than 'rogue nations', pose a danger to the future of the planet.

McGeorge Bundy, who more than any other person had close experience of decision-making during the Cuban missile crisis

(1962), has argued in his authoritative work that mathematically the danger of nuclear conflagration has reduced in every subsequent decade. Neither the USA nor the Soviet Union have ever seriously contemplated launching nuclear weapons. He does express regret that Roosevelt and Churchill did not heed the advice offered by Niels Bohr not to go ahead with the weapons programmes. Bundy, after surveying fifty years of paranoiac suspicions between the USA and the Soviet Union, however, recommends that instead of MAD (Mutual Assured Destruction), the strategy should be SANE (Survivability Adequate Nuclear Effectiveness). He urges virtues of Candor, Caution and Imagination and, above all, Courage and Hope. Bundy's counsel urged rationalization in governmental decision-making. He passed away before 9/11 and did not see how private trading in nuclear fissionable material could seriously jeopardize even SANE by non-state actors using highjacked aircrafts as missiles.

Thousands of books and articles have appeared after 9/11 but, to my mind, the most convincing case is contained in Jonathan Schell's book *The Gift of Time* and the conclusions of the Canberra Commission. Both these studies record interviews and perspectives of some decision-makers who have been at the heart of national responsibilities in different countries or have deep intellectual insights. The persons interviewed and participants include Robert McNamara, Field Marshal Carver (former Chief of Defence of the UK) General George Lee Butler (former Commander of American Strategic Forces), Generals Horner and Goodpaster of the US Army, Michael Rocard (former Prime Minister of France), Helmut Schmidt (former Chancellor of Germany), Mikhail Gorbachev, Alexander Solzhenitsyn, Andrei Sakharov, Lech Walsea, Vaclav Havel, Joseph Rotbatt, Robert O'Neill and a galaxy of others. With different reasoning these experts in their own fields saw the actual non-utility of nuclear weapons and the great danger from existing nuclear weapons, and endorsed the conclusions that these weapons should now be abolished. These knowledgeable persons discussed the many pros and cons including the hypothetical risk of a 'breakout' when, after the 'abolition', a country secretly reassembled nuclear weapons and threatened the world with its monopoly. But Schell's thesis underlines that the unexpected end of the Cold War has thrown up a challenge of opportunity and urgency. It is interesting to note the development of conventional technology. Paul Nitze whom Strobe Talbott called the 'Master of the Game' (of Disarmament negotiations), himself recommends (in an article in the *New York Times*) that nuclear weapons should be given up as not worth the hazards in their development and use. Can the nuclear powers and nuclear aspirants ignore the wisdom of these eminent men risking sensitivity to their national and global peril? Whether it is the inherent danger of weapons of mass destruction or the demonstrated irresponsibility of terror, non-proliferation requires a fresh look.*

As it happened, *The Gift of Time* has been followed by a historic turnaround in India-Pakistan relations. Until 2004, the two countries were considered the world's most dangerous nuclear twins. Countless analysts had argued that if nuclear war were to start, it would most likely be in the subcontinent. After the terrorist attack on the Indian Parliament in December 2001, our analysts advocated measures ranging from more careful vigilance to aggressive punitive action. The picture changed dramatically after the Vajpayee-Musharaff Accord of January 2004. A composite dialogue has now begun. Kashmir remains in the forefront of the agenda but it no longer holds a veto on functional cooperation and the exploration of beneficial bilateralism between the two countries. There is recognition that the long saga of beggaring each other must end. If the dismantling of the Berlin Wall symbolized the end of the Cold War, the India-Pakistan cricket series reflected the dramatic improvement in the subcontinent. Apparently after the final match, one thousand Pakistani motorcyclists with their silencers removed rode through the streets of Lahore hailing the sporting triumph of India. People are demanding normal human contacts and unshackling of the obstructions to the economic logic of promoting additional benefits of modernization for both countries. If India-Pakistan

* In the *Wall Street Journal* of 4 January 2007, four prominent Americans (Republicans: Kissinger and Perry; Democrats: Schulz and Nunn) have come round to urge that step-by-step US itself must aim for the abolition of the nuclear weapons.

do get economically enmeshed following self-interest, then, while the conventional defensive vigilance could continue, it is be obvious that a nuclear exchange between the countries would have to be ruled out. Both now have a vested interest in non-proliferation in general, but especially by irresponsible suicidal fundamentalists. To pre-empt non-state actors complicating subcontinental stability and improvement, India and Pakistan could separately but simultaneously follow the example of Libya and renounce their respective programmes of nuclear weaponry and then demand that the P5 follow suit. The boot will be on the other foot and India and Pakistan would then be on the moral high ground concerning disarmament and the abolition of nuclear weapons in a new variant of the NPT. They could go on to propose that all nations adhere to the Fissionable Material Control Treaty (FMCT) so that the production of bomb-making material is stopped everywhere; all existing fissionable material is accounted for, and future development is carefully monitored by the IAEA. It would of course be complacent to think that nuclear terror would be summarily smothered, but India and Pakistan, being geographically and civilizationally linked, are better placed to effect this dramatic transformation.

This is a far cry from Strobe Talbott's protracted conversations from 1998 onwards urging India (and presumably Pakistan) to sign the CTBT and accept the other collateral benchmarks. We could reiterate that the dissemination of knowledge and the resilience of the nationalism of equality cannot be suppressed even in the nuclear age. The discriminatory nuclear apartheid of the NPT should end and the mutation of its scope and logic initiated by India and Pakistan and become a step towards world peace. India, once again could go back to its original Nehruvian posture of being committed to total nuclear disarmament.

This suggestion, I realize, would be deemed outrageous and, possibly anti-patriotic. Most of our analysts support the Strategic Nuclear Doctrine made public in 1999, of retaining deterrent capability but combining it with the assurance of NFU. The doctrine has a reference that India must seek to develop a triad of nuclear weapons capability—on the ground, in the air and from under the sea. Bharat Karnad in his massive study argues that India's security ultimately demands that the triad must be planned for a range and sophistication which could deter even distant countries like the USA. My own guess is that such a course would almost certainly engulf India and the subcontinent into multitudinous independent flames of unsmotherable terror and dangerous internal insecurity. Karnad seems innocent of the concept of economic opportunity costs. Our states are already facing serious fiscal deficits. They are not unaware of the rising expectations, the sharpening of the rich-poor divide, and the mounting cynicism at allegedly incompetent governance. The focus of Prime Minister Manmohan Singh and the present Government of India is on invigorating allocations for health, education, infrastructure, and social justice. This would go some way towards pre-empting and reversing the incidence of terror. We have already lost decades and trillions of rupees in resources. The thesis urged here makes me self-consciously feel like a John of Gaunt in Shakespeare's *Richard II* who before the King's arrival and after uttering a most panegyric invocation to his native land, warns that the country must be aware of the shameful conquest of itself.

I have dealt at length with the question of the proliferation of nuclear weapons as it profoundly signifies the twenty-first century challenge. These weapons have an unprecedented destructive power, but instead of strengthening governments, they have exposed their limitations and highlighted the nemesis of pure militarism. It has coincided with the awakened strength of people's power and poses a challenge to diplomacy in establishing and maintaining peace. Our mindsets must be purged of historical analogies that do not grasp the political consequences of the gallop of technology in our times.

I will conclude this essay with quotes from Amartya Sen's Dorothy Hodgkin lecture at the annual session of the Pugwash conference in the year 2000 on 'India and the Bomb'. The Economics Nobel Laureate starts by perceptively acknowledging that 'Weapons of mass destruction have a peculiar fascination; they generate the warm glow of strength and power but it is carefully divorced from the brutality and genocide on which the potency of weapons depends. India's strength flows from its civilization. We could immunize the world from the pandemic of anti-Americanism as well as help to ease the irrationality of Islamophobia. Indeed, India can rediscover as Nehru always seemed to have had at the back of his mind that India's strength lies in plurality and toleration:' Sen concludes, 'The central connection between the moral and the prudential must never be overlooked.'

PART III

Now, in August 2006, there is every likelihood of approval by the US Congress of the Bush–Singh agreement on Civil Nuclear Cooperation as signed in July 2005.* It would mark a near dialectical transformation in the relations between two democracies, which were estranged for much of the second-half of the twentieth century. It signals the end of an era which began with Hiroshima, developed into the Cold War anxieties, aroused fears of militant ideological universalism and, in nervous retaliation, invited protracted 'Containment'; it coincided with the beginning of decolonization with the transfer of power and partition in the subcontinent and, as a consequence, led to apprehensions which hypnotized two generations of intellectuals and people around the world. As a result, decolonized countries and others who remained detached or neutral were dismissed as immoral. What stands vindicated now are those very principles of non-alignment and ideological agnosticism and diversity in the economic vitality of the international system, but in actual practice, the Non-aligned Movement (NAM) became a toothless and treaty-less imitation of military alliances, presuming on the permanence of the superpower confrontation. However the pursuit of peace will hereafter be based on promoting trade and functional cooperation between countries which were earlier mutually suspicious or even ideologically antagonistic. The far-reaching implications of the transition from the old 'conventional wisdom' to the present reality is not widely recognized.

* The Bush-Singh Civil Nuclear Agreement after protracted negotiations on 123 provisions has finally been approved by the US and Indian governments.

Not altogether surprisingly, the agreement has provoked strident criticism in India from extremes of the Right and the Left and abroad from firm liberals as well as staunch conservatives. In India on the one hand, it is felt it would endanger our independence and the quest for national security, and abroad that, it would jeopardize the near success of the non-proliferation regime. These perceptions are all traceable to the bequeathed sediments of the myopic paranoia of the Cold War decades. Prime Minister Manmohan Singh gave a robust defence during the debate in Parliament on 17 August 2006 with detailed point-by-point clarification, justifying the agreement, as concluded as fully consistent with the emerging priorities of developing India and in no way subordinating India's true future interests. The real challenge of the twenty-first century will not be wars—nuclear or conventional—between powerful countries but for governments—big and small—to satisfy people's rising expectations. This could pose a threat to national stability especially when fuelled by international linkages, conspired by non-state actors and so deliberately jolting the enmeshed urban conglomerates.

The agreement has reinforced the rationality of the Vajpayee-Musharraf agreement, which was reached in January 2004, condemning *all* terror (with no reservations for the so-called 'freedom fighters'). It was subsequently given bipartisan endorsement by the Musharraf–Manmohan Singh declaration in September 2005. Adversarial suspicions and mindsets will persist and incident will recur, but the bilateral understanding has already led to the restoration of much beneficial cooperation and confidence-building through the composite dialogues. This normalization may have taken the hawks in both countries by surprise but it has been openly welcomed by vast multitudes on both sides of the India–Pakistan frontier.

One aspect of the Bush–Singh Agreement has not received sufficient focus either domestically or internationally. Unlike authoritarian military governments, well-establish democracies like the US and India are greatly handicapped in their effort to modify inherited public commitments, especially when, fresh in memory, they can evoke nationalist pride or historic fears. To make contemporaneously valid improvements, therefore, demands delicate diplomatic negotiations particularly as foreign policy differences obviously continue. This would make the conclusion of the agreement a proof of courageous statesmanship and agile diplomacy on both sides.

The Non-Proliferation Treaty of 1968 (NPT) was a 'flawed' document; it sanctified a permanent nuclear 'apartheid' with a privileged licence for the so-called responsible five great powers to sophisticate their nuclear armoury; their identities happened to coincide with those of the permanent members of the UN Security Council. All other nations were denied access to even civil nuclear technology except after certified IAEA inspections. The treaty allowed for formal withdrawal but not for radical changes of regimes. (The monarchy of the Shah in Iran, which signed the NPT, was overthrown in 1979 and no formal denunciation or modification in interpretation in the letter and spirit of the previous commitment has yet been made.) Moreover, the NPT did not foresee that technological secrecy could not be preserved forever. India, therefore, had good grounds to remain a non-signatory. It was, however, insufficiently appreciated that standing aloof from an agreement, endorsed by the vast majority of states, compromised India's leadership position of the non-nuclear and have-not nations on nuclear disarmament. It aroused suspicions that India really aspired to be included in the exclusive club and had earlier paid only lip service to the abolition of weapons of mass destruction and in placing some emphasis on collective security under the UN Charter. We also did not realize that it would endanger the prospect of civil nuclear cooperation for India's own development. To my mind, it was the first time that, on a general issue (as distinct from a national one like self-determination in Kashmir or the use of armed intervention in Goa), India departed from principles and found itself justifying 'exceptionalism'. As Salman Haider, who was my colleague as deputy secretary in the Policy Planning Division of MEA, would confirm, that even then I felt that the balance of India's long-term interests would be better served by subscribing to even the 'flawed' Treaty. However, since the government with the overwhelming support of public opinion, decided to stay aloof by not joining the vast majority under the logic of built-in discrimination for the P5, I dutifully argued for our national stand. I told the British envoys, for example, that while Hiroshima was a moral outrage with dubious military justification and Stalin's action to match American nuclear capacity was understandable, for the UK, with its membership of NATO and the assurance of the US umbrella, its nuclear policy had made such weapons the badge of great power prestige and this justified our position. I added that it would actually stimulate proliferation and defeat the very objective of the Treaty by tempting other nations to develop weapons of mass destruction (WMD) for subjective prestige reason. (This alas has happened in North Korea and possibly elsewhere.)

In due course, France and China, entitled to have military reactors outside international safeguards, joined the NPT. However, enforcing non-proliferation on the rest of the world became the obsessive goal of successive US administration. After our PNE in 1974, not only was the ongoing cooperation with Canada on the building of civilian reactors terminated, but the supply of fuel for the Tarapur reactor, pledged under a bilateral Indo–US agreement, also came into question by the US law on non-proliferation. In 1977 Indo–US relations had turned friendly after the Emergency was lifted and Indian general elections were held which dislodged the Congress party government of Mrs Gandhi. During President Carter's visit to Delhi in January 1978, in a one-to-one confidential conversation, he pressed Prime Minister Morarji Desai to sign the NPT, accept IAEA safeguards and so enable the continuation of the supply of enriched fuel for Tarapur but the Indian prime minister firmly refused to accept any conditions while discrimination in favour of the P5 remained in force. Carter was irritated by Desai's adamancy and whispered his exasperation to the Secretary of the State, Cyrus Vance, sitting next to him in the formal bilateral meeting which followed immediately, 'We must write a blunt and rude letter' to the Indian prime minister. I was seated at the tail end of the Indian delegation around a circular table and was nearest to the American delegation. I did not hear—indeed no one in the room heard the whisper—but the sensitive electronic microphone in the hands of an NBC correspondent who had been collectively chosen to come for the initial photo opportunity, picked up the whisper and in accordance with the prescribed arrangements, deposited the cassette, which automatically duplicated and distributed the recorded conversation to about two hundred journalists in the Press Centre in the Ashoka Hotel. (He himself had gone sight-seeing to the Red Fort!). President Carter was greatly embarrassed by the public disclosure of his undiplomatic remark, but Morarji did not take serious offence. As Foreign Secretary, I and Jody Powell the press adviser attached to the White House were told to attempt 'damage control' the disaster to what had looked like a promising improvement of relations between the two countries. While the adverse fallout was minimized, India and US remained firmly at cross purposes on the non-proliferation issue for the next twenty-seven years.

The Bush–Singh agreement is, in fact, a compromise for both sides. While in articulation, neither side has abandoned the earlier attitudes nor the threat perceptions, both recognize the current political realities and out-dated differences. President Bush in his speech in India in 2006 acknowledged that 'Things change; times change'. Intellectuals in India are not the only ones still hypnotized by past security analogies to resist the course correction. Influential journals like *The Economist* and 'pro-non-proliferates' in the US (including Republican and Democratic Senators and Congressmen), knowledgeable and even sympathetic experts like Strobe Talbott have argued that exemption for India would open the semi-dammed floodgates to the irresponsible spread of WMDs. These eminent spokesmen abroad, however, have shown scant respect for India's vibrant democracy and many in the country honestly believe—as most in the US still seem to—that a country has the right to retain full freedom of weapon sophistication for national security. The compromise, however, is a proof of feasible flexibility even in a democracy. As sovereign countries the reasons of India and US differ but there is convergence of understanding that both are far more important to each other and both have a stake in energy augmentation.

The credit for turning around US Congressional opinion on this agreement flows from many-sided earnest efforts, which reflect the better understood strategic and economic importance of India in the twenty-first century. The administration's efforts were supported by influential people in the Indian community resident in the US, demonstrating that NRIs have by now come to grasp the American lobbying techniques. I would imagine the Indian embassy must have provided guidance to the community and to the 'India caucus'. Anyway, the present favourable Congressional majority represents a positive change from the near despondency that prevailed not many weeks ago. At this stage, it would be pointless to recall the economic penalties inflicted on India from the earlier misjudgement when governmental strategists and political thinkers in India saw prestige and national interest in advocating a unilateralist total defiance of the NPT. Although after India's explosions there was no evidence that non-nuclear neighbours like Nepal were frightened by India, it suffices that the negotiated compromise has definitive promise for India's economy and therefore it merits tribute to those who managed this course correction to rescue the future.

From Nehru's time India has never adopted the position of China, that the world can tolerate an unlimited (or, following Kenneth Waltz's thesis) a limited number of nuclear weapons powers. Though still aloof from the NPT, the present agreement is the full recognition that, unlike Pakistan, India has remained 'a responsible power' by adhering to the discipline envisaged in the Treaty in not selling nuclear weapons know-how abroad. Not accelerating its weapons programme is particularly noteworthy considering the strategic situation of India. France and the UK, both nuclear-armed powers, are neighbours but they are partners in NATO and have never targeted each other. India is the only country that has two nuclear-armed contiguous neighbours with whom there have been conflicts in the past. We are slowly repairing our relations with both but it is understandable that to safeguard national security India would want in place an independent nuclear-deterrent capability. The Sino-Indian border dispute involving fifty thousand square miles, though quiescent, is still unresolved. With Pakistan, there have been four wars; the dispute over Kashmir and the climate of distrust, though palpably improved, persists with abiding suspicious. Moreover, China has been helping Pakistan build its nuclear capability. In 1999, a meticulously planned Pakistani intrusion into Kashmir in the Kargil sector took place. According to his recent autobiography, Nawaz Sharif, the prime minister of Pakistan at the time, was taken aback when president Clinton at their meeting on 4 July 1999, informed him that the Pakistan army had alerted its nuclear batteries prior to the intrusion. India succeeded in repelling the intruders even from the commanding heights with great courage, taking terrible casualties, but it never contemplated the use of nuclear weapons and did not cross the Line of Control delineated at Simla (1972). What Nawaz Sharif does not mention, however, is that the intruding insurgents, including Afghans and the so-called jehadis, *all* complied with the Clinton's proposal of a total withdrawal to beyond the LOC. (That incidentally speaks volumes for who actually commands the so-called 'freedom fighters'.) This episode, however, also reconfirms the non-utility of nuclear weapons. This restraint by both countries was almost a replica of the Cuban missile crisis of 1962 where the adversaries saw sagacity not only in non-use and non-defiance, but preferred quiet withdrawal rather than confrontation emboldened by US national nuclear capability. However, the psychological dimensions of paranoia in both countries are not dissimilar to the national suspicious between the USA and USSR during the Cold war decades. Public opinion in India and Pakistan is still reluctant to put its faith in the enemy practising nuclear restraint. But the lesson is obvious. Since the Cuban Missile crisis of 1962, the reality remains that governments of nuclear powers would rather suffer reverses and humiliations than risk a nuclear war.

The likehood of a regional nuclear war has often been predicted by analysts in the West, implying a propensity for suicidal folly in the South Asian 'nuclear twins'. Actually, on the probability scale, this gets more and more remote. I continue to urge that we must bend our policy not so much to the 'rogue' propensities of hostile governments but initiate prophylactic action so that 'irresponsible' militant terrorists do not use crude nuclear devices. Apart from sophisticated intelligence and security vigilance to dilute the chances of such incidents, we must rely on sensitive internal political policy, more effective governance and consistent constructive diplomacy to minimize disaffection. Since 2004 the chances of another government-planned 1965 or even a repetition of Kargil 1999 have greatly diminished, but the possibility of militant terrorism (so far non-nuclear) against India (and even in Pakistan) and world governments has increased. There is a sea-change in the Indo–Pakistan atmosphere as can be seen in the cricket stadia in both countries and with the rise of national tourism in Indian Kashmir. Incidents, however, will recur, as the attack on our Parliament in 2001 or the Mumbai suburban railway explosions in July 2006. In knee-jerk instant reactions, we are apt to contemplate punitive action against Pakistan itself: armchair strategists contemplate the equivalent of the 'massive retaliation' once advocated by the US. After the attack on our Parliament in 2001, some professionals wanted India to abrogate the Indus Treaty little realizing that such a move would be masochistic. It would have provided justification to China and Nepal as upper riparians to unilaterally divert and deny the Indus and Brahmputra and even the waters of the Sutlej and the Kosi (which rise beyond the high Himalayas) to downstream India. Punitive reaction often fails to make a distinction between the current government policies of Pakistan and its inability (or even political hesitation) to effectively suppress its own sympathizers, thus risking offence to the religious susceptibilities of its own domestic constituency.

In a digression, may I recall three highjacking instances—all by pro-Pakistan sympathizers—which had starkly different results. The extensive recent comments after the release of a book by a senior politician provides an apt illustration of how to and how not to encourage terrorists. In the January 1971 high-jacking incident, the Pakistan government was actually supportive of the highjackers; anyway, after the release of the passengers, as a public demonstration, a procession rejoicing in the destruction of the Fokker Friendship aircraft paraded in Lahore with the obvious approval of the authorities. In the August 1976 incident, we firmly refused to concede to the highjackers' demand for the release of Maqbool Butt, but we got our plane and our passengers safely home. We succeeded *only* because, in an instant judgement, we felt that the Pakistan government was not behind the pro-Pakistan highjackers. Pakistan officials acted sagaciously and persuaded the highjackers to vacate the aircraft. In the Kandahar episode of IAC 814 in 2000, there was confusion and delay in decision-making in India. The local police or SPG had two hours to plan effective action to prevent the aircraft from taking off. Even so, after it had done refuelling, we should have instructed the pilot to land in Lahore and switch off the engines. The Pakistan government would have had the full responsibility for negotiating with the highjackers. Our leverage was much greater in Pakistan than in Dubai and even less in Taliban-controlled Kandahar. In the end, we were obliged to release three arch terrorists to save the passengers, with terrible future consequences. Terrorist incidents are bound to lead to increased tensions in the climate of diplomatic relations, but professionalism must not jump to populist conclusions. We actually suspended all IAC flights to Kathmandu for three months after the IAC 814 incident and inconvenienced Nepalese citizens providing yet more proof of Indian callousness. After the Mumbai explosions in July 2006, the ongoing dialogue was sought to be suspended. This shows how diplomacy becomes hostage to terrorism and sagacity succumbs to populism.

The gallop of contemporary technological progress has no parallel in history. If trade and investment are measured in terms of total wealth of goods and services, it certainly has led to unprecedented prosperity in the world. Since the Renaissance, the countries commanding a economic, scientific and technical lead heave compounded their natural advantages and accelerated their advance. But globalization is double-edged. The information revolution has politically empowered the weak and the poor—within the developing countries—and nationalism becomes more strident against the developed or larger ones. As noted earlier while access to information has stimulated expectations, also the realization that the share of benefits is unevenly distributed has also grown. This provokes disaffection, which now gets worldwide publicity and so terrorism serves as public relations of cause and complaint. Coercion and official 'terrorism' explained as *raison d'êtat* (reasons of state) revive memories of tyranny and fundamentalism but now it gets instant international public relations.

Conditioned mindsets have not, however, understood that globalization has sharpened the democratic equality of small or weak nations. The militarily powerful or fortunate in size and resources are still gripped with the old nation of imperialist conquest and easy coercion. These countries with economic surplus, no doubt, remain essential for the positive development of the handicapped nations, but they are stumped by nationalist bravado. We have entered the era of economic disparities coinciding with defiant political equality. The present agreement shifts from the old suspicion of the malevolent 'foreign hand' to negotiated cooperation for economic progress for the betterment of India.

Where this new phenomenon of revitalized nationalism has been somewhat better understood and accommodated, or where the lessons of historical experience have been quietly grasped, it has led to a slow but purposeful bonus of successful regionalism as an adjunct of globalization. This is exemplified with the progress of the European Economic Community since the Treaty of Rome (1957) and ASEAN covering countries of diverse size and potential in South-East Asia since 1967. France and Germany have buried centuries of enmity. On the other hand, the UK staying aloof from the EEC in 1957 was the manifestation of outdated confidence in Empire, but it led to a costly postponement and the UK was finally admitted in the EEC only in 1973. The sluggish progress towards SAARC may well be another example of not comprehending the modern quality of political nationalism, which geographically and economically always had an obvious logic of prospering together and not beggaring the neighbour.

The US–India relationship for long had this feature of perceived inequality but now both countries see it in their respective national interests to recognize their complimentaries and make a corrective move towards political equality. We all know that the US has suffered humiliating setbacks against small and weak nations. It is now widely disliked; even so it remains by far the largest and most indispensable economy in the world. The US Congress has incorporated declarations of its own expectations from the Bush–Singh bilateral agreement but only the signed agreement blinds democratic India. No doubt, the US is the technological donor and India the recipient but both have overcome national attitudes is superseding the earlier rigidities. The belief that by this agreement, India is in danger of becoming a US surrogate is only the leftover of the Cold War mindset; in fact, as in all trade and international treaties and agreements (unlike in military unconditional surrenders), consent is based on acknowledged limitations of national sovereignties.

In this background, I come to the crunch question, which, if evaded, may be self-destructive. Are we to follow the well-trodden intellectual imitative path of the hypothetical military scenario of a nuclear war, consistent with the capability calculus of the worst-case scenario, and prepare for a retaliatory second strike of inflicting unacceptable damage or, in the alternative, seeing the contemporaneous realities of rising non-official disaffection seek to have better distributional justice? The size of the national cake of resources, considering our population and our social demands, is small. On the probability scale, terrorism against industrialized economies looks much nearer the real menace than a nuclear attack by a hostile government. Millions of semi-educated unemployed youths, led by scientifically qualified or religiously motivated militants, conspire for violent disruption, unmindful of the loss of innocent lives. Terrorism is a manifestation of a new horizontal bipolarity of internationalism; it has no historical parallels as developed societies are threatened by militant desperate men. The lessons of the last sixty years since Hiroshima show that while the hypothetical has in fact commanded the attention and resources of the world powers, it might have been better to have identified the roots of societal inequities. It bears recalling that in 1991 the USSR, with a vast nuclear arsenal, disintegrated and almost became a failed state. Russia is, however, now climbing back to superpower status, not so much because of its nuclear capability but because of its rising energy potential. China has steadily gained in international respect and leverage because of its economic growth, notably its trade surplus with the USA. In the twentieth, and more so in the twenty-first, the ups and downs of international standing are going to be more related to economic and social development than to nuclear weapons capability.

Our strategists, who drafted or endorsed our nuclear doctrine, were probably prisoners of the outdated nations that nuclear megatonnage carried by super-fast delivery vehicles was the final arbiter of national survival and destiny. We know—as the US predicament in Iraq is embarrassingly demonstrating—that firepower does not prevail politically as it may have done in the previous centuries. National strength now has to be multifaceted; defence and internal security are ingredients and to be effective must ensure obtaining national cohesion. Sanjaya Baru in his recent book *Strategic Consequences of India's Economic Performance* (2006) quotes the Chinese think tank concept of Comprehensive National Power (CNP). The crucial factor is the willing cooperation of the people which, in turn, hinges on efficacy, resource availability and modernized social priorities for development. Viable 'strategy' in the twenty-first century will have to be more holistic; it cannot remain segregated between 'planned development' and 'non-plan' outlays.

In the perception of the world, next to China India is now perceived as on the way to becoming an economic superpower. Catering to the purchasing capacity of 300 million people in the middle-class who can afford consumer durables, provides a big attraction for domestic savings and foreign investment (300 million exceeds the total population of the US). With an 8 per cent growth, 30-50 million may be added to this number in the next five years.

Our demographic structure gives India a unique long-term inbuilt advantage in continuous addition to our workforce. But India remains a poor underdeveloped country; our internal stability is only partly compensated by our democratic constitution with defined rights and directive principles, judicial independence and layers of decentralization. What must stare the executive decision-makers (and one hopes the legislatures) in the face is that there are 400 million people below the poverty line and about an equal number hovering above subsistence level with a large proportion seething with varying degress of cynical anger and potential tinder for non-religious terror (as in Nepal). Most of the states in the Union are juggling with huge deficits and can barely afford to keep up the momentum of development or disaster relief or finding productive employment even for the educated and the qualified. There is still rampant illiteracy, inadequate health facilities, record numbers of HIV positives and the dilution of progress because of widespread corruption. There is no doubt scope for improvement in efficiency and greater discipline in expenditure, but implementing the social agenda demands exponential domestic financial resources. The number of districts under 'Naxalite' control is steadily increasing; the tally now is 172, which is nearly one-fourth of the total area of India. In Jharkhand twelve out of sixteen district are beyond the enforced rule of law. This is creating a simmering volcano, which could overwhelm the pockets of urban affluence, frustrate our great-power dream and undermine the foundation of governance and internal security. Democratic India has to find the alchemy and priority for development to ensure better distributional social justice. No nation can now segregate defence against an external danger from the people's morale and contentment. Decision-makers must make available maximum possible resources to moderate, if not eliminate the visible and definite threat of internal disaffection, which could jeopardize national stability and consequential security. No country, certainly not a poor one, can manage to cover the likely, indeed the growing and certain shadow on the future not by projecting on the theoretical and hypothetical nuclear threat. Sweden and South Africa and even Libya as non-nuclear powers are as secure as they were before abandoning nuclear militarism. In the twenty-first century, to ignore the concept of opportunity costs is inviting certain peril.

The real gain of the Bush–Singh agreement is that it implicitly recognizes not only the viability of India in the twenty-first century but also that the amelioration of people's welfare depends critically on the availability energy. According to the Tata Energy Research Institute (TERI), by 2050 India will require 8,000 BU or 1,344,000 MV of power availability. At present our energy generation is less than 130,000 MV. The domestic reserves of hydrocarbons and rising international prices of imported fuel, even if supplemented by coal, natural gas and diverse renewable sources from within the country, will still need to be supplemented and that too long before, speaking realistically, our thorium cycle matures. By 2020, according to the Nuclear Power Commission, we would make available only about 20,000 MV from nuclear fission but that too is largely contingent on the availability of enriched fuel. Imported nuclear reactors, from whatever sources no doubt will be hugely expensive but if oil prices shoot up beyond $75 a barrel, the reactors will at least ease our energy deficit. No doubt nuclear generated energy would provide only a small fraction of our total requirements, but it would be clean and could be further augmented in the future. Countries like France, Japan and many others, having planned well ahead, now rely overwhelmingly on nuclear energy for civil needs. We must, of course, develop our potential from all sources but energy availability must be given the highest priority. If nuclear energy can be made available safely, this agreement will form a critical part of the national energy security programme. In purposefully planning ahead for its energy needs, China has had no hesitation in accepting even stricter conditions under IAEA safeguards to ensure availability of enriched uranium from Australia. As a non-signatory to the NPT, the Nuclear Supply Group will set aside the stipulated constraints if the US legislation legitimizes the exception for India. If we could erase the Cold War mindsets, far from compromising non-alignment, we would be supported simultaneously by old adversaries like the USA, Russia, France, and Australia to facilitate our nuclear energy augmentation. We might as well acknowledge that we did not correctly anticipate our energy needs. We really had prophetic hunches for our foreign policy but we got deflected by Partition and the Cold War paradigm.

Our public opinion obviously wants to keep the weapons option. The 1974 and 1998 explosions can no more be undone than the partitions of 1947 and 1971. If the present thesis has any merit and democracy is our overriding asset for stability and growth (even if it does not provide foolproof immunity from acts of terrorism), the logic points to this negotiated compromise. No doubt it means that fourteen out of twenty-two reactors will be subject to IAEA safeguards, but it does not preclude a minimum deterrent. There is a unilateral commitment to desist from further nuclear testing, but it is there even on the P5. The agreement realistically (even if not theoretically) rescues us from the wholly unrealistic ambition of an independent triad defence. The triad in my view was always paranoiacally irrelevant to national priorities even in the worst-case scenarios. The tradition of non-disclosure or at least non-debate in Parliament of the budget allocations for the Atomic Energy Commission can be traced to the personal equation between Nehru and Homi Bhabha. Quite rightly, allocations and production capability for military reactors have to be secret and so too the capability for reprocessing plutonium. The size and viability of India's deterrence against hostile malevolence must remain ambiguous but the total allocation for the Atomic Energy Commission has relevance to the allocation on development plans, for agriculture, civil administration, infrastructure and social progress. This should be discussed by people's representatives as it determines the projections for 'roti, kapada aur makan' (bread, clothes and a roof). If the nuclear programme is totally compartmentalized, we may have neither sufficient 'guns' nor the 'equitable distribution and spread of butter'. This, in my view, is part of the critical choice for the apex decision-maker.

Conventional wisdom has yet to register that the twenty-first century represents a wholly new era which befuddles the analysts conditioned by outdated history. The Cold War led to bi-polar paranoia and centrifugal militarization, which has flooded the world with illegal handheld and even sophisticated weapons, but none looks more expensive, redundant and non-utilitarian than nuclear weapons. The opportunity costs must run into trillions; money which might have given greater happiness to the greatest number. It was an American president (Eisenhower) who, in his farewell message over four decades ago, warned of the tentacles of the military-industrial complex but the folly continues; above all in the USA with concepts such as 'wars in space'. Extravagant militarism and insensitive scientists endanger the earth and the environment and indirectly sharpen the feelings of frustration and deprivation of millions around the world. India had a unique tradition of toleration and plurality with historically limited proselytizing and this could more easily adjust to the process of modernization. This is, at last, being revitalized around principles which inspired its struggle for independence.

Genuine internationalism has remained entrenched in Scandinavia. It is in this context that I would like to conclude by drawing attention to the initiative of Anna Lindah, the Swedish Foreign Minister (who was later brutally murdered). She asked Hans Blix to lead a commission of highly respected international experts to study the menace of weapons of mass destruction. After two years of intense study and consultations their report was issued on 1 June 2006. Lt. General Vasantha Raghavan of the Delhi Policy Group was a member from India. Much of the concern expressed in the report is in line with the Canberra Commission and Jonathan Schell's *The Gift of Time*. The sixty specific recommendations of the Blix Commission are to rid the world of nuclear, biological and chemical arms. The idea of such a commission emanated from Dhanpala, the Shri Lankan, who was the Under Secretary General for Disarmament in the UN. The report is one of the first to recognize the danger from non-state actors using nuclear devices and underlines the urgency of the work of the commission. For compliance, the Commission envisages a critical role for the Security Council. The credentials and recommendations of the Commission deserve respect and serious attention. Apart from diverse influential institutions in many countries, the sponsoring backbone was provided by the Swedish Foreign Ministry, but it was supported by six ministries of External affairs (alas none from a developing country). I cannot help feeling that if Nehru were alive—he was the first statesman to raise alarm at nuclear explosions—he would have joined in this crusading concern at the weapons of mass destruction. It scarcely needs to be said at present that nuclear disarmament looks like a forlorn cry; but since Hiroshima the world has at least not been plunged into a nuclear Armageddon. I would argue that India's own international standing would soar if we were to again crusade unreservedly for nuclear disarmament.

The Bush–Singh agreement has the necessary ambiguity on nuclear policy but it may stand out as a small step towards turning some swords (nuclear ones) into ploughshares. The reality of the political decline of US influence, the economic rise of China, the political decline of Russia which is now banking on regaining its importance by its energy surplus, makes it all a new ball game. The Chernobyl disaster was an accident; as the crow flies, the radiation impact would affect an area whose circumference would envelop both Lahore and Lucknow if either Delhi or Islamabad were nuked. If China took the risk, it too cannot be certain that Washington or Moscow is not waiting to retaliate against Beijing and Shanghai. India would regain the leadership position of enlightened internationalization not by being a nuclear 'also ran' but if, along with Pakistan, we joined Sweden, Brazil, Argentina, South Africa and now Libya and abandoned the subjective reliance on our weapons programme. We would recapture some of our unique international standing not by precept but, in my view, by the example of our civilizational attributes of plurality, secularism, social justice and democracy. As a bonus it could accelerate regionalism in South Asia, and the boosting of UN and multilateralism. While much of the world is now descending into paranoia, India by drawing on its ancient tolerant tradition could return to moral and economic ascendancy.

The positive vision of Gandhi's country should be as John Kenneth Galbraith puts it in the final paragraph of his last book, *The Economics of Innocent Fraud* with the pithy subtitle, *Truth For Our Time*. In a chapter entitled 'The Last Word', he has a final word, which bears quoting in full:

> A final word. We cherish the progress in civilization since biblical times and long before. But there is a needed and, indeed, accepted qualification. As I write, the United States and Britain are in the bitter aftermath of a war in Iraq. We are accepting programmed death of the young and random slaughter for men and women of all ages. So, overwhelmingly, it was in World Wars I and II. So more selectively since, and still at this writing in Iraq. Civilized life, as it is called, is a great white tower celebrating human achievements, but at the top there is permanently a large black cloud. Hüman progress dominated by unimaginable cruelty and death.
>
> I leave the reader with the sadly relevant fact: Civilization has made great strides over the centuries in science, health care, the arts and most, if not all, economic well-being. But also it has given a privileged

position to the development of weapons and the threat and reality of war. Mass slaughter has become the ultimate civilized achievement.

The facts of war are inescapable—death and random cruelty, suspension of civilized values, a disordered aftermath. Thus the human condition and prospect are now supremely evident. The economic and social problems here described, as also mass poverty and starvation can, with thought and action, be addressed. So they have already been. War remains the decisive human failure.

Diplomacy for conflict resolution alone can rescue the future. Only on that path can we come nearer to Nehru's dream of India's special Tryst with Destiny.

18

Volunteerism and Social Justice

Fundamentally, the problem of volunteerism is the dichotomy between the moral impulse of the social conscience and the political concept of a social contract embodied in a modern democratic state. Both have their respective legitimacy: the strength of the former is in activist sensitivity, and that of the latter in the power it wields. The question is whether they are inherently and irreconcilably in conflict or can they evolve a mutually respecting partnership to jointly serve the shared goals of social transformation and equitable national progress. In an authoritarian political system, voluntary social action is banished into illegitimacy, and in consequence, often resorts to insurgency. In a democracy, the citizen is not only guaranteed rights but also carries obligations to the nation's collective welfare. Volunteerism, in a free society, draws its inspiration from the concept of social justice, which is enshrined in universal values and the manifold declarations on human rights. Our own constitutional directive lays down 'a social order in which justice—social, economic and political—must inform national life'. The full scope for citizen action for equal opportunity and equitable share of benefits has obvious political imperatives, but first and last, voluntary involvement in development reflects an individual's quiet zeal to move the mountain of social injustice and patiently plough a lonely furrow for a greener and more productive landscape.

What starts with an individual urge for the redressal of want and social inequities inevitably leads to problems of broadening the reach of voluntary action through institution building, creating organizational structures and finding resources and collaborators to meet the locally determined grassroots priorities. In the process, voluntary organizations (Volags) come up against entrenched orthodoxy and political conservatism which are reflected in the laws of the land even in a democratically elected government committed to building civil society to maximize drawing on social capital.

EXTERNAL AND INTERNAL CHALLENGES

In 1994, a thoughtful and informed debate took place on enlarging the scope and removing the hurdles confronting the Volags. There was a broad consensus that in all fields of social change and development, voluntary institutions must preserve their identity, distinct both from the government and from the corporate life of the country, but it was also recognized that they have a specially important role in the unorganized rural sector. The vast majority of people live in dispersed villages and therefore have been inherently handicapped to receive and wrest attention in the face of the bias of the industrial and urban-dominated establishment. Both the enormity of the problems of rural India and the negative empire of circumstances, which have given it inadequate focus, must be comprehended so that a new kind of cooperative relationship between independent rural volunteerism and the powerful modern state can be created. The challenge is to establish both external as well as internal discipline for the Volags themselves.

Let me first mention the external factors. It is generally conceded by social scientists that, contrary to what growth economists prophesied, even after three decades of planned development, an equitable share of benefits and distributive justice have not trickled down to the marginalized sections of the rural poor. It was fallacious to have assumed that restructuring society on a socialistic pattern implied that the burden of development and social transformation could be wholly consigned to the State. The welcome change is that the government, the intellectual elite and development economists have come to accept, each in their own way, that meaningful progress, particularly in the unorganized rural sector, will require the vigorous participation of the afflicted themselves.

Recent declarations at the highest level have had a more earnest emphasis on the grass-roots involvement of the people, especially in new priorities like wasteland reclamation and ecological restitution. The infamous Kudal Commission (1975) charged with examining the working of and funding by critically investigating voluntary agencies, was finally wound up after the witch hunt totally failed. For the first time, in the Seventh Five-Year Plan, funds were earmarked for allocations to non-governmental agencies. Bunker Roy, the dynamic head of a well-known voluntary organization, was appointed adviser to the Planning Commission to underline the expectations that the voluntary sector should be entrusted with a greater role in national development.

But such affirmations notwithstanding, one must not overlook that past political attitudes towards Volags have swung between positive encouragement, condescending toleration and outright hostility. Doubts about their capability and potential were reflected in years of benign neglect. Where economic stagnation got exposed by voluntary activism, political indifference tended to turn into deep suspicion and even malevolence. When Volags seemed to be coalescing behind a powerful leadership, many of them had to suffer disabilities and suppression. The voluntary sector is inherently and specially vulnerable to what John Kenneth Galbraith[1] calls 'condign power'—the power to coerce and discipline against suspected threats to the assumed exclusive prerogatives of authority. The bureaucracy at some levels gives positive encouragement to effective grass-roots organizations but in general, officialdom, all too frequently in a knee-jerk reaction, finds Volags as irritating challenges to their domains of discretion.

This ambivalence between encouragement and reservations towards the voluntary sector was evident when a draft bill to constitute a council of rural voluntary agencies was circulated in 1993. The purpose, it was explained, was to enlarge the scope for voluntary effort and to provide for redressal and protection, especially against the abuse of governmental authority. The bill also included a suggested code of conduct (ethics) for voluntary organizations, which embodied provisions for commitment to poverty eradication, accountability, professionalism, socialism and austerity. It was, however, left unclear whether registration under the act was envisaged as essential before being assigned responsibilities in the execution of governmental programmes and the right to receive foreign contributions.

While taking note of the declared purpose, many voluntary organizations were quick to question, individually and in conclaves, whether such a statutory body, with an enforceable code of behaviour, did not negate the fundamental rationale of citizen freedom for constructive endeavour. The existing laws governing the registration of societies and the Foreign Contributions Regulation Act (FCRA) already give the central and state governments the power of scrutiny and prevention of financial and other abuses. The additional powers under the enactment, it was feared, could be used by the government to discriminate arbitrarily and in the process either co-opt the more pliable or curb and undermine the more autonomous Volags. A deliberate reorientation of the conventional attitudes in the political echelons and the pyramid of officialdom will be essential if purposeful cooperation and mutual confidence between government and non-governmental organizations (NGOs) is to be fashioned. But there is a danger of escapism in the argument that the absence of such a sea change is a paralysing obstruction to voluntary action.

PROBLEMS OF FUNDING

There is a long history and great diversity of charity and social service in India. Many voluntary bodies in the social and economic life of contemporary India draw their inspiration from spiritual and religious underpinnings (Hindu, Christian, Jain, Muslim, Parsi, etc.). There are also secular organizations, some avowedly Marxist, which are impelled by universal human values and concern for social justice. All of them get support from the respect for compassion, self-denying sacrifice and service to one's fellow beings, which are all part of the ancient culture and value system of India. The great boost and inspiration for volunteerism must be traced to the advent and impact of Gandhi in our national life. While leading a mass movement for political freedom, he drew on the religious value system and insisted that political liberation must go hand in hand with social responsibility, banishing untouchability, and in regenerating village economies. He anticipated the limitations and social distortions of macro-economic planning and rampant industrialization. Gandhi is now looked upon not just as the prophet of decentralization and village-level economic self-reliance, but the inspiration for meeting the ecological disaster and human degradation brought about by modern industrial civilization.

Development professionals are not necessarily convinced of the Gandhian approach. But as social scientists, in their search for alternative strategies for development with distributive justice, they too have come round to urge a grass-roots upwards thrust. In this reoriented emphasis, the developmental professional seems at times to be drawing inspiration from the effective activism of NGOs in the affluent democracies. But the problems of volunteerism in a poor agricultural country are very different from those faced in the West. The Volags here are necessarily weaker, more fragmented, and spatially dispersed. Moreover, they cannot bank on adequate support from private philanthropy and are obliged to rely largely on institutional funding for their constructive programmes. There are, of course, some long-established Gandhian organizations and a few other dedicated groups and individual idealists who take no aid from any source and are sustained wholly with community backing. But most Volags, directly or indirectly and wholly or partially, are perforce obliged to seek governmental support. But when executing official programmes, they run up against exacting bureaucratic procedures and accounting requirements, and in the process their developmental thrust gets weakened.

It was the absence or limitations of domestic institutional funding that led to the spurt of foreign funding for Volags. Such foreign support from non-national sources comes under strict regulation. Much of it originates from non-governmental agencies of small or medium-sized countries like Canada, Scandinavia, the Netherlands, Federal Germany, the United Kingdom, Switzerland, and international agencies like UNICEF or OXFAM. As a rule, the motivations behind such funding flow from a sensitive concern for poverty in the global village and cannot be faulted for ulterior purposes or prescribing demeaning conditions.

(At home, most of these donor agencies are activists for peace, disarmament and enlightened international transfer of resources.) But even so, exclusive or excessive dependence on foreign institutional funding can be debilitating and invites suspicions of external manipulation. Whether funding is domestic or external, voluntary agencies have to be specially vigilant to maintain the highest standards of integrity, and at all times be transparently accountable and open to scrutiny.

It is worth noting that the well-reputed Volags in India were native in origin and resource base. As a rule, institutional funding sought them out; it was not the other way round. Compared to most developing countries, volunteerism in India demonstrates greater vitality with scores of pockets of solid achievement. Across the length and breadth of the country, there are some 7,000—by some accounts 100,000—small- and medium-sized voluntary organizations, many working in remote backward and tribal areas. But even so, it is estimated that Volags only cover 20,000 out of the 550,000 villages in the country. The reach of the voluntary sector in rural development is not expanding when compared to its obvious need and scope. Recognizing this, select leaders in the voluntary sector, supported by a para-governmental institution (CAPART), have been canvassing for a Common Action Programme (CAP) to attract educated youth, more particularly women, to join and extend citizen action for development and social justice. Such well-intentioned campaigns may recruit some foot soldiers but the leaders, the institution builders, and the trailblazers of Volags, who are pushing the frontiers of voluntary action to the vast neglected rural hinterland, will only be found from amongst self-impelled volunteers.

The more difficult problem for voluntary organizations is not in relation to the government or donors, but internal to the organizations themselves. Volunteerism, which starts with individual motivation, predicates higher values and self-imposed discipline. Volags must function democratically in programming, but they must not allow this attitude to overlook the imperative of public accountability. They must be vigilant against factionalism. It would be pretentious to claim that Volags are inoculated against corruption. The need for financial prudence and discipline of work ethics, essential for an organizational framework, can degenerate into individual or institutional authoritarianism. Finding the right mix to ensure sustained vitality is a difficult challenge for Volags. To guard against such perils, it is always instructive to recall the high-minded founders of voluntary organizations and treat them as the moral lodestars. Volags must exemplify the spirit of dedication, rejecting ulterior ambitions and monetary affluence, and so earn respect for voluntary activism.

OTHER MAJOR PROBLEMS

But the ordinary run of supporting personnel in the voluntary sector is bound to be a mixed lot in quality and motivation. The lure of security and prestige associated with government service and the envy of earnings in the corporate sector siphons off much of the meritocracy from grass-roots organizations. Not that those who come forward to join Volags under economic pressures of unemployment are necessarily incapable of adjusting to the ethos of Volags. But the voluntary organizations must provide living wages and upgrade them to keep up with creeping inflation. The more pernicious influence on the Volags comes from the environment of consumerism, corruption, moral degeneration and the social ascendancy of the unprincipled. As in politics, the posture of higher public virtue and a romanticized idealism of public service is almost a professional hazard but a psychological necessity in volunteerism. In fact, and not surprisingly, claiming commitment to the social environment associated with volunteerism provides cover for individual ambitions, career-building and the quest for public recognition. These exist side by side with wholly sincere commitment to social service without expectations of the conventional rewards. Any survey of Volags will show hundreds of highly motivated men and women, both retired and professionally qualified youth, who have rejected other opportunities to tether themselves to grass-roots voluntary organizations.

To enhance the bargaining power of the Volags, efforts are underway to build various kinds of collective lobbies and a united front of the voluntary sector. Some tentative initiatives were restricted to organizations engaged in a specific sector, like wasteland development or adult education. Other proposals envisaged the incorporation of representatives of every kind of voluntary organizations in a national or state-wide forum. Such ideas have gathered support, but in concept and feasibility, they remain bedevilled with built-in difficulties. People-based organizations, by definition, must be localized and are bound to be diverse in priorities and approach. A coalition of Volags could more readily be catalysed around a specific issue or an imminent common threat, but this might be short-lived. While Volags are understandably on guard to preserve their separate identities, they are not above competing with each other for funds or trained workers or poaching and piggybacking on the work of other voluntary organizations. Further, unwittingly, they can be tempted to flatter the corporate sector by imitation, by tending towards gigantism and dog-eat-dog propensities, which are legitimate as modalities and measures of success in the market economy but are fundamentally repugnant to volunteerism. With such complexities, forging even a loose confederation of voluntary organization which would enhance credibility of the sector as a whole, is not going to be easy. As a precondition to such success there should be a greater flexibility to subscribe to a common allegiance and combine it with genuine mutual respect for each other. Volunteerism must be grounded in a firm faith in plurality and adherence to a voluntarily determined code of conduct. What needs to be reiterated is that even without such a countervailing power, the opportunity of inching progress in grass-roots confidence-building is not necessarily doomed.

Another institutional problem for the Volags is to graft relevant technology, managerial talent and professional skills to catalyse faster progress in the rural sector. Many institutions, including the Rural Management Academy in Anand (Gujarat), are addressing themselves to this problem imaginatively. Even so, in general, graduates in rural management or agricultural engineering are understandably reluctant to live and work in the villages for long years. Nevertheless, it is encouraging that more and more motivated professionals are coming forward to make careers in the voluntary sector. When inducting qualified personnel, one has to be on guard that the emoluments of professionals (even if less than those of their peers in the corporate sector) do not lead to widening the alienating gulf from the village poor. There could also be friction with the typical grass-roots worker who is less educated but a better communicator and catalyst for confidence-building at the people's level. Similarly, innovative new models, which are built with concentrated technical and capital inputs, have to be constantly assessed as to whether they could be replicated by the people themselves. If this is not kept in mind, it could only reinforce the old habit of psychological dependence amongst the rural poor. In building the capacity of indigenous absorption of new strategies, the resident grass-roots worker and the development professional have to find ways to forge a harmonious compact so that they can jointly determine the modalities and pace in grass-roots-upward development.

Finally, there is the difficult question of the attitude of the Volags in rural development to conventional politics. In a democracy, political parties have a legitimate right to marshal the people to their particular persuasion through party cells. There has emerged the idea of a coalition of grass-roots organizations forming a broad nationwide non-party political front for social justice as an alternative development strategy. But the Volags, who straddle social and developmental goals on the one hand with preferences in electoral politics on the other, must be prepared for the unsavoury games of the political marketplace. If a Volag is perceived as identifying with or opposed to a political party, it could come under competitive pressures. If the grass-roots strength is unshakeable and collateral outside support can give it a staying power, a strong Volag can win in a confrontation with established authority on specific issues and even deepen its hold amongst the people. In brief, every voluntary agency, after carefully determining its own strength and priorities, will require careful helmsmanship to steer through political eddies and storms so that collective solidarity and the interests of the poor are not undermined. All this underlines that outside involvement in promoting volunteerism carries serious responsibilities and patient long-term commitment to bring about rural regeneration.

These are difficult problems in the odyssey of volunteerism. There can be no firm answers but there is a need to reflect on the conceptual approach and the specific dilemmas. I myself do so with limited experience and superficial insights. What çan be confidently affirmed is that in a poor country like India, which has got habituated to democracy and seeks to strengthen civil society, the challenge and scope for social and developmental goals through collateral voluntary effort is boundless. The strength and value of the Volags must not be measured merely by the macroeconomic calculus. In the final instance, one must end where one began: voluntary action flows from a sensitive conscience and demands sustained dedication. The catalogues of possible impediments are sometimes imaginary or irrelevant but only occasionally insuperable. Volunteerism can hold its own and even thrive if there is the mental fortitude to plough the lonely furrow in a vast parched landscape towards the distant horizon of the social and economic liberation of the land.

SEVA MANDIR

Seva Mandir was established with the faith that shoring up democracy and achieving true economic and social liberation requires citizen involvement and heightened social responsibility. Seva Mandir eschews party politics but it does not shy away from supporting people on specific issues involving civic rights, social disabilities, denial of justice under the law and demanding a fairer share of development resources for the rural poor. In 1995 we have two-hundred whole-time workers and several hundred village collaborators covering four hundred and fifty villages, spread in pockets over several thousand square kilometres of a rugged, unusually depressed area which is threatened with ecological doom. Seva Mandir is purposefully but gingerly engaged in all aspects of rural problems. But we are not complacent about our success and not unaware of the diverse inner problems and external hurdles that continually beset us. We know we need institutional self-discipline, and a measure of rectitude amongst the workers at all levels, to stay the course for a long march. We also know that we will falter if we betray the trust of the people with whom we work and we will certainly fail if we lose faith. Eventual success and satisfaction will only come when we can see the growth of confidence in the people's capacity to economic self-reliance so that one day we may become redundant.

Index